CENSORED

"Project Censored is one of the organizations that we should listen to, to be assured that our newspapers and our broadcasting outlets are practicing thorough and ethical journalism."—Walter Cronkite

"[Censored] should be affixed to the bulletin boards in every newsroom in America. And, perhaps read aloud to a few publishers and television executives."—Ralph Nader

"[Censored] offers devastating evidence of the dumbing-down of mainstream news in America.... Required reading for broadcasters, journalists and well-informed citizens."—Los Angeles Times

"A distant early warning system for society's problems."
—American Journalism Review

"One of the most significant media research projects in the country."
—I. F. Stone

"A terrific resource, especially for its directory of alternative media and organizations.... Recommended for media collections."—Library Journal

"Project Censored shines a spotlight on news that an informed public must have...a vital contribution to our democratic process."
—Rhoda H. Karpatkin, President, Consumer's Union

"Buy it, read it, act on it. Our future depends on the knowledge this collection of suppressed stories allows us."—San Diego Review

"This volume chronicles 25 news stories about events that could affect all of us, but which we most likely did not hear or read about in the popular news media."—Bloomsbury Review

"Censored serves as a reminder that there is certainly more to the news than is easily available or willingly disclosed. To those of us who work in the newsrooms, it's an inspiration, an indictment, and an admonition to look deeper, ask more questions, then search for the truth in the answers we get."—Creative Loafings

"This invaluable resource deserves to be more widely known."
—Wilson Library Bulletin

CENSORED 2004

The Top 25 Censored Stories

PETER PHILLIPS & PROJECT CENSORED

INTRODUCTION BY AMY GOODMAN
CARTOONS BY TOM TOMORROW

SEVEN STORIES PRESS
New York / London / Melbourne / Toronto

PN
4888
.P6
C462 2003

Cover image: On February 5, 2003, the day Secretary of State Colin Powell gave his
speech to the United Nations Security Council presenting the U.S. case for war against
Iraq, U.N. officials covered the tapestry reproduction of Picasso's *Guernica* that hangs at
the entrance of the Security Council building. Picasso's mural was inspired by the bombing of the tiny Basque village of Guernica during the Spanish Civil War and is a chilling
protest against modern warfare. Who requested the censoring of Picasso's work remains
unclear, but the profound symbolism of the act is most transparent, and a reminder of the
lies and public relations spin leading up to the U.S. invasion of Iraq.

CENSORED 2004 IS DEDICATED TO FREE SPEECH RADIO
PACIFICA NETWORK AND DEMOCRACY NOW!

Pacifica Sisters

KPFA (Berkeley) 94.1 FM in the Berkeley signal area.

KPFK (Los Angeles) 90.7 FM in the Los Angeles metro signal area.

KPFT (Houston) 90.1 FM in the Houston metro signal area.

WBAI (New York) 99.5 FM in the New York metro signal area.

WPFW (Washington, DC) 89.3 FM in the Washington, DC, metro signal area.

Pacifica Affiliates East

WBGU 88.1 FM, Bowling State University, OH

WCBN 88.3 FM, Ann Arbor, MI

WDBX 90.1 FM, Carbondale, IL

WEFT 90.1 FM, Champaign, IL

WEOS 89.7 FM, Geneva, NY

WERU 89.8 FM, Orland, MN

WGDR 91.1 FM, Plainfield, VT

WHUS 91.7 FM, Storrs, CT

WJFF 90.5 FM, Jeffersonville, NY

WLUW 88.7 FM, Chicago, IL

WMNF 88.5 FM, Tampa, FL

WMUH 91.7 FM, Muhlenberg College, PA

WNCU 90.7 FM, Durham, NC

WOJB 88.9 FM, Hayward, WI

WORT 89.9 FM, Madison, WI

WREK 91.1 FM Georgia Tech, Atlanta, GA

WRFG 89.3 FM, Atlanta, GA

WRFL 88.1 FM, University of Kentucky, Lexington, KY

WRPI 91.5 FM, Troy, NY

WSIA 88.9 FM, Staten Island, NY

WSMU 91.9 FM, North Dartmouth, MA

WSNC 90.5 FM, Winston-Salem State University, NC

WUSB 90.1 FM, University of Stony Brook, NY

WWSP 89.9 FM, University of Wisconsin, Stevens Point, WI

WWUH 91.3 FM, University of Hartford, CT

WXOU 88.3 FM, Rochester, MI

WZRD 88.3 FM Northeastern Illinois University, Chicago, IL

Pacifica Affiliates West

KAOS 89.3 FM, Evergreen State College, Olympia, WA

KAZI 88.7 FM, Austin, TX

KBCS 91.3 FM, Bellevue, WA

KCRL 90.9 FM, Salt Lake City, UT

KCSB 91.9 FM University of California–Santa Barbara, CA

KDUR 91.9 FM and 93.9 FM, Fort Lewis College, CO

KDVS 90.3 FM, University of California–Davis, CA

KEOS 81.9 FM, College Station, TX

KFAI 90.3 FM, Minneapolis, MN

KGNU 88.5 FM, Boulder, CO

KHSU 90.5 FM, Humboldt State University, Arcata, CA

KKCR 90.9 AND 91.9 FM, Hanalei, HI

KKFI 90.1 FM, Kansas City, MO

KMUD 88.3, 88.9, and 91.1 FM, Redway, CA

KOPN 89.5 FM, Columbia, MO

KRZA 88.7 FM, Alamosa, CO

KSJK 1230 AM, South Oregon University, Ashland, OR

KSUA 91.5 FM, Fairbanks, AK

KSVR 91.7 FM, Mount Vernon, WA

KUGS 89.3 FM, Western Washington University, WA

KUNF 88.7, 90.9, and 99.1 FM, Paonia, CO

KUNM 89.9 FM, University of New Mexico, Albuquerque, NM

KUOI 89.3 FM, University of Idaho, ID

KWVA 88.1 FM, University of Oregon, Eugene, OR

KXCI 91.3 FM, Tucson, AZ

KZYX 90.7 and 91.5 FM, Philo, CA

Contents

Preface 11

Acknowledgments.. 15

Introduction by Amy Goodman, *Democracy Now!* 25

How Project Censored Stories Are Selected 29

CHAPTER 1   The Top Censored Stories of 2002 and 2003
            by Peter Phillips, Katie Sims, Trish Boreta, Dana Balicki,
            Licia Marshall, Chris Salvano, Jason Spencer, and
            the Spring 2003 Sociology of Censorship Class.................. 31

  1 The Neoconservative Plan for Global Dominance 34

  2 Homeland Security Threatens Civil Liberty 38

  3 U.S. Illegally Removes Pages from Iraq U.N. Report 42

  4 Rumsfeld's Plan to Provoke Terrorists..................................... 44

  5 The Effort to Make Unions Disappear...................................... 46

  6 Closing Access to Information Technology 50

  7 Treaty Busting by the United States 52

  8 U.S./British Forces Continue Use of Depleted Uranium Weapons
    Despite Massive Evidence of Negative Health Effects 57

  9 In Afghanistan: Poverty, Women's Rights, and Civil Disruption
    Worse than Ever 61

 10 Africa Faces New Threat of New Colonialism 64

11 U.S. Implicated in Taliban Massacre 68

12 Bush Administration Behind Failed Military Coup
   in Venezuela 70

13 Corporate Personhood Challenged 74

14 Unwanted Refugees a Global Problem 77

15 U.S. Military's War on the Earth 79

16 Plan Puebla-Panama and the FTAA..83

17 Clear Channel Monopoly Draws Criticism..............................87

18 Charter Forest Proposal Threatens Access to Public Lands 91

19 U.S. Dollar vs. the Euro: Another Reason
   for the Invasion of Iraq 94

20 Pentagon Increases Private Military Contracts...........................98

21 Third World Austerity Policies:
   Coming Soon to a City Near You 100

22 Welfare Reform Up for Reauthorization,
   But Still No Safety Net...103

23 Argentina Crisis Sparks Cooperative Growth 107

24 U.S. Aid to Israel Fuels Repressive Occupation in Palestine.....110

25 Convicted Corporations Receive Perks Instead of Punishment...113

   Censored 2004 Runners-Up 116

CHAPTER 2 *Censored* Déjà Vu: A Review and Update on Important
           Censored Stories from Prior Years by Peter Phillips
           and the Project Censored Writing Team: Derek Fieldsoe,
           Michael Kaufmann, Courtney Sessler, Matt Hamburg,
           Dana Balicki, Keith Harmon Snow, Kagiso Molethe,
           Jason Spencer, Josh Sisco, Veronica Lopez, Corey Clapp,
           Mitzila Valdes, and Donald Yoon 125

           MEDIA MOMENTS BY MICHAEL PARENTI..125

CHAPTER 3 Junk Food News and News Abuse
           by Jason Spencer and Christina Cutaia..............................163

CHAPTER 4 The Big Five Media Giants by Mark Crispin Miller 171

CHAPTER 5   Media Democracy in Action by Peter Phillips, DaveyD,
             Marc Sapir, and the Project Censored Writing Team:
             Kagiso Molefhe, Michael Kaufman, Matt Hamburg,
             Donald Yoon, and Josh Sisco 181

CHAPTER 6   From Saving Private Lynch To The "Top Gun" President:
             The Made-for-TV "Reality" War On Iraq
             by Robin Andersen..219

CHAPTER 7   Weapons of Mass Deception by
             Sheldon Rampton and John Stauber, *PR Watch* *231*

CHAPTER 8   Iraq War: Before and Beyond by Norman Solomon,
             Peter Phillips, Marcus Borgman, and Tom Lough 247

CHAPTER 9   The USA Patriot Act: Uncensored
             by Herb Forestel and Nancy Kranich 265

CHAPTER 10   FAIR's Third Annual "Fear & Favor" Report, 2002:
             How Power Shapes the News
             by Janine Jackson, Peter Hart, and Rachel Coen..............283

CHAPTER 11   Bearing Bad News by Rohan Jayasekera,
             associate editor, *Index on Censorship* *297*

CHAPTER 12   Why Japan Remains a Threat to Peace and Democracy
             in Asia: The Problem of Lap Dog Journalism
             by Kenichi Asano 309

APPENDIX A   *Censored 2004* Resource Guide:
             Top 25 *Censored* Sources 319

APPENDIX B   *Censored 2004* Resource Guide:
             Our Favorite National/International News Sources 327

APPENDIX C   *Censored 2004* Resource Guide:
             Media Activist Organizations..339

APPENDIX D   Our Favorite Web Site E-zines....................................349

Index 353

About the Editor..367

How to Support Project Censored 368

THIS MODERN WORLD

by TOM TOMORROW

THEY'RE THE ALTERNATIVE TO THE ALTERNATIVE... THE OPPOSITION TO THE OPPOSITION! THEY'RE...

CONSERVATIVES WITH AN ATTITUDE!

WHAT ARE YOU REBELLING AGAINST, JOHNNY?

OH, YOU KNOW--PROGRESSIVE TAX-ATION, ENVIRONMENTAL PROTECTIONS, ABORTION RIGHTS--THINGS LIKE THAT...

HE'S SO DREAMY!

UNDAUNTED BY THE P.C. THOUGHT POLICE, THESE RIGHT-WING REBELS AREN'T AFRAID TO PAY THE PRICE FOR SPEAKING THEIR MINDS!

--AND IF YOU ASK ME, WE SHOULD ALL SUPPORT THE PRESIDENT AND HIS POLICIES!

CAREFUL! SOME LIBERAL MIGHT HEAR YOU--AND--UH--WRITE A LETTER TO THE EDITOR OR SOMETHING!

THEY ARE VOICES IN THE WILDERNESS, FIGHTING A LONELY BATTLE AGAINST OVERWHELMING ODDS...

ACTOR RICHARD DREYFUSS HAS EXPRESSED HIS RESER-VATIONS ABOUT THE WAR WITH IRAQ!

MANY COLLEGE PROFESSORS HAVE ALSO BEEN CRIT-ICAL!

DAMN THIS PERVASIVE LIBERAL HEGEMONY!

...BUT SOMEHOW THEY PERSEVERE--FUELED BY LITTLE MORE THAN THEIR RAGE AT AN UNJUST WORLD----AND, UM, COPIOUS QUANTITIES OF MONEY, POWER, AND INFLUENCE--AS WELL AS A VIRTUAL STRANGLE-HOLD ON THE BASIC TERMS OF THE DEBATE...

YES--BUT WE ARE UP AGAINST THE LIKES OF RICHARD DREYFUSS--AND ALL THOSE COLLEGE PROFESSORS!

NOT TO MENTION THE OCCASIONAL NEWSPAPER CARTOONIST!

Preface

BY PETER PHILLIPS

2002 and 2003 were years of particularly dangerous censorship and deception. That being the case, it should come as no surprise that in addition to the top 25 "most censored" stories covered in Chapter 1, this year, we have brought together the largest group of guest writers and researchers ever presented in a *Censored* volume. Michael Parenti's wit starts out Chapter 2, which is our annual review of stories from prior years. Chapter 3 contains our annual summary of "junk food news," the frivolous stories that dominated the media. Mark Crispin Miller's media ownership maps are updated in Chapter 4. Hip-hop historian and deejay DaveyD outlines the importance of music and culture to the political movements of our times in Chapter 5. Media and war is the theme of Robin Andersen's Chapter 6, which focuses on the images of the war from Private Lynch to the "Top Gun" president. Sheldon Rampton and John Stauber from *PR Watch* cover issues of deception and misinformation in Chapter 7. Norman Solomon joins us again with an update on his trip to Iraq and media lies in Chapter 8. The USA Patriot Act is the topic of Chapter 9 by Herbert Foerstel and Nancy Kranich. We are very pleased to include this year FAIR's third annual "Fear & Favor" Report, 2002, "How Power Shapes the News," by Janine Jackson, Peter Hart, and Rachel Coen. Rohan Jayasekera, associate editor of the *Index on Censorship* in London, provides a global update of media in Chapter 11. And Kenichi Asano gives us a strong critique of media in Japan in Chapter 12.

Freedom of information in American society is in serious danger. Corporate media is trying to maintain access to most official sources of news—and having a startling degree of success. Consolidation of media has brought the total news sources for most Americans to less than a handful, and these news groups have an ever-increasing dependency on prearranged content.

The 24-hour news shows on MSNBC, Fox, and CNN are closely inter-connected with various governmental and corporate sources of news. Maintenance of continuous news shows requires a constant feed and supply of stimulating and entertaining events and breaking soundbites. Advertisement for mass consumption drives the system and prepackaged sources of news are vital within this global news process. Ratings demand continued cooperation from multiple sources for ongoing weather reports, war stories, sports scores, business news, and regional headlines. Print, radio, and TV news also engages in this constant interchange with news sources.

The preparation for and following of ongoing wars and terrorism fits well into the visual kaleidoscope of preplanned news. Government public relations specialists and media experts from private commercial interests provide ongoing newsfeeds to the national media distributions systems. The result is an emerging macrosymbiotic relationship between news dispensers and news suppliers. Perfect examples of this relationship are the press pools organized by the Pentagon both in the Middle East and in Washington, DC, which give pre-scheduled reports on the war in Iraq to selected groups of news collectors (journalists) for distribution through their individual media organizations.

Embedded reporters (news collectors) working directly with military units in the field must maintain cooperative working relationships with unit commanders as they feed breaking news back to the U.S. public. Cooperative reporting is vital to continued access to government news sources. Therefore, rows of news-story reviewers back at corporate media headquarters rewrite, soften, or spike news stories from the field that threaten the symbiotics of global news management.

Journalists who fail to recognize their roles as cooperative news collectors will be disciplined in the field or barred from reporting, as in the celebrity cases of Geraldo Rivera and Peter Arnett.

Journalists working outside of this mass media system face increasing dangers from "accidents" of war and corporate-media dismissal of their news reports. Massive civilian casualties caused by U.S. troops, extensive damage to private homes and businesses, and reports that contradict the official public relations line were downplayed, deleted, or ignored by corporate media, while content is analyzed by experts (retired generals and other approved collaborators) from within the symbiotic global news structure.

Symbiotic global news distribution is a conscious and deliberate attempt by the powerful to control news and information in society. The Homeland Security Act Title II Section 201(d)(5) specifically asks the directorate to "develop a comprehensive plan for securing the key resources and critical infrastructure of the United States including... information technology and telecommunications systems (including satellites)... emergency preparedness communications systems." The government's goal is total information control, and the continuing consolidation of media makes this process easier to achieve.

Freedom of information and citizen access to objective news is rapidly fading in the United States and the world. In its place is a complex entertainment-oriented news system, which protects its own bottom line by servicing the most powerful military-industrial complex in the world.

For the majority of Americans who depend on corporate media for their daily news, this monolithic news structure creates intellectual celibacy, inaction, and fear. The result is a docile population, whose principal function within society is to simply shut up and go shopping. The powerful would like us quiet and consumptive and the corporate media is delivering that message on a daily basis.

So as we now stand on the threshold of losing news freedom, we must push our own agenda of free speech and grassroots news. To this end project, Project Censored presents *Censored 2004*, a book reflective of a world at war, a nation in fear, and a repressive secretive government. The 200 of us working together on this annual publication stand with our brothers and sisters worldwide who are calling for equality, freedom, civil rights, and peace.

The Project Censored crew (SSU Faculty, students, and PC staff)

Acknowledgments

Project Censored is managed through the Department of Sociology in the School of Social Sciences at Sonoma State University. We are an investigative sociology and media analysis project dedicated to the freedom of information thoughout the United States.

Over 200 people were directly involved in the production of *Censored 2004*. University and program staff, students, faculty, community experts, research interns, guest writers, and our distinguished national judges all contributed time, energy, and money to make this year's book an important resource for the promotion of freedom of information in the United States.

I want to personally thank those close friends and intimates who have counseled and supported me through another year of Project Censored. Most important, I thank my wife Mary Lia-Phillips, who as my lover, friend, and partner provides daily consultative support to Project Censored. The men in the Green Oaks breakfast group, Noel Byrne, Bob Butler, Rick Williams, Colin Godwin, and Bill Simon, are personal advisors and confidants who help with difficult decisions. Thanks go also to Carl Jensen, founder of Project Censored, and director for 20 years. His continued advice and support are very important to the project. Trish Boreta, Project Censored coordinator, is an important daily associate administrator of the project. Her dedication and enthusiasm are greatly appreciated. Katie Sims, our story coordinator and student advisor, deserves a special thank-you, she supervised the processing of over 700 story nominations for this year's book and advises the Project Censored TV news team.

A big thanks goes to the people at Seven Stories Press. They are more than a publishing house; rather they have become close friends who help edit our annual book in record time and serve as advisors in the annual release process of the most *Censored* stories. Publisher Dan Simon is a free spirit centered in human betterment through knowledge and literature. He deserves full credit for assembling an excellent support crew. Kudos and and thanks for their excellent work to: operations director Jon Gilbert; managing editor India Amos; editors Mikola De Roo, Ria Julien, and Greg Ruggiero; academic market director Tara Parmiter; publicists Lars Reilly, Phoebe Hwang, and Ruth Weiner; and book designer Cindy LaBreacht.

Thanks also to Bill Mokler and the sales staff at Consortium Books, who will see to it that every independent bookstore, chain store, and wholesaler in the U.S. is aware of *Censored 2004*. Thanks to Hushion House, our distributors in Canada, as well as Turnaround Publishers Services Ltd. in Great Britain and Palgrave Macmillan in Australia.

Thank you to Amy Goodman who wrote the introduction to the *Censored 2004* edition. Amy Goodman and *Democracy Now!* are inspirational examples of freedom of information through quality investigative reporting.

Thanks also to the authors of the most *Censored* stories for 2004, for without their often unsupported efforts as investigative news reporters and writers, the stories presented in *Censored* would not be possible.

Our guest writers this year are Robin Andersen, Kenichi Asano, Marcus Borgman, Rachel Coen, DaveyD, Herb Foerstel, Peter Hart, Janine Jackson, Rohan Jayasekera, Nancy Kranich, Tom Lough, Mark Crispin Miller, Michael Parenti, Sheldon Rampton, Norman Solomon, and John Stauber. They represent a unique combination of scholars, journalists, and activists dedicated to media democracy through a diversity of news and opinion. Thank you to each and all for your unique contribution to *Censored 2004*.

This year's book again features the cartoons of Tom Tomorrow. "This Modern World" appears in more than 90 newspapers across the country. We are extremely pleased to use Tom Tomorrow's wit and humor throughout the book.

Our national judges, some of whom have been involved with the project for 27 years, are among the top experts in the country concerned with First Amendment freedoms and media. We are honored to have them as the final voice in ranking the top 25 most *Censored* stories.

An important thanks goes to our financial donors, including Sonoma State University Instructionally Related Activity Fund, the School of Social Sciences at Sonoma State University, and especially the over 4,000 individuals who purchase books and send us financial gifts each year. You are our financial angels who continue to give year after year to this important student-run media research project.

This year we had 92 faculty/community evaluators assisting with our story assessment process. These expert volunteers read and rated the nominated stories for national importance, accuracy, and credibility. In March, they participated with the students in selecting the final top 25 *Censored* stories for 2004.

Most of all, we need to recognize the Sonoma State University students in the Spring 2003 Media Censorship class and the Fall 2002 Sociology of Media class, who worked long hours nominating and researching some 700 underpublished news stories. Students are the principle writers for the censored news synopsis in the book each year and 82 students served as interns for the project, working on various teams including: public relations, Web design, news story research, office support, events/fund raising, and TV news production. Student education is the most important aspect of Project Censored, and we could not do this work without the dedication and effort of our student interns.

Daryl Khoo is our Webmaster. The Project Censored Web site, <www.projectcensored.org>, has expanded under his supervision.

Lastly, I want to thank our readers and supporters from all over the United States and the world. Hundreds of you nominated stories for consideration as the most *Censored* news story of the year. Thank you very much!

PROJECT CENSORED 2002 & 2003 STAFF

Peter Phillips, Ph.D.	Director
Carl Jensen, Ph.D.	Director Emeritus and Project Advisor
Tricia Boreta	Coordinator/Editor
Katie Sims	Story Management/TV News Team Leader
Beverly Krystosek	Bookkeeping
Odilia Pablo	Office Support
Daryl Khoo	Webmaster
Dana Balicki	Teaching Assistant
Licia Marshall	Teaching Assistant
Chris Salvano	Teaching Assistant
Jason Spencer	Teaching Assistant

Spring & Fall 2002 & 2003 Interns and Community Volunteers

Mette Adams, Serena Ahlgren, Dylan Alter, Ramsey Anderson, Dana Balicki, Eduardo Barragan, Jennifer Berger, Dan Bluthardt, Patrick Cadell, Vanessa Cavallaro, William Corey Clapp, Eric Common, Suze Cribbs, Dylan Citrin Cummins, Christina Cutaia, Alessandra Diana, Stephen Dietrich,

Grace Farasey, Derek Fieldsoe, Terri Freedman, Matt Hamburg, Larissa Heeren, Laura Huntington, David Immel, Kristen Jacobs, Leo James, Evan Johnson, Michael Kaufmann, Patrick Kelleher, Sean Kelson, Daryl Khoo, Kristina Kronenberger, Brooke Krystosek, Tom Larsen, Ron Liskey, Ed Longnecker, Veronica Lopez, Omar Malik, Licia Marshall, Kim Meister, Courtney Meyer, Kagiso Molefhe, Justin Myers, Jesse Narvaez, Casey Neth, Kellie Noe, Vanessa Nutter, Michael Oliva, Victoria Pellinen, Jason Pennetta, Jessica Peterson, Sarah Potts, Annette Powell, James Ramirez, Sean Roney, Vanessa Richter, Leandra Rouse, Chris Salvano, Courtney Sessler, Ben Sheppee, Allan Silverman, Marcia Simmons, Josh Sisco, Dana Small, Hanah Snavely, Jason Spencer, Josh Stithem, Elise Symonds, Angelica Tercero, S'leta Thorp, Joshua Travers, Colin Umphryes, Mitzie Valdez, Christina Van Straalen, Erik Wagle, Bria Ward, Melanie Westbrook, Josh Wittman, and Donald Yoon.

Student Researchers in Sociology of Media Class, Fall 2002

Sarah Anderson, David Cole, Leanna Del Zompo, Derek Fieldsoe, Michael Kaufmann, Omar Malik, Alice Reece, and Casey Stenlund.

Student Researchers in Media Censorship Class, Spring 2003

Lisa Badenfort, Lindsey Brage, Tony Cullen, Dylan Citrin Cummins, Jessie Esquivel, Scott Frazier, Terri Freedman, Kathleen Glover, Sherry Grant, Melissa Jones, T. Grayson Kent, Daryl Khoo, Emilio Licea, Jen Scanlon, Josh Sisco, Alyssa Speaker, Pat Spiva, Tara Spreng, Effren Trejo, and Weston White.

In Memoriam

David Immel
1975–2002
A dedicated Project Censored Intern, 2001–2002

PROJECT CENSORED 2004 NATIONAL JUDGES

ROBIN ANDERSEN, associate professor and chair, Department of Communication and Media Studies, Fordham University

RICHARD BARNET, author of 15 books and numerous articles for *The New York Times Magazine*, *The Nation*, and *The Progressive*

LIANE CLORFENE-CASTEN, cofounder and president of Chicago Media Watch, a volunteer watchdog group that monitors the media for bias, distortions, and omissions. She is an award-winning journalist with credits in national periodicals such as *E Magazine*, *The Nation*, *Mother Jones*, *Ms.*, *Environmental Health Perspectives*, *In These Times*, and *Business Ethics*. She is the author of *Breast Cancer: Poisons, Profits, and Prevention*.

LENORE FOERSTEL, Women for Mutual Security, facilitator of the Progressive International Media Exchange (PRIME)

DR. GEORGE GERBNER, dean emeritus, Annenberg School of Communications, University of Pennsylvania; founder of the Cultural Environment Movement; author of *Invisible Crises: What Conglomerate Media Control Means for America and the World* and *Triumph and the Image: The Media's War in the Persian Gulf*

ROBERT HACKETT, professor, School of Communications, Simon Fraser University; director of NewsWatch Canada

DR. CARL JENSEN, founder and former director of Project Censored; author of *Censored: The News That Didn't Make the News and Why* (1990–1996) and *20 Years of Censored News* (1997)

SUT JHALLY, professor of communications and executive director of the Media Education Foundation, University of Massachusetts

NICHOLAS JOHNSON,* professor, College of Law, University of Iowa; former FCC Commissioner (1966–1973); author of *How To Talk Back To Your Television Set*

RHODA H. KARPATKIN, president of Consumers Union, non-profit publisher of *Consumer Reports*

CHARLES L. KLOTZER, editor and publisher emeritus, *St. Louis Journalism Review*

NANCY KRANICH, past-president of the American Library Association (ALA)

JUDITH KRUG, director of the Office for Intellectual Freedom, American Library Association (ALA); editor of *Newsletter on Intellectual Freedom; Freedom to Read Foundation News;* and *Intellectual Freedom Action News*

WILLIAM LUTZ, professor of English, Rutgers University; former editor of *The Quarterly Review of Doublespeak;* author of *The New Doublespeak: Why No One Knows What Anyone's Saying Anymore* (1966)

JULIANNE MALVEAUX, PH.D., economist and columnist, King Features and Pacifica radio talk show host

ROBERT W. McCHESNEY, research associate professor in the Institute of Communications Research and the Graduate School of Library and Information Science at the University of Illinois, Urbana-Champaign; author of *Rich Media, Poor Democracy*; *Telecommunications, Mass Media, and Democracy: The Battle for the Control of U.S. Broadcasting 1928–35*; and other books on media

MARK CRISPIN MILLER, professor of Media Ecology, New York University; director of the Project on Media Ownership

JACK L. NELSON,* professor, Graduate School of Education, Rutgers University; author of 16 books, including *Critical Issues in Education* (1996), and more than 150 articles

MICHAEL PARENTI, political analyst, lecturer, and author of several books, including *Inventing Reality; The Politics of News Media; Make Believe Media; The Politics of Entertainment;* and numerous other works

DAN PERKINS, political cartoonist, pen name Tom Tomorrow, and creator of "This Modern World"

BARBARA SEAMAN, lecturer; author of *The Greatest Experiment Ever Performed on Women: Exploding the Estrogen Myth* (Hyperion, 2003); *The Doctors' Case Against the Pill; Free and Female; Women and the Crisis in Sex Hormones;* and other books; cofounder of the National Women's Health Network

ERNA SMITH, professor of journalism, San Francisco State University, author of several studies on mainstream news coverage on people of color

NORMAN SOLOMON, syndicated columnist on media and politics; coauthor of *Target Iraq: What the News Media Didn't Tell You* (Context Books, 2003); executive director of the Institute for Public Accuracy

SHEILA RABB WEIDENFELD,* president of D.C. Productions, Ltd.; former press secretary to Betty Ford

---

*Indicates having been a Project Censored judge since its founding in 1976

PROJECT CENSORED 2004 FACULTY, STAFF, AND COMMUNITY EVALUATORS

Julia Allen, Ph.D.	English
Melinda Barnard, Ph.D.	Communications
Philip Beard, Ph.D.	Modern Languages
Jim Berkland, Ph.D.	Geology
Barbara Bloom, Ph.D.	Criminal Justice Administration
Andrew Botterell, Ph.D.	Philosophy
Maureen Buckley, Ph.D.	Counseling
Elizabeth Burch, Ph.D.	Communications
Noel Byrne, Ph.D.	Sociology
James R. Carr, Ph.D.	Geology
Ray Castro, Ph.D.	Chicano & Latino Studies
Liz Close, Ph.D.	Nursing (Chair)
Lynn Cominsky, Ph.D.	Physics/Astronomy
Bill Crowley, Ph.D.	Geography
Victor Daniels, Ph.D.	Psychology
Laurie Dawson, Ph.D.	Labor Education
Randall Dodgen, Ph.D.	History
Tamara Falicov, M.A.	Communication Studies
Fred Fletcher	Community Expert, Labor
Dorothy (Dolly) Friedel, Ph.D.	Geography
Susan Garfin, Ph.D.	Sociology
Patricia Leigh Gibbs, Ph.D.	Sociology
Robert Girling, Ph.D.	Business, Economics
Mary Gomes, Ph.D.	Psychology
Myrna Goodman, Ph.D.	Sociology
Scott Gordon, Ph.D.	Computer Science
Diana Grant, Ph.D.	Criminal Justice Administration
Velma Guillory-Taylor, Ed.D.	American Multicultural Studies
Chad Harris, M.A.	Communication Studies
Daniel Haytin, Ph.D.	Sociology
Laurel Holmstrom, M.A.	Academic Programs
Jeffrey Holtzman, Ph.D.	Environmental Sciences
Sally Hurtado, Ph.D.	Education
Pat Jackson, Ph.D.	Criminal Justice Administration
Tom Jacobson J.D.	Environmental Studies & Planning
Sherril Jaffe, Ph.D.	English

Paul Jess	Community Expert, Environmental Law
Cheri Ketchum, Ph.D.	Communications
Mary King, M.D.	Health
Jeanette Koshar	Nursing
John Kramer, Ph.D.	Political Science
Heidi LaMoreaux, Ph.D.	Liberal Studies
Virginia Lea, Ph.D.	Education
Benet Leigh, M.A.	Communications Studies
Wingham Liddell, Ph.D.	Business Administration
Tom Lough, Ph.D.	Sociology
John Lund	Business & Political Issues
Rick Luttmann, Ph.D.	Mathematics
Robert Manning	Peace Issues
Regina Marchi, M.A.	Communication Studies
Ken Marcus, Ph.D.	Criminal Justice Administration
Perry Marker, Ph.D.	Education
Daniel Markwyn, Ph.D.	History
Doug Martin, Ph.D.	Chemistry
Elizabeth Martinez, Ph.D.	Modern Languages
Phil McGough, Ph.D.	Business Administration
Eric McGuckin, Ph.D.	Liberal Studies
Robert McNamara, Ph.D.	Political Science
Andy Merrifield, Ph.D.	Political Science
Ann Neel, Ph.D.	Sociology
Catherine Nelson, Ph.D.	Political Science
Leilani Nishime, Ph.D.	American Multicultural Studies
Linda Nowak, Ph.D.	Business
Tim Ogburn	International Business
Tom Ormond, Ph.D.	Kinesiology
Wendy Ostroff, Ph.D.	Liberal Studies
Ervand M. Peterson, Ph.D.	Environmental Sciences
Keith Pike, M.A.	Native American Studies
Jorge E. Porras, Ph.D.	Modern Languages
Arturo Ramirez, Ph.D.	American Multicultural Studies
Jeffrey T. Reeder, Ph.D.	Modern Languages
Michael Robinson, Rabbi	Religion
R. Thomas Rosin, Ph.D.	Anthropology
Richard Senghas, Ph.D.	Anthropology/Linguistics
Rashmi Singh, Ph.D.	American Multicultural Studies

Cindy Stearns, Ph.D.	Women's Gender Studies
John Steiner, Ph.D.	Sociology
Meri Storino, Ph.D.	Counseling
Elaine Sundberg, M.A.	Academic Programs
Scott Suneson, M.A.	Sociology/Political Science
Bob Tellander, Ph.D.	Sociology
Laxmi G. Tewari, Ph.D.	Music
Karen Thompson, Ph.D.	Business
Suzanne Toczyski, Ph.D.	Modern Languages
Carol Tremmel, M.A.	Extended Education
Charlene Tung, Ph.D.	Women's Gender Studies
David Van Nuys, Ph.D.	Psychology
Francisco H. Vazquez, Ph.D.	Liberal Studies
Greta Vollmer, Ph.D.	English
Alexandra Von Meier, Ph.D.	Environmental Sciences
Albert Wahrhaftig, Ph.D.	Anthropology
Tim Wandling, Ph.D.	English
Tony White, Ph.D.	History
Rick Williams J.D.	Attorney at Law
Richard Zimmer, Ph.D.	Liberal Studies

Sonoma State University Supporting Staff and Offices

Bernard Goldstein: Chief Academic Officer and staff

Elaine Leeder: Dean of School of Social Sciences and staff

William Babula: Dean of School of Arts and Humanities

Barbara Butler and the SSU Library staff

Paula Hammett: Social Sciences Library Resources

Jonah Raskin and Faculty in Communications Studies

Susan Kashack and staff in SSU Public Relations Office

Colleagues in the Sociology Department: Noel Byrne, Kathy Charmaz, Susan Garfin, Dan Haytin, Robert Tellander, Myrna Goodman, and department secretary Bev Krystosek

Introduction

BY AMY GOODMAN, *DEMOCRACY NOW!*

Pacifica Radio was founded more than 50 years ago by war resisters. Lou Hill came out of a detention camp after World War II and said, "There has to be a media outlet that is not run by the corporations that profit from war or beating the drums for war." And so Pacifica was born and the first station KPFA in Berkeley was run by a non-profit organization as a public media space. University of Pennsylvania professor George Gerbner says, "Corporations have nothing to tell and everything to sell." Pacifica is a network run by journalists and artists, and I believe that is what all media should be in this country.

I want to express my concern about the increasing commercialization and privatization that is overtaking media in this country and around the world. It is a profit-driven agenda of those in power that threatens the ever-shrinking public media spaces that we share. Public media spaces serve as a vital component of our civic discourse and our democracy. We together in the public media world see our role as providing a forum for national discourse and international debate around the most important issues of our day, especially now in this time of war, invasion, and occupation.

It is absolutely critical that all the media open up the dialogue and discussion to the great diversity of voices in this country. Before the invasion of Iraq, the majority of people in the country were opposed to war, but you didn't hear them in the mainstream media. In fact, Fairness and Accuracy in Reporting (FAIR) did a study that showed in the week before and the week after Secretary of State Colin Powell made his case for war at the United Nations, the four major nightly newscasts—ABC, NBC, CBS, and

PBS's *NewsHour with Jim Lehrer*—conducted 393 interviews that were focused on the pending war. Only three of the people interviewed, less than 1 percent, were opposed to war. This sort of news coverage does not represent the diversity of opinion in this country. The 1 percent of the people interviewed by the corporate media who opposed the war actually represented not a fringe minority, not even the silent majority, but rather they represented the silenced majority—silenced by the mainstream corporate media that have become even more homogeneous and exclusive since the June 2 vote at the Federal Communications Commission (FCC).

As a journalist, it is the first red flag when we learn that something is being done secretly, that there isn't transparency. The secret proposals within the FCC to allow greater consolidation of the media, which were not made public until June 2, are a clear example of the dismissal of democratic process. That on an issue of this kind of grave import there was only one little publicized formal public hearing held in Richmond, Virginia, is an another silencing of the majority.

At least we can thank the two FCC commissioners, Michael Copps and Jonathan Adelstein, who did go around the country holding informal hearings in support of democratic discussion. It is absolutely critical that the public weighs in on media issues. The airwaves are not just public for the public media, like Pacifica or NPR or PBS. The airwaves are owned by the public. And even the private corporations—like Viacom, which owns CBS, General Electric, which owns NBC, and Disney, which owns ABC—are in actuality leasing the public's airwaves. Corporate media have a responsibility, as we do, to use the airwaves responsibly and to serve a democracy.

My colleague Juan Gonzalez, who is co-host of *Democracy Now!*, is also president of the National Association of Hispanic Journalists (NAHJ). He testified at the informal FCC forum held last January at Columbia Law School in New York organized by FCC Commissioner Copps. Juan released the NAHJ Seventh Annual Network Brownout Report, which found that in 2001, less than one percent of all news stories on the network evening newscasts of ABC, CBS, NBC, and CNN were related to Latino issues. Juan said the stories that were related to Latinos often portrayed them stereotypically: as living in the U.S. as illegal immigrants, prone to violence, and residing in slums.

This year a study by FAIR found that 92 percent of all U.S. news sources interviewed on the nightly newscasts of ABC, NBC, and CBS in 2001 were white. It also found that of those more than 14,600 reports, only .6 percent was Latino.

Ben Bagdikan, the author of *Media Monopoly*, testified at one of the informal FCC hearings in California and he talked about his experience going into a major radio network studio in San Francisco. He was told not to mention the day of the week or the weather in his interview. He was also told not to say where he was, nor to describe the studio he was in. The host explained that the program is used in the network's cities around the country. He said they wanted people in those cities to think they are listening to a "local" program.

Real local media programs are being lost to the increasing consolidation of ownership in the hands of fewer media conglomerates. The loss of local control can endanger our communities. In Minot, North Dakota, a train derailed in the early hours of a January morning 2002 and a toxic cloud of anhydrous ammonia emanated from the accident. When law enforcement officials tried to warn the local community by calling radio station KCGB, they couldn't get through to anyone. It turns out that media giant Clear Channel owns all six of Minot's radio stations and that all six were served by one news employee who was unreachable at the time of the accident. (See *Censored* #17.) More than 300 people ended up being hospitalized. It is absolutely critical that we have local community media.

Communication is vital. In just a few years since the media deregulation of 1996, Clear Channel has gobbled more than 1,200 radio stations. Many do not have a single live person on the premises as the signal is piped through, state after state, with no local mediation or participation, giving new meaning to the term "clear channeling."

This issue of media consolidation breaks down liberal and conservative lines—Democrat and Republican. You now have the National Rifle Association (NRA) joining with progressive groups against further media consolidation. It was under the Democrats in 1996 that Vice President Al Gore pushed through the 1996 Telecommunications Act. That legislation authorized what may be the largest giveaway of public resources in history. Between $70 and $90 billion worth of broadcast spectrum were turned over to private media conglomerates.

Media consolidation subverts democracy in so many ways. The media now defines who are serious political candidates. Over a decade ago, Ross Perot ran for president; he didn't have a party at first, and most people didn't know his name, but when he promised to pour vast sums of his personal fortune into political advertising, he got major media coverage and the media got their payments for advertisements. And then, of course, Perot got lots of free airtime. But without the money, third-party candidates are largely ignored. Political advertising is a major revenue source for corporate media. That is why the National Association of Broadcasters (NAB) is one of the main lobby groups working against campaign finance reform in this country.

Media consolidation also hurts kids. A study by Children Now of Oakland, California, shows that media consolidation leads to fewer children's programs in favor of more lucrative programs for adults. According to the Children Now study, the top seven broadcast stations in Los Angeles have half as much children's programming as they did five years ago. In one case, a station owned by Viacom dropped 89 percent of its children's programming. As Patti Miller, head of Children Now said, "The study gives us a frightening peek into the world of children's television in an age of media consolidation."

Another important example of how media giants are hurting our democracy is the case of low-power FM broadcast, LPFM. In the late '90s, there was a broad-based grassroots movement to restore Class D licensing. This would have created a blossoming of small independent radio stations in communities from coast to coast. Sadly, Congress, strongly lobbied by the NAB and National Public Radio (NPR), prevented any significant growth of low-power FM.

We have to turn the tide. We need local community control. The chorus is larger than we thought. Activist groups like Project Censored, FAIR, and many others are pushing for stronger local control and are helping to build the media democracy movement. We have to challenge the powers that be and rebuild media from the bottom up.

I think we must remember that media homogenization serves the state. Media's role in democracy is to hold the state accountable. I trust that public media collaboration will challenge the mainstream media and demand that they too become what should be the role of all the media—that is to be the exception to the rulers. We must go to where the silence is and tell the truth to power.

Amy Goodman is the host of *Democracy Now!*, a national daily news program. The program is currently aired at some 120 stations nationwide, including the Pacifica radio stations, Pacifica affiliates, <WBXI.org>, public-access television stations, Free Speech TV (Dish Network Channel 9415), short-wave radio (Radio for Peace Intention), and <www.democracynow.org>.

How Project Censored Stories Are Selected

Sonoma State University Project Censored students and staff screen several thousand stories each year. About 700 of these are selected for evaluation by faculty and community evaluators. Our 89 faculty/community evaluators are experts in their individual fields and they rate the stories for credibility and national importance. Often more than one of our evaluators will examine and rate the same story. The top ranked 200 stories are then researched for national mainstream coverage by our upper division students in the annual Media Censorship class. The class examines the corporate media's coverage of the story and takes a second look at the credibility and accuracy of the story in relationship to other news articles on the topic. About 125 stories each year make the final voting level. A collective vote of all students, staff, and faculty narrows the stories down to 60 in early November. A second vote is taken a week later, after a short 300-word summary of each of the top 60 stories is prepared, and sent out with a voting sheet to all faculty/community evaluators, students, staff, and self-selected national judges. This Project-wide vote by some 150-plus people establishes which 25 stories will be listed in our annual book. The final ranking of stories is decided by our national judges, who receive a synopsis and full text copy of the top 25 stories.

While selection of these stories each year is a long, subjective process, we have grown to trust this collective effort as the best possible means of fairly selecting these important news stories. This process, we believe, gives us an annual summary list of the most important undercovered news stories in the United States.

PROJECT CENSORED MISSION STATEMENT Project Censored, founded in 1976, is a nonprofit project within the Sonoma State University Foundation, a 501(c)3 organization. Our principle objective is the advocacy for, and protection of, First Amendment rights and freedom of information in the United States. Through a faculty/student/community partnership, Project Censored serves as a national media ombudsman by identifying and researching important news stories that are underreported, ignored, misrepresented, or censored in the United States. We also encourage and support journalist, faculty, and student investigations into First Amendment and freedom of information issues. We are actively encouraging the development of a national interconnected, community-based media news service that will offer a diversity of news and information sources via print, radio, television, and internet to local mainstream audiences.

HOW TO INVEST IN FREEDOM OF INFORMATION Project Censored is a nonprofit tax-exempt organization. Funds for the Project are derived from sales of this book, and donations from hundreds of individuals. You can send a support gift to us through our website at www.projectcensored.org, or by mail to:

> Project Censored
> Sonoma State University
> 1810 East Cotati Avenue
> Rohnert Park, CA 94931

CHAPTER 1

The Top Censored Stories of 2002 and 2003

By Peter Phillips, Katie Sims, Trish Boreta, Dana Balicki,
Licia Marshall, Chris Salvano, Jason Spencer,
and the spring 2003 Sociology of Censorship Class

In the mid-1700s, the French philosopher Montesquieu suggested that the best way to preserve civil liberties was to guard against unequal distributions of power. A generation later another statesman, Thomas Jefferson, advised his countrymen that the only way to guard against unbalanced distributions of power was to ensure equal access to information. The way to accomplish this, he said, was to maintain a free and independent press that critically scrutinized the governing bodies and the individuals that lead them.

The events of the past year demonstrate the importance of these two statements more concisely now than at any other time in our country's history. Perhaps the *most* censored subject of this year is the growing concern among both liberals and conservatives that a dangerous trend is emerging within our political institutions. This trend has a name that is proclaimed loudly within the independent press, on both the right and the left, but is rarely mentioned in the editorial columns of our daily newspapers and only hinted at on network and cable television. Some call it jingoism, others nationalism or, more strongly, fascism. Whatever the term, it names a fear that has begun to grip those brave enough to pay attention and sharp enough to see the signs.

Thus, many of the best investigations this year were preoccupied with the erosion of civil and human rights, U.S. policies overseas, and the drive toward war. Yet the stories with the most significant findings went largely ignored by mainstream media. The deeper the analysis went, the more shallow the coverage seemed to become.

Problems related to the environment, health, and education did not disappear this year. But in the current climate, the powerful forces with the ability to change the structure of our nation far into the future have eclipsed the problems that currently surround us in our daily lives. Reflecting this perspective, the more than 200 voters to Project Censored made some important decisions regarding the top 25 list. Many of our choices focus on the United States' impact on other countries (*Censored* #8, #9, #11, #15, #24, and #25), the world's poor (*Censored* #10, #14, #16, #23 and #24), and global relationships (*Censored* #1, #3, #4, #7, #12, #16, and #19).

On the domestic front, emphasis was placed on broad policy decisions that have the potential to impact the rights and privileges of the American people both today and tomorrow (*Censored* #2, #5, #6, #18, #21, and #22). While a few of our stories this year centered on corporate corruption and influence peddling (*Censored* #12, #17, #18, #20, and #25).

Our 2004 edition contains articles critical of the present administration. Of course, much of this criticism extends to policies established by the prior administration. But it also reveals a reluctance on the part of many journalists, since 9/11, to cover stories that, though truthful, may run counter to the current political climate. We do not, however, consider political sway to be a valid excuse for bad editorial decisions. Project Censored has never based its story choices on political correctness and is certainly not inclined to start now. We are committed to recognizing and exposing examples of important research by independent journalists and authors that went ignored by mainstream media.

We think this year's selections are a reflection of this commitment.

Here are the 25 stories separated by category:

POLITICAL
  #1 The Neoconservative Plan for Global Dominance
  #2 Homeland Security Threatens Civil Liberty
  #3 U.S. Illegally Removes Pages from Iraq U.N. Report
  #7 Treaty Busting by the United States

MILITARY

#4 Rumsfeld's Plan to Provoke Terrorists

#8 U.S./British Forces Continue Use of Depleted Uranium Weapons Despite Massive Evidence of Negative Health Effects

#11 U.S. Implicated in Taliban Massacre

LABOR

#5 The Effort to Make Unions Disappear

CORPORATE

#6 Closing Access to Information Technology

#13 Corporate Personhood Challenged

#17 Clear Channel Monopoly Draws Criticism

#20 Pentagon Increased Private Military Contracts

#25 Convicted Corporations Receive Perks Instead of Punishment

ENVIRONMENT

#15 U.S. Military's War on the Earth

#18 Charter Forest Proposal Threatens Access to Public Lands

GLOBAL TRADE

#10 Africa Faces New Threat of Colonialism

#16 Plan Puebla-Panama and the FTAA

#19 U.S. Dollar vs. the Euro: Another Reason for the Invasion of Iraq

#23 Argentina Crisis Sparks Cooperative Growth

FOREIGN POLICY

#9 In Afghanistan: Poverty, Women's Rights, and Civil Disruption Worse Than Ever

#14 Unwanted Refugees a Global Problem

#15 Bush Administration Behind Failed Military Coup in Venezuela

#24 U.S. Aid to Israel Fuels Repressive Occupation in Palestine

DOMESTIC POLICY

#21 Third World Austerity Policies: Coming Soon to a City Near You

#22 Welfare Reform Up For Reauthorization, But Still No Safety Net

Last year, Project Censored moved to a new cycle for the release of our annual *Censored* stories. The *Censored* book is now released in September of each year, moving the process forward six months. The stories reviewed, therefore, were published between the months of April 2002 and March 2003.

Sonoma State University Project Censored students and staff screened several thousand stories during that 12-month period. Almost 700 stories were selected for evaluation by members of our faculty and community. Our 90 Faculty/Community Evaluators are experts in their individual fields and they rate the stories for credibility and national importance. Some 150 stories this year made it to the final voting level. Project-wide voting by more than 150 people established the 25 most important stories for *Censored 2004*. The top 25 stories were then ranked by our national judges, including Michael Parenti, Robin Andersen, Carl Jensen, Lenore Foerstel, and some 20 other national journalists, scholars, and writers.

While selection of these stories each year is a subjective judgmental process, we have grown to trust this collective method as the best possible means of fairly sorting and selecting important news stories censored by the mainstream press.

We hope you agree.

1 The Neoconservative Plan for Global Dominance

Sources:
Harper's, October 2002
Title: "Dick Cheney's Song of America"
Author: David Armstrong

Mother Jones, March 2003
Title: "The 30-Year Itch"
Author: Robert Dreyfuss

<Pilger.com>, December 12, 2002
Title: "Hidden Agendas"
Author: John Pilger

Faculty Evaluators: Phil Beard and Tom Lough
Student Researcher: Dylan Citrin Cummins

Corporate media coverage: Jay Bookman, "The President's Real Goal in Iraq," *The Atlanta Journal-Constitution*, September 29, 2002

Over the last year, corporate media have made much of Saddam Hussein and his stockpile of weapons of mass destruction. Rarely did the press address the possibility that larger strategies might also have driven the decision to invade Iraq. Broad political strategies regarding foreign policy do indeed exist and are part of the public record. The following is a summary of the current strategies that have formed over the last 30 years, strategies that eclipse the pursuit of oil and that preceded Hussein's rise to power:

In the 1970s, the United States and the Middle East were embroiled in a tug of war over oil. At the time, American military presence in the Gulf was fairly insignificant and the prospect of seizing control of Arab oil fields by force was pretty unattainable. Still, the idea of this level of dominance was very attractive to a group of hard-line, promilitary Washington insiders that included both Democrats and Republicans. Eventually labeled "neoconservatives," this circle of influential strategists played important roles in the respective Defense Departments of Gerald Ford, Ronald Reagan, and George Bush Sr. at conservative think tanks throughout the 1980s and 1990s and today occupies several key posts in the White House, Pentagon, and State Department. The principals among them are:

➤ Dick Cheney and Donald Rumsfeld, our current vice president and defense secretary, respectively, who have been closely aligned since they served with the Ford Administration in the 1970s;

➤ Deputy Defense Secretary Paul Wolfowitz, the key architect of the postwar reconstruction of Iraq;

➤ Richard Perle, former chairman and current member of the Pentagon's Defense Policy Board, which has great influence over foreign military policies;

➤ William Kristol, editor of *The Weekly Standard* and founder of Project for a New American Century, the powerful, neoconservative think tank.

In the 1970s, however, neither high-level politicos nor the American people shared the priorities of this small group of military strategists. In 1979, the Shah of Iran fell and U.S. political sway in the region was greatly jeopardized. In 1980, the Carter Doctrine declared the Gulf "a zone of U.S. influence." It warned (especially the Soviets) that any attempt to gain control of the Persian Gulf region would be regarded as an assault on the vital interests of the U.S. and repelled by any means necessary, including military force. This was followed by the creation of the Rapid Deployment Force—a military program specifically designed to rush several thousand U.S. troops to the Gulf on short notice.

Under President Reagan, the Rapid Deployment Force was transformed into the U.S. Central Command that oversaw the area from eastern Africa to Afghanistan. Bases and support facilities were established throughout the Gulf region, and alliances were expanded with such countries as Israel, Saudi Arabia, and Iraq.

Since the first Gulf War, the U.S. has built a network of military bases that now almost completely encircle the oil fields of the Persian Gulf.

In 1989, following the end of the Cold War and just prior to the Gulf War, Dick Cheney, Colin Powell, and Paul Wolfowitz produced the Defense Planning Guidance report advocating U.S. military dominance around the globe. The plan called for the United States to maintain and grow in military superiority and prevent new rivals from rising up to challenge us on the world stage. Using words like "preemptive" and military "forward presence," the plan called for the U.S. to be dominant over friends and foes alike. It concluded with the assertion that the U.S. can best attain this position by making itself "absolutely powerful."

The 1989 plan was spawned after the fall of the Soviet Union. Without the traditional threat to national security, Cheney, Powell, and Wolfowitz knew that the military budget would dwindle without new enemies and threats. In an attempt to salvage defense funding, Cheney and company constructed a plan to fill the "threat blank." On August 2, 1990, President Bush called a press conference. He explained that the threat of global war had significantly receded, but in its wake, a new danger arose. This unforeseen threat to national security could come from any angle and from any power.

Iraq, by a remarkable coincidence, invaded Northern Kuwait later the same day.

Cheney et al. were out of political power for the eight years of Bill Clinton's presidency. During this time, the neoconservatives founded the Project for the New American Century (PNAC). The most influential product of the PNAC was a report entitled "Rebuilding America's Defense," <www.newamericancentury.org>, which called for U.S. military dominance and control of global economic markets.

With the election of George W. Bush, the authors of the plan were returned to power: Cheney as vice president, Powell as secretary of state, and Wolfowitz in the number-two spot at the Pentagon. With the old Defense Planning Guidance as the skeleton, the three went back to the drawing board. When their new plan was complete, it included contributions from Wolfowitz's boss Donald Rumsfeld. The old "preemptive" attacks have now become "unwarned attacks." The Powell-Cheney doctrine of military "forward presence" has been replaced by "forward deterrence." The U.S. stands ready to invade any country deemed a possible threat to our economic interests.

UPDATE BY DAVID ARMSTRONG: Just days after this story appeared, the Bush Administration unveiled its "new" National Security Strategy (NSS), which effectively validated the article's main thesis. The NSS makes clear that the administration will pursue a policy of preemption and overwhelming military superiority aimed at ensuring U.S. dominance. Since that time, the major media have generally come around to the point of view presented in the article. *The New York Times*, which originally rejected the article's premise, now makes a virtual mantra of the notion that the current security strategy is little more than a warmed-over version of the policy drafted during the first Bush Administration of preventing new rivals from rising up to challenge the U.S. in the wake of the Soviet Union's collapse. The article circulated widely, particularly in the run-up to the war in Iraq, and was entered into the Congressional Record. It also became a topic of discussion on such outlets as the BBC, NPR, MSNBC, various talk radio shows, and European newspapers. In the process, it has substantially helped shape the debate about the Bush Administration's foreign policy.

UPDATE BY BOB DREYFUSS: For months leading up to the war against Iraq, it was widely assumed among critics of the war that a hidden motive for military action was Iraq's oil, not terrorism or weapons of mass destruction. In fact, "No Blood for Oil" became perhaps the leading slogan and bumper sticker of the peace movement. Yet there was very little examination in the media of the role of oil in American policy toward Iraq and the Persian Gulf, and what coverage did exist tended to pooh-pooh or debunk the idea that the war had anything to do with oil. So I set out to place the war with Iraq in the context of a decades-long U.S. strategy of building up a military presence in the region, arguing that even before the war, the U.S. had turned the Gulf into a U.S. protectorate. Perhaps most importantly, I showed that a motive behind the war was oil as a national security issue, as a strategic commodity, not as a commercial one, and that, in fact, most of the oil industry itself was either opposed to or ambivalent about the idea of war against Saddam Hussein. Yet the neoconservatives in the Bush Administration, whose forebears had proposed occupying the oil fields of the Gulf in the mid-1970s, sought control of the oil in the region as the cornerstone of American empire.

Since the end of this war, it has become clear that the United States (and the U.K.) have aggressively sought to maintain direct control over Iraq's oil industry. When looters devastated Baghdad, only the Ministry of Oil was unscathed because U.S. marines protected it. Since then, handpicked Iraqi officials have been installed in the ministry, under the supervision of U.S. military and civilian officials, and there is movement toward privatization of Iraq's oil industry, a point that I emphasized in my writing on the topic before the war. Not only that, but it is increasingly clear that France, Russia, and China are likely to be excluded from either rebuilding the industry and securing contracts for future Iraqi oil delivery.

I can't say that the media followed up on my exposure of this issue, except that a few alternative print periodicals, such as *Mother Jones* and *The American Prospect*, covered the story, and I appeared on a number of radio and television talk show programs as a result of my writing on Iraq, including C-Span, CNBC, and CBC-TV in Canada. I was also invited to make a presentation on "The 30-Year Itch" at the Transnational Institute in Amsterdam. According to *Mother Jones*, the article drew more traffic to its Web site than any other article.

2 Homeland Security Threatens Civil Liberty

Sources:
Global Outlook, Winter 2003
Title: "Homeland Defense: Pentagon Declares War on America"
Author: Frank Morales

Center for Public Integrity, <publicintegrity.org>
Title: "Justice Department Drafts Sweeping Expansion of Terrorism Act"
Authors: Charles Lewis and Adam Mayle

<infowars.com>, <Rense.com>, February 11, 2003 and *Global Outlook*, Vol. 4
Title: "Secret Patriot II Destroys Remaining U.S. Liberty"
Author: Alex Jones

Faculty Evaluators: Robert Manning, Rashmi Singh, and Andrew Botterell
Student Researchers: Sherry Grant and Dylan Citrin Cummins

Corporate media coverage: E. Moscoso and N. Achrati, "Patriot Act II," *The Atlanta Journal-Constitution*, May 11, 2003; Cassio Furtado, "Patriot Act II," *The Tampa Tribune*, March 28, 2003; and Rajeev Goyle, "Patriot Act Sequel Worse than First," *Baltimore Sun*, February 21, 2003.

As reported widely in the mainstream press, the new Department of Homeland Security (DHS) represents the most extensive restructuring of the U.S. government since 1947—the year the Department of War was combined with the army, navy, marines, coast guard, and air force to create the Department of Defense (DOD). The new Department of Homeland Security (DHS) combines more than 100 separate entities of the executive branch, including the secret service, the coast guard, and the border patrol, among others. The DHS employs over 170,000 federal workers and commands a total annual budget of $37 billion. But what does this mean for the people of the United States? What sort of long-term effects will it have on the day-to-day lives of average Americans? These questions have received scant attention in the corporate media.

The concept of homeland security was thrown around the Pentagon long before the events of 9/11. Originally titled "Homeland Defense," it was placed within the Pentagon's "Operations Other Than War (OOTW)" command, under the stand-alone civil disturbance plan called the "Garden Plot." Over the years, homeland defense has been extended by a host of presidential decision directives and executive orders.

Now, following the events of 9/11, the initial concept has ballooned into a vast, powerful, and far-reaching department.

One DHS mandate largely ignored by the press requires the FBI, CIA, and state and local governments to share intelligence reports with the department upon command, without explanation. Civil rights activists claim that this endangers the rights and freedoms of law-abiding Americans by blurring the lines between foreign and domestic spying (as occurred during the COINTELPRO plan of the '60s and '70s). According to the ACLU, the Department of Homeland Security will be "100 percent secret and 0 percent accountable." Meanwhile, the gathering, retention, and use of information collected is a central focus of the Bush Administration's new agenda. Officially established to track down terrorists, information can be collected on any dissenter, American citizen or not, violent or not. The classification of recent peace marches and protests as "terrorist events" within DOD and FEMA (Federal Emergency Management Agency) documents is one example of the dangerous potential of these mandates.

As part of homeland security, the USA Patriot Act of 2001 allows the government increased and unprecedented access to the lives of American citizens and represents an unrestrained imposition on our civil liberties. Wiretaps, previously confined to one phone, can now follow a person from place to place at the behest of government agents and people can now be detained on the vague suspicion that they might be a terrorist—or assisting one. Detainees can also be denied the right to legal representation (or the right of private counsel when they are allowed to meet with their attorneys).

William Safire, a writer for *The New York Times*, defined the first Patriot Act as a presidential effort to seize dictatorial control. No member of Congress was given sufficient time to study the first Patriot Act that was passed by the house on October 27, 2001. In some cases, while driving the act through Congress, Vice President Cheney would not allow the legislation to be read, publicly threatening members of Congress that they would be blamed for the next terrorist attack if they did not vote for the Patriot Act.

The Domestic Security Enhancement Act of 2003 (Patriot Act II) is accused of posing even greater hazards to civil liberties. The draft proposal of Patriot Act II was leaked from John Ashcroft's staff in February of 2003 and was stamped "Confidential —Not for Distribution." Patriot Act II was widely editorialized against in the U.S. media but full disclosure of the contents, implications, and motivations were underdeveloped. In particular, there are three glaring areas that warranted greater coverage by the American media:

➤ The second Patriot Act proposes to place the entire federal government and many areas of state government under the exclusive jurisdiction of the Department of Justice (DOJ), the Office of Homeland Security, and the FEMA NORTHCOM military command.

➤ Under Section 501, a U.S. citizen engaging in lawful activity can be picked off the streets or from home and taken to a secret military tribunal with no access to or notification of a lawyer, the press, or family. This would be considered "justified" if the agent "inferred from conduct" suspicious intention. One proposed option is that any violation of federal or state law could designate a U.S. citizen as an "enemy combatant" and allow him or her to be stripped of citizenship.

➤ Section 102 states that any information gathering can be considered as the pursuit of covert intelligence for a foreign power—even legal intelligence gathering by a U.S. reporter. This provision could make newsgathering illegal, and therefore, an act of terrorism.

In addition, the Bush Administration is calling for a repeal of the Posse Comitatus Act of 1878, a law passed after the Civil War to prohibit the deployment of federal military forces onto American streets to control civil action—otherwise known as martial law.

One fear among civil rights activists is that, now that the details of the Domestic Security Enhancement Act/Patriot Act II have been revealed, the proposals contained therein will be taken apart, renamed, and incorporated into other, broader pieces of legislation within the Department of Homeland Security.

UPDATE BY FRANK MORALES: To further prepare for new "law enforcement" missions for the military within America overseen by the Northern Command, the Center for Law and Military Operations, based in Charlottesville, Virginia, recently published the legal rationale for these developments. Entitled *Domestic Operational Law Handbook for Judge Advocates*, the document reflects the growing momentum towards the repeal of the Posse Comitatus Act. Virtually unreported in any media, and published prior to 9/11, the document states that although "the founding fathers' hesitancy to raise a standing army and their desire to render the military subordinate to civilian authority" is "rooted in the Constitution," "exceptions to the restrictions on employment of federal armed forces to assist state and local civil authorities are also grounded in the Constitution, which provides the basis for federal legislation allowing military assistance for civil disturbances." The JAG handbook attempts to solidify, from a legal standpoint, Pentagon penetration of America and its "operations other than war," essentially providing the U.S. corporate elite with lawful justification for its class war against the American people, specifically those that resist the "new world law and order" agenda.

The handbook notes that "the Department of Defense Civil Disturbance Plan, named Garden Plot, provides guidance and direction for planning, coordination, and executing military operations during domestic civil disturbances." Operation Garden Plot, originating in 1968 and continually updated, is according to the JAG handbook, tasked with the mission of conducting "civil disturbance operations throughout the United States," providing "wide latitude to a commander to use federal forces to assist civil law enforcement in restoring law and order." And it's exactly this type of "wide latitude" that we've witnessed at recent protests in New York City and Oakland.

United States Army Field Manual 19–15, entitled *Civil Disturbances*, issued in 1985, is designed to equip soldiers with the "tactics, techniques, and procedures" necessary to suppress dissent. The manual states that "crowd control formations may be employed to disperse, contain, or block a crowd. When employed to disperse a crowd, they are particularly effective in urban areas because they enable the control force to split a crowd into smaller segments." Sound familiar? If you were at the February 15 New York City peace rally, it certainly does. The manual goes on to state that "if the crowd refuses to move, the control force may have to employ other techniques, such as riot control agents or apprehensions…" The army "civil disturbance" manual, correlated to present-day realities, also makes the point that "civil disturbances include acts of terrorism," which "may be organized by disaffected groups," who hope to "embarrass the government," and who may, in fact, "demonstrate as a cover for terrorism."

The sophistry involved in turning a peace rally into a pro–Al Qaeda rally is precisely the logic that is operative within Pentagon driven civil disturbance planning situated within the broader context of so-called "homeland defense." In fact, rather than protest being the occasion of "terrorism," the "War on Terrorism" is the cover for the war on dissent. But don't take my word for it. Listen to what the California Anti-Terrorism Information Center spokesman Mike Van Winkle had to say recently to the *Oakland Tribune* (May 18, 2003): "You can make an easy kind of link that, if you have a protest group protesting a war where the cause that's being fought against is international terrorism, you might have terrorism at that protest… You can almost argue that a protest against that is a terrorist act."

FOR FURTHER STUDY:

Frank Morales, "Operations Other Than War: Los Angeles, 1992," in *Police State America*, ed. Tom Burghardt (Arm The Spirit, 2002). Contact <www.kersplebedeb.com>.

Headquarters, Department of the Army, *United States Army Field Manual 19–15*, *Civil Disturbances*, Washington, DC, November 25, 1985, <www.adtdl. army. mil/cgi-bin/atdl.dll/fm/19–15/toc.htm>.

Center for Law and Military Operations, *Domestic Operational Law Handbook for Judge Advocates*, April 15, 2001, <www.jagnet.army.mil/clamo/publications>.

Frank Morales, "U.S. Military Civil Disturbance Planning: The War at Home," <www.cryptome.org/garden-plot.htm>.

3 U.S. Illegally Removes Pages from Iraq U.N. Report

Source:
The Humanist and *ArtVoice*, March/April 2003
Title: "What Bush Didn't Want You to Know about Iraq"
Author: Michael I. Niman

Faculty Evaluator: Tom Lough
Student Researchers: Lindsey Brage and Licia Marshall

First covered by Amy Goodman on *Democracy Now!*

Throughout the winter of 2002, the Bush Administration publicly accused Iraqi weapons declarations of being incomplete. Yet the truth of the situation is that it was the United States itself that had removed more than 8,000 pages of the 11,800-page original report.

This came as no surprise to Europeans however, as Iraq had made extra copies of the complete weapons declaration report and unofficially distributed them to journalists throughout Europe. The Berlin newspaper *Die Tageszeitung* broke the story on December 19, 2002, in an article by Andreas Zumach.

At the same time, the Iraq government sent out *official* copies of the report on November 3, 2002. One, classified as "secret," was sent to the International Atomic Energy Agency, and another copy went to the U.N. Security Council. The U.S. convinced Colombia, chair of the Security Council and current target of U.S. military occupation and recipient of financial aid, to look the other way while the report was removed, edited, and returned. Other members of the Security Council such as Britain, France, China, and Russia, were implicated in the missing pages as well (China and Russia were still arming Iraq) and had little desire to expose the United States' transgression. So all members accepted the new, abbreviated version.

But what was in the missing pages that the Bush Administration felt was so threatening that they had to be removed? What information were Europeans privy to that Americans were not?

According to Niman, "The missing pages implicated 24 U.S.-based corporations and the successive Ronald Reagan and George Bush Sr. Administrations in connection with the illegal supplying of Saddam Hussein's government with myriad weapons of mass destruction and the training to use them." Groups documented in the original report that were supporting Iraq's weapons programs prior to Iraq's 1990 invasion of Kuwait included:

- ➤ Eastman Kodak, DuPont, Honeywell, Rockwell, Sperry, Hewlett-Packard, and Bechtel;
- ➤ U.S. government agencies such as the Department of Energy (DOE), Department of Agriculture (DOA), and Department of Defense (DOD);
- ➤ nuclear weapons labs such as Lawrence-Livermore, Los Alamos, and Sandia.

Beginning in 1983, the U.S. was involved in 80 shipments of biological and chemical components, including strains of botulism toxin, anthrax, gangrene bacteria, West Nile fever virus, and dengue fever virus. These shipments continued even after Iraq used chemical weapons against Iran in 1984. Later, in 1988 Iraq used the chemical weapons against the Kurds.

But perhaps most importantly, the missing pages contain information that could potentially make a case for war crimes against officials within the Reagan and the Bush Sr. Administrations. This includes the current Defense Secretary Donald Rumsfeld—for his collaboration with Saddam Hussein leading up to the massacres of Iraqi Kurds and acting as liaison for U.S. military aid during the war between Iraq and Iran.

UPDATE BY MICHAEL I. NIMAN: The first time I had a story nominated for a Project Censored award was in 1989 after I went into the bush on Costa Rica's remote Osa Peninsula to track pirate gold miners and the U.S. military. I drank stagnant water to battle dehydration and picked ticks from my body. In short, I went after the story.

This was different. I didn't break this story. It was broken by German reporter Andreas Zumach and brought to the U.S. by Amy Goodman on her *Democracy Now!* radio show. No media outlet in my hometown of Buffalo covered it, so I added some media analysis, a few observations about censorship, and ran it in Buffalo's weekly *ArtVoice*. Since the national media never picked up the story, *The Humanist* took my story nationwide. I didn't use primary sources for this story. I just monitored the alternative and foreign press. With such thorough self-censorship in the U.S. press, reading the international press is now akin to going into the remote bush.

It is now five months later and there are still no new developments regarding this story. No corporate or government figures have been indicted. There is no investigation. The major media still hasn't carried the story. In its place, however, most media outlets ran false pronouncements from the Bush Administration about pending Iraqi weapons programs. We now know that these weapons no longer existed and that the Bush Administration was able to hijack the U.S. into war based on a combination of misinformation and missing information.

4 Rumsfeld's Plan to Provoke Terrorists

Source:
CounterPunch, <www.counterpunch.org/floyd101.html>, November 1, 2002
Title: "Into the Dark"
Author: Chris Floyd

Faculty Evaluators: Catherine Nelson and Meri Storino
Student Researcher: Jennifer Scanlan

Corporate media coverage: William Arkin, "The Secret War," *Los Angeles Times*, October 27, 2002

According to a classified document, "Special Operations and Joint Forces in Countering Terrorism," prepared for Secretary of Defense Donald Rumsfeld by his Defense Science Board, a new organization has been created to thwart potential terrorist attacks on the United States. This counterterror operations group—the Proactive Preemptive Operations Group (P2OG) will require 100 people and at least $100 million a year. The team of covert counterintelligence agents will be responsible for secret missions designed to target terrorist leaders. The secret missions are designed to "stimulate reactions" among terrorist groups, provoking them into committing violent acts which would then expose them to "counterattack" by U.S. forces.

This means that the United States government is planning to use secret military operations in order to provoke murderous terrorist attacks on innocent people. In a strange twist of logic, it seems the plan is to somehow combat terrorism by causing it. According to the report, other strategies include stealing money from terrorist cells or tricking them with fake communications. The Defense Department already maintains a secretive counterterror operations group known as Delta Force that is called in when a crisis happens.

Exactly what type of actions would be required to "stimulate reactions" by terrorist groups has yet to be revealed. When asked questions regarding what measures would be taken, Pentagon sources responded, "Their sovereignty will be at risk."

The current P2OG program is not entirely new to the United States. One similar program was Operation Northwoods. In 1963, America's top military brass presented a plan to President John Kennedy that called for a fake terrorist campaign—complete with bombings, hijackings, plane crashes, and dead Americans—to provide "justification" for an invasion of Cuba, a Mafia/corporate fiefdom that had recently been lost to Castro. Kennedy rejected the plan and was killed a few months later. Now Rumsfeld has resurrected Northwoods, but on a far grander scale, with resources at his disposal undreamed of by his predecessors and no counterbalancing global rival to restrain him.

Former President Richard Nixon wanted such a group, but Congress denied it; President Reagan tried to use the National Security Council instead, but ran into trouble with the Iran-Contra affair. Now, President Bush may finally realize the dream.

UPDATE BY CHRIS FLOYD: Appropriately enough for a story about the deepest possible covert operation—penetrating terrorist cells and provoking them into action—the saga of the Pentagon's Proactive Preemptive Operations Group (P2OG) went straight back into the dark after strutting its brief hour upon the stage. There has been no new information about the group since it was first mentioned nationally in the *Los Angeles Times* as part of a larger story on Pentagon plans for new "secret armies." Was it funded? Is it operational? Has it "flushed out" any terrorists lately by goading them into "action"? Are any of the post-Iraq War spate of terrorist atrocities linked to P2OG activities? We don't know. And with Donald Rumsfeld's openly avowed penchant for "strategic misinformation," how will we ever know? Certainly the mainstream press has done nothing to enlighten us. Although the *CounterPunch* article (which appeared simultaneously in *The Moscow Times*) provoked a lively response in the "alternative" media (print, Web, and radio), there has not been a single subsequent mention of the group in the U.S. national press. In the U.K., John Pilger has raised warning flags about P2OG in *The New Statesman* and the *Daily Mirror*, while *The Ecologist* also ran a version of the *CounterPunch* article. The rest is silence. At first glance, this decided lack of interest might seem a curious reaction, given the American media's insatiable—and profitable—obsession with terrorism. But the media's equally intense, and equally profitable, abhorrence of moral ambiguity—especially when it involves possible American complicity in mayhem and murder—makes the silence easier to understand.

FOR ADDITIONAL INFORMATION:

William Arkin, "The Secret War," *Los Angeles Times*, October 27, 2002, <www.commondreams.org/views02/1028–11.htm>.

David Isenberg, "P2OG Allows Pentagon to Fight Dirty," *Asia Times*, November 5, 2002, <www.atimes.com/atimes/Middle_East/DK05Ak02.html>.

An excerpt from the partially classified Defense Science Board briefing that proposed the creation of P2OG at <www.serendipity.li/more/dsbbrief.ppt>.

"Friendly Fire: Operation Northwoods," ABCNews.com, May 1, 2001, <abcnews.go.com/sections/us/DailyNews/jointchiefs_010501.html>

John Pilger, *The New Statesman*, December 12, 2002, <pilger.carlton.com/print/124759>.

5 The Effort to Make Unions Disappear

Sources:
International Socialist Review, September/October 2002
Z Magazine, September 20, 2002
Title: "Employers Attack: Unions Blink"
Author: Lee Sustar

War Times, October/November 2002
Title: "Unions Face National Insecurity"
Author: David Bacon

The Progressive, February 2003
Title: "Brazen Bosses"
Author: Anne-Marie Cusac

The American Prospect, March 2003
Title: "Class Warfare, Bush-Style"
Author: Robert L. Borosage

Faculty Evaluators: Fred Fletcher, Diana Grant,
Francisco Vazquez, and Laurie Dawson
Student Researchers: Rebecca Grant, Jessie Esquivel, and Sarah Zisman

For more than a quarter-century, big business has engaged in a successful campaign of weakening unions, redistributing income away from the working class, and writing business-friendly rules for the global economy. Yet the current political climate makes the last 25 years look like a golden era for workers' rights. Called the "most pro-corporate president in history," George W. Bush has been, particularly since 9/11, engaged in a relentless, yet largely covert, effort to undermine labor unions and worker protections.

In March 2001, Bush told 10,000 workers of Northwest Airlines that they could not strike for 80 days. The president also told United Airlines strikers that unless they agreed to further concessions the administration would refuse the $1.8 billion that the airline needed to avoid bankruptcy. After 9/11, Bush invoked the Taft-Hartley Act forcing workers of the Pacific Maritime Association to return to work.

Immigrant workers have suffered the most from the "war on unions." Prior to 9/11, immigrant workers began receiving better wages and working conditions. The Service Employees International Union (SEIU) negotiated a new contract for baggage screeners raising their pay from minimum wage to $10 an hour. Also, the AFL-CIO called for the repeal of the law that makes it illegal for undocumented workers to work in the U.S. The Immigration and Naturalization Service (INS) was also beginning to reduce the number of raids it carried out to find undocumented workers.

In the wake of 9/11, the Bush Administration used the specter of national security to justify its attack on public-sector unions, and to stall passage of the homeland security bill until receiving the right to exempt the 180,000 employees of the new department of most civil-service protections. Congress passed legislation that created the Transportation Security Authority (TSA), which oversees baggage screeners at airports and requires all baggage screeners to be federal government employees. But because the TSA is part of the Homeland Security Department, employees may not form or join a union. Congressional legislation also allows Homeland Security Director Tom Ridge to suspend civil service regulations, allow discrimination, abolish whistleblower protections, and exempt the department from Freedom of Information Act regulations (FOIA). The House has passed legislation that also exempts the Homeland Security Department from Title 5 of the Civil Service Act, which protects the collective bargaining rights of federal employees.

After 9/11, to ensure that screeners were American citizens, the INS launched Operation Tarmac. Operation Tarmac began by picking up immigrant workers who had access to airplanes. But as time moved on, the operation began cracking down on immigrant workers in all sections of airports, even food service. In one instance, the Hotel and Restaurant Employees Union claims that immigrant workers were called to an employee meeting where they were arrested by INS agents.

In December of 2002, the Labor Department issued new reporting and itemization regulations for unions—an administrative nightmare that will cost unions millions of dollars. Having asked the new Congress to pass strict penalties for unions that fail to meet reporting deadlines, the Bush budget increased spending for auditing, investigating, and punishing union violations. At the same time, the budget cut money for enforcing workplace health and safety laws and for investigating corporate violations of worker protections. In his first two years in office, Bush has already blocked more strikes than any president in history.

As was reported in the mainstream press, the Bush Administration has announced plans to accelerate the process of contracting out federal work to private companies, putting the jobs of nearly 850,000 federal employees at risk. This invites anti-union, low-wage contractors to compete for what are now, in most cases, decent-paying, union jobs with good benefits. But what went unreported is that this is proving to embolden conservative governors who are seeking wholesale privatization and de-unionization of state and local work forces as well.

UPDATE BY ANNE-MARIE CUSAC: It is hard to overstate the importance of this story. The near loss of the right to organize has the potential to affect every single worker in the country, though it most drastically affects poor and working-class people. As the right to organize disappears, so, too, do other rights: the right to health care, livable wages, and leisure time.

One of the most disturbing aspects of this story is the blatant mistreatment of those workers who are brave enough to attempt to bring unions into their places of work. The outright physical abuse, the propensity to fire organizers, the threats to lay off or cut benefits to any who vote for the union—all of these are effective strategies that contribute to the sinking rates of union membership in the United States. The government has little power to stop employers from using such tactics, and some employers evidently feel that it pays to break the law. Millions of workers want a union and do not have one. Less than 10 percent of the private sector is now unionized, down from a high of 36 percent in the early 1950s.

Since my piece appeared in *The Progressive*, the National Labor Relations Board (NLRB) has issued more complaints showing that companies routinely attempt to suppress unions.

In late April, the *Washington Post* reported, President Bush took advantage of a congressional recess to avoid Senate oversight in his appointments of two more officials to positions connected with the NLRB.

Bush chose Peter Eide to serve as the general counsel at the Federal Labor Relations Authority. Eide is now in charge of enforcing labor laws that apply to federal employees. Formerly, Eide directed labor-law policy at the United States Chamber of Commerce.

Bush also appointed Neil Anthony Gordon McPhie to the Merit Systems Protection Board, which, among other obligations, oversees personnel and disciplinary procedures that government agencies take against workers.

More information on particular companies that fire or otherwise mistreat workers who are trying to bring in unions is available on the NLRB Web site: <www.nlrb.gov/>. Two experts on these issues, Kate Bronfenbrenner and Lance Compa, are both associated with Cornell University and the School of Industrial and Labor Relations: <www.ilr.cornell.edu/>. Bronfenbrenner is the author of several excellent books, and Compa's 2000 report on union organizing and human rights issues in the United States is available on the Human Rights Watch Web site: <www.hrw.org/reports/2000/uslabor/>. Anyone interested in these issues is also welcome to contact me at *The Progressive*, Tel: (608) 257-4626.

UPDATE BY LEE SUSTAR: It's revealing that the story of a labor movement with more than 13 million members can be censored with relative ease. The dominant media view in recent years has been that unions are artifacts of an earlier era and are simply no longer relevant in the "new" information economy. Full-time labor beat reporters, once fixtures in big-city newsrooms, virtually disappeared years ago.

Since the onset of economic crisis, however, some journalists have resurrected an older media stereotype: that of big labor, selfishly protecting its "special" interests at the expense of the greater economic good. Developments since the publication of "Employers Attack" make this clear.

The most important example was the contract battle by the West Coast dockworkers in the International Longshore and Warehouse Union (ILWU). Journalists typically portrayed the ILWU as a barrier to progress—even though it was an employers' lockout that shut down the ports for 10 days in September and October 2002. President George W. Bush's use of the antilabor Taft-Hartley Act, ostensibly aimed at ending the lockout, in fact gave the employers' dictates the backing of the federal courts—a fact barely noted in the mainstream press.

Similarly, reporters blamed the crisis gripping the airlines largely on labor. *New York Times* labor reporter Steven Greenhouse wrote in an article published April 27, 2003, "The pilots, the machinists, and other airline unions have obtained some of the highest wages in organized labor in decades past, helping push their airlines' operating costs so high that the airlines became vulnerable to downturns and more recently to the emergence of low-cost upstarts like Jet Blue." In fact, unionized workers at United Airlines accepted massive concessions in 1994—and the company ended up bankrupt anyway. Few reporters have examined the human costs of an estimated $35 billion in airline labor concessions—lost jobs, cut wages, broken families, and worse. The same is true of the series of steel industry bankruptcies, which have wiped out health insurance and cut pensions for tens of thousands of retirees.

Fortunately, alternatives exist. The reportage and analysis in "Employers Attack" were expanded in a subsequent article in the *International Socialist Review*, "Labor's War at Home" (March/April 2003, online at <www.isreview.org>). Web sites such as LaborNet, <www.labornet.org>, *Socialist Worker*, <www.socialistworker.org>, *Labor Notes*, <www.labornotes.org>, ZNet, <www.zmag.org>, and *CounterPunch*, <www.counterpunch.org> regularly post news and analysis of organized labor. These outlets have followed one of the most important political developments in the unions in many years—widespread opposition to the U.S. war on Iraq and the formation of the organization "U.S. Labor Against the War." They also frequently cover union reform efforts ignored by the media.

6 Closing Access to Information Technology

Source:
Dollars and Sense, September 2002
Title: "Slamming Shut Open Access"
Author: Arthur Stamoulis

Faculty Evaluator: Scott Gordon
Student Researcher: Daryl Khoo

Technological changes, coupled with deregulation, may soon radically limit diversity on the Internet.

The 7,000 Internet Service Providers (ISPs) still available today are quickly dwindling to just two or three for any one locale. They are being bought out by large monopolies that also control your local phone, cable, and possibly, satellite Internet.

The Federal Communications Commission (FCC) and Congress are currently overturning the public-interest rules that have encouraged the expansion of the Internet up until now. Much of this is due to the lobbying tactics that cable and phone industries use to mute the competition, take advantage of technological changes, and push for deregulation to consolidate market control.

A policy of open access currently makes it possible for people to choose between long-distance phone providers. This open-access policy has also allowed one to choose between AOL, MSN, Jimmy's Internet Shack, and thousands of other ISPs for dial-up Internet access. Phone companies would like to use their monopoly ownership of the phone wires to have total control over phone-based Internet services as well, but telecom regulations are in place that prevent them from blocking out other companies.

Unfortunately, as the general shift from dial-up to broadband Internet access gets underway, the FCC is moving in with a series of actions that threaten to shut down open access. In 2002, the FCC decided to characterize high-speed cable Internet connection—largely controlled by AOL Time Warner, AT&T Broadband, and other large corporate players—as an "information service" rather than a "telecommunications service." This designation frees cable broadband from telecom rules, giving the cable companies that own broadband lines the ability to deny smaller ISP companies access over their cable lines. Cable itself is a monopoly in most towns, so anyone who signs up for cable Internet will typically have no choice other than to use the cable company's own ISP.

Such degree of market control spells trouble for freedom of information on the Internet. Cable and phone monopolies would become clearinghouses for information.

Corporations and government agencies will hold tremendous power to filter and censor content. ISPs already have the capability to privilege, or block out, content traveling through their Web servers. With the demise of open access regulations, Internet content will likely resemble the "monotonous diet of corporate content" that viewers now receive with cable television.

The monopoly power being handed over to the cable and phone companies will enable them to sell different levels of Internet access, much like they do with cable television. For one price, you could access only certain pre-approved sites; for a higher price, you could access a wider selection of sites; and only for the highest price could you access the entire World Wide Web. This is already the way that many wireless Internet packages operate. It's clear that "marginal" content that isn't associated with e-commerce, big business, or government would have a hard time making it into the first-tier, "basic" packages. This isn't censorship, we'll be told. It's just that there is only so much bandwidth to go around, and customers would rather see CNN, the Disney Channel, and porn than community-based Web sites, such as <www.indymedia.org>.

UPDATE BY ARTHUR STAMOULIS: Most people still do not understand how differences in regulations governing different technologies threaten the future of the Internet—and industry is continuing to use that to their advantage.

In November 2002, the FCC approved Comcast's $47.5-billion purchase of AT&T Broadband, creating the largest cable company in the world. Neither the FCC nor the Department of Justice (DOJ) imposed any rules forcing the newly formed behemoth to offer customers the ISP of their choice. Thus, 30 percent of cable subscribers now have little-to-no say over what high-speed cable broadband ISP they will use. It's simply Comcast or nothing.

Senator McCain's effort to allow phone companies to bar other ISPs from the DSL lines—the Consumer Broadband Deregulation Act—thankfully went nowhere during the 107th Congress. While behind-closed-doors lobbying has undoubtedly continued, the FCC has also done little on this front in the first half of 2003, focusing instead on dismantling the few remaining media ownership regulations for television, radio, and newspapers.

Of course, the elimination of ownership rules for television broadcasters could also have an impact on the Internet. In 1996, television stations were given the right to the "digital" spectrum free of charge, another one of Congress' gifts to industry worth billions upon billions of dollars. This digital spectrum gives owners the option to broadcast as many as five channels on the space previously needed for just one. As television stations typically get preferred treatment with cable companies in terms of transmission deals or must-carry regulations, media conglomerates that can buy up lots of TV stations now will likely have considerable access to cable bandwidth.

This is especially valuable as TV and the Internet merge into next-generation inter-active television (ITV) applications.

Whether public-interest or community-access programming will have a place in this brave new Internet world will depend upon how loudly people demand it. Fortunately, the biggest untold media story of 2003 is that people are coming together to demand their media rights. The Bush Administration's deregulatory bonanza was met with loud protest from groups as disparate as the National Organization for Women (NOW) and the National Rifle Association (NRA), the Catholic Conference of Bishops, and the AFL-CIO. Online progressive organizations like <MoveOn.org> and Common Cause have also mobilized their members in the fight for media democracy. People from coast to coast have protested in the streets on these issues.

Readers interested in learning more about how regulations and technological changes affect the Internet should turn to the Center for Digital Democracy, <democraticmedia.org>, a group that has provided the best policy analysis expertise on these issues for years. Activists should also get in touch with Media Tank, <mediatank.org>, a leader in grassroots media democracy organizing. Finally, people should follow the progress of Free Press, <mediareform.net>, a new project aimed at becoming a national clearinghouse on media issues, started by veteran media critic Robert W. McChesney.

7 Treaty Busting by the United States

Sources:
Connections, June 2002
Title: "Rule of Power or Rule of Law?"
Authors: Marylia Kelly and Nicole Deller

The Nation, April 2002
Title: "Unsigning the ICC"
Author: John B. Anderson

Asheville Global Report (*AGR*), June 20–26, 2002
Title: "U.S. Invasion Proposal Shocks the Netherlands"
Compiled by: Eamon Martin

Global Outlook, Summer 2002
Title: "Nuclear Nightmare"
Author: John Valleau

Faculty Evaluators: Lynn Cominsky, Rick Luttmann,
Mary Gomes, Robert MacNamara, and Diana Grant
Student Researchers: Pat Spiva and Tara Spreng

The United States is a signatory to nine multilateral treaties that it has either blatantly violated or gradually subverted. The Bush Administration is now rejecting outright a number of those treaties, and in doing so places global security in jeopardy as other nations feel entitled to do the same. The rejected treaties include: The Comprehensive Test Ban Treaty (CTBT), the Treaty Banning Antipersonnel Mines, the Rome Statute of the International Criminal Court (ICC), a protocol to create a compliance regime for the Biological Weapons Convention (BWC), the Kyoto Protocol on global warming, and the Anti-Ballistic Missile Treaty (ABM). The U.S. is also not complying with the Treaty on the Non-Proliferation of Nuclear Weapons (NPT), the Chemical Weapons Commission (CWC), the BWC, and the U.N. framework Convention on Climate Change.

The ABM Treaty alone is a crucial factor in national security; its demise will destroy the balance of power carefully crafted in its original blueprint. The Bush Administration has no legitimate excuse for nullifying the ABM Treaty because the events that have threatened the security of the United States have not involved ballistic missiles, and none of them are in any way related to the subject matter of the ABM Treaty. Bush's withdrawal violates the U.S. Constitution, international law, and Article XV of the ABM Treaty itself. The Bush Administration says it needs to get rid of the ABM Treaty so it can test the SPY radar on the Aegis cruisers against Inter Continental Ballistic Missiles (ICBM) and so that it can build a new test facility at Fort Greely, Alaska. In addition, some conservatives have willingly dismissed the ABM Treaty because it stands as the major obstacle towards development of a "Star Wars" missile defense system.

The NPT is crucial to global security because it bars the spread of nuclear weapons. The U.S. is currently in noncompliance with the NPT requirements, as demonstrated in the January 2002 U.S. *Nuclear Posture Review*. Moreover, critics charge that the National Ignition Facility (NIF) under construction at Livermore lab violates the Comprehensive Test Ban Treaty (CTBT), which the U.S. signed in 1996, but has not ratified. The CTBT bans nuclear explosions, and its language does not contain any "exceptions allowing laboratory thermonuclear explosions."

The twentieth century was the bloodiest in human history, with a total of 174 million people killed in genocide and war. As the world becomes increasingly globalized, it increasingly needs an international legal framework through which the people of the world can be protected from heinous criminal acts, such as genocide, war crimes, and crimes against humanity. It is an understanding of this reality that may explain the votes of the 139 countries that signed the Rome Treaty and the 67 ratifications that have resulted in the establishment of the International Criminal Court (ICC).

Former U.S. president, Bill Clinton, signed the Rome Treaty supporting the ICC when he held office. However, in an unprecedented action, George W. Bush actually erased Clinton's signature (a United States president has never before "unsigned" a treaty). And his administration has declared it has no intention whatsoever of co-operating with the ICC.

Furthermore, in what is being called the Hague Invasion Act, the GOP-controlled House Appropriations Committee voted to authorize the use of military force to "rescue" any American brought before the ICC. Erica Terpstra, a parliamentary representative in the Netherlands, where The Hague and ICC are located, states that this "is not only a gesture against the Netherlands...but against the entire international community."

While proponents of ICC consider it the most important development in international law since the Nazi war crimes Nuremberg Tribunal after World War II, the Bush Administration insists it would limit U.S. sovereignty and interfere with actions of the U.S. military.

This unprecedented rejection of and rapid retreat from global treaties that have in effect kept the peace through the decades will not only continue to isolate U.S. policy, but will also render these treaties and conventions invalid without the support and participation of the world's foremost superpower.

FOR ADDITIONAL INFORMATION:

Dr. Robert Bowman, Lt. Col., USAF (ret.), "The ABM Treaty: Dead or Alive?" *Space and Security News*, February 2002.

UPDATE BY MARYLIA KELLY: The United States, a progenitor of the concept that national and international affairs should be subject to "rule of law," is now actively undermining that rule. By so doing, the United States is simultaneously decreasing the security of its own and all the world's people. "Rule of Power or Rule of Law?" and the longer report on which it is based document how the U.S. flaunts its treaty obligations and international law. Moreover, the article and report create a needed foundation for public debate on the long-term consequences of the Bush Administration's increasing penchant for using the U.S. military, new weapons, and a unilaterally-powerful "Fortress America" as its foreign policy basis.

Since the article was published in May 2002, the U.S. has undertaken a series of actions to further weaken international law as a framework for achieving just resolution of conflict. The action that first comes to many minds is the recent war on Iraq. However, a number of lesser-known U.S. actions to undermine international treaties may also have serious, deleterious impacts on domestic and global security. Two key examples can be found in U.S. disregard for the Treaty on the Non-Proliferation of Nuclear Weapons (NPT) and the Biological Weapons Convention (BWC).

The Bush Administration actively negated its central disarmament obligation under the NPT by adding billion of dollars to the budget for nuclear weapons activities, including its 2004 budget request to speed the weapons labs' development of a "Robust Nuclear Earth Penetrator" bomb, conduct research on a variety of new mini-nuke concepts, enhance U.S. readiness to conduct a full-scale underground nuclear test and design and build a new plutonium pit factory capable of producing Cold War production levels of more than 500 new bomb cores per year. The administration's Nuclear Posture Review and the subsequent National Security Strategy of the United States promulgate a policy of "preemptive" or "preventive" first use of nuclear weapons. It is no coincidence that North Korea and Iran, targeted by new U.S. nuclear policy initiatives, have apparently stepped up their nuclear programs. North Korea has announced its withdrawal from the Non-Proliferation Treaty. Iran has embarked on a more aggressive nuclear power program, albeit in current compliance with the International Atomic Energy Agency requirements. The U.S. demands, "do as we say, not as we do."

U.S. actions have similarly led to a dangerous weakening of the Biological Weapons Convention. As recently as November 2002, the Bush Administration continued to quash negotiations on verification and enforcement measures needed to detect and prevent violations to the BWC. Then, the U.S. announced its intention to build and operate biowarfare agent facilities at its two premier classified nuclear weapons laboratories, Lawrence Livermore in California and Los Alamos in New Mexico. The co-location of biowarfare agent and nuclear weapons design capabilities is proceeding without environmental impact statements, public hearings, or proliferation reviews.

Many good resources for further study are available from nongovernmental organizations and on the Web. Tri-Valley CAREs' site is <www.trivalleycares.org>. The "Rule of Power or Rule of Law?" report was written by the Institute for Energy and Environmental Research, <www.ieer.org>, and the Lawyers Committee on Nuclear Policy, <www.lcnp.org>. In 2003, Apex Press released an expanded book-length version under the same title, with Nicole Deller, Arjun Makhijani, and John Burroughs.

UPDATE BY JOHN VALLEAU: The mass media continued to ignore the implications of the U.S. Missile Defense (MD) plans. Some activist organizing continued among peace groups. When the Canadian government was forcefully urged, by delegations and letters and briefs, to oppose publicly the MD plans, the consequences were pointed out: both for nuclear proliferation and the introduction of U.S. space weaponry. In view of the longstanding Canadian opposition to space weapons (in the U.N. Conference on Disarmament and elsewhere), we were disillusioned by our government's unwillingness to speak out; we hoped that if Canada spoke out, as a friendly nation that belongs to NATO and NORAD, it might well have some inhibiting effect on the U.S. plans.

In the last few weeks (I write in early June 2003) the issue has suddenly become prominent in the mainstream media, but for the most disappointing of reasons: the Canadian government is moving to "negotiate" with the U.S. about cooperation in MD— the direct opposite of our hopes—and using evasive arguments, which suggests they never read the briefs. The context of this shift in policy involves signals of U.S. displeasure over Canada's refusal to take direct part in the illegal aggression on Iraq: the embarrassing response in Ottawa has been to seek to curry renewed U.S. favor, at whatever cost of principle. This is life on the periphery of power. On the positive side, a vigorous public debate has been provoked and it has focused substantially on the key MD issues of nuclear proliferation and the path to space weapons; one can hope that articles like mine and others have contributed somewhat at least to this ready public awareness of the issues at stake.

WEB SITES FOR INFORMATION AND INVOLVEMENT:

Union of Concerned Scientists, <www.ucsusa.org>: Detailed studies and commentary.
Global Network Against Weapons and Nuclear Power in Space, <www.space4 peace.org>: Up-to-date news and commentary; news list; activism.
Project Ploughshares, Canada, <www.ploughshares.ca>: Detailed information; policy.

UPDATE BY EAMON MARTIN: At the time this story broke, *Asheville Global Report* editors noticed that with the exception of one, modest article released on the Reuters newswire, coverage was limited to a few articles published outside of the United States. Here, the U.S. Administration of George W. Bush was already asserting a controversially unilateralist foreign policy, going so far as to threaten an invasion of a sovereign nation, all for the sake of shielding its personnel from the scrutiny of human rights observers and thus, world opinion. In light of the extremely provocative and hostile nature of this diplomatic posture, one might wonder whether the mainstream news media themselves were protecting the U.S. from accountability by not finding this story to be newsworthy.

The United Nations Security Council (UNSC) has recently extended its exemption from the jurisdiction of the ICC for a second straight year. "The [U.N.] resolution is an attempt to satisfy domestic political ideology and legislation, and… subordinate a multilateral institution to U.S. power," said William Pace, convenor of the Coalition for the ICC, in a report by Jim Lobe for Inter Press Service published on June 9, 2003.

Lobe writes that rights groups and government backers of the ICC are demanding an open debate on the issue. They argue that the Security Council lacks the legal authority to grant exemptions because the U.N. Charter does not grant it power to amend an international treaty. Pace's group, which represents dozens of human rights groups around the world, strongly lobbied member nations of the UNSC to reject Washington's request.

Of the 15 members of the council, only the United States, China, and Pakistan have not signed the Rome Statute. The other 12 have either signed or ratified it. As of May 2003, all NATO members, except the United States and Turkey, have ratified the ICC treaty, as have all members of the European Union (EU) and all candidate EU members, except the Czech Republic.

That the Bush Administration would demonstrate such resistance to the ICC at a time of unprecedented U.S. military expansionism, while trumpeting a National Security Strategy of "preemptive" defense, has invited suspicion about the White House's quest for absolute impunity.

As top U.S. officials such as Vice President Dick Cheney continue to portray their global campaign against "terror" as potentially being a "war without end," and as the deployment of U.S. forces abroad escalates from Colombia to the Horn of Africa to the Philippines, and beyond, the U.S. refusal of a world criminal court may have alarming geopolitical implications.

For more information, see Jim Lobe, "U.S. Looks to Renew Exemption from World Criminal Court," Inter Press Service, June 9, 2003; Eamon Martin, "Bush Declaration: Global Military Domination," *Asheville Global Report*, No. 193, September 25, 2002, <www.agrnews.org/issues/193/worldnews.html>.

8 U.S./British Forces Continue Use of Depleted Uranium Weapons Despite Massive Evidence of Negative Health Effects

Sources:
Hustler, June 2003
Title: "Toxic Troops: What Our Soldiers Can Expect in Gulf War II"
Author: Dan Kapelovitz

Children of War, March 2003
Title: "The Hidden Killer"
Author: Reese Erlich
Faculty Evaluator: Rick Williams
Student Researchers: Darrel Jacks and Jason Spencer

British and American coalition forces are using depleted uranium (DU) shells in the war against Iraq and deliberately flouting a U.N. resolution that classifies the munitions as illegal weapons of mass destruction.

Nobel Peace Prize candidate Helen Caldicott states that the tiny radioactive particles created when a DU weapon hits a target are easily inhaled through gas masks. The particles, which lodge in the lung, can be transferred to the kidney and other vital organs. Gulf War veterans are excreting uranium in their urine and semen, leading to chromosomal damage. DU has a half-life of 4.1 billion years. The negative effects found in one generation of U.S. veterans could be the fate of all future generations of Iraqi people.

An August 2002 U.N. report states that the use of the DU weapons is in violation of numerous laws and U.N. conventions. Maj. Doug Rokke, ex-director of the Pentagon's DU project says, "We must do what is right for the citizens of the world— ban DU." Reportedly, more than 9,600 veterans have died since serving in Iraq during the first Gulf War, a statistical anomaly. The Pentagon has blamed the extraordinary number of illnesses and deaths on a variety of factors, including stress, pesticides, vaccines, and oil-well fire smoke. However, according to top-level U.S. Army reports and military contractors, "short-term effects of high doses (of DU) can result in death, while long-term effects of low doses have been implicated in cancer." Our own soldiers in the first Gulf War were often required to enter radioactive battlefields unprotected and were never warned of the dangers of DU. In effect, George Bush Sr. used weapons of mass destruction on his own soldiers. The internal coverup of the dangers of DU has been intentional and widespread.

In addition to Doug Rokke, the Pentagon's original expert on DU, ex-army nurse Carol Picou has been outspoken about the negative effects of DU on herself and other veterans. She has compiled extensive documentation on the birth defects found among the Iraqi people and the children of our own Gulf War veterans. She was threatened in anonymous phone calls on the eve of her testimony to Congress. Subsequently, her car, which contained sensitive information on DU, was mysteriously destroyed.

UPDATE BY DAN KAPELOVITZ: Just as "Toxic Troops: What Our Soldiers Can Expect in Gulf War II" hit the newsstands, the U.S. military was dropping a fresh batch of depleted-uranium tipped shells on Iraq. The story couldn't have been more timely; yet the mainstream media blatantly ignored *Hustler*'s coverage of the hazards of depleted uranium (DU) and largely failed to report any DU-related stories.

Rather than being ashamed that a porn magazine was more willing than they were to publish the truth, major media outlets kidded themselves into believing that the story didn't need to be covered, claiming it was "old news." While it's true that there has been some limited coverage of DU ever since the first Gulf War, the average American has not heard of depleted uranium. Those who have most likely saw reports focusing on DU's awesome armor-piercing abilities, not its harmful long-term effects on people and the environment.

Had the mainstream media informed Americans about the hazards to the military men and women caused by our own government, U.S. citizens might not have been so gung-ho to send our troops to Iraq again. Instead, TV pundits constantly told the American people that we attacked the Iraqi people in order to "liberate" them. Thanks to U.S. efforts, the Iraqi population is now free to live in a radioactive battlefield.

As with the first Gulf War, there were relatively few immediate American casualties. But with each passing year, more and more Gulf War veterans are sick and dying, very possibly due to exposure to depleted uranium. The latest Persian Gulf conflict was basically a low-level nuclear war, and our new recruits are destined to suffer DU-related illnesses and fatalities.

While there has been grassroots activism against the use of depleted uranium, the American military has ignored the concerns and have even discounted their own report, completed six months prior to the first Gulf War, which concluded that DU was indeed dangerous. At least this time around, more soldiers seem to be aware of the possible hazards of DU and are taking precautions to avoid exposure. Some are even placing signs in Arabic to warn Iraqi children not to play with radioactive shells or on contaminated tanks. After the war, the British government, which also used DU weapons, asserted that it should help clean up the radioactive mess that it created. If the American media did its job exposing the truth, perhaps the U.S. government, which was responsible for most of the damage, would be shamed into sharing England's concerns.

RESOURCES:

International Action Center (IAC), <www.iacenter.org>: The IAC published the book *Metal of Dishonor Depleted Uranium*

Dr. Helen Caldicott, *The New Nuclear Danger: George W. Bush's Military-Industrial Complex*, <www.nuclearpolicy.org>

Military Toxics Project, <www.miltoxproj.org/>

National Gulf War Resource Center, <www.ngwrc.org>

Uranium Medical Research Center, <www.umrc.net>

Campaign Against Depleted Uranium, <www.cadu.org.uk>

UPDATE BY REESE ERLICH: The Pentagon loves using depleted uranium ammunition because it penetrates and helps blow up enemy targets. They care little about the long-term health effects on enemy soldiers, civilians, or even U.S. military vets. As I investigated the issue further, I began to realize the government may well be covering up a health scandal, just as it hid the effects of Agent Orange in Vietnam.

In Basra, before the U.S. invasion of 2003, doctors showed me a photo album of horribly deformed children, some born without noses or eyes. They compiled a cancer registry of children suffering from leukemia and other cancers. Children exposed to DU in southern Iraq saw a fourfold increase in cancer and birth defects since 1990.

In "The Hidden Killers," I combined original reporting from Iraq and Bosnia with interviews of U.S. military veterans. Too many Iraqi and Bosnian civilians exposed to DU are showing up with the same kinds of cancers as American Gulf War vets.

I also learned that the Pentagon doesn't like critics. Military officers and scientists who criticize the Pentagon's position can come under withering attack. After the Gulf War, Maj. Doug Rokke was assigned to develop official procedures for soldiers at sites where DU was used. He and his committee mandated that soldiers wear special protective clothing because of the cancer risk. The Pentagon overruled him, claiming DU is safe. Rokke, who is on disability as a result of his DU exposure, later had his disability benefits cut off.

The topic of depleted uranium ammunition has surfaced in the mainstream media over the years, but strong denials from the military and the complexity of the topic have muted many of the stories. I've had editors at prestigious publications tell me they won't touch the DU story because it's "too controversial." In my opinion, few reporters or editors are willing to risk the career danger inherent in criticizing the Pentagon or taking on a popular president during "wartime."

Since "The Hidden Killers" came out, the Uranium Medical Research Center, <www.umrc.net>, has published studies showing the devastating impact of DU in the Afghanistan War, and the *Christian Science Monitor* (May 15, 2003) featured an

THIS MODERN WORLD   by TOM TOMORROW

excellent report on the impact of DU use in urban areas during the Iraq invasion.

I'd like to particularly thank the Stanley Foundation, a non-profit in Muscatine, Iowa, for its support in producing "Children of War: Fighting Dying, Surviving," the public radio documentary in which "The Hidden Killers" was featured.

9 In Afghanistan: Poverty, Women's Rights, and Civil Disruption Worse than Ever

Sources:
The Nation, October 14, 2002
Title: "Afghanistan Imperiled"
Author: Ahmed Rashid

Left Turn, February/March 2003
Title: "Afghanistan: Lies and Horrible Truths"
Author: Pranjal Tiwari

The Nation, April 29, 2002
Title: "An Uneasy Peace"
Author: Jan Goodwin

Mother Jones, July/August 2002
Title: "Childhood Burdens"
Authors: Photo Essay by Chien-Min Chung/Saba, Text by Scott Carrier

Corporate media coverage: Michele Landsburg, "Afghanistan Documentary Exposes Bush's Promises," *Toronto Star*, March 2, 2003.

Faculty Evaluators: Richard Zimmer, Greta Vollmer, Rick Williams, and Maureen Buckley
Student Researchers: Kathleen Glover and Dylan Citrin Cummins

While all eyes have been turned to Iraq, the people of Afghanistan have continued to suffer in silence in what is considered to be their worst poverty in decades. The promised democratic government is too concerned with assassination attempts to worry about the suffering of its people. They still have no new constitution, no new laws, and little food. Ethnic and political rivalries plague the country and the military power of the warlords has increased. While the International Security Assistance Force (ISAF), the 4,500-strong foreign peacekeeping unit, is assigned to defend only the capital, private armies of an estimated 700,000 people roam Afghanistan continuing a traditional system of fiefdoms.

The Nation covered the failure of the improvement of women's rights after the U.S. invasion. Despite the fanfare (stripping the burqa and the signing of the Declaration of Essential Rights of Afghan Women), little has changed for the average Afghani woman. Many women have yet to stop wearing the burqa due to fear of persecution and the new Interior Ministry still requires women to receive permission from their male relatives before they travel. According to former Women's Affairs Minister Dr. Sima Samar, the ministry is severely underfunded. As of April 2002, Dr. Samar had no access to the Internet and was unable to afford to operate her satellite phone. She was also receiving many death threats. Dr. Samar resigned later that year and is currently working as a human rights commissioner. Hafiza Rasouli, a UNICEF project officer, stated, "We felt safer under the Taliban." As for the future *loya jirga*, or grand council, that will help determine governmental policies, only 160 seats out of 1,450 have been guaranteed to women.

As of July 2002, the life expectancy for the people of Afghanistan is 46 years. The average yearly income per capita is $280. As for the children, 90 percent are not in school. After 23 years of war, the adult male population has been decimated, and many children have taken the place of their fathers and mothers as the breadwinners in their families. Some scavenge for scrap metal, wood, or bricks, while others hammer sheet metal, fill potholes, or build coffins. They are lucky to earn five cents an hour. More than one out of every four children in Afghanistan will die before the age of five. The growth of more than half these children is moderately or severely stunted from malnutrition. A UNICEF study has found that the majority of children are highly traumatized and expect to die before reaching adulthood. Beyond this, the region is just overcoming a three-year drought, which killed half the crops and 80 percent of livestock in some areas.

In January 2002, the Tokyo conference pledged $4.5 billion for reconstruction, of which donor nations promised $1.8 billion this year. Nearly one year later, barely 30 percent of what was promised had been delivered. The U.S. government's own contribution has been half that of the European Union. The $300 million granted in 2002 was quickly spent. The U.S. government has been hesitant to put funding into the ISAF or reconstruction-oriented groups and has been more focused on building an Afghan national army. However, the simultaneous funding of local warlords, now being referred to as "regional leaders," is undermining this work.

UPDATE BY PRANJAL TIWARI: News about Afghanistan seemed to drop off the mainstream radar following the U.S. invasion. For a while we heard about the new postwar Afghanistan: radios being turned on for the first time in years, women going to school, men shaving beards, and the onset of the Kharzai era. But what we didn't hear about in the mainstream press forms the bulk of Afghanistan's grim and continuing postwar history. To help negotiate some of the blind spots, excellent resources include the Human Rights Watch (HRW) reports cited in the article: "Afghanistan's Bonn Agreement One Year On," <www.hrw.org/backgrounder/asia/afghanistan/bonn1yr-bck.htm>.

"All Our Hopes Have Been Crushed," <www.hrw.org/reports/2002/afghan3/>.

Also, Human Rights Watch's "Key Documents on Afghanistan" has a number of other reports and alerts on the subject: <www.hrw.org/campaigns/afghanistan/>

ZNet's "Afghanistan Watch" section: <www.zmag.org/terrorwar/znet_afghanistan.htm>.

"Unworthy Victims," <www.globalexchange.org/september11/apogreport.pdf>.

Robert Fisk Reports from Afghanistan, <www.robert-fisk.com/index_fisk_articles.htm>

The Revolutionary Association of Women in Afghanistan (RAWA), <rawa.fancymarketing.net/recent2.htm>

Project on Defense Alternatives, <www.comw.org/warreport/index.html> and <www.comw.org/pda/index.html>.

The English-language Pakistani daily *Dawn*, <www.dawn.com>. Humeira Iqtidar's article "Reconstruction of Iraq," for example, appeared in *Dawn* on April 7 2003.

10 Africa Faces Threat of New Colonialism

Sources:
Left Turn, July/August 2002
Title: "NEPAD: Repackaging Colonialism in Africa"
Author: Michelle Robidoux

Briarpatch, Vol. 32, No. 1, excerpted from *The CCPA Monitor*, October 2002
Title: "Ravaging Africa"
Author: Asad Ismi

Peacework, October 2002
Title: "Africa: The New Oil and Military Frontier"
Author: Dena Montague

New Internationalist, January/February 2003
Title: "How (Not) to Feed Africa"
Author: Dr. Tewolde Berhan Gebre Egziabher

Faculty evaluator: Heidi LaMoreaux
Student Researchers: Kathleen Glover, Laura Huntington, Kagiso Molefhe, and Dana Balicki

Today, Africa is the most war-torn continent in the world. Over the past 15 years, 32 of the 53 African countries experienced violent conflict. During the Cold War years (1950–1989), the U.S. sent $1.5 billion in arms and training to Africa thus setting the stage for the current round of conflicts. From 1991 to 1995, the U.S. increased the amount of weapons and other military assistance to 50 of the total 53 African countries. Over the years, these U.S.-funded wars have been responsible for the deaths of millions of Africans and the subsequent displacement, disease, and starvation of many millions more.

In June 2002, leaders from the eight most powerful countries in the world (the G8) met to form a New Partnership for Africa's Development (NEPAD) as an "antipoverty" campaign. One glaring omission, however, is the consultation and representation of the African nations. Not one of the eight leaders was from Africa. The danger of the NEPAD proposal is that it fails to protect Africa from exploitation of its resources. NEPAD is akin to Plan Columbia in its attempt to employ Western development techniques to provide economic opportunities for international investment. Welcomed by the G8 nations, this development plan reads like a mad dash to grab up as much of Africa's remaining resources as possible.

According to Robert Murphy of the U.S. State Department's Office of African Analysis, Africa is important to "the diversification of our sources of imported oil" away from the Middle East. The U.S. currently gets 15 percent of its total oil imports from the African continent. By 2015, that figure will be 25 percent. Rather than a plan to reduce African poverty, NEPAD is a mechanism for ensuring that U.S. and other Western investments are protected.

All over Africa activists, trade unionists, and women's organizations are mobilizing against NEPAD. It is clear to them that the "solutions" put forward by NEPAD are in direct contradiction to what is really needed to deal with the problems faced by Africa today. The objective of NEPAD will be to provide "increased aid to developing countries that embrace the required development model." The harrowing effects of International Monetary Fund (IMF) and World Bank debt on the African continent will neither be addressed nor revoked by the new program. Under NEPAD, Africa's natural riches will continue to be bought and sold by the autonomous Western powers-that-be under the namesake of "development" and with the feigned support of the African people.

Meanwhile, the food shortage in Africa is now widespread. Dr. Tewolde Berhan Gebre Egziabher, general manager of the Environmental Protection Authority in Ethiopia, explains that drought is not the cause of famine in Africa. Storage and transport are the two big problems. The year before last in Ethiopia, when there was a surplus of food, farmers could not sell their produce (locally or on the foreign market) and thus, did not get the capital they needed for future crops. One hundred kilos of maize would sell for as little as $4 and Saudi Arabia wanted to buy this cheap maize. However, by the time the maize got to the port, its price tripled because transport costs are so high. It was marginally cheaper for Saudi Arabia to instead buy maize that came all the way from the U.S. The U.S. is underselling starving nations and the food shortages are actually exasperated by this practice.

Loans provided by the IMF, World Bank, and G8 have traditionally included strategies known as Structural Adjustment Programs (SAPs), which came in to effect in Africa in 1980. SAPs require that governments reduce public spending (especially on health, education, and food/storage) in order to pay Western banks. They must also increase exports of raw materials to the West, encourage foreign investment, and privatize state enterprises. Instead of reducing the debt, since 1980, SAPs have increased African debt by 500 percent, creating a domino effect of disasters (prolonged famine, conflict, abject poverty, and environmental exploitation) linked to an estimated 21 million deaths and, in the process, transferring hundreds of billions of dollars to the West.

UPDATE BY ASAD ISMI: My article shows how Western prosperity is based on the destruction of Africa. The story details the U.S. imperial design for Africa, which involves fostering wars and destroying economies in order to plunder natural riches. The U.S. has created a holocaust in Africa by backing wars and imposing structural adjustment programs, which have allowed it to loot hundreds of billions of dollars from the continent.

Since the story was first published in October 2002, 1.5 million more people have died in the Congo War, bringing the total up to a shocking 4 million since 1998. This is a war foisted on the Democratic Republic of the Congo (DRC)—the richest country in Africa—by the U.S. through its proxies Rwanda and Uganda, who have occupied the country, stolen its abundant natural wealth, and sent it to the West. A peace agreement signed in September 2002 in which Rwanda and Uganda agreed to withdraw, is not working because Uganda has reoccupied parts of the eastern Congo and Rwanda keeps raiding the country. Recently, Rwandan troops burnt down thousands of homes in the eastern Congo. Uganda has armed two ethnic groups, the Hema and Lendu in Ituri Province, and encouraged them to fight, resulting in 11,400 deaths so far; the two groups have laid siege to the provincial capital, Bunia, where bloody massacres continue. This shows the extent to which the U.S. will go to plunder Africa.

Those interested can also go to my Web site, <www.asadismi.ws>, for more on Africa.

OTHER RESOURCES:

Larry Elliot, "Africa Betrayed: The Aid Workers' Verdict: G8 Rescue Plan Labeled 'Recycled Peanuts,'" *The Guardian* (London), June 28, 2002.

William D. Hartung and Bridget Moix, "Deadly Legacy: U.S. Arms to Africa and the Congo War" (Report), World Policy Institute, New York, 2000, <www.world-policy.org/projects/arms/reports/congo.htm>.

William Blum, *Killing Hope: U.S. Military and CIA Interventions Since World War II* (Maine: Common Courage, 1995).

Ellen Ray, "U.S. Military and Corporate Recolonization of the Congo," *CovertAction Quarterly*, Spring/Summer 2000.

Ellen Ray and Bill Schaap, "NATO and Beyond: The Wars of the Future," *Covert Action Quarterly*, Winter 1999.

Human Rights Watch, World Report 1999: "The Democratic Republic of Congo."

Alex de Waal and Rakiya Omaar, "Somalia: Adding 'Humanitarian Intervention' to the U.S. Arsenal," *CovertAction Quarterly*, Spring 1993.

BBC Reports on Angola, <news.bbc.co.uk/hi/english/world/africa/newsid_ 2117000/2117049.stm>

Ann Talbot, "The Angolan Civil War and U.S. Foreign Policy," *World Socialist*, April 13, 2002, <www.wsws.org/articles/2002/apr2002/ango-a13.shtml>.

Eric Toussaint (CADTM COCAD, <users.skynet.be/cadtm/>), "Debt in Sub-Saharan Africa on the Eve of the Third Millennium," <attac.org/fra/toil/doc/cadtm3en.htm>.

Gregory Simpkins, "Africa Will Continue To Matter To The New Administration," The Foundation for Democracy in Africa, Press Release, December 21, 2000, <democracy-africa.org/afrmatters.htm>.

"Africa: Mining Overview," <www.mbendi.co.za/indy/ming/af/p0005.htm>.

Gordon Barthos, "Diamonds of Death Haunt Africa," *Toronto Star*, March 10, 2000.

"Africa in Turmoil: Ongoing Armed Conflicts," *Toronto Star*, May 14, 2000.

Robert Naiman and Neil Watkins, "A Survey of IMF Structural Adjustment in Africa: Growth, Social Spending and Debt Relief," Center for Economic and Policy Research (CEPR), April 1999.

Structural Adjustment Participatory Review International Network (SAPRIN), "The Policy Roots of Economic Crisis and Poverty: A Multi-Country Participatory Assessment of Structural Adjustment," April 2002.

Richard Feinberg et al., eds., *Between Two Worlds: The World Bank's Next Decade* (New Brunswick, NJ: Transaction Books, 1986).

Walden Bello, "The Role of the World Bank in U.S. Foreign Policy," *CovertAction Quarterly*, Winter 1991–92.

Walden Bello, Shea Cunningham, and Bill Rau, "IMF/World Bank: Devastation by Design," *CovertAction Quarterly*, Winter 1993–94.

Asad Ismi, "Plunder with a Human Face: The World Bank," *Z Magazine*, February 1998.

World Bank, "Making Monterrey Work For Africa: New Study Highlights Dwindling Aid Flows, Mounting Challenges," Press Release, April 10, 2002, <www4.worldbank.org/afr/stats/adi2002/default.cfm>.

United Nations, Development Program (UNDP), Human Development Report, 2001.

UPDATE BY MICHELLE ROBIDOUX: What NEPAD shows is that regardless of the actual causes of the hardships facing the world's poorest countries, there is only one prescription on offer by the world's leaders: neoliberal market-driven measures of privatization and deregulation. The mass protests against NEPAD at the World Summit on Sustainable Development in Johannesburg challenged the notion that African civil society is prepared to accept the disastrous policies THAT have left 40 million Africans at risk of starvation this year.

FOR MORE INFORMATION, SEE:

Alternative Information and Development Center, <www.aidc.org.za/web/about. php?id=6>.

11 U.S. Implicated in Taliban Massacre

Sources:
Asheville Global Report (*AGR*), No. 179, June 20–26, 2002
Title: "Documentary Implicates U.S. Troops in Taliban Prisoner Deaths"
Compiled by: Kendra Sarvadi

In These Times, September 2, 2002
Title: "Secret History?"
Author: Adam Porter

Faculty Evaluators: Maureen Buckley and Ray Castro
Student Researchers: Tara Spreng and Emilio Licea

A documentary entitled *Massacre at Mazar*, released in 2002 by Scottish film producer Jamie Doran, implicates U.S. troops in the torturing and deaths of approximately 3,000 men from Mazar-i-Sharif, Afghanistan.

Doran's documentary follows the finding of Physicians for Human Rights (PHR), which concluded that there was evidence of the disposal of human remains at two mass gravesites near Mazar-i-Sharif. In the documentary, two witnesses claim that they were forced to drive into the desert with hundreds of Taliban prisoners who were held in sealed cargo containers. The witnesses alleged that the orders came from a local U.S. commander. Prisoners, who had not yet suffocated to death inside the vans, were shot by Northern Alliance gunmen, while 30 to 40 U.S. soldiers stood watching.

Irfan Azgar Ali, a survivor of the trip, informed *The Guardian* (London) newspaper, "They crammed us into sealed shipping containers. We had no water for 20 hours. We banged on the side of the container. There was no air and it was very hot. There were 300 of us in my container. By the time we arrived in Sheberghan, only 10 of us were alive." One Afghani truck driver, forced to drive the containers, says the prisoners began to beg for air. "Northern Alliance commanders told us to stop the trucks and we came down," he said. "After that, they shot into the containers to make air holes. Blood came pouring out. They were screaming inside." Another driver in the convoy estimated that an average of 150 to 160 people died in each container. When the containers were unlocked at Sheberghan, the bodies of the dead tumbled out. Another witness states they observed a U.S. soldier break an Afghani prisoner's neck and pour acid on others.

In addition to bodies of Taliban prisoners, the filmmakers allege that thousands of Afghanis, Pakistanis, Uzbeks, Chechens, and Tajiks may also be buried there.

Afghani warlord General Abdul Rashid Dostum, the man whose forces allegedly carried out the killings, admits there were only 200 such deaths and that the prisoners died before the transfer.

One Northern Alliance soldier who spoke to Doran claims that U.S. troops masterminded a cover-up. The soldier informed Doran, "The Americans told the Sheberghan people to get rid of them [the bodies] before satellite pictures could be taken." One witness told *The Guardian* (London) that an U.S. Special Forces vehicle was parked at the scene as bulldozers buried the dead. Doran's footage showed areas of compacted red sand, apparently caked with blood, as well as "clothing, bits of skull, matted hair, jaws, femurs, and ribs jutting out of the sand, despite a sloppy attempt to remove evidence after the fact" (*Melbourne Sunday Herald Sun*, February 9, 2003). Additionally, bullet casings littered the site, offering a grim testimony that some Taliban prisoners, who were still alive, were executed before being dumped in the desert. United Nations (U.N.) and human rights officials have found the grave, but have not estimated the number of bodies it contains.

Says Doran, "I took the footage to the European Parliament because… I have a great fear that the graves may be tampered with. I had to take it to the highest level in Europe." According to the Glasgow *Herald* (December 19, 2002), Doran stated "They're hiding behind a wall of secrecy, hoping this story will go away, but it won't." Doran also feared for the safety of the witnesses, two of whom have subsequently been murdered. Doran's key researcher, Najibullah Quarishi, was almost beaten to death in an unsuccessful attempt to gain a copy of incriminating footage.

The screening of the film at the European Parliament prompted calls for an international commission to investigate the charges. Andrew McEntree, former chairman of Amnesty International, said that "very credible evidence" in the documentary needed to be investigated. McEntree said that he believed that war crimes had been committed not only under international law, but also under U.S. law.

A Pentagon spokesman denied the allegations: "U.S. Central Command looked into it… when allegations first surfaced that there were graves discovered in the area of Sheberghan prison. They looked into it and did not substantiate any knowledge, presence, or participation of U.S. service members." A U.S. Embassy spokesperson in Berlin also rejected the allegations made in the documentary saying, "The claims are completely false that American soldiers were involved in the torture, execution, and disappearance of Taliban prisoners. In no way did U.S. troops participate or witness any human rights violations." But in a statement to United Press International wire service (August 29, 2002), Doran said, "It is beyond doubt that a number of American soldiers were at Sheberghan Prison. Either they walked around blindfolded with earmuffs for eight days or they saw what was going on."

UPDATE BY ADAM PORTER: The situation in Afghanistan has changed little since the U.S. appointed government of Hamid Kharzai came to power. The situation in Mazar is comparable. Opium production, the main source of income for deputy defense minister Rachid Dostum, alleged architect of the slaughter in Mazar, has increased by 1,847 percent (U.N. figures) and the feared ministry of virtue and vice has been restarted. Women are not permitted to wear makeup in public and the Taliban have staged a comeback in the southeast of the country, killing a number of Kharzai's troops. Dostum's men have been involved in a variety of "clashes" with other warlords in the north.

As far as the massacre in Mazar goes, little has happened on the ground, except that some of the witnesses are dead, and some bodies have been exhumed and dumped elsewhere. The film made by Irish filmmaker Jamie Doran and his excellent team at Atlantic Films has been shown on mainstream television in the U.K.

Doran's film is still tugging at the sleeves of the powerful. Shown in 14 countries on television, the documentary was, at last, shown to the Italian and German Parliaments in December 2002. On January 15, 2003, Doran was also able to get the film shown to members of the British Parliament. As a result, quietly, the United Nations has agreed to undertake an investigation into the incident. How far that investigation will go is anyone's guess.

12 Bush Administration Behind Failed Military Coup in Venezuela

Sources:
The Guardian (London), April 17, 2002
Title: "Don't Believe Everything You Read in the Papers about Venezuela"
Author: Greg Palast

The Guardian (London), April 22, 2002
Title: "The Coup"
Author: Duncan Campbell

Global Outlook, Summer 2002
Title: "Venezuela: Bush Administration Behind Failed Coup"
Author: Joe Taglieri

People's Weekly World, July 27, 2002
Title: "Coup-Making in Venezuela: the Bush and Oil factors"
Author: Karen Talbot

NACLA Report on the Americas, July/August 2002
Title: "Venezuela: The Revolution Will Not Be Televised"
Author: Jon Beasley-Murray

Faculty Evaluators: Carol Tremmel, Robert Manning, Andrew Botterell, Tamara
Falicov, Sally Hurtado, and Elizabeth Martinez
Student Researchers: David Immel, Licia Marshall, Scott Frazier, Effren Trejo,
Sherry Grant, and Josh Sisco

The April 11, 2002, military coup in Venezuela was supported by the United States
government. As early as last June, American military attaches had been in touch
with members of the Venezuelan military to examine the possibility of a coup. During the coup, U.S military were stationed at the Colombia-Venezuela border to provide support and to evacuate U.S. citizens if there were problems. According to
intelligence analyst, Wayne Madsen, the CIA actively organized the coup. "The
CIA provided Special Operations Group personnel, headed by a lieutenant colonel
on loan from the U.S. Special Operations Command at Fort Bragg, North Carolina,
to help organize the coup against Chavez," he said.

Since his 1998 election, President Hugo Chavez had increasingly socialized
the Venezuelan government. One of his most controversial moves was to double
the royalties charged to foreign oil companies by Venezuela's national oil company, PDUSA, abolishing a 60-year-old agreement with these companies.
Venezuela is the fourth largest oil-producing nation, and the third largest oil
provider to the U.S. As the leader of OPEC, Chavez has encouraged lowering oil
production to raise prices.

Chavez has irritated the U.S. in many ways. In 1999, he altered the constitution, changing the law to provide unused land to the landless (who make
up more than half of the population of 24 million) and angering powerful plan-
tation owners. Chavez also refused to allow U.S. planes to fly over Venezuela during their military activities in Colombia. President Chavez was also the first head
of state to visit Saddam Hussein in Iraq since the embargoes in 1990.

Because of the close relationship that many of Venezuela's wealthy have with
the United States, the coup took place with little opposition from Venezuela's long-
established business and political community. The Bush Administration was quick
to endorse the change in government, which put Pedro Carmona, a wealthy busi-
nessman and former business associate of George Bush Sr., into office. Carmona's
first move as president was to "dissolve the Constitution, national legislature,
Supreme Court, attorney general's office, and comptroller's office."

In the United States, corporate press covered the coup from a sympathetic anti-
Chavez perspective. On April 11, the alleged murder of 17 anti-Chavez protest-

ers (itself a response to sniper fire that killed protestors at a pro-Chavez demonstration) was pointed to as justification for Chavez's removal. Yet the two following days, which resulted in the killing of as many as 40 pro-Chavez protesters, the deaths were hardly mentioned.

Television stations in Venezuela refused to cover the anticoup protests, choosing instead to run their regular program schedule. Five out of the six major networks are owned by a single owner, who supported U.S. involvement in Venezuela. CIA Special Operations psychological warfare (PSYOPs) produced television announcements, purportedly by Venezuelan political and business leaders, saying Chavez "provoked the crisis by ordering his supporters to fire on peaceful protestors in Caracas."

Despite the distorted media coverage in Venezuela, a huge anticoup civil protest involving hundreds of thousands of people began. Several branches of the Venezuelan military joined the anticoup forces. The streets of Caracas were flooded with protestors and soldiers vehemently chanting anti-Carmona slogans. Within two days, Carmona stepped down and Chavez returned to power.

UPDATE BY DUNCAN CAMPBELL: The conflict in Venezuela is still unresolved, but there are currently tentative agreements to move towards a referendum on the rule of Hugo Chavez. November 2003 has been suggested as a date, but this is not confirmed and much may happen in between. Chavez has introduced new plans to punish the press and media for stirring up the opposition and encouraging what he sees as treason. The opposition see this as state censorship. Chavez supporters say that this is the fault of the media for inflaming the people with inaccurate information. But journalists and human rights groups have condemned these moves. Pedro Carmona left the country and went into exile. Other ex-military figures who led the opposition have also gone into exile. The U.S. has distanced itself from tacitly supporting the coup although Ambassador Charles Shapiro got into trouble in May, when a guest at a U.S. embassy party gave an anti-Chavez puppet show. The predicted bloodbath has not at this moment happened, thankfully. There is weariness on both sides with the future uncertain.

Chavez weathered the storm and proved more resilient than his opponents anticipated and the oil industry, although damaged, started to function again. The lesson seems to be that the country was not prepared to accept a coup and that the plotters miscalculated the national and international mood. There was strong opposition to the coup from the Organization of American States, which the U.S. followed after its early diplomatic misstep. Otto Reich has been demoted and given another minor post after it became clear that the Senate would never authorize his appointment. He has been the one big loser in the affair so far. (See Chapter 2, *Censored* #11 2003.)

UPDATE BY JOE TAGLIERI: From what I've seen of the mainstream American press' political coverage of South and Central America over the years, way too often it's hook, line, and sinker, Washington's official line-style reporting.

As *Narco News*'s Al Giordano quips, the mainstream's "horsemen of simulation" journalism present a skewed, Swiss cheese–like, sometimes flat out dishonest portrait of the shenanigans the U.S. government has perpetrated south of the border throughout the last century. From Teddy Roosevelt's "gunboat diplomacy" to Guatemala in 1954 to Chile's Allende in '73 to '80s Contra cocaine and on through to today's "Plan Colombia/Andean Initiative," Uncle Sam has had lots to say about what goes down in "his hemisphere."

The botched coup against Venezuelan President Hugo Chavez in April 2002 and an attempted general strike organized late last year by the same coup plotters (see <www.fromthewilderness.com/free/ww3/123102_strike_wasnt.htm>) seemingly come straight out of State Department lifer Otto Reich's "Latin American Chaos" playbook.

It was unfortunate, though not surprising given its track record, to see much of the U.S. press dutifully relaying Otto and his ilk's anti-Chavez propaganda all over the globe. So as far as a mainstream response to my little story, I haven't heard a peep from anyone.

Fortunately for Chavez and his poor majority, good press from America doesn't seem all that necessary. The former paratrooper seems to have some kind of guardian angel keeping him up there in Miraflores Palace. Time and time again he has emerged victorious despite the half-baked efforts at opposition by Venezuela's industrial and media oligarchs and their "consultants" from U.S. intelligence.

The bottom line fact is Chavez is still the president because the 80 percent poor majority wants it that way, period. The nation's vastly outnumbered rich kids and tired American spooks like Otto Reich don't seem to have the juice to displace someone with Chavez's kind of energy and overwhelming popular support.

Bear in mind, however, that at the rate the U.S. war machine is moving, "intervention" in a future Venezuelan "crisis," like maybe another coup against Chavez, is definitely not a far-fetched notion.

Another important bottom line to always keep in mind when discussing Venezuela is that black lifeblood of the modern world—oil. Chavez is at the helm of a nation that is one of America's top suppliers. So, similar to relations with the Middle East, the U.S. government and its Big Oil sponsors have a serious economic stake in Venezuelan politics.

The "sp-oil-s" of President Bush's conquest of Iraq, which along with Iran and Saudi Arabia holds the bulk of the earth's remaining usable oil reserves, may take some of the heat off Chavez for now, but only time will reveal the answer to that kind of speculation game.

Right now, those interested in keeping up with what's happening in Venezuela should check these Web sites: Vheadline, <www.vheadline.com/main.asp> and the *Narco News Bulletin*; <www.narconews.com/>.

13 Corporate Personhood Challenged

Sources:
Common Dreams, January 1, 2003 and *Impact Press*, February/March 2003
Title: "Now Corporations Claim the Right to 'Lie'"
Author: Thom Hartmann

Wild Matters, February 2003
Title: "Americans Revolt in Pennsylvania: New Battle Lines Are Drawn"
Author: Thom Hartmann

The Hightower Lowdown, April 2003
Title: "How a Clerical Error Made Corporations 'People'"
Author: Jim Hightower

Corporate media coverage: *The New York Times*, *Los Angeles Times*, *USA Today*, *Fortune*, and *Ottawa Citizen*.

Faculty Evaluators: Mary Gomes and Ken Marcus
Student Researchers: Chris Salvano, Sherry Grant, and Melissa Jones

Since the founding of our country, a debate has raged over the nature of corporations and whether they should be entitled to the same right to legal "personhood" as actual people. This idea of corporate personhood has recently come under scrutiny.

It was back in 1886 that a Supreme Court decision (*Santa Clara County v. Southern Pacific Railroad Company*) ostensibly led to corporate personhood and free speech rights, thereby guaranteeing protections under the First and Fourteenth Amendments. However, according to Thom Hartmann, the relatively mundane court case never actually granted these personhood rights to corporations. In fact, Chief Justice Morrison Waite wrote, "We avoided meeting the Constitutional question in the decision." Yet when writing up the case summary—which has no legal status—the court reporter, a former railroad president named J.C. Bancroft Davis, declared: "The defendant Corporations are persons within the intent of the clause in Section 1 of the Fourteenth Amendment to the Constitution of the United States, which forbids a state to deny any person within its jurisdiction the equal protection of the laws." But the court had made no such legal determination. It was the clerk's opinion and misrepresentation of the case in the headnote upon which current claims of corporate personhood and free speech entitlements now rests.

In 1978, however, the Supreme Court further entrenched the idea of corporate personhood by deciding that corporations were entitled to the free speech right to give money to political causes—linking free speech with financial clout. Interestingly, in a dissent to the decision, Chief Justice William Rehnquist pointed out the flawed 1886 precedent and criticized its interpretation over the years saying, "This court decided at an early date, with neither argument nor discussion, that a business corporation is a 'person' entitled to the protection of the Equal Protection Clause of the Fourteenth Amendment."

But more recently, in December 2002, Porter Township, Pennsylvania, unanimously passed an ordinance denying corporate claims to personhood. The township is the first and only local government in the United States to deny these civil and constitutional rights to corporations. Porter Township and neighboring Rush Township have laws that govern the local dumping of Pittsburgh-generated sludge by charging the dumping companies a "tipping fee." In 2000, Synagro Corporation, one of the largest dumping companies in the nation, sued Rush Township, claiming that as a corporate citizen, the township violated Synagro's Fourteenth Amendment rights. In response, Porter Township, passed its precedent-setting ordinance claiming that the dumping company, or any corporation within its jurisdiction, may not wield personhood and free speech privileges.

A more high-profile challenge to corporate personhood involves a lawsuit against Nike and its claims on Third-World labor practices. In 1998, Nike CEO Phil Knight wrote a *New York Times* op-ed piece responding to criticisms of Nike's Asian labor practices. As was widely reported in the mainstream press in mid-April of 2003, San Francisco consumer advocate Marc Kasky filed a lawsuit against Nike, believing the company misled the public about its labor practices. Nike, however, claims that the First Amendment protects Nike's statements, making it irrelevant whether the statements are true or false.

In May 2002, the California Supreme Court ruled against Nike, saying its statements were commercial speech and can therefore be regulated by the Federal Trade Commission. This ruling, writes Justice Joyce L. Kennard, "means only that when a business enterprise, to promote and defend its sales and profits, makes factual representations about its own product or its own operations, it must speak truthfully."

On April 26, 2003, the *Ottawa Citizen* provided some pro-Nike coverage of the current case against Nike saying, "The case began some years ago when anti-globalizers accused Nike of exploiting workers at its factories abroad. The Nikebashing was unrelenting, and the company fought back." Hartmann's article also notes *The New York Times'* editorial support for Nike saying, "In a real democracy, even the people you disagree with get to have their say." That's true, says Hartmann, but Nike is not a person—it's a corporation.

On June 26, the Supreme Court sidestepped the potential landmark decision by dismissing the Nike case, sending it back to San Francisco. The court agreed that the case presented "novel First Amendment issues" and that a California trial would help resolve the facts. The case should go to trial in San Francisco by fall 2004.

UPDATE BY JIM HIGHTOWER: Anyone seeking to preserve America's fragile democracy must first understand the scope and magnitude of the powers aligned against it. We live in an age in which corporations have been enthroned and corruption in high places has enabled power and wealth to be aggregated into an increasingly smaller number of hands. As citizens concerned with the future of human rights in a democratic republic, it's vital that we now speak up and spread the word about "corporate personhood," which lies at the heart of the challenge facing us today.

On April 23, 2003, the U.S. Supreme Court heard oral arguments in *Nike v. Kasky*, the Nike Corporation's appeal of an April 2002 California Supreme Court ruling. In *Kasky v. Nike*, the California court rejected claims by Nike's lawyers that the First Amendment immunized Nike from being sued under state consumer protection laws (for allegedly misrepresenting facts in a public relations campaign). The U.S. Supreme Court (where the case was *Nike Inc., et al. v. Marc Kasky* because Nike was the party appealing) issued a ruling in late June dismissing Nike's claim of exemption from the California law under the First Amendment. The court majority asserted that it was premature to take up the free-speech issues raised by Nike and sent the case back to California.

Up to June 2003, the story in *The Hightower Lowdown* received no additional coverage by mainstream media sources. However, the *Nike v. Kasky* case has generated a substantial amount of interest, although the opinions are predictable. As of May 25, 2003, four of the five largest U.S. newspapers had editorialized on behalf of Nike. Though all five had received submissions from nationally published writers, none had published dissenting commentaries. *The Rocky Mountain News* was alone among the top-50 papers in allowing space for a dissent to their pro-Nike editorial. *The Sacramento Bee* thus far is the only paper to critique Nike's "free speech" claims in an editorial (while arguing that the Supreme Court should dismiss Kasky's suit on other grounds).

FOR MORE INFORMATION GO TO:
ReclaimDemocracy.org, P.O. Box 532, Boulder, CO 80306; Tel: (303) 402-0105; Web site: <www.reclaimdemocracy.org>.

Program on Corporations Law and Democracy, P.O. Box 246, South Yarmouth, MA 02664; Tel: (508) 398-1145; Web site: <www.poclad.org>.

Alliance for Democracy, 760 Main Street, Waltham, MA 02451; Tel: (781) 894-1179; Web site: <www.thealliancefordemocracy.org>.

14 Unwanted Refugees a Global Problem

Sources:

In These Times, October 14, 2002
Title: "The World Isn't Watching–The Forgotten Refugee Crisis"
Author: Daniel Swift

Mother Jones, March 2003
Title: "Outback Nightmares and Refugee Dreams"
Author: Charles Bowden

Bulletin of Atomic Scientists, November/December 2002
Title: "Neglect is Never Benign"
Author: Bill Frelick

Faculty Evaluators: Richard Zimmer, Charlene Tung, and Diana Grant
Student Researchers: Tara Spreng and Sherry Grant

In the last 10 years, the number of displaced people has exploded. Known as refugees, asylum seekers, illegal aliens, or unauthorized economic migrants, many are the indigenous of their region and almost all are the poorest of the poor.

According to the 2002 World Refugee Survey, there are as many as 40 million displaced people throughout the world. Fifteen million are seeking asylum in other countries. In addition, there at least 22 million "internally displaced" within their country of origin, who are not protected by international law and are therefore at even greater risk of oppression and abuse.

The terrorist attacks of September 11 and the subsequent War on Terrorism launched by the United States and its allies have had a spillover effect on the lives of refugees worldwide.

Failed states, where warlords, gangsters and terrorists can operate with impunity, are producing hopeless and desperate people—a dangerous breeding ground for political and religious fanaticism. Often, the international response to terrorist acts is to blame the refugees, even when they themselves are the victims.

The international community is unwilling to devote necessary resources to help resolve those conflicts or at least to fully address the social and humanitarian issues.

Living in the margins of unwilling host communities, long-term refugees are victims not only of the war and persecution that forced them from their homes, but of the neglect that denies them hope of political settlements that would resolve the underlying causes of their affliction. Herded into huge refugee camps, where the prospect of emigration is slim, they can be deported at any time.

Corporate profiteers from developed countries are finding ways of benefiting from this global misfortune. Wackenhut, one of the largest operators of for-profit prisons, is now setting up, with local subsidies, for-profit internment camps that charge penniless exiles a daily fee and then deport them when they are unable to pay.

The cycle of political upheaval, economic flight, and expatriation that leads to international terrorism is unlikely to resolve itself if the people of the rich nations in the world continue to neglect the world's homeless.

UPDATE BY CHARLES BOWDEN: The story of how Australia has handled refugees (basically, prison in Australia and then eventually, the contracting of incarceration out to Pacific Island nations) is neither a story about Australia nor about one group of displaced people. It is a salvo announcing the future. War, poverty, overpopulation, and the wrenching change caused by a global economy have hurled millions of people into a void, where they cannot stay put and cannot move without being perceived as illegal interlopers. Australia, one of the fairest nations on Earth, has become the poster child for barbarism in its harsh reaction to these displaced people, but it is highly unlikely that other nations will react to the same problem with more kindness. I live 60 miles from the Mexican border in a desert where at least 200 illegal immigrants will die of thirst and heat this summer and where the rest will be hunted like animals by U.S. law enforcement. Technically, they are not refugees, but then the category of refugee is one invented by the powerful to sort out the weak and to dismiss them into a legal limbo.

Since my story was published, Australia has witnessed the collapse of refugees seeking entry as a naval blockade and word of the harsh treatment has staunched the flow. Also, Australia has become a role model for European nations (Great Britain, Italy, Greece, and Spain, for example) facing similar invasions of the poor. The movement of people, of course, has increased as war in the Middle East and the global chill in trade has made difficult living conditions lurch toward the impossible.

The mainstream press has reacted to the story with total silence. In part, this is because the war with Iraq has devoured news space. But I think, in the main, it is because the Draconian laws passed by a panicked Congress after September 11, 2001, have made Australia's policies look too much like our own imprisonment of people without open legal hearings both within the United States and at our base in Cuba. And of course, the folk movement of Mexicans (the largest such migration now occurring on the surface of the earth) cannot be really examined by the U.S. press without acknowledgment of decades of failure, including both the 1986 reforms of our immigration laws and the passage of NAFTA.

The key source for anyone pursuing this story, both in Australia and globally, is Human Rights Watch, <www.hrw.org>.

15 U.S. Military's War on the Earth

Sources:
Dollars and Sense, March/April, 2003
Title: "War on Earth"
Author: Bob Feldman

Washington Free Press, September/October 2002
Title: "Disobeying Orders"
Authors: David S. Mann and Glen Milner

Wild Matters, October 2002
Title: "Military Dumping"
Author: John Passacantando

Faculty Evaluators: Bill Crowley and Mary Gomes
Student Researchers: Jen Scanlan and Grayson Kent

The world's largest polluter, the U.S. military, generates 750,000 tons of toxic waste material annually, more than the five largest chemical companies in the U.S. combined. This pollution occurs globally, as the U.S. maintains bases in dozens of countries. In the U.S., there are 27,000 toxic hot spots on 8,500 military properties. Washington's Fairchild Air Force Base is the number-one producer of hazardous waste, generating over 13 million pounds of waste in 1997. Not only is the military emitting toxic material directly into the air and water, it's poisoning the land of nearby communities, resulting in increased rates of cancer, kidney disease, birth defects, low birth weight, and miscarriage.

The military currently manages 25 million acres of land providing habitat for some 300 threatened or endangered species. Groups such as Defenders of Wildlife have sued the military for damage done to endangered animal populations by bomb tests. The testing of low-frequency sonar technology is accused of having played a role in the deaths of whales around the world.

Rather than working to remedy these problems, the Pentagon claims that the burden of regulations is undercutting troop readiness. The Pentagon already operates military bases in and outside of the U.S. as "federal reservations" which fall outside of normal regulation. Yet the Department of Defense (DOD) is seeking further exemptions in Congress from the Migratory Bird Treaties Act, the Wildlife Act, the Endangered Species Act, the Clean Air Act, and the National Environmental Policy Act.

The Pentagon now employs 10,000 people with an annual budget of $2 billion to deal with the legalities that arise from the military's toxic droppings. New Justice Department policies frustrate attempts by the public to obtain knowledge. In one case, the U.S. Navy demanded $1,500 for the release of documents related to compliance with environmental laws at the Trident nuclear submarine base in the Puget Sound. Other requests are simply not processed and attempts at legal countermeasures are thwarted. The Pentagon has also won reductions in military whistleblower protection laws. These measures disregard the Freedom of Information Act and obstruct the notion of a democratic state.

UPDATE BY DAVID S. MANN AND GLEN MILNER: Since our article appeared in the *Washington Free Press* in September 2002, there have been numerous attempts by the U.S. military and the Bush Administration to secure military exemptions from environmental law. In a rare defeat, the Pentagon failed in 2002 to win concessions from Congress for exemptions from the Endangered Species Act, Marine Mammal Protection Act, and other environmental laws.

A December 10, 2002, document, *Sustainable Ranges 2003 Decision Briefing to the Deputy Secretary of Defense*, unleashed a three-year campaign to systematically exempt all U.S. military activity from every perceived environmental restriction. Included in the briefing is a "2002 Lessons Learned" section, citing the need for better quantification of encroachment impacts and a sustained aggressive campaign addressing concerns of the GAO and Congress. Other targeted critics are state attorneys general, media, industry, and non-governmental organizations (NGOs).

In a March 7, 2003, memo, Deputy Defense Secretary Paul Wolfowitz asked the army, navy, and air force secretaries for examples of military readiness hindered by compliance to environmental law. Even though current law has never been used for such purposes, Wolfowitz's aim is to allow the president to invoke environmental exemptions deemed necessary for national defense.

Other attempts for environmental exemption for the military have been less than obvious. An April 2003 proposal by Defense Secretary Donald Rumsfeld, the Defense Transformation for the Twenty-First Century Act, suspended whistleblower protections for Department of Defense personnel. In another, an executive order from President Bush is being considered establishing the Department of Defense as the first among equals in any disagreement between agencies. Added to this are new restrictions on the implementation of the Freedom of Information Act and a reduced budget for the Environmental Protection Agency for fiscal year 2004.

Efforts for environmental justice continue. In the Pacific Northwest, we have begun a mix of public education and legal action concerning the U.S. Navy and environmental compliance. We have found that coalitions of long-time "peace" and "environmental" organizations make effective action groups.

In March 2001, two environmental organizations and three peace organizations filed a 60-day notice against the navy's Trident II (D-5) missile upgrade at the Trident nuclear submarine base at Bangor, Washington. The case, by David Mann, is now in the Ninth Circuit Court of Appeals with a decision expected in the fall of 2003.

Two other lawsuits involving David Mann and Glen Milner and the Freedom of Information Act (FOIA) have gone to court. In the first, filed in April 2002, concerning explosive Trident rocket motor shipments, the navy conceded it had lost the case. The navy then paid attorney fees and reclassified the documents exempt under national security. This case and another filed in March 2003, involving accident assessments for explosive material at the Bangor submarine base, are still pending.

In December 2002, a FOIA request by Glen Milner revealed the Navy has been firing 20 mm depleted-uranium rounds into prime fishing waters off the coast of Washington State during routine calibration and testing of the navy's Close-In Weapons System (CIWS). Numerous FOIA requests have shown the navy is not in compliance with Nuclear Regulatory Commission (NRC) licensing agreements. A preliminary complaint has been filed with the NRC. Our goal is a NEPA lawsuit and injunction against the navy over the firing of depleted-uranium rounds into U.S. waters.

For information on our lawsuit against the U.S. Navy visit <www.gzcenter.org>. Organizations involved are Waste Action Project, Washington Physicians for Social Responsibility, and Peace and Justice Alliance, all based in Seattle, Washington; Ground Zero Center for Nonviolent Action in Poulsbo, Washington; and Cascadia Wildlands Project in Eugene, Oregon.

UPDATE BY BOB FELDMAN: Despite the increased size of recent antiwar protests around the globe, the Pentagon's "war on the earth" still continues. Since the story was published, a new wave of environmental destruction in Iraq was produced by the U.S. war machine's March and April 2003 missile attacks and its bombardment, invasion, and occupation of that country.

A report on Iraq of the United Nations Environmental Program [UNEP]'s Post-Conflict Assessment Unit noted that the heavy Pentagon bombing and the movement of large numbers of Pentagon military vehicles and troops in Iraq "further degraded natural and agricultural ecosystems."

The UNEP Post-Conflict Assessment Unit report also observed the Pentagon's intensive use of depleted uranium (DU) weapons. Significant levels of radioactive contamination were found at four sites in Baghdad in May 2003, by *Christian Science Monitor* reporter Scott Peterson (*Christian Science Monitor*, May 15, 2003). Much of this radioactive contamination was likely produced by the DU bullets fired into the center of Baghdad at the Iraqi Ministry of Planning by the Pentagon's A-10 Warhog aircraft, Abrams tanks, or Bradley fighting vehicles. According to the *Monitor*, Pentagon figures indicate that about 250,000 DU bullets were fired by A-10 Warhog aircraft in March and April 2003, leaving an estimated additional 75 tons of DU in Iraq as a result of the Pentagon's attack.

Local air pollution and soil contamination in Iraq also increased as a result of the recent war. The Pentagon's bombing of Baghdad, for instance, ignited fires producing toxic, black smoke that contained dangerous chemicals, which caused harm to Iraqi children and to Iraqi adults with respiratory problems, and further polluted Iraqi ecosystems.

The mainstream press showed no interest in *Dollars and Sense*'s "War on the Earth" story. But U.S. alternative media outlets responded with some interest. WMBR-Cambridge's *No Censorship Radio* invited me to appear on its weekly show to talk about the "War on the Earth" article, as did a producer at the *Making Contact* radio show. *AlterNet*'s environmental editor selected this *Dollars and Sense* article for posting on the *AlterNet* Web site and there was some mention in the *Utne Reader*.

The impact of the article among green/antiwar readers was due, I think, in large part to the *Dollars and Sense* magazine editors' decision to use maps to visually reflect the domestic and global extent of the Pentagon's pollution activity. Also, the article initially appeared just a few days before the U.S. warfare state launched its attack on Iraq. So the article's implied argument, that to be a friend of the earth, a green activist must also mobilize against U.S. global militarism, probably seemed like an historically timely one.

Since the article appeared in *Dollars and Sense*, the U.S. Navy—in response to years of protest—has finally closed its base on Puerto Rico's Isla de Vieques. But the environmentally destructive target practice that the U.S. Navy used to do on the Isla de Vieques has been transferred to Florida.

To both get more information contact the Military Toxics Project, P.O. Box 558, Lewiston, ME 04243; Tel: (207) 783-5091; or E-mail: <steve@miltoxproj.org>; Web site: <www.miltoxproj.org>. Seth Shulman's early 1990s book, *The Threat At Home: Confronting the Toxic Legacy of the U.S. Military*, also contains information about the Pentagon's "War on the Earth" within the U.S.'s borders.

16 Plan Puebla-Panama and the FTAA

Sources:
CorpWatch, <corpwatch.org>, September 19, 2002
Title: "PPP: Plan Puebla Panama, or Private Plans for Profit?"
Author: Miguel Pickard

Public Citizen's Trade Watch, 2002 Report
Title: "Unveiling 'NAFTA for the Americas'"
Author: Timi Gerson

Labor Notes, April 02, 2002
Title: "Plan Puebla-Panama: The Next Step in Corporate Globalization"
Authors: Tom Hansen and Jason Wallach

Asheville Global Report/Extra!, February 03, 2003
Title: "The FTAA is None of Your business"
Author: Rachel Coen

Faculty Evaluators: Francisco Vasquez and Richard Zimmer
Student Researchers: Jessie Esquivel and Dana Balicki

The Free Trade Area of the Americas (FTAA) is a trade agreement intended to spread NAFTA's trade rules to an additional 31 Latin American nations by 2005. Working in conjunction with FTAA is Plan Puebla-Panama (PPP), a multibillion-dollar development plan in progress that would turn southern Mexico and all of Central America into a colossal free-trade zone, competing in the worldwide race to drain wages, working conditions, environmental protection, and human rights.

PPP is the brainchild of Mexican president, and former Coca-Cola executive, Vicente Fox. Fox set priorities when he first took office, stating, "My government is by entrepreneurs, for entrepreneurs." Not surprisingly then, the PPP emerges not as a strategy to end the endemic poverty in this region, but rather to induce private investment/colonization as it turns over control of the area's vast natural resources—including water, oil, minerals, timber, and ecological biodiversity—to the private sector, mostly multinational corporations. Seven hundred and eighty companies of all sizes (including Harkin, Union Pacific-Southern, International Paper, Exxon, Mobil, Dow Chemical of Mexico, Union Carbide, and Monsanto) sent representatives to the PPP informational meeting in Yucatan during the summer of 2002.

The ideas for the PPP area consist of: the construction of new ports, airports, railroads, bridges, and 25 dams for hydroelectric generation; the upgrading of telecommunications facilities, including a fiber-optic network; the upgrading of electrical grids; highway construction; and the creation of wildlife reserves to help facilitate "bioprospecting" by various multinational seed, chemical, and pharmaceutical companies.

The Inter-American Development Bank (IDB) is the main backer of the Plan Puebla-Panama. The cost of $3.5 billion, which is 84 percent of the funds, will initially go for massive road construction and improvement on two stretches of highways. One of the highways will be from the Central America's Caribbean coast up 1,745 km to the Mexican border with Texas, and the other highway will run 3,150 km from central Mexico going into Panama City. As trade routes, these two highways are intended to open the entire Mexican and Central American corridor for business. The taxpayers of the eight PPP countries will be the ones paying for the development of the public-works projects that will benefit private transnational capital and assure profits for corporate investors.

Fox wants to transplant the *maquiladora*, production-for-export model that has been applied with disastrous results in northern Mexico. The American isthmus, the narrowest part of the Americas, will be turned into a state-of-the-art foreign product assembly station. Twenty-first century commodities are increasingly produced in the Pacific Rim, with China's 1.2 billion people leading the way with the largest and lowest-paid work force in the world. But transportation is a problem when the largest consumer bases are located on the U.S. Atlantic Coast and in the upper Midwest. It is much cheaper to ship these goods unassembled, using modern containerized shipping, but they still must be assembled into finished products before reaching the market. Thus, the isthmus offers unique strategic advantages as the shortest land route between Pacific production and Atlantic consumption.

According to journalist Miguel Pickard this project will turn 9 southern Mexico states and all of Central America into a massive free-trade zone, competing in a race to the bottom of the list of the world's wages, working conditions, environmental regulations, and human rights policies.

Under the FTAA, multinational corporations could leverage exploited workers in Mexico against even more desperate workers in Haiti, Guatemala, or Brazil. The FTAA would intensify NAFTA's "race to the bottom" and deepen the negative effects of NAFTA already seen in Canada, Mexico, and the U.S. PPP is one more "development" plan instituted by transnational corporations and international financial institutions that will benefit the corporate bottom line, but result in more poverty and displacement. More than 18 percent of the inhabitants of the future PPP area belong to indigenous communities, 40 percent are under age 15, and the majority live below the poverty line.

UPDATE BY MIGUEL PICKARD: The Plan Puebla-Panama (PPP) was proposed in 2001 by Mexican President Vicente Fox and was widely commented on in the area it covers, i.e., Mexico and Central America. But within the United States, there had been very little information, in spite of the fact that the initiative benefits mostly U.S. multinational corporations. The fact that *CorpWatch* published the article on its Web page meant that it was immediately picked up by numerous activist organizations and given wide circulation, especially to readers in the north. The article helps make clear how enormous areas of land (in the case of the PPP, 102 million hectares, with 64 million inhabitants in eight countries), are being "prepared" for multinational corporation (MNC) exploitation, under the guise of infrastructure "development," with no informed consent of the people living therein.

Due to efforts of activist organizations in the south, the threat posed by the PPP to people, and especially indigenous communities in the area, was given wide dissemination, especially through well-attended regional meetings that brought together social and civil organizations from Mexico and Central America. Opposition activities ensued from these encounters in practically all of the 9 countries of the PPP, alerting governments that civil society was demanding to be heard and consulted and that alternatives needed to be discussed. Alternatives obviously had to contemplate the interests of inhabitants, and civil society in general, and not just those of MNCs.

The Mexican government realized by late 2002 that opposition to the PPP had grown enormously and that simply signaling a project as part of the PPP was enough to draw unwanted activist scrutiny and mobilization. In essence, PPP publicity, which touted it as a way out of poverty for an especially underdeveloped area, had failed. Rhetoric extolling the social virtues of the PPP was exposed as so much veneer for a project that puts natural and human resources at the behest of corporations. In essence the Fox government had to backpedal on the PPP, purging almost all references to it in official discourse, until new "packaging" could be found.

PPP discourse to date continues "on hold" within the Fox government. Its official PPP Web site, for example, was removed from the Internet during 2002. What is important to stress, however, is that the PPP megaprojects are continuing full steam ahead, even though they may not be labeled as such. Although now more difficult to detect, activists within Mexico and Central America are on alert and mobilizing to stop large-scale "development" projects that are bereft of civil society input.

A follow-up story on the PPP and additional information on the PPP are available at "The Lacandon Jungle's Last Stand Against Corporate Globalization," <www.corpwatch.org/issues/PID.jsp?articleid=4148>.

UPDATES:
<www.ciepac.org/bulletins/ingles/ing329.htm>
<www.ciepac.org/bulletins/ingles/ing312.htm>
<www.ciepac.org/bulletins/index02.htm>

UPDATE BY TIMI GERSON: The North American Free Trade Agreement (NAFTA) has had disastrous consequences in Canada, the U.S., and Mexico. It has forced millions of Mexican farmers off of their land and into sweatshops along the U.S./Mexico border; created ghost towns in the American Midwest and South with the shuttering of steel and textile factories; and led to successful attacks by chemical companies on Canadian federal bans on toxic substances. NAFTA's race to the bottom in labor and environmental standards is well-known, but equally damaging is its attack on democracy. NAFTA allows corporations to sue governments in secret tribunals when companies feel that "investor rights" have been violated by public health and safety laws, local zoning ordinances, or almost anything else that cuts into profit. It is this model—a slow-moving *coup d'etat* on democracy—that is being expanded via the proposed Free Trade Area of the Americas (FTAA).

On November 20–21, 2003 the 34 Trade Ministers of the Americas and the Caribbean (all countries except Cuba) are coming back to where it all began—Miami, Florida, where negotiations were launched in 1994. Per usual, multinational CEOs will court and lobby ministers at the Americas Business Forum. Outside the security perimeter, plans for a People's Gala, a march and rally, teach-ins, and other activities showing the diversity of opposition to NAFTA for the Americas are being coordinated by a broad coalition including: the AFL-CIO, Public Citizen, Sierra Club, Jobs with Justice, the Citizens Trade Campaign, Oxfam America, the National Family Farm Coalition, the Alliance for Responsible Trade, and the Latin America Solidarity Coalition, and others working with local Florida organizations like the Miami Workers Center, the Coalition of Immokalee Workers, Unite for Dignity, and the Florida Fair Trade Campaign.

Despite mounting evidence to the contrary, U.S. media pundits cling to the ideological conviction that "free" trade lifts all boats. The reality is that a malaise with Washington consensus policies of privatization and market fundamentalism is sweeping across the continent (witness the election of corporate globalization critics in Brazil, Argentina, and Ecuador). To date, and with almost no coverage in the American press, almost 10 million Brazilians have voted against the FTAA in an informal plebiscite; Americans, Argentines, Ecuadorians, Mexicans, and Uruguayans are engaged in similar processes of *consulta popular* or people's referendum; and national or regional Forums Against the FTAA have been held in Argentina, Bolivia, the Caribbean, Central America, Colombia, and Ecuador. In the face of rising international and domestic opposition, the Bush Administration seeks to lock down as many countries as possible in bilateral NAFTA-style agreements as soon as possible. A Central American Free Trade Agreement (CAFTA) with Costa Rica, El Salvador, Guatemala, Honduras, and Nicaragua is set to be complete by January 1, 2004. The U.S.-Chile free trade agreement was signed June 6, 2003, and will soon be voted on by Congress. These agreements are pieces in the FTAA puzzle. The Bush Administration is pushing a January 1, 2005, deadline for completion of FTAA negotiations with implementation by January 1, 2006. NAFTA was an experiment that failed; the FTAA will be more of the same.

To help stop the FTAA, contact Public Citizen's Global Trade Watch at <gtwfield@citizen.org> or (202) 546-4996 and check out our Web site at <www.tradewatch.org>.

17 Clear Channel Monopoly Draws Criticism

Source:
MediaFile, September 2002
Title: "Clear Channel Stumbles"
Author: Jeff Perlstein

Corporate media coverage: *NOW With Bill Moyers*, April 26, 2002, and April 4, 2003; *The New York Times*, January 30, 2003, and February 3, 2003; and *Wall Street Journal*, January 31, 2003.

Faculty Evaluators: Scott Gordon and Jorge Porras
Student Researchers: Melissa Jones and Chris Salvano

Clear Channel Communications of San Antonio, Texas may not yet be a household name, but in the past seven years, the radio station conglomerate has rocketed to a place alongside NBC and Gannett as one of the largest media companies in the United States.

Before passage of the 1996 Telecommunications Act, a company could not own more than 40 radio stations in the entire country. With the act's sweeping relaxation of ownership limits, the cap on radio ownership was virtually eliminated. As a result, Clear Channel has dominated the industry by growing from 40 radio stations nationally in the mid-'90s, to approximately 1,225 stations nationally by 2003. The station also dominates the audience share in 100 of 112 major markets. In addition to its radio stations, Clear Channel also owns television station affiliates, billboards, and outdoor advertising, and owns, operates, or exclusively books the vast majority of live entertainment venues, amphitheaters, and nightclubs in the country. According to *NOW with Bill Moyers*, Clear Channel controls the nation's largest concert and events promoters, and in 2001, Clear Channel sold 27 million concert tickets. That is 23 million more than the closest competitor.

In 2001, Denver concert promoter Jesse Morreale sued Clear Channel. Morreale's suit claims that Clear Channel's use of its billboards to advertise Clear Channel-booked shows of Clear Channel-owned music is, in essence, a breach of antitrust law. The suit also alleges that Clear Channel stations have threatened to withdraw certain music from rotation unless the artist's book concerts through Clear Channel and play at Clear Channel-owned music venues.

Clear Channel has also drawn criticism for using "voice tracking." Voice tracking is when one deejay produces a standardized national broadcast and formats it into their radio stations nationwide—giving the semblance of a local broadcast. By this process, Clear Channel can produce its radio format in San Antonio, Texas, and play it on its 1,225 radio stations without regard to local music, culture, or issues.

In January 2002, a train carrying 10,000 gallons of anhydrous ammonia derailed in the town of Minot, North Dakota, causing a spill and a toxic cloud. Authorities attempted to warn the residents of Minot to stay indoors and to avoid the spill. But when the authorities called six of the seven radio stations in Minot to issue the warning, no one answered the phones. As it turned out, Clear Channel owned all six of the stations, and none of the station's personnel were available at the time.

Senator Byron Dorgan of North Dakota grilled Federal Communications Commission (FCC) chairman Michael Powell over the consolidation of media in the U.S., using the Minot incident as a warning and an example. At a Senate Commerce Committee meeting Dorgan warned that as large media companies like Clear Channel buy up the last remaining independent media outlets across the country, the public suffers. According to Powell, there is strong evidence that many independently run local stations cannot afford to produce quality local news. However, a recent study by Columbia University's Project for Excellence in Journalism found that TV stations owned by smaller media firms generally produce better newscasts.

Such branding and consolidation is counter to the FCC's mandate of encouraging media diversity. Nevertheless, the FCC is doing very little about the results of increased media concentration. This may be a result of the relationship that exits between the FCC commissioners and the broadcast companies and their lobbyists. According to the Center for Public Integrity (CPI), media companies and lobbyists developed a very cozy relationship. As Chuck Lewis of CPI notes, "We found that 1,400 trips [by FCC commissioners]—all-expense-paid trips—were paid for by broadcasters. How can the FCC judge and discuss media ownership if they're taking trips from these guys?"

The FCC is, in fact, investigating one complaint made against Clear Channel. An advertiser in Ohio claims that Clear Channel is circumventing existing ownership limits by operating stations through shell companies in a practice known as "parking" or "warehousing" stations. Clear Channel has sold off stations to alleged front companies, which allows Clear Channel to continue operating the properties while also providing an easy way to buy back the stations now that the FCC has further relaxed ownership limits.

On June 2, 2003, the FCC approved new ownership limit caps giving a green light for further media consolidation. (See Amy Goodman's Introduction and Chapter 2, *Censored* #1 2003.)

UPDATE BY JEFF PERLSTEIN: It's been 9 months since I wrote this article, and Clear Channel is now widely seen as the poster child for what's wrong with our hyperconsolidated media environment and the free-market government policies that are to blame. One strong indicator that media activists have succeeded in moving this issue into the political mainstream and building political pressure is the recent June 2 vote at the FCC, which loosened a whole host of restrictions on broadcast media—except in the area of radio ownership. In fact, the commissioners actually voted to tighten some of the radio rules and Congressional antitrust committees are following up to examine anticompetitive practices in the industry.

But these days one need not look to DC to hear about the latest Clear Channel debacle. Egregious examples of the company's behavior are part and parcel of water cooler conversations, hundreds of e-mail lists and Web sites, and regular coverage by the independent media. Just ask people and they'll recite the litany for you: the banning of the Dixie Chicks and more than 200 peace-related songs, including "Imagine" by John Lennon; the many station-sponsored pro-war rallies; the intense union busting; automated on-air programming and the train wreck in Minot, North Dakota; and the "derelict rodeo roundup."

Yes, the so-called "derelict rodeo roundup," in which employees give homeless people a $20 bill, a 40-ounce bottle of malt liquor, and a bus ticket to the edge of town, was pioneered in spring of 2003 by a Clear Channel station in Cincinnati. Unconscionable behavior like this has fanned the flames of public outrage and provided the opportunity for media activists to build powerful coalition with media workers' unions, peace and justice networks, artists, youth organizers, attorneys, hip-hop activists, children's advocates, women's rights groups, and more.

Not only did these coalitions succeed in using Clear Channel as a lightning rod to mobilize unprecedented numbers against further deregulation by the FCC, but they're following up to build on the momentum at the local and national levels.

Community-driven campaigns in New York City and the San Francisco Bay Area are providing powerful models for engaging communities in holding corporate media accountable to their needs and ensuring local voices are a part of the mix. The Turn Off the Radio Campaign in New York is a media boycott taking place each Thursday for 12 hours, in which participants refrain from listening to radio and TV stations that broadcast a disproportionate share of offensive material.

The Community Coalition for Media Accountability (CCMA) in the Bay Area worked with youth-led organizations to issue a report rigorously documenting how local Clear Channel station KMEL-FM's nonmusic coverage was dominated by crime, drugs, and violence. Founded by the Youth Media Council and Media Alliance, the CCMA has followed up to build a broad coalition and win a number of concessions from the region's number-one hip-hop and R&B station. The coalition is actively encouraging allies in cities around the country to seize this model and adapt it in ways that make sense and are powerful.

On the national level, Clear Channel is facing a rapidly growing number of legal challenges, Congressional hearings and investigations, and targeted campaigns by a variety of unions. Congressional co-sponsorship and public support is growing for Senator Feingold's bill targeting Clear Channel's brutal domination of the radio and concert industries.

Even the corporate media couldn't ignore the growing public outrage and organized pressure by media activists. Clear Channel's behavior and the policies that created this monster were finally picked up by *Wall Street Journal* and a handful of other big media outlets.

At this writing, the grassroots momentum for accountability and transformation of corporate media structures continues to build, and Clear Channel is worried: the company recently hired a top Wall Street PR firm to deal with their "image problem."

Please continue to bolster the work of independent media and support the organizing for true media justice.

RESOURCES/LINKS:
<www.Salon.com>: Search for "Boehlert"
<www.Clearchannelsucks.org>
<www.Media-Alliance.org>; Tel: (415) 546-6334; E-mail: <info@media-alliance.org>
<www.Youthmediacouncil.org>; Tel: (510) 444-0640

18 Charter Forest Proposal Threatens Access to Public Lands

Sources:
Earth First!, Eostar 2002
Title: "Privatization's Trojan Horse"
Edited by: Kristin Robison

The American Prospect, September 9, 2002
Title: "Park Wars"
Author: Jon Margolis

Faculty Evaluator: Eric McGuckin
Student Researchers: Dana Balicki and Lisa Badenfort

Corporate media coverage: "Charter Forests Spell Trouble," *Ventura County Star*, May 15, 2002, and Jon Margolis, "Park Wars," *Washington Post*, September 9, 2002: 29.

The Bush Administration's Charter Forest Proposal is an attempt to privatize and profit from public forestland. Under this proposal, public-land management will be transferred from public hands to local privately controlled oversight boards. The Charter Forest Plan is the Bush Administration's attempt to further commodify and privatize the collective public domain of national forests by implementing ideas formulated by the American Recreation Coalition (ARC). ARC represents resort developers, more than 100 motorized recreation industries and touts the Walt Disney Corporation as their most prominent member. According to its own description, the ARC "strives to catalyze public/private partnerships for outdoor recreation opportunities." The ARC guided the development of President Clinton's Recreation Fee Demonstration Program as well as the current Charter Forest Proposal.

The Charter Forest Plan would transfer authority of some national forests from the U.S. Forest Service to local "trusts" (board of trustees) consisting largely of "user groups." This plan will decentralize forest management, allowing industry and local governments to wrest control of public lands from the federal government. Public domain makes up one-third of the country and includes national parks, national forests, and wilderness areas.

This Charter Forest Proposal promotes a "free-market environmentalism" which makes market demand the determiner for how public lands will be used. A chartered forest board of trustees, left on its own to raise revenue and manage a natural area, "discovers" that they can raise more money by charging $20 a night for a developed campground site, versus $6 a night for an undeveloped space. Advertising would target wealthy patrons, offering "forest-based" lodging with a wide variety of items for purchase at convenient and tastefully rustic shops.

The charter forest concept goes hand in hand with the Clinton era Recreation Fee Demonstration Program, charging people high fees to enjoy public lands; in essence imposing "double taxation" on areas for which Americans already pay taxes (for the management of these public forestlands). This is a pay-to-play plan requiring citizens to pay for access to national forests at hundreds of sites across the U.S. These proposals would allow corporations to decide through their boards of directors who uses the land and how. The ARC already shares responsibility with the Forest Service for the implementation of the fee program through the Challenge Cost Share Agreement of 1996. Under this agreement they are in charge of preparing and distributing all press releases and fact sheets regarding the privatization and development of natural forest areas.

The ARC represents resort developers and strives to create new, highly profitable outdoor recreation opportunities for businesses, such as the Walt Disney Corporation. Local boards would have complete control over these lands and would be categorized as a corporation. The lands are to be privatized and developed, and outdoor recreation will be their product for sale (at up to $50 a day).

Francis Pandolfi (former chair of ARC's Recreation Roundtable before he was chosen as chief of staff of the Forest Service) stated at a 1997 Forest Service staff meeting, "the next step is to use the recreation fee pilot project to pull together a first-class business management plan… For the first time, we are selling a product." As incorporated entities, the boards would also have the freedom to grant logging and mining contracts. The new proposal would obstruct the legal avenues currently available to environmental groups seeking to preserve public lands.

Wild Wilderness, an environmental organization, is working to prevent this occurrence. Scott Silver, executive director of Wild Wilderness, states, "Rec fees and the Charter Forest Proposal are just the first visible manifestations of an entirely new federal land management paradigm, one that strongly emphasizes and promotes highly developed, intensively motorized recreation."

UPDATE BY KRISTIN ROBISON: "In wildness is the preservation of the world," wrote Henry David Thoreau more than 100 years ago. Consider the recent implications of wildness being commercialized, privatized and turned into recreation opportunities by federal land managers and the private sector. Consider what happens when wildness is Disneyfied, marketed and sold to paying customers.

In light of Thoreau's warning, the corporate takeover of nature is more than just another example of creeping privatization. And that is the story that was presented in the March/April 2002 issue of *Earth First!*.

Following the publication of "Privatization's Trojan Horse," 35 coordinated demonstrations took place in 16 states in an attempt to gain visibility for this issue. Our mission was to explain the value of preserving free access to wild nature and to warn the public that big changes were in the works.

For the most part, the corporate media failed to report upon these events. In some cases, reporters attended protests, but failed to get their stories printed. Others published stories consisting of only a few sentences that neglected to address the real issues. In those rare cases in which lengthy articles were printed, government and recreation industry spokespersons put their own twisted spin upon the issues. Today, the Bush Administration is racing to privatize everything of value. It is actively creating a fiscal crisis with policies revolving around tax cuts and empire-building. With the crisis becoming firmly entrenched, President Bush and his team can say, "We have no money, we must make cuts, cuts, and still more cuts. And when cuts are not enough, we must turn to the private sector for help."

Seeing this coming and sounding the alarm, *Earth First!* reported the news, while the corporate media looked the other way.

Perhaps there's hope in the fact that the Bush Administration is so blatant in its war upon democracy and its rush to strip citizens of everything they hold in common. The public is finally starting to get a whiff of what's in the air.

With the threat of privatization of our national forests looming large, the question becomes, "Will our message be heard broadly enough so that this takeover agenda can be stopped in whatever time remains?"

For those wishing to learn more, contact Wild Wilderness, Tel: (541) 385-5261; E-mail: <ssilver@wildwilderness.org>. The Wild Wilderness Web site, <www.wildwilderness.org>, documents threats to wildness that Thoreau could have never imagined.

19 U.S. Dollar vs. the Euro: Another Reason for the Invasion of Iraq

Sources:
The Sierra Times, February 9, 2003
Title: "The Real Reasons for the Upcoming War with Iraq"
Author: William Clark

Feasta, January 2003
Title: "Oil, Currency, and the War on Iraq"
Author: Cóilín Nunan

The Nation, September 23, 2002
Title: "The End of Empire"
Author: William Greider

Faculty Evaluators: Wingham Liddell, Tony White, Phil Beard, and Tom Lough
Student Researchers: Effren Trejo, Kathleen Glover, and Dylan Citrin Cummins

President Richard Nixon removed U.S. currency from the gold standard in 1971. Since then, the world's supply of oil has been traded in U.S. fiat dollars, making the dollar the dominant world reserve currency. Countries must provide the United States with goods and services for dollars—which the United States can freely print. To purchase energy and pay off any IMF debts, countries must hold vast dollar reserves. The world is attached to a currency that one country can produce at will. This means that in addition to controlling world trade, the United States is importing substantial quantities of goods and services for very low relative costs.

The euro has begun to emerge as a serious threat to dollar hegemony and U.S. economic dominance. The dollar may prevail throughout the Western Hemisphere, but the euro and dollar are clashing in the former Soviet Union, Central Asia, sub-Saharan Africa, and the Middle East.

In November 2000, Iraq became the first OPEC nation to begin selling its oil for euros. Since then, the value of the euro has increased 17 percent, and the dollar has begun to decline. One important reason for the invasion and installation of a U.S. dominated government in Iraq was to force the country back to the dollar. Another reason for the invasion is to dissuade further OPEC momentum toward the euro, especially from Iran, the second largest OPEC producer, which was actively discussing a switch to euros for its oil exports.

Because of huge trade deficits, it is estimated that the dollar is currently overvalued by at least 40 percent. Conversely, the euro-zone does not run huge deficits, uses higher interest rates, and has an increasingly larger share of world trade. As the euro establishes its durability and comes into wider use, the dollar will no longer be the world's only option. At that point, it would be easier for other nations to exercise financial leverage against the United States without damaging themselves or the global financial system as a whole.

Faced with waning international economic power, military superiority is the United States' only tool for world domination. Although the expense of this military control is unsustainable, says journalist William Clark, "one of the dirty little secrets of today's international order is that the rest of the globe could topple the United States from its hegemonic status whenever they so choose with a concerted abandonment of the dollar standard. This is America's preeminent, inescapable Achilles' heel." If American power is ever perceived globally as a greater liability than the dangers of toppling the international order, the U.S. systems of control can be eliminated and collapsed. When acting against world opinion—as in Iraq—an international consensus could brand the United States as a "rogue nation."

UPDATE BY WILLIAM CLARK: Only time will tell what will happen in the aftermath of the Iraq war and U.S. occupation, but I am hopeful my research will contribute to the historical record and help others understand one of the important but hidden macroeconomic reasons for why we conquered Iraq. The Bush/Cheney Administration probably believes that the occupation of Iraq and the installation of a large and permanent U.S. military presence in the Persian Gulf region will stop other OPEC producers from even considering switching the denomination of their oil sales from dollars to euros. However, using the military to enforce dollar hegemony for oil transactions strikes me as a rather unwieldy and inappropriate strategy. Regrettably, President Bush and his neoconservative advisors have exacerbated "anti-

American" sentiments by applying a military option in Iraq that is, in essence, an economic problem. History may not look kindly upon their actions.

Despite the U.S. media reporting to the contrary, the current wave of "global anti-Americanism" is not against the American people or against American values—but against the hypocrisy of militant American imperialism. The foreign polices of the neoconservatives may be creating the regrettable emergence of a possible European-Russian-Chinese alliance in an effort to counter American imperialism. It appears that the structural imbalances in the U.S. economy, along with the Bush Administration's flawed tax, economic, and most principally their overtly imperialist foreign policies, could result in the dollar's reserve currency status or oil transaction currency status being placed in jeopardy or at the very least significantly diminished over the next one to two years. In the event that my hypothesis materializes, the U.S. economy will require restructuring in some manner to account for the reduction of either of these two pivotal advantages.

What is needed is a multilateral meeting of the G8 nations to reform the international monetary system. Given that future wars will become more likely over oil and the currency of oil, the author advocates that the global monetary system be reformed without delay. This would include the dollar and euro being designated as equal international reserve currencies, and placed within an exchange band along with a dual-OPEC oil transaction currency standard. Additionally, the G8 nations should also explore a future third reserve currency option regarding a yen/yuan bloc for East Asia. A compromise on the euro/oil issues via a multilateral treaty with a gradual phase-in of a dual-OPEC transaction currency standard could minimize economic dislocations within the U.S.

While these proposed multilateral reforms may lower our ability to finance our current massive levels of debt and maintain a global military presence, the benefits would include improving the quality of our lives and that of our children by reducing animosity towards the U.S., while we rebuild our alliances with the EU and world community. Creating balanced domestic fiscal polices along with global monetary reform is in the long-term national security interest of the United States and necessary for the global economy. Hopefully, these proposed monetary reforms could mitigate future armed or economic warfare over oil, ultimately fostering a more stable, safer, and prosperous global economy in the twenty-first century.

UPDATE BY COILIN NUNAN: At the time this article was written, the suggestion that Iraq's move to selling oil for euros had something to do with the U.S. threatening war against the country was just a theory. It still is a theory, but a theory that subsequent U.S. actions have done little to dispel: the U.S. has invaded Iraq and installed its own authority to rule the country, and as soon as Iraqi oil became available to sell on the world market, it was announced that payment would be in dollars only.[1] But the story doesn't end there: the U.S. trade deficit is still widening and the dollar falling. More and more, oil exporters are talking openly about selling their commodity for euros instead of greenbacks. While Indonesia has only been considering it,[2] Prime Minister Dr. Mahathir of Malaysia has been strongly encouraging his country's oil industry to actually do it,[3] which has led European Union's Energy Commissioner Loyola de Palacio to comment that she could see the euro replacing the dollar as the main currency for oil pricing.[4] Meanwhile, Iran has been giving all the signs that it is about to switch to the euro: it has been issuing eurobonds, converting its foreign exchange reserves from dollars to euros, and having warm trade negotiations with the EU. According to one recent report, it has even started selling its oil to Europe for euros and encouraging Asian customers to pay in euros too.[5] Should U.S. talk of "regime change" in Iran not be seen in the light of these facts? The media largely appear to think not, as there has been little discussion of the dollar-euro connection with the "War on Terror." What discussion there has been may well be expanded upon in the future, as neither the threat to the dollar and the U.S. economy nor the U.S. threat to world peace are likely to go away any time soon.

1. Carola Hoyos and Kevin Morrison, "Iraq Returns to International Oil Market," *Financial Times*, June 5, 2003, <news.ft.com/servlet/ContentServer?pagename=FT.com/Story FT/FullStory&c=StoryFT&cid=1054416466875>.
2. Kazi Mahmood, "Economic Shift Could Hurt U.S.-British Interests In Asia," March 30 2003, <IslamOnline.net>.
3. Shahanaaz Habib, "'Use Euro for Oil Prices,' says Dr. M," *The Star*, June 16, 2003, <thestar.com.my/news/story.asp?file=/2003/6/17/nation/sboil&sec=nation>.
4. Reuters, "EU Says Oil Could One Day be Priced in Euros," June 16, 2003, <biz.yahoo.com/rf/030616/energy_euro_2.html>.
5. C. Shivkumar, "Iran Offers Oil to Asian Union on Easier Terms," June 16, 2003, <thehindubusinessline.com/stories/2003061702380500.htm.

20 Pentagon Increases Private Military Contracts

Sources:
Fortune, March 3, 2003
Title: "The Pentagon's Private Army"
Author: Nelson D. Schwartz

CorpWatch, <corpwatch.org>, March 20, 2003
Title: "Halliburton Makes a Killing on Iraq War"
Author: Pratap Chatterjee

The Observer (London), April 13, 2003
Title: "Battle for Iraq: Scandal-hit U.S. Firm Wins Key Contracts"
Author: Antony Barnett

Faculty Evaluator: Tom Lough
Student Researcher: Josh Sisco

President Dwight Eisenhower's final remarks upon vacating the White House were "Beware the military-industrial complex." With the war on Iraq, the government rapidly increased the already growing privatization of much of its military operations. Staffed largely by ex-military and Defense Department officials, private companies—such as Kellogg, Brown & Root; DynCorp; Cubic; ITT; and MPRI—have been aggressively snatching up government contracts. One estimate, cited by Nelson Schwartz in *Fortune* magazine, says that 8 percent, or $30 billion, of the Pentagon's total budget for 2003 will go to private companies. Following 9/11, the Defense Department released a study that concluded, "Only those functions that must be performed by the Defense Department should be kept by the Defense Department. Any function that can be provided by the private sector is not a core government function." The U.S. military has contracted with private military companies on everything from kitchen and laundry duty to domestic recruiting efforts.

Kellogg, Brown & Root (KBR) is a subsidiary of Halliburton, the energy company formerly headed by Vice President Dick Cheney. By the time Cheney left Halliburton for the vice presidency, the company had extensive involvement with the Pentagon. While secretary of defense for Bush Sr., Cheney awarded Halliburton a $3.9 million contract to "study and then implement the privatization of routine army functions." Adm. Joe Lopez (ret.), former commander in chief for U.S.

forces in southern Europe, as well as Cheney's aid under the elder Bush, is now the senior vice president at KBR and responsible for military contracting.

KBR was given a 10-year contract entitled Logistics Civil Augmentation Program (LOGCAP). This is a "cost-plus-award-fee, indefinite-delivery/indefinite-quantity service," an open-ended mandate for privatization anywhere in the world, according to journalist Pratap Chatterjee. Whereas it used to take 120 to180 days to deploy private companies to foreign military bases, a 72-hour notice is now all that is required. KBR was also given $16 million to build a 408-bed prison for Afghanistan's enemy combatants in Guantanamo Bay, Cuba.

Last year, DynCorp won a State Department contract to protect Afghan president Hamid Kharzai. The protection force consists of former members of Delta Force and other elite military units. DynCorp, in conjunction with several other companies such as Airscan and Northrop Grumman, receives roughly $1.2 billion a year to spray suspected coca fields in Columbia.

In April 2003, DynCorp was also awarded a multimillion-dollar contract to build a private police force in post-Saddam Iraq. Potential officers do not need to speak Arabic and must be U.S. citizens and current or former police officers, according to the London *Observer*. Private police provided by DynCorp working for the U.N. in Bosnia were accused of buying and selling prostitutes, including a 12-year-old girl. Others were accused of videotaping the rape of one of the women. Ecuadorian peasants are suing the company, alleging that chemicals sprayed over Colombia spread into Ecuador killing legal crops and children. DynCorp has been accused of destruction of legal crops and of committing serious human rights violations.

UPDATE BY PRATAP CHATTERJEE: War profiteering has risen to an all time high under the Bush Administration. For the first time in history, one in 10 people deployed during a war was a private contractor. From building the tent cities, to maintaining the fighter jets and training the troops in live-weapons fire, private companies made a killing in the invasion of Iraq. What is even more significant is that the vice president of the United States has directly benefited from these contracts in his former job (he gets compensation of $180,000 a year from the company) and his staff continues to receive advice from his company.

Since *CorpWatch* and the *San Francisco Bay Guardian* broke the story that Halliburton had stationed employees in Uzbekistan to run United States military bases in April 2002, the value and number of the company's war machine contracts have vastly expanded. As the first bombs rained down on Baghdad, thousands of Halliburton employees were working alongside U.S. troops in Jordan, Kuwait, and Turkey under a package deal worth well over $1 billion. In addition the company has contracts to support troops in Afghanistan, Djibouti, and Georgia in the former Soviet Union.

Cheap labor is a primary reason for outsourcing services, says Maj. Toni Kemper, head of public affairs at one of the Turkish bases: "The reason that the military goes to contracting is largely because it's more cost effective in certain areas. I mean there was a lot of studies years ago as to what services can be provided via contractor versus via military personnel. Because when we go contract, we don't have to pay health care and all the other things for the employees; that's up to the employer."

For more information, check out <www.corpwatch.org>.

21 Third World Austerity Policies: Coming Soon to a City Near You

Sources:
Harper's, March 2003
Title: "Resolved to Ruin"
Author: Greg Palast

CovertAction Quarterly, Spring 2002
Title: "Global Rollback"
Author: Michael Parenti

The Texas Observer, January 17, 2003
Title: "Mistakes Were Made" (a book review of *Globalization and Its Discontents* by Joseph Stiglitz)
Author: Gabriella Bocagrande

Faculty Evaluators: Eric McGuckin and Linda Nowak
Student Researchers: Tony Cullen and Scott Frazier

Policies traditionally carried out overseas by international lending institutions such as the United States–led World Bank or International Monetary Fund (IMF) are quickly becoming part of the U.S. domestic economy. Privatization, loss of social services, bifurcation of the economy, and an overall decline in the lives of working people are an ongoing reality in the U.S.

Officially, IMF and World Bank measures were imposed to curb inflation, increase exports, and strengthen the fiscal condition of debtor nations, allowing them to pay back their loans. In actuality, however, the common result of structural adjustments has been depressed wages, reduced consumer purchase-power, and environmental degradation, while boosting profit rates for multinational investors. Small farmers, having lost their subsidies and import protections, are driven off their land into overcrowded cities. According to a number of economists, including the former chief economist for the World Bank, Joseph Stiglitz, as Western investment in the Third World increased throughout the '90s, so did poverty and social instability.

The World Bank and IMF have a four-step "reform" formula for each country. The formula includes capital-market liberalization, privatization, market-based pricing, and, finally, the introduction of "free trade." In step one, capital is freed up to flow in and out across the borders. Generally, the result is the increased flow of capital out to external businesses with no guarantee that the money will flow in through foreign investment.

Privatization is the second step. This refers to the transfer of traditionally state-run services and utilities like gas, oil, roads, water, post offices, and banks to private companies. The problem, say critics, is that private ownership of a country's framework leaves it unable to protect its citizens or natural resources from abuses of power.

Step three of the program, market-based pricing, is the point at which consumer purchase-power drops and the local economy really begins to suffer. The country's political leaders no longer have the ability to place local controls on economic trends and the country and its citizens become vulnerable to the whims of the global market.

The final step in the formula is free trade. But "free" is a relative term when referring to import/export values and global trade agreements. Third World nations are not on the same economic footing as their industrialized trade partners. Industrialized countries, influenced by their corporate backers, usually override attempts at import protections by Third World countries in order to procure local industries, cheap labor, and natural resources.

Many of these policies had been established slowly in the United States over a number of years, but the intensity and speed with which they are now emerging is unprecedented. After 9/11, with much of the public distracted by terrorism and the desire for national defense, business litigators and antilabor politicians stepped up the process of rolling back laws enacted over the last 100 years to protect workers, the public, and the environment from the excesses of industry. Just as with World Bank/IMF policies in other countries, the goal is to privatize profits and socialize losses. The vast majority of profits made by a company will be concentrated in a few private hands, while economic losses will be borne by the taxpayers through increased taxation and denial of social benefits. This is a trend that represents a huge shift in social and economic policy in the United States, with long-term implications.

UPDATE BY GABRIELLA BOCAGRANDE: The appearance of Joseph Stiglitz's book *Globalization and Its Discontents* in 2002 was widely greeted as a radical departure by a World Bank insider from the neoliberal policies of the international financial institutions in Washington. While it was gratifying to see Mr. Stiglitz lambaste the IMF for promoting indigence, unemployment, and organized crime every time it gained control over a distressed economy in the developing world, an alternative interpretation of Mr. Stiglitz's observations suggests that he recommended no fundamental changes in the neoliberal approach to "development." He suggested milder forms of fiscal intervention in economies in crisis and more generous "social safety nets," but this is rather like recommending the distribution of pith helmets to protect people from nuclear combat.

Nor has the IMF changed its ways. Throughout 2002 and 2003, it continues to strangle the economy of Argentina by exacting continuing budget cuts in repayment of the external debt. Most recently, the IMF has threatened the new Argentine government with another credit cutoff for not allowing private banks holding household mortgages to foreclose more rapidly on delinquent homeowners, 50 percent of whom are now impoverished, thanks to the IMF itself. Stiglitz's response to this position would most likely be to argue that it is not sound economic policy to create more homeless people because it weakens consumer demand. After all, homeless people are only a market for canned goods, plastic sheeting, and pots and pans to bang, while people who own residences buy appliances and cookware, not to mention PlayStations, Next Day Blinds, and DVDs.

There is something fundamentally wrong with the IMF and the World Bank, but Joseph Stiglitz did not finger it: These institutions represent the interests of First World finance capital, but they are never charged with this—not by Mr. Stiglitz and not by the mainstream press. They represent themselves publicly as charitable institutions sincerely seeking to promote job growth and prosperity around the world, and Mr. Stiglitz let them get away with it. Coverage of them by Stiglitz and the press attributes increasing world misery to well-intentioned "mistakes" on their part, rather than the systematic operation of the structural machinery of greed.

Organizations that genuinely oppose the policies of the IMF and the World Bank are Public Services International, which advocates on behalf of public sector trade unions, <www.world-psi.org>; the Bank Information Center, which promotes transparency at the Banks, <www.bicusa.org>; and the Citizens' Network for Essential Services, <www.challengeglobalization.org>.

22 Welfare Reform Up for Reauthorization, But Still No Safety Net

Sources:
Mother Jones, May/June 2002
Title: "Without a Safety Net"
Authors: Barbara Ehrenreich and Frances Fox Piven

In These Times, September 2, 2002
Title: "Bad to Worse"
Author: Neil deMause

The American Prospect, Summer 2002
Title: "What Does Minnesota Know?"
Author: Dave Hage

Dollars and Sense, September/October 2002
Title: "Good Times, Bad Times: Recession the Welfare Debate"
Author: Heather Boushey

Faculty Evaluators: Maureen Buckley, Barbara Bloom, and Wingham Liddell
Student Researchers: Jen Scanlan, Jessie Esquivel, Sarah Zisman, and Alyssa Speaker

In 1996, President Bill Clinton enacted legislation that ended 61 years of federal aid designed to lift families out of poverty and ushered in a commitment to lower welfare rolls by forcing recipients to work. The 1996 law, entitled Temporary Assistance for Needy Families (TANF), is set to be reviewed in the summer of 2003. Poverty and unemployment are on the rise in the U.S. and the welfare safety net for needy children no longer meets basic needs. Yet the Bush Administration is seeking to reduce the safety net even more.

As part of its plan to reauthorize TANF, the White House has proposed new work requirements that promise to exacerbate the plight of the unemployed by undercutting state programs that managed to make partial successes of the 1996 bill. Under the 1996 provisions, states had the right to adopt local policies to accommodate the job training and education needs of clients. New rules being proposed in Washington would replace state-level policies with more rigid, mechanistic limitations imposed by the federal government. Programs like employment skills training, guided job searches, and bilingual education would be constricted or discontinued altogether.

Prior to 1996, the federal government had matched a percentage of the state's welfare spending. With the passage of TANF, each state had an annual grant of a set amount. Some states were able to take the grant and work with client families to move them from assistance to reasonable employment and out of poverty, but in most states as the welfare rolls declined, poverty actually increased.

While the 1996 welfare law required parents to work in order to receive TANF benefits, in practice, a good bit of leeway remained for parents to attend school and job training programs. But now, with very little input from state agencies, the White House has decided to impose new restrictions that would eliminate states' flexibility regarding the application of their yearly grants. States would be required to verify that 70 percent of their welfare clients worked 40 hours a week.

A study released by the *Christian Science Monitor* indicates that mothers on welfare received an average of $13,000 a year, well below the poverty line. Since government assistance diminishes as job income rises, recipients are still unable to cover food, rent, and utilities. One-fifth of all mothers in the study had to cut the size of meals they serve their children because they could not afford to buy more food. To earn more money, the mothers work more hours, leaving the kids without their mothers for longer periods at a time. This also means that mothers have to pay more for child care.

According to a recent survey by the National Governors Association, the new welfare requirements will "dismantle effective programs that reduce nonmarital births, improve job retention, encourage completion of secondary education by teenagers and young adults, and reduce substance abuse." Many state legislators are angry that they were never consulted before the push for the new rules began. This move toward the imposition of big government over states' rights seems an ironic policy for a conservative Republican Administration.

In 1996, the assumptions underlying welfare reform were that a job could lift a family out of poverty and that there were enough jobs for anyone willing to work. In today's economy, families living close to the poverty line are increasingly likely to fall over the edge.

UPDATE BY DAVID HAGE: The landmark federal law known as "welfare reform" received intense news coverage during 1995 and 1996, when Congress was debating the measure and battling with President Bill Clinton. By 2000, however, it had dropped off the national radar screen. Lawmakers considered welfare reform a finished project because they had debated and passed legislation, and most reporters moved on to other stories when no obvious crises emerged.

On the ground, however, it was very much a live story. The law had triggered a revolution at the local level, as states converted their welfare offices into employment agencies, and workers in the trenches were just beginning to figure out what worked and what didn't in the daunting and unprecedented task of moving millions of poor, underskilled single parents into the job market.

By 2002, some welfare advocates and poverty scholars were actually looking forward to reauthorization of the federal law. They hoped that Congress would learn from six years of experience and give them tools to handle the emerging problems: the crushing costs of child care for poor single mothers; the fact that most welfare "leavers" remained mired in poverty-level jobs; the discovery that millions of welfare recipients had mental illnesses, chronic disabilities, borderline IQs, and other disadvantages that barred them from holding steady work.

Instead, in 2002, the Bush Administration offered a bill that capped federal funds to the states, imposed demanding new work requirements on welfare recipients, and effectively banned many of the most promising state-level experiments. That proposal, which alarmed many governors and welfare scholars, died by late summer when the Republican House failed to reach agreement with the Democratic Senate.

In mid-2003, however, the Bush Administration submitted essentially the same proposal, and the Republican leadership in both chambers promised to adopt it. Ironically, and sadly, this occurred just as the welfare experiment was experiencing its first crisis at the local level: the job market was contracting, welfare caseloads were rising, and state governments were facing their worst fiscal crisis since the Depression. Most welfare reporters seemed fatigued by the story, and a cynic would have predicted that they would return to the story only when poor families turned up sleeping on park benches.

If there was any promise in the 1996 welfare law, it was that society might actually look at the families on public assistance and ask what might be required to give them better lives. By all appearances, seven years into the experiment, Congress and much of the public had never looked or simply shrugged.

In Washington, the Center for Law and Social Policy (CLASP) and the Center on Budget and Policy Priorities have done fine work in tracking the consequences of the 1996 law, and the Urban Institute undertook a comprehensive study of the fate of poor families under the "new federalism." But it remains unclear whether anyone in a position of power was paying attention.

UPDATE BY NEIL DEMAUSE: In the nine months since *In These Times* published "Bad To Worse," if anything, things have gotten even more dismal for women trying to survive on welfare. Congress never did pass a TANF reauthorization law in 2002, and with Republicans regaining control of the Senate in the November elections, it's even more likely that what legislation eventually emerges will be heavy on punitive restrictions like increased work hours and full-family sanctions, with more progressive measures likely to be pushed to the side. Meanwhile, the economy-ravaged (and tax-cut-ravaged) federal government is even more strapped for cash, making it more unlikely that federal child care funds will be increased, even as need is on the rise. According to a Government Accounting Office study, 23 states have cut child-care funding in the last two years because of their own fiscal crises.

All this has taken place far from the public eye, as media coverage of welfare, once a staple of nightly news broadcasts, has all but vanished—just when the effects of "welfare reform," no longer masked by the 1990s economic boom, are finally becoming clear: more homelessness, more hunger, and lessened ability to escape from poverty. (Recent studies have found, in fact, that low-income single mothers were the one demographic group whose fortunes slipped even during the height of the boom times.) Instead, the myth that reform has worked persists, largely because caseloads dropped precipitously upon implementation of the 1996 law and have remained low. But as Mark Greenberg of the Center for Law and Social Policy notes, "That raises big questions: Some people point to that as evidence of the continued success of state efforts, while others ask why welfare caseloads *aren't* going up when unemployment is going up?"

Instead of asking these questions, Congress has largely focused on following the course set out by the 1996 law—one recent Senate committee hearing was titled "Welfare Reform: Building on Success." And President Bush is now moving to bring similar "reform" to other programs, proposing to convert Medicaid, Head Start, and Section 8 housing vouchers into "block grant" programs that, like TANF, would freeze federal funding levels while allowing states unprecedented leeway in denying services.

Meanwhile, the coalition of groups that first organized to track the TANF reauthorization process continues to press for more equitable policies for America's poor.

Among the groups to contact for more information: the DC-based Center for Law and Social Policy, Tel: (202) 906-8000, Web Site: <www.clasp.org>; Center on Budget and Policy Priorities, Tel: (202) 408-1080, Web site: <www.cbpp.org>; the Welfare Made a Difference Campaign, a network of grassroots low-income organizers, Tel: (212) 894-8082, Web site: <www.wmadcampaign.org>; and the Welfare Information Network's comprehensive Web site at <www.financeprojectinfo.org/win>.

23 Argentina Crisis Sparks Cooperative Growth

Sources:
Yes!, Fall 2002
Title: "Starting Over"
Author: Lisa Garrigues

Utne Reader, January/February 2003
Title: "Don't Cry For Argentina"
Author: Leif Utne

Faculty Evaluator: Patricia Leigh Gibbs
Student Researchers: Emilio Licea, Jennifer Scanlan, and Dana Balicki

The citizens of Argentina are cooperatively rebuilding their country, rising above the financial devastation caused by decades of privatization and military leadership. In December 2001, the International Monetary Fund (IMF) recipe had gone sour, destroying currency values and employment levels. The IMF "recipe" had used loans to prop up an overvalued peso, as well as to push the multinational privatization of Argentine companies.

The resulting crisis left thousands of people unemployed. Fearing a run on the banks, the government froze accounts, enraging a public that was already nervous about losing its life savings. Millions took to the streets throughout the country shouting, "*Que se vayan todos!*" (roughly, "Throw the bums out!")

The president resigned and within a month Argentina defaulted on $132 billion of foreign debt and suffered a 25 percent unemployment rate, a middle class rapidly slipping into poverty, widespread hunger, and mounting crime. What had once been the world's seventh richest nation found itself in complete economic, political, and social collapse.

Alva Sotelo was a seamstress at a Brukman Factory in Buenos Aires, where, like many other debt-burdened factories, the owners cut their losses and abandoned the plant. With the idea of survival fueling the factory's former employees, they began sleeping in the factory hoping their employers would come back and pay their salaries. Eventually, with no other alternative, the workers at Brukman and hundreds of other previously employed factory workers began to slowly run the factory themselves. The workers at Brukman elected a six-member commission to coordinate the work; they managed to pay off the debts with factory profits and managed to pay workers an equal amount by dividing the remaining profits.

The middle and lower classes have joined in a grassroots movement to take back the country. The power vacuum is being filled by an array of grassroots democratic organizations. *Asambleas populares* (popular assemblies) are occurring all over the country including over 200 neighborhoods in Buenos Aires alone. These assemblies consist of people gathering in parks or plazas to address problems facing their communities: food distribution, health care, day care, welfare, and transportation. "The spirit on the streets and in the assemblies is that people can govern themselves," notes *SIC* magazine. According to one poll, one-third of Argentines have attended a popular assembly, and "35 percent say the assemblies constitute 'a new form of political organization.'" Many people have even disengaged themselves from the formal peso economy by joining "barter clubs"—neighborhood-based economic networks that let citizens trade goods and services without dealing with the banks. The barter system now accounts for $400–$600 million worth of business.

The spirit of the cooperative is alive and well in cities, rural areas, and neighborhoods all over Argentina. Neighborhood assemblies have organized alternative forms of survival such as street-corner soup kitchens. Food donations are now replacing money as the price of entrance to cultural events. Community gardens are prospering.

The most extraordinary of these new forms of survival are worker cooperatives like the Brukman factory. There are about 100 legal, worker-owned cooperatives in Argentina, which range in size from eight employees to over 1,000. Roughly 10 businesses a month are being taken over and run by the employees. Most of them share a model similar to Brukman's, in which the workers elect the managers of the company and the profits are split among the workers. The original owners often attempt to evict workers, but are unsuccessful either because they are legally challenged or because members of the local neighborhood assemblies show up and hold nonviolent protests and vigils against the eviction of the workers.

Argentina is awash in economic and political chaos; however, it is clear that the Argentine people have decided to take control of their communities. The current rebuilding process does not depend on IMF recipes or capitalist promises, but rather on the cooperation of hundreds of Argentines. It's an enormous social experiment that could prove to be the first great popular rebellion against capitalism of the twenty-first century. When an entire people wake from the trance of political passiveness, it seems that anything is possible.

UPDATE BY LISA GARRIGUES: Most U.S. media covered, at least briefly, the food rioting and looting that broke out in Argentina in December 2001, as a result of its economic collapse. But few discussed the economic alternatives, experiments in direct democracy, and solidarity that began to take shape after the Argentine collapse. As the corporate-driven world economy marginalizes more and more people, it becomes increasingly important to investigate the alternatives that are "growing through the cracks in the system."

How can we learn from the Argentine experiment, its successes and failures?

The workers at the Brukman factory, which was featured in the article, were evicted in April 2003 in a violent confrontation between demonstrators and police in which police fired rubber and lead bullets, then chased demonstrators 20 blocks into a children's hospital and lobbed tear gas into the hospital. As of this writing, the workers are attempting to work out an arrangement to continue to operate in another location. However, workers throughout Argentina continue to occupy and run factories, and unemployed groups are still squatting unoccupied land, baking bread, and starting cooperative businesses.

The barter clubs had faded out by the end of 2002. Most Argentines say that they ceased to function because of corruption, counterfeiting of barter "credits," and because many people simply ran out of items to trade.

The neighborhood assemblies operate on a much smaller level, with 10 to 50 people per assembly. Some assemblies took over abandoned public and private property banks, empty lots, and buildings and turned them into soup kitchens and cultural centers. Most of these groups have since been evicted by the government.

Some people who left the assemblies say they fell victim to takeover by established left-wing political parties, an inability to work together, and increased marginalization from the middle class that had spawned them. However, the assemblies continue to take on important tasks within the neighborhood, like sending food to malnourished children, and organizing vaccinations and health fairs, and one assembly has recently received official recognition by the government.

The feeling of renewed solidarity among the Argentine people has continued. As one sociologist I interviewed last year said, "It's not important whether the neighborhood assemblies succeed or fail, what's important is that the Argentine people have begun to think differently."

It is this "thinking differently," thinking beyond the ways that have been handed down to them by a collapsing system, that has remained. And this, I believe, is the lesson, not just for the citizens of this country who have finally woken up from the fear of their own neighbor that was instilled in them during the dictatorship, but for all of us.

When the system fails us, or when we see that the system is failing our neighbor, who might live down the street or on the other side of the world, we can choose to begin to think differently, to build a system that includes all of us.

<argentinanow.tripod.com.ar>: Narratives and analyses of the social and economic experiments in Argentina; news and photos from 2001–2002.
</www.znet.org>: Ongoing coverage and analysis of events in Argentina.
<www.indymedia.org>: Go to the Argentina section for news updates in English.

24 U.S. Aid to Israel Fuels Repressive Occupation in Palestine

Sources:
CovertAction Quarterly, Spring 2002, No. 72
Title: "Palestine in the Crosshairs: U.S. Policy and the Struggle for Nationhood"
Author: John Steinbach

Left Turn, March 4, 2002
Title: "U.S. Aid Lifeblood of the Occupation"
Author: Matt Bowles

Wartimes, April 2003
Title: "Israel Erecting 'Great Wall' Around Palestine"
Author: Bob Wing

Faculty Evaluator: Rabbi Michael Robinson
Student Researchers: Kathleen Glover, Josh Sisco, Lindsey Brage, Dana Balicki, Allyssa Speaker, and Colin Umphryes

U.S. aid to Israel over the course of its 54 years of nationhood has fueled the illegal occupation of Palestinian land superceding Palestinian rights to self-government.

Jimmy Carter raised the ire of the American Israel Public Affairs Committee (AIPAC) and other Zionist pressure groups when he expressed support for a "Palestinian Homeland" and criticized Israel's settlement policies. However, he never favored the creation of a Palestinian state and did nothing to slow the settlements in the West Bank and Gaza. U.S. support of Israel was greatly increased during the Reagan era, which represented "a quantum leap in efforts to promote Israel and delegitimize the Palestinians in the United States." Illicit arms technology transfers to Israel resulted in a greatly enhanced Israeli military.

Under the Clinton Administration, even while the "peace process" and the Final Status Talks were ongoing between the Palestinians and Israel, U.S. economic and military aid to Israel continued to accelerate. From 1949 to 1997, U.S. aid to Israel, which has a population of 4.8 million, totaled over $134 billion. The total U.S. foreign aid to Israel for the same period exceeded the total aid to all of sub-Saharan Africa, Latin America, and the Caribbean combined, which has a combined population of 486 million.

During the last 25 years U.S. aid to Israel has been about 60 percent military aid and 40 percent economic aid. There is a new plan to phase out all economic aid by 2008 in order to have all the aid going to military. Israel receives about $3 billion a year in direct aid and $3 billion a year in indirect aid in the form of special loans and grants. Under the Arms Export Control Act the U.S. can only supply weapons that are used "for legitimate self defense." The U.S. Foreign Assistance Act prohibits military assistance to any country "which engages in a consistent pattern of gross violations of internationally recognized human rights." The Proxmire Amendment bans military assistance to any government that refuses to sign the Treaty on the Non-Proliferation of Nuclear Weapons and to allow inspections of its nuclear facilities. All three of these laws are currently being broken with aid to Israel.

Since 1982, the aid to Israel has been transferred in one lump sum at the beginning of each fiscal year. Aid to other countries is distributed in quarterly installments throughout the year and they must account for specific purchases. Israel is not required to account for the specific purchases that the aid is being used for; it can be spent on anything—including expansion of colonial settlement projects.

It is with this aid that Israel has been able to continue the comprehensive and unrelenting occupation of the West Bank and Gaza. Today, Israel is bulldozing Palestinian farmers' olive trees in order to build an encompassing 30-foot-high cement wall with gun towers and electric fencing to imprison Palestinians and the entire West Bank. Israeli forces have commandeered the Western Aquifer, which constitutes 50 percent of the West Bank water supply, and thousands of acres of Palestinian agricultural land. The wall around Jerusalem will bring the now-divided Holy City fully under Israeli control and effectively strangle West Bank economy and agriculture. The wall includes a 15-foot-deep, 20-foot-wide trench (Amy Goodman of *Democracy Now!* reported it would be filled with raw sewage), a dirt path that will be a "killing zone" for Palestinians who try to access it, an electrified fence, and a two-lane Israeli patrol road.

Since Israel barred most Palestinians from working inside Israel, unemployment in the West Bank has soared to over 50 percent. Agriculture is therefore more important than ever. Square foot by square foot, olive tree by olive tree, village by village, Israel is relentlessly taking over Jerusalem, the West Bank, and Gaza with the full support of the American taxpayer.

UPDATE BY BOB WING: The story is a monumental example of the illegality and brutality of the Israeli occupation of Palestine, the numerous but unreported nonviolent attempts by Palestine to resist, and of U.S. silence/complicity with Israel.

Since publication of my article, the Israelis continue building the wall, taking over more and more Palestinian land, destroying or stealing olive trees and snatching the Palestinian water supply. Resistance by the Palestinians, especially olive growers and by residents between East Jerusalem and Bethlehem has also been constant, but still ineffective at halting the building of the separation barrier.

None of the mainstream press carried my story. A few, like *The New York Times*, carried stories about the wall buried deep in their papers. Even the alternative press failed to carry the story in any significant way. Although a deputy editor supported my story, the main editor of *Village Voice* rejected it, telling the deputy editor that *The New York Times* had already said all there needed to be said on the subject.

For information on what you can do, go to the following Web sites: <www.btselem.org> and <www.gush-shalom.org/English>.

UPDATE BY MATT BOWLES: Since the writing of this article, conditions have worsened for Palestinians and for international solidarity activists working to support the Palestinians. Ariel Sharon has continued construction of the "Apartheid Wall," demolishing entire villages along the way. Israeli policies of economic strangulation and collective punishment have become more severe, making Palestinian survival a daily struggle for many. And the Israeli military has taken aim at the nonviolent peace activists who have come to support the Palestinians via the International Solidarity Movement (ISM) and other organizations. Rachel Corrie, a 23-year-old college student from Olympia Washington, was murdered by the Israeli Defense Forces (IDF) on March 16, 2003, as she was intentionally run over by an Israeli driven Caterpillar bulldozer. Two other ISM activists were shot in the head, and many more injured, beaten, and deported.

On the upside, however, the resistance is mounting. The International Solidarity Movement—a Palestinian led movement that uses nonviolent direct action to resist Israeli occupation—is refusing to be intimidated by the Israeli crackdown, and continues to organize activists to go to Palestine. Stop U.S. Tax-Funded Aid to Israel Now (SUSTAIN)—a nonhierarchical grassroots organization committed to popular education and nonviolent creative/direct action in America—has had a surge in chapter start-ups and has begun organizing regional strategy summits. SUSTAIN is currently focusing on a campaign against the Caterpillar Corporation, which supplied the bulldozer used to kill Corrie as well as bulldozers used for the destruction of civil society, private property, and other war crimes against the Palestinian people. SUSTAIN has occupied Caterpillar offices across the country, issuing them "demolition orders" by activists dressed up in IDF costumes. SUSTAIN also organizes street theater, as in January of 2003 when 200 people re-enacted the Israeli invasion of Jenin in a popular nightspot-area of Washington, DC. And SUSTAIN promotes the Palestinian arts as a means of cultural resistance and survival.

You can get involved with a SUSTAIN chapter in your area or start up a new one. To learn more about SUSTAIN, read our seasonal newsletter, or find a chapter near you, please visit the Web site at <www.sustaincampaign.org/>. You can also participate in the International Solidarity Movement (ISM) and go to Palestine. Visit the ISM Web site at <www.palsolidarity.org>. Both organizations are in desperate need of money, as we are grassroots organizations with no funding or sponsors. Please contribute financially through the Web sites.

And finally, analytically speaking, since my article was published, other SUSTAIN activists have written articles in *Left Turn* and have drawn out other nuances in the U.S.-Israel relationship. Topics such as the right-wing Zionism of the neoconservatives, who now wield huge amounts of power under the Bush Administration, are timely topics to study, especially as Washington, DC, just hosted an "Interfaith Zionist Leadership Conference" that was the convergence of Christian fundamentalism, white supremacy, and Zionism. It has also been noted that the total U.S. aid to Israel since 1948, if adjusted for inflation and interest, becomes $247 billion (*Left Turn*, May/June 2003).

25 Convicted Corporations Receive Perks Instead of Punishment

Sources:
Asheville Global Report, No. 183, July 18–24, 2002
Title: "Corrupt Corporations Still at Work in Developing World"
Author: Emad Mekay

Mother Jones, May/June 2002
Title: "Unjust Rewards"
Author: Ken Silverstein

Faculty Evaluators: Laurie Dawson and Diana Grant
Student Researchers: Lindsey Brage and Terri Freedman

American energy giant Enron and telecommunications company WorldCom committed massive corporate fraud and illegal acts. Declaring bankruptcy in December 2001, they left thousands of American workers jobless and without pensions. The Institute for Policy Studies in Washington, DC and *CorpWatch*, a multinational watchdog group, has uncovered evidence of bribery scandals, environmental degradation and violations of international and labor laws. Yet Enron still has 25 percent interest in a Bolivian oil company called Transredes. Working with Shell Oil, the company is building a pipeline through Bolivia's Chaco Forest region, an area internationally known for its biodiversity and endangered species and the ancestral homeland of the indigenous Guarani and Guianeck peoples. In December 2002, Transredes was granted $220 million in loans from the International Development Bank, to be backed by U.S. taxpayer dollars.

Enron was also responsible for cutting down the last intact, dry tropical forest in the world, Bolivia's 15-million acre Chiquitano Forest, for another gas pipeline. The Chiquitano Forest was home to the endangered marsh deer, maned wolf, jaguar, ocelot, and the hyacinth macaw. The World Wildlife Fund ranked the area one of the world's 200 most endangered ecoregions. During the Clinton Administration in 1999, the Overseas Private Investment Corporation (OPIC) approved loans for Enron's pipeline, which could have skirted the forest at an additional expense to the company. Officially, OPIC is mandated to protect ecologically sensitive areas.

WorldCom still profits from its extensive telephone and Internet networks throughout Latin American, Asia, Europe and Africa. Enron has additional business interests throughout Central and South America. In northwest India a power plant, which they co-own with Bechtel and General Electric, is so controversial that Enron officials face threats of being arrested on the spot if they enter the country. According to Nadia Martinez of the Institute for Policy Studies, "Enron and WorldCom are just symptoms of the way companies are able to do business without accountability."

In 2000, Bill Clinton issued an order that provided clear guidelines regarding the awarding of federal contracts. The new "contractor responsibility rule" specified that federal officers should weigh "evidence of repeated, pervasive, or significant violations of the law," such as cheating on prior contracts, antitrust activities; and violating environmental and safety laws, labor-rights laws, and consumer-protection laws. President Bush quietly killed the rule requiring officials to ban federal contractors with a record of violations of workplace safety and other laws.

The Congressional Research Service issued an opinion concluding that the secret suspension of the rule (there was no issuing of public notice or soliciting of comments) was probably illegal, but the move went virtually unreported in the media. The government does not maintain a central database to store information on contractors' records of compliance with the law. The Environmental Protection Agency (EPA) and the Occupational Safety and Health Administration (OSHA) maintain their own lists of corporate violations, but parent companies are not always linked to their subsidiaries. "There's no process built into the review system," says Gary Bass, executive director of OMB Watch, a Washington-based advocate of government accountability.

A six-month investigation by *Mother Jones* of the nation's 200 largest contractors found that the government continues to award lucrative contracts to dozens of companies that it has repeatedly cited for serious workplace and environmental violations. Among the findings: 46 of the biggest contractors were prosecuted by the Justice Department and ordered to pay cleanup costs after they refused to take responsibility for dumping hazardous waste and various other environmental violations. General Electric (GE)—which received nearly $9.8 billion from the government, making it the nation's tenth largest contractor—topped the list with 27 cases of pollution for which it was held solely or jointly liable. Subsequently GE was fined a total of only $369,363 for its combined EPA and OSHA violations (27 and 48, respectively).

UPDATE BY EMAD MEKAY: The story was an attempt to direct public attention to the corporate mismanagement, executive greed and malpractice of multinational corporations—particularly the same ones that stirred public controversy last year in the U.S. over their fraudulent dealings—in the developing countries.

Unless they are well-regulated and well-supervised, the economies of the poor nations tend to be a subject for all kinds of abuse by fly-by-night operators. But because of pressure from public international financial institutions, like the World Bank and the International Monetary Fund (IMF), to deregulate their economies and dismantle public monitoring agencies, the risk of multinational engaging in corrupt activities overseas is far higher.

According to recent documents obtained from the U.S. Treasury Department, U.S. energy company Enron, one of the companies referred to in the story, managed to secure government assistance to its problematic overseas investments through hefty contributions to different U.S. Administrations and access to government officials.

Enron has regularly sought aid from staff from the Treasury Department and the State Department to favorably resolve its problems and disputes with foreign governments over its subsidiaries, activities particularly in countries like Argentina, India, Nigeria, the Dominican Republic, and Turkey.

According to Public Citizen, which is using the Freedom of Information Act to obtain documents from the U.S. Treasury Department, the shamed company also played a major role in exporting California-style deregulation to poor countries. This has often proved catastrophic for the citizens of those countries. Brazil, for example, now says it will investigate allegations that U.S. energy giant AES Corp. and Enron conspired to rig the 1998 bidding process for Latin America's largest electric utility, Eletropaulo. Enron decided not to bid for the project in return for other potentially lucrative energy deals with AES.

Brazil now wants to know whether the utility could have fetched a higher price and to what extent the under-the-counter deal between the two multinationals hurt the Latin American country's interests.

The U.S. government also continued to back another company caught in financial scandals and mentioned in the story, WorldCom, despite its now established record of fraud. In May, MCI, the telephone division of bankrupt giant WorldCom, said it had received a contract from the U.S. Defense Department to install wireless phone service in Iraq. The company declined to discuss details of the contract, citing "an agreement with our client."

Despite the laudable attention the mainstream media gave to the Enron scandal in the United States, very little has been published about the role of the same company in the defenseless poor nations.

Some corporate monitors like *CorpWatch*, Public Citizen and the Institute of Policy Studies have all devoted time and effort to follow the Enron case and other cases in which international business giants are abusing their mandates in the poor nations. Their Web sites respectively are:<www.corpwatch.org>, <www.citizen.org/>, and <www.ips-dc.org>. Inter Press Service is also a news agency that seeks to cover development news and the unethical practices of some major companies. It can be found at<www.ipsnews.net>.

Censored 2004 Runners-Up

SUCCESSFUL ORGANIZING SPARKS
LAND REDISTRIBUTION IN BRAZIL

Source: *Clamor* #17, November/December 2002
Title: "Struggle for Land"
Author: Michelle Steinberg
Student Researcher: Melissa Jones

The Landless Workers' Movement (*Movimento dos Trabalhaores Rurais Sem Terra or MST*) is possibly one of the most successful grassroots land-reform movements in the world. Landless families tired of living in poverty formed MST in 1985. In Brazil, much of the land is owned by only a small number of people, who then rent out the land to families. The families work the land year-round and must contribute anywhere from 50–80% of their yield to the landowners.

MST operates in 23 of the 27 Brazilian states. The states are divided into regions geographically. Each region works with MST settlements (legalized land occupation) to form municipalities that work with the state and national levels of MST. Every five years, all of the states meet in a national congress to discuss issues and make plans for future fights. Every two years, national, state and regional meetings take place in which movement coordinators are elected. Unlike most other organizations, one person does not hold a leadership position for an extended period of time. This serves two purposes: it eliminates the privilege of such a position and keeps people from becoming power-hungry. Another essential element to the success of MST is the organization's perseverance. The MST also seeks to break the Latin idea of machismo by allowing women equal opportunities to participate in leadership positions and in the financial gains.

PROMISE OF ALTERNATIVE ENERGY HANDICAPPED BY CONFLICTS OF INTEREST

Source: *Utne Reader*, September/October 2002
Title: "Fossil Fools"
Author: Matt Bivens
Faculty Evaluator: Dolly Freidel
Student Researcher: Terri Freedman

The U.S. Congress continues to subsidize polluting fossil fuel plants, while renewable energy sources such as wind and solar power struggle for a fraction of federal funds. In early 2002, Congress extended a $55 million federal subsidy for wind power technology and at the same time awarded $35 billion to the fossil fuel industry—coal, oil, gas, and nuclear energy.

The Department of Energy acknowledges that "green energy"—wind, solar, and hydrogen storage cells—is clean and safe. Although prices are still slightly higher than fossil fuels, there are no added health or pollution costs.

Europe is building its future with wind farms, providing a potential model for the U.S. and Canada. Offshore wind parks are a source of electricity in many northern European countries and Canada has plans for an offshore wind park. The U.S. has promising areas for developing wind and solar power, but will not be able to develop these sustainable technologies if the federal government continues to underfund these attempts and subsidize the fossil-fuel industries.

SURPRISE! U.S. HAS ITS OWN SECRET BIOWEAPONS PROGRAM

Sources:

GeneWatch
Title: "Biowar and Peace"
Author: Lauren Davis

Asheville Global Report
Author: Frida Berrigan

Student Researcher: Jessie Esquivel

The U.S has initiated a secret weapons program in violation of the 1972 Biological Weapons Convention Treaty. The treaty prohibits the development, production, and stockpiling of biological agents that have no "prophylactic, protective, or other peaceful purpose." Signers of the treaty agreed not to make or obtain weapons that were made for hostile purposes or for use in armed conflicts.

The U.S. has not complied with rules that were set by the treaty. Both the Nixon and Bush Administrations rejected regular inspections called for in the treaty. The Clinton Administration, along with the Energy and Defense Departments and the CIA, tested bombs that could spread biological agents over a wide area; also the Pentagon's Threat Reduction Agency built a bioweapons plant to demonstrate that these kinds of projects could be created without suspicions. The U.S. claims to be using these programs as a mode of defense. However, some say that U.S. behavior suggests that our biodefense program might be larger than we are willing to admit.

IS CHINA NEXT?

Source:
Global Outlook, Issue 2, Summer 2002
Title: "Encircling China"
Student Researcher: Emilio Licea

Although China is not officially labeled a "rogue state," it is nonetheless listed by the Pentagon as "a country that could be involved in an immediate or potential contingency." The strongest U.S. military buildups have been in areas of the South China Sea, the Taiwan Straights, the Korean Peninsula, and the Sea of Japan, as well as in the heartland of Central Asia.

Supported by the Bush Administration, Taiwan has been "conducting active research aimed at developing a tactical ballistic missile capable of hitting targets in mainland China." The alleged purpose of these missiles is to degrade the strike capability of the People's Liberation Army (PLA), including missile infrastructure and non-missile infrastructure (airfields, harbors, missile sites, etc.) In turn, U.S. military presence in Pakistan and Afghanistan (and in several other former Soviet republics) on China's Western border, are being coordinated with Taiwan's naval deployment in the South China Sea.

EAST TIMOR TRYING TO AVOID GLOBAL TRADE BODIES

Source:
Peacework, May 2002
Title: "East Timor: The World's Newest Country Threatened by Economic Chains"
Student Researcher: Pat Spiva

East Timor became independent on May 20, 2002, and views this independence as an opportunity to avoid the downward economic trap of accepting loans from IMF and World Bank. Third World dealings with IMF and World Bank create inescapable debt and dependence upon the unfair policies and terms of these institutions. Instead of spending revenues to pay the interest rates on loans financed by already wealthy states, the East Timor government plans to use its income from taxation for health care, education, and to alleviate poverty.

THE IMF "SAPS" THE LIFE OUT OF WORLD'S FORESTS

Source:
Earth First!, Eostar, March-April 2002
Title: "How the IMF Is Destroying the World's Forests"
Author: Jason Tockman
Student Researcher: Colin Umphryes

The World Bank and the International Monetary Fund (IMF) were created, in part, to help alleviate poverty and to create higher standards for developing countries, but they have fallen short of this task. One of the tactics they use to create jobs in developing countries is to strip down red tape so that countries are better able to extract and export their natural resources. Due to the enormous needs that these countries face in caring for their populations, they often see no other way but to industrialize in this fashion. Unfortunately, it is these countries that are the least prepared for the fallout of environmental damage resulting from the economic liberalizations that, more often than not, leave their forests ravaged.

To stimulate foreign investment, a key ingredient of economic development, the IMF uses a program called structural adjustment programs (SAPs). These programs essentially call for the deregulation of environmental policy. They shift industry priorities from a focus on domestic goods to an export orientation. Because the IMF acts as a banker in this situation, it wants to control its investment to ensure that the loan itself is paid back.

The net result for many of these developing countries is that they experience a surge in exports for their natural resources at the expense of the native populations and the environment. While job growth is created in certain industries, the effect is so devastating, it uproots many people from their once productive lives living off the land and thrusts them into a new situation for which they are ill-equipped. Due to overgrazing, excessive mining, and severe deforestation, farmers and fisherman are no longer able to make a living. Often the jobs created by these new industries benefit only a few at the expense of the greater population and the entire local environment.

ECUADORIAN FARMERS AND DYNCORP

Source:
Eat the State, March 13, 2002
Title: "Rumble from the Jungle: Ecuadoran Farmers Take on DynCorp"
Authors: Jeffrey St. Clair and Alexander Cockburn
Student Researchers: Kathleen Glover and Lindsey Brage

DynCorp is being sued by International Labor Rights on behalf of 10,000 Ecuadorian peasant farmers and Amazonian Indians, charged with infanticide, wrongful death, and torture.

International Labor Rights has filed suit in U.S. federal court against DynCorp on behalf of 10,000 Ecuadorian peasant farmers and Amazonian Indians. DynCorp is being charged with torture, infanticide, and wrongful death due to the aerial spraying of toxic pesticides in the Amazonian jungle. Federal judge Richard Roberts denied DynCorp's motion to dismiss the case on the grounds that their work involved national security.

In Colombia, DynCorp employees not only fly fumigated planes but train soldiers and police on how to resist insurgent groups. Plan Colombia awards DynCorp $600 million to fumigate coca fields. They have sprayed 14 percent of Colombia.

PRESS FORGETS UNSCOM SPIES

Source:
Extra!, December 30, 2002
Title: "Press Rewrites History of Iraq Arms Inspections"
Author: Norman Solomon
Student Researcher: Terri Freedman

Although major U.S. newspapers reported that U.N. weapons inspectors were doing double-duty work for the CIA prior to the 1998 bombing of Iraq, the story dropped from sight by mid-1999. The very same papers would only allude to the "inspector-spies" and would make no reference to their own earlier investigative reports.

America's major newspapers seem to be willing to rewrite history from year to year. In 1999, *The New York Times* (January 7, 1999), *Washington Post* (January 6, 1999; January 17, 1999; and March 2, 1999), *Boston Globe* (January 6, 1999), and *USA Today* (March 3, 1999) all ran scandalizing, front-page stories about the CIA's covert use of United Nations arms inspectors–UNSCOM inspectors—to spy on Iraq. The inspectors were in the country to carry out their U.N. mission to search for Iraqi weapons.

However, in stories run by the same newspapers between August 1999 and September 2002, reporters referred only to allegations and accusations of spying, conveniently avoiding any allusion to the earlier reports.

CIA CONTINUES PENTAGON'S TERMINATED OSI PROGRAMS

Source:
Extra!, November 27, 2002
Title: "The Office of Strategic Influence Is Gone, But Are Its Programs in Place?"
Student Researcher: Chris Salvano

The Federation of American Scientists has pointed to a startling revelation by Secretary of Defense Donald Rumsfeld that mainstream media have missed. In remarks during a recent press briefing, Rumsfeld suggested that though the controversial Office of Strategic Influence (OSI) no longer exists in name, its programs are still being carried out.

The OSI came under scrutiny last February, when *The New York Times* reported that the new Pentagon group was "developing plans to provide news items, possibly even false ones, to foreign media organizations" (February 19, 2002). It is almost certain that any large-scale disinformation campaign directed at the foreign press would have led, sooner or later, to a falsified story being picked up by U.S. media.

In remarks made at a November 18 media briefing, Rumsfeld suggested that though the exposure of OSI's plans forced the Pentagon to close the office, they certainly haven't given up on its work. Rumsfeld told reporters, "And then there was the Office of Strategic Influence.... There's the name. You can have the name, but I'm gonna keep doing every single thing that needs to be done and I have."

AGRIBUSINESSES ASSERT CONTROL OVER FARMERS THROUGH SPY TECHNOLOGY

Source:
GeneWatch, November/December, 2002
Title: "Precision Farming: Agribusiness Meets Spy Technology"
Author: Carmelo Ruiz-Marrero
Student Researcher: Daryl Khoo

New agribusiness technologies may bode ill for sustainable agriculture and democratic governance and could impose new forms of dependence on farmers. Hope Shand, research director of ETC Group (an action group on erosion, technology, and concentration) argues, "precision farming is about commodification and control of information and it is among the high-tech tools that are driving the industrialization of agriculture, the loss of local farm knowledge and the erosion of farmers rights." She adds that precision farming seeks to legitimate and reinforce the uniformity and chemical-intensive requirements of industrial agriculture under the guise of protecting the environment and improving efficiency.

Remote sensing is a key component of precision agriculture. For example, it has the ability to quantifiably measure a crop's health status. But it also is being used by the Tasmanian government as part of an identity protection pilot program and the Argentine government to verify farmers' tax reporting of the size of their fields.

Remote sensing has also been used to gather information in order to sue small, independent farmers. When organic farmer Percy Schmeiser complained that his organic canola crop had been genetically contaminated by a GM canola field somewhere upwind, Monsanto's lawyers sued him for illegally planting the corporation's patented seed.

CITIGROUP'S BID TO GLOBALIZE BANKING SERVICES

Source:
Multinational Monitor, April 2002
Title: "Servicing Citi's Interests"
Author: Antonia Juhasz
Student Researcher: Licia Marshall

The current goal of powerful banking multinational Citigroup is to control banking services worldwide. It hopes to use the World Trade Organization's General Agreements on Trade in Services to pry open new markets around the world while restricting the ability of governments to regulate their behavior.

Citibank is a key player in the corporate coalition pushing for liberalization of trade in services both in the U.S. and abroad. Historically countries would require that foreign banks form minority partnerships with domestic banks in order to protect against draining capital out of the country. Citigroup wants to have the ability to enter a foreign country and buy existing banks or financial service providers without having to have a domestic partner. Such a provision in NAFTA allowed Citigroup to acquire Mexico's largest commercial bank, Banamex, and they would like to have this opportunity worldwide.

THIS MODERN WORLD

by TOM TOMORROW

CHAPTER 2

Censored Déjà Vu

A REVIEW AND UPDATE ON IMPORTANT CENSORED STORIES FROM PRIOR YEARS

BY PETER PHILLIPS AND THE PROJECT CENSORED WRITING TEAM
Derek Fieldsoe, Michael Kaufmann, Courtney Sessler, Matt Hamburg,
Dana Balicki, Keith Harmon Snow, Kagiso Molethe, Jason Spencer,
Josh Sisco, Veronica Lopez, Corey Clapp, Mitzila Valdes, and Donald Yoon

Media Moments

BY MICHAEL PARENTI

For some time now, I have been suffering from what I call "media moments."
We have all heard of "senior moments," a term used mostly by people of
mature years who suddenly experience a lapse in recall. The mind goes
blank and the individual complains, "I'm having a senior moment." A media
moment is a little different. It happens when you are reading or hearing
what passes for the news. You are appalled and frustrated by the conservative bias, the evasions, the non sequiturs, and the outright disinformation.
Your mind does not go blank; you simply wish it would.

I recall one media moment I experienced while listening to the BBC
News. The BBC supposedly provides coverage superior to what is heard on
U.S. mainstream media. It occasionally runs stories on European and Third
World countries that are not likely to be carried by U.S. newscasters. And
BBC reporters ask confrontational questions of the personages they inter-
view, applying a critical edge rarely shown by U.S. journalists. But the truth
is, when it comes to addressing the fundamental questions of economic

power, corporate dominance, and Western globalization, BBC journalists and commentators are as careful as their American counterparts not to venture beyond certain orthodox parameters.

The recent BBC segment that gave me my media moment was a special report on asthma, of all things. It began by noting that the number of asthma sufferers has been increasing at the alarming rate of 50 percent each decade. "Scientists are puzzled," for there is "no easy explanation," the narrator tells us. One factor is "genetic predisposition." We hear from a British scientist who says, yes, there is definitely a hereditary factor behind asthma; it tends to run in families. Sure, I say to myself, asthma is increasing by 50 percent a decade because people with a genetic tendency toward the disease are becoming more sexually active and procreative than everyone else. I feel a media moment coming on.

There are other contributing factors to the asthma epidemic, the narrator continues, for instance, "lifestyle." He interviews another scientist who confirms this "scientific finding." People are keeping cleaner homes, using air conditioning, and in general creating a more antiseptic lifestyle for themselves, the scientist says. This means they do not get enough exposure to pollen, dust, and dirt the way people did in the good old days. Hence, they fail to build up a proper defense to such irritants.

These comments made me think back to my younger years when I lived next to a construction site that deposited daily clouds of dust over my abode for months on end. Rather than building up a hardy resistance, I developed an acute sensitivity to dust and mold that has stayed with me to this day. Does exposure to a toxic environment really make us stronger? Looking at the evidence on cancer, lung diseases, and various occupational ailments, we would have to conclude that exposure does not inoculate us; rather it seems to suppress or overload our immune systems, leaving us more, not less, vulnerable.

The BBC report on asthma then takes us to India for some *actualité*. A young man suffering from the disease is speaking in a rasping voice, telling of his affliction. This is accompanied by the squishing sound of a hand-held respirator. The victim says he has no money for medication. The narrator concludes that the disease persists among the poor in such great numbers because they cannot afford medical treatment. I say to myself, yes, but this doesn't tell us what causes asthma in the first place.

Another "expert" is interviewed. He says that in India, as in most of the world, asthma is found in greatest abundance in the congested cities, less so in the suburbs, and still less in the countryside. No explanation is given for this, but by now I can figure it out for myself: the inner-city slum dwellers of Calcutta enjoy too antiseptic a lifestyle; too much air conditioning and cleanliness has deprived them of the chance to build up a natural resistance. At this point, I can feel the media moment drawing ever closer.

The BBC report makes no mention of how neoliberal "free market" policies have driven people off the land, causing an explosion in slum populations throughout the world. These impoverished urban areas produce the highest asthma rates. And the report says nothing about how, as cigarette markets in the West become saturated, the tobacco companies vigorously pursue new promotional drives in Asia, Africa, and Latin America, leading to a dramatic climb in Third World smoking rates, which certainly does not help anyone's respiratory system.

Finally the BBC narrator mentions pollution. He says it "may" be a factor, but more study is needed. May? Furthermore, he asks, "Is pollution really a cause or is it merely a trigger?" He seems to be leaning toward "trigger," although by now I am having trouble seeing the difference. The media moment has come upon me full force. I begin talking back at my radio, posing such cogent and measured comments as, "You jackass BBC flunky announcer!"

Media apologists like to point out that journalists face severe constraints of time and space and must necessarily reduce complex realities into brief reports; hence, issues are conflated, and omissions and oversights are inevitable. But this BBC report went on for some 10 minutes, quite a long time by newscast standards. There would have been ample opportunity to say something about how the use of automobiles has skyrocketed throughout the entire world, causing severe damage to air quality, especially in cities. There would have been enough time to mention how the destruction of rain forests and the dramatic increase in industrial emissions have contributed to an alarming CO_2 buildup and a commensurate decline in the atmosphere's oxygen content. The BBC could have told us how the oil cartels have kept us hooked on fossil fuel, while refusing to develop nonpolluting, inexpensive tidal, wind, thermal, and solar energy systems.

But mainstream media bosses would dismiss such revelations as "editorializing" and ideologically motivated. Instead, this BBC report chose to be "balanced" and "objective" by blaming the victims, their genetic predispositions, their antiseptic lifestyles, and their inability to buy medications.

Newscasters who want to keep their careers afloat learn the fine art of evasion. We should never accuse them of doing a poor and sloppy job of reporting. If anything, with great skill they skirt around the most important points of a story. With much finesse, they say a lot about very little, serving up heaps of junk news filled with so many empty calories and so few nutrients. Thus do they avoid offending those who wield politico-economic power. It is enough to take your breath away.

Michael Parenti's most recent books are *The Terrorism Trap: September 11 and Beyond* (City Lights) and *The Assassination of Julius Caesar: A People's History of Ancient Rome* (The New Press).

CENSORED #1 2003
FCC MOVES TO PRIVATIZE AIRWAVES

For almost 70 years, the Federal Communications Commission (FCC) has administered and regulated the broadcast spectrum as an electronic "commons" on behalf of the American people. The FCC issues licenses to broadcasters that allow them, for a fee, to use, but not own, one or more specific radio or TV frequencies. Thus, the public has retained the ability to regulate, as well as influence, access to broadcast communications.

Several years ago, the Progress and Freedom Foundation, in their report "The Telecom Revolution: An American Opportunity," recommended a complete privatization of the radio frequencies, whereby broadcasters with existing licenses would eventually gain complete ownership of their respective frequencies. They could thereafter develop them in markets of their choosing or sell and trade them to other companies. The few nonallocated bands of the radio frequency spectrum would be sold off, as electronic real estate, to the highest bidders. With nothing then to regulate, the FCC would eventually be abolished.

Michael K. Powell, FCC chairman, and son of Secretary of State Colin Powell, in a recent speech compared the FCC to the Grinch, a kind of regulatory spoilsport that could impede what he termed a historic transformation akin to the opening of the West. "The oppressor here is regulation," he declared. In April 2001, Powell dismissed the FCC's historic mandate to evaluate corporate actions based on the public interest. That standard, he said, "is about as empty a vessel as you can accord a regulatory agency." In other comments, Powell has signaled what kind of philosophy he prefers to the outdated concept of public interest. During his first visit to Capitol Hill as chairman, Powell referred to corporations simply as "our clients."

Challenges to this proposed privatization of airways have emerged from a number of sources. One group, the Democratic Media Legal Project (DMLP) in San Francisco, argues that even the existing commercial media system, aided by the Telecommunications Act of 1996, is unconstitutional because it limits diversity of viewpoints, omits or misrepresents most social, political, and cultural segments, and is unaccountable to the public.

The course of wireless broadcasting is approaching an unprecedented and critical crossroad. The path taken by the United States and by the other industrialized nations that may follow our lead will profoundly influence the ability of the citizenry of each country to democratically control the media.

SOURCES: Jeremy Rifkin, "Global Media Giants Lobby to Privatize Entire Broadcast System," *The Guardian* (London), April 28, 2001 and *MediaFile*, Fall 2001, Vol. 20, No. 4; Brendan L. Koerner, "Losing Signal," *Mother Jones*, September/October 2001; and Dorothy Kidd, "Legal Project to Challenge Media Monopoly," *MediaFile*, May/June 2001.

UPDATE BY DEREK FIELDSOE: The passage of the 1996 Telecommunications Act resulted in massive media consolidation. One conglomerate, Clear Channel, took great advantage of this, scooping up more than 1,200 radio stations thanks to the passage of this act. By scrapping most of their rules, the FCC basically rendered itself useless. The FCC oversees an infrastructure of airwaves, telephone lines, and cable conduits that are the backbone of a $950 billion-a-year industry. As the financial stakes have risen, the corporate media lobbyists have become increasingly adept at peddling their probusiness agenda to the FCC.

On January 2, 2003, Fox, NBC, and Viacom issued a joint filing to the FCC, claiming that "there's no longer any public-interest need served by the commission's ownership rules." These conglomerates say that the FCC shouldn't make any distinctions among media outlets at all, because there's no difference in terms of impact that a TV station or major daily has compared to a weekly paper or Web site. There are two rules in particular that the three networks were asking the FCC to reform:

1. Raise the ban on broadcasters owning television stations that reach more than 35 percent of the country and all mergers between the four largest TV networks.
2. Eliminate the prohibition on owning a newspaper and broadcast outlet in the same market.

The three networks that submitted the filing claim that the FCC isn't necessary and that current antitrust rules and "properly functioning markets" are enough to ensure competition and healthy journalistic diversity.

On June 2, 2003, the FCC finally voted to ease the rules on ownership. The limit on the percentage of TV audience a media entity can reach has gone from 35 percent to 45 percent. There was also a relaxing of the crossownership rules, lifting a 1970 radio/television and a 1975 newspaper/broadcast ban on crossownership.

Democratic FCC Commissioner Michael Copps said, "There is a growing concern about a rush to judgment here at the commission, and relatively few in the population knew this issue was out there." Copps had sought more public comment on the media ownership review, stating that some 99 percent of the comments arriving at the FCC were opposed to the lessening of the media owner regulations.

On May 23, the Center for Public Integrity issued a report on the cozy relationship between the FCC and media organizations. The report shows that FCC officials have taken 2,500 trips costing nearly $2.8 million over the past eight years, most paid for by corporate media. Trips included hundreds of conferences and other events in locations all over the world including Paris, Hong Kong, and Rio de Janeiro. Top destinations listed were Las Vegas (330 trips), New Orleans (173 trips), and New York (102 trips). FCC officials were put up in the plush Bellagio Hotel in Las Vegas.

On June 2, 2003, Reuters reported that a bipartisan group of senators opposed to television networks expanding their reach expressed confidence that they had the votes to roll back a rule adopted by the FCC. The group said it was pressing ahead with legislation to retain limits keeping a network from owning stations that together reach more than 35 percent of the national audience.

SOURCE: <www.publicintegrity.org>.

CENSORED #2 2003
NEW TRADE TREATY SEEKS TO PRIVATIZE GLOBAL SOCIAL SERVICES

A global trade agreement being negotiated seeks to privatize nearly every government-provided public service and allow transnational corporations to run them for profit.

The General Agreement on Trade in Services (GATS) is a proposed free-trade agreement that will attempt to liberalize/dismantle barriers that protect government-provided social services. These are social services bestowed by the government in the name of public welfare. The GATS was established in 1994, at the conclusion of the "Uruguay Round" of the General Agreement on Tariffs and Trade (GATT). In 1995, the GATS agreement was adopted by the newly created World Trade Organization (WTO).

Corporations plan to use the GATS agreement to profit from the privatization of educational systems, health care systems, child care, energy and municipal water services, postal services, libraries, museums, and public transportation. If the GATS agreement is finalized, it will lock in a privatized, for-profit model for the global economy. GATS/WTO would make it illegal for a government with privatized services to ever return to a publicly owned, non-profit model. Any government that disobeys these WTO rulings will face sanctions. What used to be areas of common heritage like seed banks, air and water supplies, health care, and education will be commodified, privatized, and sold to the highest bidder on the open market. People who cannot afford these privatized services will be left out.

This potential expansion of GATS/WTO authority into the day-to-day business of governments will make it nearly impossible for citizens to exercise democratic control over the future of traditionally public services. One American trade official summed up the GATS/WTO process by saying, "Basically, it won't stop until foreigners finally start to think like Americans, act like Americans, and most of all shop like Americans."

SOURCE: Maude Barlow, "The Last Frontier," *The Ecologist*, February 2001.

UPDATE BY DONALD YOON: The purpose of the GATS is the liberalization of trade in services and the weakening of government barriers to privatization by the service industries. This facilitates access to government contracts by transnational corporations in areas such as education, health care, child care, energy, municipal water systems, postal services, libraries, museums, and public transportation, to name a few. Through a set of legally binding constraints backed by WTO-enforced trade sanctions, the agreement prevents the government from taking actions on behalf of its citizens. Once a service contract has been given to a corporation, it *cannot* be revoked, even if the prices are so high they lead to social unrest and violence.

Part of what makes this all the more troubling is that, currently, these service contracts are being reviewed behind closed doors, so citizens have no idea which services their governments are trading away to the highest bidder. Since the GATS is a multilateral framework agreement, it is subject to new sectors and rules being added. In December 2001 at the WTO Ministerial meeting in Doha, Qatar, a new provision was added that commits countries to take down "tariff and nontariff barriers" to environmental services, including water.

Public services like libraries are paid for by tax support. A broadened definition of "services" includes almost anything that is not a physical commodity. Under national treatment rules, a company could, for example, demand the same subsidies and tax support that public libraries get if they can prove themselves to be "information services." Rather than giving the new company funds to equalize, chances are the library would get its funds cut. Imagine having to pay a high fee to check out library books due to cuts in public funding—caused a company from outside your own country!

The latest news regarding GATS is that members of the WTO's Committee on Trade and Development have been unable to agree on the mandate to strengthen the Special and Differential Treatment provision (S&D) for developing nations. The idea here is that because of their fragile economic status, developing countries would receive increased access to the international commodities markets in return for opening their service markets to the developed world. Negotiations that took place in Tokyo on February 14–16, 2003, failed to deliver results. The developing nations are being put under increased pressure to privatize their social services, even without this increased access.

During mid-year 2002, all WTO member countries made confidential wish lists of services they want privatized. On February 25, 2003, confidential European GATS negotiating documents were released by NGOs exposing the true nature of the GATS agenda. The Canadian Polaris Institute obtained copies of the ECU's confidential GATS requests and these documents are now in the public domain. The 109 request lists submitted by WTO countries include everything from professional and business services to education and environmental services. Even recreational and cultural services were listed by some countries, including theatre, live performance, libraries, and museums.

The latest news on GATS can best be accessed at progressive sites like <www.gatswatch.com> and <www.polarisinstitute.org>.

CENSORED #3 2003

UNITED STATES' POLICIES IN COLOMBIA SUPPORT MASS MURDER

In July 2000, the U.S. Congress approved a $1.3 billion war package for Colombia to support President Pastrami's "Plan Colombia." Plan Colombia is a $7.5 billion counternarcotics initiative. In addition to this financial support, the U.S. also trains the Colombian military.

Colombia's annual murder rate is 30,000. It is reported that around 19,000 of these murders are linked to illegal right-wing paramilitary forces. Many leaders of these paramilitary groups were once officers in the Colombian military, trained at the U.S. Military run School of the Americas.

According to a Human Rights Watch 120-page report titled "The 'Sixth Division': Military-Paramilitary Ties and U.S. Policy in Colombia," Colombian armed forces and police continue to work closely with right-wing paramilitary groups.

Journalists Alexander Cockburn and Jeffrey St. Clair contend that the war in Colombia isn't about drugs. It's about the annihilation of popular uprisings by Indian peasants fending off the ravages of oil companies, cattle barons, and mining firms. It is a counterinsurgency war, designed to clear the way for American corporations to set up shop in Colombia.

Cockburn and St. Clair examined two Defense Department–commissioned reports, the RAND Report and a paper written by Gabriel Marcella, titled "Plan Colombia: the Strategic and Operational Imperatives." Both reports recommend that the U.S. step up its military involvement in Colombia. In addition, the reports make several admissions about the paramilitaries and their links to the drug trade, regarding human rights abuses by the U.S.-trained Colombian military, and about the irrationality of crop fumigation.

Another problem resulting from the Colombian "drug war" has been the health consequences of the U.S.-sponsored aerial fumigation. Since January 2001, Colombian aircraft have been spraying toxic herbicides over Colombian fields in order to kill opium poppy and coca plants. These sprayings are killing food crops that indigenous Colombians depend on for survival, as well as harming their health. Children are especially susceptible to the harmful effects. In addition, the sprayings have killed fish, livestock, and contaminated water supplies.

SOURCES: *CounterPunch*, Alexander Cockburn and Jeffrey St. Clair, "Blueprints for the Colombian War," July 15, 2001; Jim Lobe, "Colombian Army and Police Still Working With Paramilitaries," *Asheville Global Report*, October 4, 2001; Dan Kovalik and Gerald Dickey, "Colombian Trade Unionists Need U.S. Help," *Steelabor*, May/June 2001; and Rachel Massey, "Echoes of Vietnam," *Rachel's Environment & Health News*, December 7, 2000.

UPDATE BY COREY CLAPP: With bombings, assassinations, and other issues unfolding almost daily, any story on Colombia runs the risk of becoming almost obsolete by publishing time. Still, there are significant stories that have come up since the *Censored 2003* publication that deserve attention because of the neglect they received in major U.S. media sources:

The fumigation story has been severely neglected and spun in the major U.S. media in 2002 and 2003, with recent stories claiming that "Plan Colombia" and the war on drugs is paying off. In 2003 many of the major media outlets such as the *Washington Post*, depicted Plan Colombia and the war on drugs as a success, with the State Department findings of a decreased coca production in Colombia for 2002, from 169,800 to 144,000 hectares. Articles such as the one published in the *Post* only show the face value of the results of aerial fumigation and fail to reveal the many problems that the sprayings have caused, including the deaths of children.

The Earth Justice Organization claims that the production of coca, historically concentrated in Colombia, has spread throughout the Andean region and neighboring countries since widespread U.S. supported fumigation began in 1996. In most cases, the target areas for spraying seem to be conveniently located in territory held by the Revolutionary Armed Forces of Colombia (FARC), a leftist insurgency in southern Colombia, even though coca cultivation is widespread throughout paramilitary strongholds as well. The fumigation planes usually spray during the night, resulting in extremely inaccurate, widespread fumigation of food crops and villages.

Roundup, the principal agent being used in Columbia, is produced by Monsanto of St. Louis, Missouri, a private U.S. contractor that provides Colombia with chemicals, spraying supplies, and training. In February 2003, the Colombian government discretely announced plans to increase the concentration of the chemical sprayed from 8.0 to 10.4 liters per hectare.

The FARC-EP is the oldest group of insurgents in Latin America. Fighting against a corrupt government and the affiliated paramilitary, they have funded their operations through coca and opium production since the 1980s. Seeking political justice and social equality, the FARC made an attempt to organize politically late in the 1980s, forming the Patriotic Union (UP). Jeremy McDermott of BBC News reported that the UP ended up being completely eliminated by right-wing death squads sponsored by drug traffickers with links to the Colombian government. After the murder of over 3,000 UP members including their 1990 presidential candidate Bernardo Jaramillo, the FARC's political road to power had been effectively closed. In the late '90s, the FARC were granted a 42,000–sq. km. safe haven by former President Pastrana, and they began peace negotiations with the Colombian government shortly after. Human Rights Watch reports that in 2002, after three years of peace talks, President Pastrana, with U.S. support, announced the end of negotiations and ordered the immediate recovery of the FARC territory by Colombian authorities. In 2002, newly elected Colombian president Alvaro Uribe Velez, continued this hard line against FARC forces.

With kidnappings and bombings occurring almost daily, the violence in Colombia has only escalated since *Censored 2003*. On February 7, 2003, after a car bomb killed 37 and injured many others in an prominent club frequented by members of the paramilitary and superrich, Colombian officials were quick to blame FARC for the attack. Many U.S. publications swiftly published this story, condemning the rebel group for the bombing which killed innocent civilians and children. The *New Zealand Herald* was one of several publications that published a very short, news brief almost a month later, claiming that after an intense internal investigation in early March, FARC-EP leaders determined that not a single member or unit of the FARC-EP had participated in the February 7 bombing. Doug Stokes, writing for the *Narco News Bulletin*, claims the Colombian government used the February 7 incident to legitimize their new national security plan, which includes the banning of public rallies (often organized or backed by left-wing oppositions or some social justice organization), searches without court order, and the imposition of public curfews.

In late February the Inter Press Service (IPS) news agency covered the Colombian governments new antiterrorism bill. The new law threatens prison sentences between 8 and 10 years for anyone who publishes statistics considered counterproductive to the "fight against terrorism," as well as the suspension of the publication that produced the article. The IPS stated that both punishments also apply to those who "divulge reports that could hamper the effective implementation of military or police operations, endanger the lives of public forces personnel or private individuals," or commit other acts that undermine public order "while boosting the position or image of the enemy."

After a U.S.-funded plane crashed in rebel territory on February 13, Nelson D. Schwartz from *Fortune* was one of the few writers who explicitly exposed the fact that the Americans were not civilians, that they were actually contracted employees from the U.S. private military company, Northrop Grumman. While some U.S. journalists and civilian tourists have been kidnapped in Colombia in the past, this was the first U.S. casualty and the first time a U.S. employee had been kidnapped in their four-decade war. This has been a significant turning point in U.S. involvement with Colombia. In mid-February, under presidential authority, George W. Bush sent 150 American Special Forces troops to train the Colombian military and help conduct a search and rescue operation. In an early March press release, the Council on Hemispheric Affairs now places over 411 U.S. troops currently stationed in Colombia, exceeding the limit of 400 set by Congressional order, with all signs pointing toward increasing military involvement.

As of this writing, the Colombian government is still the world's third largest recipient of U.S. military aid. The Colombian military still has one of the worst human rights records in the Western hemisphere with well-documented ties to the United Self Defense Forces (AUC), one of the larger and more well-known paramilitary outfits. According to David Stokes, over 8,000 political assassinations were committed in Colombia last year, and the country's paramilitary groups performed approximately 80 percent of these murders. Stokes explains how President Alvaro Uribe (who came to power with paramilitary support) and the Colombian government have begun negotiations with the AUC as of the winter of 2003, recognizing the AUC as a distinct political actor, and moving towards further cooperation between the two groups.

Several U.S. and European organizations are working to stop the spray campaigns. Information and updates are available from Amazon Alliance, Tel: (202) 785-3334, Web site: <www.amazonalliance.org>; Center for International Policy, Tel: (202) 232-3317, Web site: <www.ciponline.org>; Earth Justice, Tel: (510) 550-6700, Web site: <www.earthjustice.org>; Institute for Science and Interdisciplinary Studies, Tel: (413) 559-5582, Web site: <isis.hampshire.edu; Latin America

Working Group, Tel: (202) 546-7010, Web site: <www.lawg.org.; and Transnational Institute, Web site: <www.tni.org/drugs/>. For listings of new documents on the spray campaigns, see the U.S. Fumigation Information Web site, <www.usfumigation. org>. To join a delegation to Colombia and interact with Colombian citizens who are working for peace there, contact: Witness for Peace, Tel: (202) 588–1471, Web site: <www.witnessforpeace.org>.

SOURCES: Javier Baena, "Colombia Ombudsman Challenges Government Decision to Up Concentration of Herbicides to Kill Drug Crops," Associated Press, February 28, 2003; Anna Cederstav " Coca Cultivation in Colombia–The Story Behind the Numbers," *Earth Justice*, February 27, 2003, <www.earthjustice.org/news/display.html?ID=550>; Neil T. Duren and Thomas Gorman, "The Slippery Slope Approaches in Colombia," Council on Hemispheric Affairs Press Release, March 4, 2003, <www.scoop.co.nz/mason/stories/WO0303/S00034.htm>; Karen DeYoung, "U.S.: Coca Cultivation Drops in Colombia—Decrease Called Historic Change," *Washington Post*, February 28, 2003; Human Rights Watch, "World Report 2003: Colombia: Human Rights Developments," <hrw.org/wr2k3/americas4.html>; News Brief, *New Zealand Herald*, March 3, 2003, <www.nzherald.co.nz/storyprint.cfm? storyID=3200279>; Nelson D. Schwartz, "The War Business: The Pentagon's Private Army," *Fortune*, March 3, 2003; and Douglas Stokes, "Worthy Victims: Colombia's War on Terror," *Narco News Bulletin*, March 8, 2003.

CENSORED #4 2003
BUSH ADMINISTRATION HAMPERED FBI INVESTIGATION INTO BIN LADEN FAMILY BEFORE 9/11

A French book *Bin Laden, la verite interdite* (*Bin Laden, The Forbidden Truth*) claims that the Bush Administration halted investigations into terrorist activities related to the bin Laden family and began planning for a war against Afghanistan before 9/11.

In 1996, George W. Bush and his administration initially halted investigations into terrorism, while bargaining with the Taliban to deliver Osama bin Laden in exchange for economic aid and political recognition. The book goes on to reveal that former FBI deputy director John O'Neill resigned in July of 2001 in protest over the obstruction of terrorist investigations. According to O'Neill, "The main obstacles to investigating Islamic terrorism were U.S. oil corporate interests and the role played by Saudi Arabia in it." The restrictions were said to have worsened after the Bush Administration took over. Intelligence agencies were told to "back off" from investigations involving other members of the bin Laden family, the Saudi royals, and possible Saudi links to the acquisition of nuclear weapons by Pakistan. John O'Neill died on 9/11 in the World Trade Center.

According to the book, long before the September 11 attacks, the United States had decided to invade Afghanistan in the interest of profits. In February of 1998, at the hearing before a subgroup of the Committee on International Relations, Congress discussed ways to deal with Afghanistan to make way for an oil pipeline. *Jane's Defense Newsletter* reported in March 2001 that an invasion of Afghanistan was being planned.

Times of India reported that in June of 2001, the U.S. Government told India that there would be an invasion of Afghanistan in October of that year. By July of 2001 George Arney, with the BBC, also reported the planned invasion.

SOURCES: Amanda Luker, "French Book Indicts Bush Administration," *Pulse of the Twin Cities*, January 16, 2002; Rashmee Z. Ahmed, "Bush Took FBI Agents OFF Bin Laden Family Trail," *Times of India*, November 8, 2001; and Greg Palast and David Pallister, "FBI and U.S. Spy Agents Say Bush Spiked bin Laden Probes Before September 11" *The Guardian* (London), November 7, 2001.

Corporate media coverage: *Los Angeles Times*, January 13, 2002

UPDATE BY MATT HAMBURG: An abundance of mainstream and alternative news stories and books have emerged since last year on the security failures of 9/11. For many independent scholars, academics, and freelance journalists, the idea that the Bush Administration hampered investigations into the bin Laden family has become a much larger issue. Mainstream journalism, however, has focused on the need for a restructuring of the agencies involved in the multiple intelligence failures on 9/11. A *Washington Post* article asserts "FBI and CIA officials failed to grasp the magnitude of the terrorism threat on U.S. soil." Additionally, George Will argues that certain "fact patterns" about pre-9/11 activities in America had not been discerned or properly analyzed by the FBI and that information had not been properly disseminated with the FBI. Several books have also advocated for the FBI/CIA incompetence theory. A book called *The Cell, Inside the 9/11 plot, and Why the FBI and CIA Failed to Stop* focuses on the incompetence of the frontline FBI agents. When independent authors have come forward to suggest the government might not be telling all they know they have been dismissed. For instance, the *Washington Post* reviewed Keith Richburg's book, *Shadow of a Doubt.* The review asserted, "Nowhere do the authors offer any evidence—or even quote anyone making the assertion—that the Bush Administration pursued an early dialogue with the Taliban out of the desire to build an oil pipeline."

However, British author Nafeez Ahmed, in his book *The War on Terror*, does put forward powerful evidence that suggests the Bush Administration had early dialogue with the Taliban and even had plans to invade Afghanistan prior to 9/11. To date, his book has put forward the most scholarly analysis of the relationship between FBI/CIA security blocks and the Al Qaeda network. He details the extent to which information regarding the time, place and identity of the 9/11 terrorists was available but suppressed by the highest levels of military intelligence.

The few threads of the 9/11 story that the mainstream press has picked up have been limited in scope. The New York *Daily News, Boston Globe, Boston Herald,* and *Newsday* reported on the saga of John O'Neill, former FBI terror expert, who had warned of the immanence of an Al Qaeda attack and resigned to take a job as head of security at the World Trade Center just prior to 9/11. The Zacarias Moussaoui trial has also garnered some attention. Most recently, the Justice Department appealed a court ruling that would have allowed Mr. Moussaoui's lawyers to interrogate a captured leader of Al Qaeda. Moussaoui's case may be moved from civilian trial to a military tribunal.

Rather than pursuing evidence suggesting that the FBI/CIA suppressed information regarding Al Qaeda prior to 9/11, the press has focused on agency incompetence. The leading advocates of the incompetence theory range from the conservative pundit George Will to David Corn of *The Nation* and Michael Albert of ZNet. Albert, for instance, points out that these are the same U.S. intelligence agencies that can't find the "perpetrators of the recent anthrax attacks, even though the anthrax came from Fort Detrick, Maryland, and even though, given the skills required, the number of possible culprits is a handful."

SOURCES: Nafeez Mosaddeq Ahmed, *The War on Freedom: How and Why America Was Attacked* (Media Messenger Books, 2002); "NY Times Relatives Say 9/11 Facts May Stay Hidden," Associated Press, February 14, 2003: Pointing out that the "federal commission assigned to investigate the attacks includes members of law firms that lobby for the airline industry"; David Corn, "Capital Games," *The Nation,* May 30, 2002; Michael Albert, "What Did Bush Know and When," ZNet, May 22, 2002; Philip Shenon, "Justice Department Will Appeal Ruling in Trial Linked to 9/11," *The New York Times,* February 8, 2002; Gore Vidal, </9/11congress.netfirms.com/ Vidal.html>; Eric Lichtblau, "FBI and CIA to Move their Counterterror Units to a Single Location," *The New York Times,* February 15, 2003; "Review of *Shadow of a Doubt,* By Keith B. Richburg," *Washington Post Book Review,* September 8, 2002; George Will, "Preserving the Bureau," *Washington Post,* February 9, 2003; Verne Gay, "The FBI Agent Who Knew… Before 9/11," *Newsday,* October 3, 2002; and Craig Cox, "Secrecy Surrounds 9/11 Investigation," Utne.com, February 2003, <www.com/web_special/web_specials_ 2003–02/articles/10292–1.html>.

U.S. INTENTIONALLY DESTROYED IRAQ'S WATER SYSTEM

During the first Gulf War, the United States deliberately bombed Iraq's water system. After the war, the U.S. pushed sanctions to prevent importation of necessary supplies for water purification. These actions resulted in the deaths of thousands of innocent Iraqi civilians, many of whom were young children. Documents have been obtained from the Defense Intelligence Agency (DIA), which prove that the Pentagon was fully aware of the mortal impacts on civilians in Iraq and was actually monitoring the degradation of Iraq's water supply. The destruction of civilian infrastructures necessary for health and welfare is a direct violation of the Geneva Convention.

After the Gulf War, the United Nations applied sanctions against Iraq, which denied the importation of specialized equipment and chemicals, such as chlorine for purification of water. There are six documents that have been partially declassified and can be found on the Pentagon's Web site at <www.gulflink.osd.mil>. These documents include information that prove the United States was fully aware of the costs to civilians, especially children, by upholding the sanctions against purification of Iraq's water supply.

The United States' insistence on using this type of sanction against Iraq is in direct violation of the Geneva Convention. The Geneva Convention was created in 1979 to protect the victims of international armed conflict. It states, "It is prohibited to attack, destroy, remove or render useless, objects indispensable to the survival of the civilian population, such as foodstuffs, crops, livestock, drinking water installation and supplies, and irrigation works, for the specific purpose of denying them for their sustenance value to the civilian population or to the adverse party, whatever the motive, whether in order to starve out civilians, to cause them to move away, or for any other motive." The United States, for nearly a decade, has "destroyed, removed, or rendered useless" Iraq's "drinking water installations and supplies."

The United Nations estimates that more than 500,000 Iraqi children have died as a result of sanctions and that unclean water is a major contributor to these deaths.

SOURCE: Thomas J. Nagy, "The Secret Behind the Sanctions: How the U.S. Intentionally Destroyed Iraq's Water Supply," *The Progressive*, September 2001, <www.progressive.org>.

UPDATE BY JASON SPENCER: The update concerning the destruction of the Iraqi water supply is that it has happened again in the 2003 Gulf War. The corporate media has ignored the issue of U.S. destruction of civilian infrastructure as an acceptable tactic of war. As Thomas Nagy illustrated in his article featured in *Censored 2003*, declassified documents prove that U.S. officials knew of the horrible consequences for civilians and willingly employed the destruction of infrastructure including, but not limited to, water treatment systems.

After extensive national news database searches, only one mainstream newspaper was found to have run an article discussing the Defense Department documents and the predicted effects on the Iraqi civilian population. *The Seattle Times*, a Gannett News Service paper ran an article on August 4, 2002. Greg Barrett's article not only mentions the documents Nagy uncovered, but also points out that the U.N. reported that Saddam Hussein lived up to his end of the oil-for-food plan and the U.S. still blocked crucial water-sanitation supplies.

Concerning the hypocrisy of the U.S. policy on civilians in war, *The Seattle Times* article quotes Nagy as saying, "Imagine if the document had read, 'U.S. Water Treatment Vulnerabilities,' and it described in detail how to spread an epidemic to the U.S. civilian population. It would be called terrorism, or worse, genocide." The rest of the corporate media seem to have completely avoided the hypocrisy of U.S. foreign policy and the subject of the U.S. war tactics that are violations of the Geneva Convention and even resemble the traditional definition of terrorism.

The Center for Economic and Social Rights (CESR) has commissioned a report on the crisis in Iraq and charges that the U.S. and U.K. risk committing war crimes again by depriving Iraqi civilians of safe water in the 2003 war on Iraq. "International law on this matter is unambiguous—depriving people of life-sustaining resources is a war crime," said Roger Normand, executive director of CESR. The January 2003 CESR report states clearly that the international agencies are not adequately prepared to respond to the humanitarian consequences of war. The CESR report also states that "military attacks on electricity... and other necessities of modern civilian life would cause the immediate collapse of Iraq's water purification, sanitation," and other systems, which will trigger many more civilian deaths than the bombs alone. The report also asks the very questions that the American media should have been asking of its administration: "What are the contingency plans to prevent repetition of the 'cycle of death' caused by increased malnutrition and disease, especially among children?" and "Why are humanitarian response plans being developed in secrecy and without necessary coordination among key actors?"

CENSORED #6 2003
U.S. GOVERNMENT PUSHING NUCLEAR REVIVAL

The U.S. government is blazing a trail of nuclear weapon revival leading to global nuclear dominance. A nuke-revival group, supported by people like Stephen Younger, Associate Director for Nuclear Weapons at Los Alamos, proposes a "mini-nuke" capable of burrowing into underground weapon supplies and unleashing a small, but contained nuclear explosion. "Mini-nukes" have a highly accurate ability to penetrate underground stockpiles of weapons and command centers.

The nuclear weapons advocacy group is comprised of nuclear scientists, Department of Energy (DOE) officials, right-wing analysts, former government officials, and a congressionally appointed oversight panel. The group wants to ensure that the U.S. continues to develop nuclear capacity into the next half-century.

The recent interest in such weapons is based on two premises: 1) the belief that only nuclear weapons can destroy underground networks and that the "mini-nuke" would deter other countries from using these underground systems and 2) that these new bombs would give government the option to launch a nuclear strike to take out a small target while delivering minimal civilian casualties.

Princeton theoretical physicist Robert W. Nelson has studied the question for the Federation of American Scientists. Nelson concluded, "No earth-burrowing missile can penetrate deep enough into the earth to contain an explosion with a nuclear yield even as small as 1 percent of the 15-kiloton Hiroshima weapon. The explosion simply blows out a massive crater of radioactive dirt, which rains down on the local region with an especially intense and deadly fallout."

The Panel to Assess the Reliability, Safety, and Security of the United States Nuclear Stockpile has recommended spending $4 billion to $6 billion over the next decade to restore the production capabilities of plutonium pit plants in the U.S. The DOE is currently spending $147 million on pit production at Los Alamos this year and is requesting $218 million for 2002. A renovated Los Alamos will be capable of producing up to 20 pits a year by 2007. Last year, the DOE received $2 million to design a new pit plant capable of producing 450 cores of plutonium a year.

SOURCE: Stephen I. Schwartz, "The New-Nuke Chorus Tunes Up," *Bulletin Of The Atomic Scientists*, July/August 2001.

UPDATE BY DANA BALICKI: "We've got all options on the table because we want to make very clear to nations that you will not threaten the U.S. or use weapons of mass destruction against us or our allies or friends."—President George W. Bush, March 2002

"The fact is, no one wants to use nuclear weapons. What we want to do is have a range of capabilities that makes their use less likely."—National Security Advisor Condoleezza Rice, March 2002

The nuclear revival continues. On May 26, 2003, the Senate lifted a 10-year-old ban on research on a new generation of low-yield nuclear weapons. Senate Democrats won a concession that congressional approval would be necessary before full-scale development. Concurrently, a comparable bill for a "study" of low-yield "mini-nukes" was passed in the House. Final approval is pending as of this writing, but it seems likely that Congress will give the approval the Bush Administration wants for the study of low-yield nuclear weapons.

During the week of May 23, 2003, Donald Rumsfeld insisted the Pentagon had no immediate plans to develop the new weapons such as deep-penetrating bunker-busters aimed at underground facilities, or mini-nukes—smaller than five kilotons—that would be designed to destroy biological and chemical stockpiles. He insisted the Pentagon only wanted to find out whether such bombs would be practical. However, on June 3, the Bush Administration announced plans for a factory known as a "Modern Pit Facility" that can produce new kinds of nuclear weapons triggers. The new facility would have the capability of building plutonium-containing triggering devices used in thermonuclear warheads. The plant would have the ability to rapidly change from building one type of trigger device to another, as well as designing new triggers for mini-nukes.

Tom Clements of Greenpeace International stated, "There is no justification whatsoever to proceed with plans for this new nuclear bomb factory."

SOURCES: *The Atlanta Journal-Constitution,* June 3, 2003; *The Houston Chronicle,* May 27, 2003; and *Financial Times* (London), May 23, 2003.

CENSORED # 7 2003
CORPORATIONS PROMOTE HMO MODEL
FOR SCHOOL DISTRICTS

For decades, public schools have purchased innumerable products and services from private companies—from textbooks to bus transportation. Within the last decade, however, privatization has taken on a whole new meaning. Proponents of privatized education are now interested in taking over entire school districts. While Educational Management Organizations (EMOs) are being promoted as the new answer to impoverished school districts and dilapidated classrooms, the real emphasis is on investment returns rather than student welfare and educational development.

Bush's proposal for national standardized testing is helping to pave the way for these EMOs. Bush wants yearly standardized testing in reading and math for every student in the country between the third and eighth grades. The effect of Bush's testing plan will be nothing less than a total reconstruction of curriculum and instruction across the country. Schools with already limited resources, serving poor and minority communities, will be those under the greatest pressure to boost scores or face loss of funding.

Only public school students take the standardized tests; kids whose parents can afford private schools don't have to agonize year after year about potential failure.

Privatization opponents say that public education should serve and be run by the public, especially teachers and parents, as opposed to shareholders who run the for-profit companies.

SOURCES: Barbara Miner, "Business Goes to School: The For-Profit Corporate Drive to Run Public Schools," *Multinational Monitor*, January/February 2001; Frosty Troy, "Dunces of Public Education Reform," *The Progressive Populist*, November 15, 2000; Dennis Fox, "Corporate-Sponsored Tests Aim to Standardize Our Kids," *North Coast Xpress*, Winter 2000; and Linda Lutton, "Testing, Testing: The Miseducation of George W. Bush," *In These Times*, June 2001.

UPDATE BY MICHAEL KAUFMANN: EMOs claim to be able to prop up failing and bankrupt school districts by delivering quality education for less—in other words, by cutting costs and trimming "unnecessary" personnel from the district's payroll. The companies have also made promises of upgrading the dilapidated, sometimes dangerous, environment of neglected inner-city schools and restoring pride and self-esteem to students. But the primary marketing angle employed by the EMOs has been to tap into one of the most emotionally charged issues of the current education crisis—that of failing test scores.

Taking their cue from the Bush Administration's obsession with raising students' test scores through increased standardized testing (exemplified by such legislation as the No Child Left Behind Act), EMOs have been quick to make promises of improving students' scores at even the most resource-challenged schools. As the EMOs would have it, the key to raising the academic level of failing schools is standardized testing. Instead of the "frills" of a traditional liberal-humanist education with its notion of bettering the whole person and not measuring success solely by test scores, these companies place a premium on bottom-line results.

Standardized testing, however, has shown itself to be especially problematic when it comes to an increasingly important sector: immigrant children, who are already suffering the effects of the elimination of bilingual education. The combination of relentless standardized testing with lack of language skills has been devastating for Latino children in particular and has led to charges against some EMOs that the companies are trying to force out students who may be lowering average test scores.

Edison Schools, a for-profit education management company, has been in business for ten years, the company has yet to show a quarterly profit. And, of course, as a for-profit enterprise, one of Edison's paramount concerns is investor return. Dow Jones Business News reported that, in the fall of 2002, Edison Schools, already plagued by an ongoing SEC investigation of its accounting practices, was warned by NASDAQ that the company was in danger of being dropped from the stock index because of its low share price. Founder H. Christopher Whittle immediately set out to buy up company stock in order to bolster the company's sagging share price. But by September 2002, Edison share had fallen from a high of $40 to less than $1.00. Additionally, according to the Dow Jones report, despite the company's continuing claims that their first ever quarterly profit is just around the corner, Edison recently announced yet another loss of more than $9 million for the second quarter ending December 31, 2002.

Meanwhile, 2002 and 2003 showed a mixed track record for Edison in one of the company's most hyped areas: that of test score improvement. While the data are often times contradictory, with Edison frequently claiming substantial gains in failing districts, opponents of the company maintain that many of the schools and districts taken over by Edison showed little to no improvement. Others saw their test scores drop after being adopted by Edison. Caroline Grannan, on her Parents Advocating School Accountability (PASA) Web site, <pasaf.org> points out, Edison has been known to use different methodologies in different situations in order to produce figures proving that the private company outperforms public schools. In other cases, such as in the San Francisco City School District, according to PASA, Edison has been accused by the California Office of Education of publishing false test score results. The PASA Web site has compiled a list of 16 school districts, from Texas to Pennsylvania, which have terminated their relationships with Edison, citing everything from lack of promised improvement in test scores to high teacher turnover as a result of the company's "lean" management policies.

One of Edison's most important market niches has been that of low-income, minority, and inner-city schools. In a scathing article in the *New York Amsterdam News*, "The Edison Schools Inc.: Crapola For Our Children," Wilbert A. Tatum accuses the city's administrators of selling out to for profit companies, abandoning their educational responsibilities toward Black children in the process.

EMOs have gotten a major legislative shot in the arm from the Bush Administration with the passing of the Elementary and Secondary Education Act (ESEA) in 2002. ESEA, popularly known as the No Child Left Behind Act, contains provisions that directly benefit private services. Barbara Miner, in her article "Privatizers' Trojan Horse" in the spring 2003 edition of *Rethinking Schools*, points out that under ESEA, "low-income families from schools in their second year of 'needing improvement' are eligible for before-or-after school services in reading, language arts, and math." The money for these supplemental services will be taken directly out of districts' budgets and represent a potential gold mine for EMOs more traditional "learning centers" such as Huntington and Sylvan and other new, more innovative private education providers. So despite the less than stellar results logged by companies such as Edison, entrepreneurs have not given up on the potential gold mine that is privatized education.

CENSORED # 9 2003

U.S. FACES NATIONAL HOUSING CRISIS

The national housing crisis affects nearly 6 million American families and is growing worse. Over 1.5 million low-cost housing units have recently been lost, and millions of children are growing up in housing that is substandard and dangerous.

Politicians refuse to add federal-funded housing to the U.S. budget. Low-cost housing programs are slowly being drained of funding. More than 100,000 federally subsidized units have been converted to market-rate housing in the past three years. While the $5-billion Federal Housing Administration surplus is tied up in Washington, neither major political party seems responsive to the current housing crisis. Neither party is addressing issues of living wage, adequate health care, or affordable housing.

Homelessness has become the result for many families across the nation. The economic slowdown, the welfare reform of 1996, and the events of September 11 are pushing hard-working Americans into the street. In New York alone, it is estimated that 30,000 people are living in shelters, and many thousands more live on the street.

In Chicago, over 20,000 units of public housing units have been removed from service and some 50,000 people now reside in the streets.

SOURCE: Randy Shaw, "There's No Place Like Home," *In These Times*, November 2000.

UPDATE BY VERONICA LOPEZ: Since the publication of the original article, "There's No Place Like Home," the shortage of affordable housing has continued to be a critical issue facing the nation. Despite a weakening economy and a growing need for affordable housing, Congress continues to ignore the problem. Meanwhile, the Bush Administration has proposed sweeping changes in vital HUD programs that promise to exacerbate the already dire situation. Regrettably, the mainstream media remains disinterested in covering this issue at the national level.

According to Kim Schaffer and a report from the National Low-Income Housing Coalition (NLIHC), "The need for housing for people with the lowest incomes continues to be high. Five million homes would need to be constructed over the next 20 years to close the gap between the number of households with extremely low incomes and the supply of housing they can afford."

Despite the tireless efforts of the NLIHC, Congress has continued to defeat passage of an initiative that would provide for a National Housing Trust Fund. According to NLIHC, the trust fund would "provide communities with funds to build, rehabilitate, and preserve 1.5 million homes over the next 10 years."

In the face of Bush's currently proposed 2004 HUD budget, the need for a National Housing Fund has become even more crucial. The budget includes the elimination of the HOPE VI Revitalization program, calls for the restructuring of the Section-8 program, and cuts funding to many other smaller programs that provide funds to local housing agencies. The cut in HOPE VI funds have hit especially hard because such funds are essential to local agencies for providing the rehabilitation, maintenance, and replacement of old and dilapidated housing units.

Journalist Meredith Kruse of the *Virginia Pilot* wrote, "The U.S. Department of Housing and Urban Development proposed the local funding cut to deal with a $250 million deficit created when HUD administrators failed to accurately estimate how much local authorities needed." Many of the smaller cuts to local agencies have been widely felt by jurisdictions across the country. Local housing departments are faced with the dilemma of having to cut programs, including assistance to the elderly and disabled and programs that allow families to become self-sufficient. The cuts are part of an attempt to balance the budget in the wake of a $250 million budget shortfall that occurred as a result of "poor accounting systems," according to HUD officials.

In addition to these proposed changes, the new budget will include the phasing out of the Section-8 program, which provides rent subsidies to low-income tenants. Section 8 has been seen by many as one of HUD's most successful programs. It will be replaced by Housing Assistance for Needy Families (HANF). Under the proposed change, states would receive funds directly from HUD to spend at their discretion. With a lack of oversight and established infrastructure, it's not difficult to imagine a scenario in which cash-strapped states are forced to divert HUD funds to general spending purposes.

While local housing shortages are being covered in regional media, coverage of the housing crisis on a national level continues to be absent from corporate media.

SOURCES: Kevin Dias, " HUD Error Could Lead to Public Housing Cuts," *Star Tribune*, January 25, 2003; Julie Hauserman, "Bush Plan Siphons Entrusted Tax Funds," *St. Petersburg Times*, February 3, 2003; HUD, "Bush Administration Announces More than $60 million in Housing and Economic Development Funds for the State of Florida," HUD News Release, August 14, 2002, <www.hud.gov>; Meredith Kruse, "Planned Budget Cuts Stun Housing Officials," *The Virginia Pilot*, January 13, 2003; Encarnacion Pyle, "Shut Out; Lack of Low-Income Housing and Subsidies Puts Thousands of Local Families at Risk," *The Columbus Dispatch*, December 22, 2002; Kim Schaffer, "Bush Tax Plan Ignores the Housing Needs of Low-income Americans," National Low-Income Housing Coalition, February 11, 2003, <www.nlihc.org/>.

BUSH APPOINTS FORMER CRIMINALS TO KEY GOVERNMENT ROLES

George W. Bush has brought several top government officials convicted for their involvement in the Iran-Contra scandal under President Reagan back into the fold.

In February 2001, John Poindexter was appointed to head the new Information Awareness Office (IAO), an offshoot of the Pentagon-based Defense Advanced Research Projects Agency (DARPA). His task will be to supply federal agents with "instant" analysis of all electronic communication. After serving as Reagan's national security advisor, John Poindexter was charged and found guilty of conspiracy, obstruction of justice, and the destruction of evidence as he played a central role in the Iran-Contra affair.

Elliot Abrams was recently appointed to the National Security Council (NSC) as director of its Office for Democracy, Human Rights, and International Relations. In 1991, Abrams plead guilty to withholding evidence from Congress regarding his role in the Iran-Contra affair. As Reagan's assistant secretary of state for human rights and humanitarian affairs, he oversaw U.S. foreign policy in Latin America and was active in covering up some of the worst atrocities of the war. George Bush, Sr. subsequently pardoned him.

John Negroponte, the new ambassador to the U.N., served under Reagan as ambassador to Honduras from 1981 to 1985. He is known for his role in the coverup of human rights abuses by CIA trained paramilitaries throughout the region. Soon after he took his new office, he unsuccessfully attempted to undermine the treaty that established the International Criminal Court (ICC) by threatening the Security Council with removing U.S. peacekeepers out of East Timor unless U.S. personnel are exempt from ICC proceedings.

Otto Reich has been appointed as assistant secretary of state for Western hemisphere affairs (which includes Latin America). The Bush Administration used a "recess appointment" during January 2002 to sidestep the Senate confirmation hearing otherwise required of the appointment. Reich was instrumental in the failed Venezuelan coup in April. In the 1980s, Reich was head of the office for Public Diplomacy, which was censured by Congress for "prohibited covert propaganda activities" after influencing the media to favorably cover the Reagan administration's position.

SOURCES: Peter Kornbluh, "Bush's Contra Buddies," *The Nation*, May 7, 2001; Terry Allen, "Public Serpent; Iran-Contra Villain Elliott Abrams is Back in Action," *In These Times*, August 6, 2001; Terry Allen, "Scandal? What Scandal?" *Extra!*, September/October 2001; Duncan Campbell, "Friends of Terrorism," *The Guardian* (London), February 8, 2002; John Sutherland, "No More Mr. Scrupulous Guy," *The*

Guardian (London), February 18, 2002; Michael Zuckerman," True or False: Iran-Contra's John Poindexter is Back at the Pentagon," *Washingtonian*, February 2002.

UPDATE BY JOSH SISCO: After the theft of the last presidential election, many thought that George W. Bush was strategically elected to continue the work of his father. When the administration began targeting Iraq late in 2002, after bombing Afghanistan into submission, these opinions intensified. While campaigning, numerous promises were made to curtail the corruption and moral decay that America presumably was undergoing during eight years of Democratic leadership. However, instead of ending administrative corruption altogether, Bush Jr. decided to mark a return to the wrongdoing of Reagan and his father. Next to Watergate, the Iran-Contra Affair, which Poindexter, Abrams, Negroponte, and Reich were all heavily involved in, was one of the largest and most far-reaching scandals that the United States government has faced in the latter half of the 20th century.

When questioned about Abrams' criminal record, Ari Fleischer replied, "The president thinks that is a matter of the past and was dealt with at the time." If a person admits guilt in lying to their boss, they will more than likely be fired. However, when Abrams plead guilty to two counts of "withholding information" from the United States Congress, the president pardoned him.

Since being reappointed by Bush, these men have resumed right where they left off: meddling in the affairs of legitimately elected governments in the name of democracy and homeland security. The outcry against Otto Reich was at least strong enough to force two demotions before he finally found a permanent home. Bush chose to nominate Reich as assistant secretary of state for Latin American affairs after Congress had recessed at the beginning of last year to avoid confirmation hearings. This is the State Department's highest position in Latin America. When Congress began a new session last November, he lost his position. Senator Richard Lugar (R–Indiana), who was newly appointed to head the Senate foreign relations committee, replacing conservative kingpin Jesse Helms, vowed not to confirm Reich in his original post. "I think we really need a very, very strong leader who has strong bipartisan confidence." Senator Christopher Dodd (D–Connecticut), another key member of the committee, also vowed to defeat Reich if he was nominated again.

The administration ultimately decided not to renominate Reich and instead temporarily made him special envoy to Latin America, where he would work at the State Department and report to Colin Powell. State Department spokesman Richard Boucher did not give reporters the specifics of the special envoy position. However, according to Duncan Campbell at *The Observer*, Powell was said to have become uncomfortable with such a controversial figure in the State Department and Reich was demoted again to a "minor role" at the National Security Office.

Elliot Abrams, John Negroponte, and Otto Reich were all instrumental in the failed April 2002 Venezuelan coup. They began meeting with leaders of the coup in the summer of 2001. These included Pedro Carmona, the short-lived president, Venezuelan military General Efrain Vasquez, and Gustavo Cisneros, who owns four of the five television stations and who is a long-time friend of the Bush family. During the planning stages, Elliot Abrams gave the unofficial "nod for the coup." *People's Weekly World* author John Gilman writes that during right-wing anti-Chavez demonstrations, "Cisneros jammed the one government TV station and focused on the right-wing counter democracy mob." Bush Administration officials have admitted that Reich had been on the phone to coup leaders the morning that it took place. After Pedro Carmona took power, Reich summoned Caribbean and Latin American ambassadors to his Washington office and told them Venezuela's new government is supported by the United States and that because Chavez "resigned," democracy will still be in place. The return of these Reagan hard-liners seems to be lining up with the surge of left-wing governments in Latin America including Venezuela, Brazil and Ecuador.

Posted at <www.maryknoll.org>, the *Los Angeles Times* reported that after Negroponte's nomination for U.N. ambassador, "the U.S. government revoked the visa of General Luis Alonso Discua Elvir, who was Honduras' deputy ambassador to the U.N. General Discua was the commander of the Battalion during Negroponte's tenure as [Nicaraguan] ambassador." The general claims to have information providing direct links between Negroponte and human rights abuses of Honduran military unit Battalion 3–16. John Negroponte as ambassador to the U.N. has played a key role in the drive for war with Iraq, where he was crucial in helping the U.S. steal the report and delete 8,000 pages.

At the beginning of last December, Elliot Abrams, in addition to his National Security Council position, was named, special assistant to the president and senior director for Near East and North African affairs, including Arab-Israeli relations and U.S. efforts to promote peace and security in the region. Abrams was one of the signers of a letter to President Clinton in 1998 encouraging the invasion of Iraq.

John Poindexter is barred from Costa Rica for drug trafficking, and although he was convicted of five felony counts of lying to Congress, he was pardoned by the elder Bush for simply admitting his guilt. Now he heads the government's domestic spy programs and has been given $200 million to compile databases on all Americans culled from electronic communication and public video surveillance. Poindexter is now head of the Information Awareness Office (IAO) within the Homeland Security Department.

SOURCES: David Greenburg, "Back, But Not by Popular Demand," *National Post*, December 8, 2002; Matt Welch, "Rubbing Salt in Old Wounds: Bush's Appointments of Iran-Contra Scandal Alumni Add Insult to Unhealed Injuries of the Cold War," *National Post*, December 14, 2002; Oliver Knox, "Bush Taps Reich as Latam Envoy," Agence France Presse, January 9, 2003; Duncan Campbell, "Bush Sidelines his Cuban Hardman," *The Guardian* (London), January 10, 2003; Johanna Neuman, "Anti-Communist Reich Given State Department Position," *Los Angeles Times*, January 12, 2002; Jim Lobe, "Fate of Anti-Castro Latin American Aid Uncertain," *Asheville Global Report*, December 5–11, 2002; Michael I. Niman, "What Bush Didn't Want You to Know about Iraq," *The Humanist*, March/April 2003; Susan Webb, "Carter Urges Peace, Bush Undermines U.N.," *People's Weekly World*, December 14, 2002; Karen Talbot, "Coup-Making in Venezuela: the Bush and Oil Factors," *People's Weekly World*, July 27, 2002; Emile Schepers, "Corporate Media Hide Truth About Venezuelan Coup," *People's Weekly World*, April 27, 2002; John Gilman, "The U.S. Role in the Venezuelan Coup," June 15, 2002; Office of the Press Secretary, December, 2, 2002; Ed Vulliamy, "Two Men Driving Bush into War," *The Observer*, February 23, 2003; <www.maryknoll.org>, "Stop Human Rights Obstructor John Negroponte: Act Immediately to Prevent Senate Approval of Negroponte for Ambassador to the U.N.," July 17, 2001, <www.maryknoll.org/GLOBAL/ALERTS?no_negroponte.htm>; Jim Lobe, "Congress Delays Pentagon's '1984' Spy Scheme," *Asheville Global Report*, February 20–26, 2003; Dorothy L. Wake, "'Big Brother' is Convicted Felon: John Poindexter at the Helm of TIA Program," *Because People Matter*, March/April 2003; and Michael I. Niman, "Baghdad on the Hudson; Let the Blitzkreig Begin?" *ArtVoice*, February, 12, 2003.

HENRY KISSINGER AND GERALD FORD LIED TO THE AMERI-CAN PUBLIC ABOUT EAST TIMOR

Declassified documents released in December of 2001 made it clear that former President Gerald Ford and Secretary of State Kissinger gave then-President Suharto a green light for Indonesia's 1975 invasion of East Timor. Kissinger had denied that the U.S. met with and encouraged Suharto to invade East Timor. The declassified documents included a dialogue between Kissinger, Ford, and Suharto adding significantly to what is known about the role the U.S. played in condoning the Indonesian invasion. The invasion left 230,000 East Timorese dead as the result of the invasion and subsequent 23 year occupation of the country.

SOURCES: Jim Lobe (IPS), "Documents show U.S. Sanctioned Invasion of East Timor," *Asheville Global Report*, December 13, 2001.

UPDATE BY MATT HAMBURG: The documents declassified in December 2001 have reached the mainstream press to some degree. Christopher Hitchens's book, *The Trial of Henry Kissinger*, has been the wellspring of this coverage. While Hitchen's book has not been well publicized by the mainstream press, his book did inspire a documentary, *The Trials of Henry Kissinger. Trials* has, in fact, been reviewed rather favorably by the mainstream press. The documentary, made by filmmakers Ales Gibney and Eugene Jackson, provides, as reviewer Ann Hornaday described it, "a damning legal brief against the former secretary of state." It is worth noting that many of these film reviews were dated during the several weeks before Kissinger's resignation from his chairmanship of the 9/11 investigative panel. The lead sentence from a *Newsday* article dated December 1, 2002, states, "If Henry

Kissinger had any shame, he would decline his new appointment and, while on bended knee, also return his 1973 Nobel Peace Prize." As the New York *Daily News* described it, the documentary "serves as a reminder that American foreign policy has not had anything against vicious despots per se, only those who are not acting in our interests." Additionally, the *Washington Post* has described how former President Ford, with Secretary of State Kissinger, gave the "green light for the invasion of East Timor leading to the murder of some 200,000." While the 200,000 figure might be lower than other estimates, the evidence of Ford and Kissinger's complicity in the atrocities has now been well documented.

SOURCES: Christopher Hitchens, *The Trial of Henry Kissinger* (New York, Verso, 2001); "U.S. Backed Indonesian Terror," *Washington Post,* October 31, 2002; Les Payne, "9/11 Deserves Better than Kissinger," *Newsday,* December 1, 2002; Ann Hornaday, "The Trials of Henry Kissinger," *Washington Post,* October 11, 2002; Manohla Dargis, "A Chilling Case Against Kissinger," *Los Angeles Times* movie review, October 25, 2002; Jack Matthews, "Regarding Henry," New York *Daily News*, September 25, 2002; and "Kissinger: Peacemaker of War-Maker," *Pittsburgh Post-Gazette*, January 3, 2003.

CENSORED # 14 2003
NEW LAWS RESTRICT ACCESS TO ABORTIONS IN U.S.

A quiet war against abortion rights is being conducted by many local governments in the United States. Cities and counties are placing repressive legal restrictions on abortion providers under the guise of women's health laws. These restrictions can include: width of hallways, jet and angle type of drinking fountains, the heights of ceilings, and how long one must wait between initially seeing the doctor and when the procedure can be performed.

Known as TRAP (Targeted Regulation of Abortion Providers) laws, these legal ordinances attempt to restrict all aspects of the physical environment related to an abortion.

TRAP laws have been passed in numerous states including Utah, Connecticut, Louisiana, South Carolina, Wisconsin, Alabama, Colorado, Mississippi, New Mexico, Oklahoma, Kentucky, Illinois, Nebraska, and Texas. Complying with TRAP laws can be very expensive. Remodeling modifications such as hallway width, angle and jet types for drinking fountains, ceiling height, doorway width, counseling room dimensions, air-circulation rates, outdoor weed-control practices, and separate changing rooms for men have resulted in the closing of cash-poor abortion clinics. Sometimes the clinics are closed only temporarily, but often the repairs are simply too expensive and the clinic is forced to cease operating altogether.

In 1992, when the *Planned Parenthood v. Casey* ruling established continued support for the 1973 *Roe v. Wade* decision, a new stealthier strategy was shaped by pro-life campaigners. Right-to-life advocates began thinking about other ways to attack abortion rights that were not so overtly challenging to the *Roe v. Wade* decision. By claiming that abortions take place in dirty facilities and cause such illnesses as depression and breast cancer, right-to-lifers have subtly moved away from the moral and legal debate and into a nebulous realm of "women's health."

Louisiana's newest anti-abortion law, known as the civil-liability law, would allow any woman who has had the procedure to sue the doctor for up to 10 years— not just for her own injuries, but also for "damages occasioned by the unborn child." While still being challenged in court, this civil-liability law threatens the viability of clinics in the entire state of Louisiana.

The Supreme Court has repeatedly supported a woman's right to abortion, but these laws are quietly taking that right away. If these laws remain unchallenged it may mean the end of legal abortions in the United States.

SOURCE: Barry Yeoman, "The Quiet War on Abortion," *Mother Jones*, September/October 2001.

UPDATE BY KAGISO MOLETHE: Barry Yeoman's article did so well that it won the *Washington Monthly's* December 2002 award. A Humboldt State college professor made it part of her syllabus for her class on terrorism. Westchester Coalition for Legal Abortion featured it on their Web site. The story stirred up a few court cases and a few appeals. Despite all this, the mainstream media still fails to give this story a closer look and grant it the full coverage it merits. As a result, it is no surprise that not much has changed. Thirty years after *Roe v. Wade*, it seems that the fight is headed right back where it started, with abortion being illegal. According to <crlp.org>, before abortion was legalized, 200,000 to 1.2 million illegal abortions were performed annually, causing 5,000 to 10,000 deaths.

The silent war on abortion still continues. More and more states are incorporating restriction laws. According to the *St. Louis Dispatch*, about 32 states require the parental consent or notification for minors. Fourteen states require the 24-hour waiting period. At least four states require the woman to meet with the physician 24 hours before the procedure. In this visit the physician is expected to provide the still disputed information that abortion can increase the risk of breast cancer. The American Cancer Society (ACS) has admitted that there is still no evidence of a link between abortion and breast cancer. This requirement forces the women to make two trips, often presenting a hardship for women coming from communities far from clinics.

The TRAP laws continue to be passed in more states. Abortion clinics unable to afford required remodeling are being forced to close. Physician are increasingly backing away from the abortion procedure due to fear of potential civil-liability law suites.

One of the first things President Bush did in the beginning of 2001 was to sign an executive order cutting federal funding to international agencies that support women seeking an abortion. "It is my conviction that taxpayer's funds should not be used to pay for abortion, either here or abroad," Mr. Bush wrote in his executive memorandum (BBC). One month later, the Bush Administration decided to make embryos and developing fetuses eligible for government health care. Although the Bush Administration claimed it was just helping poor mothers to get prenatal care, supporters of abortion rights fear that this could lay legal ground work toward establishing rights of a fetus and the reversal of *Roe v. Wade*.

CENSORED #16 2003
CIA KIDNAPS SUSPECTS FOR OVERSEAS TORTURE AND EXECUTION

Since September 11 the United States began involving itself more heavily in the business of abducting terrorist suspects. These suspects are denied legal counsel and detained without specific charges. Often being shipped to other countries where torture and other human rights violations are allowed, terrorist suspects are not even being protected by any U.S., foreign, or international human rights laws.

One particular abductee, Muhammad Saad Iqbal Madni is believed by the CIA to be an Al Qaeda member with possible links to the "shoe bomber," Richard Reid. In January 2002, the CIA provided the Indonesian government with information that led to Iqbal's arrest. Days later, Egyptian intelligence officials (who have close ties to the CIA) requested that Iqbal be extradited to their country. Two days later, without being charged or having access to a lawyer, Muhammad was put on an unmarked U.S. jet, arranged by the CIA, and flown from Jakarta to Egypt, where he could be subjected to numerous interrogation tactics that are illegal in the U.S.

Although such movement of opposition suspects has been used in the past, the recent events since 9/11 have shown a dramatic increase and visibility of this practice.

SOURCES: Don Greenlees, "Love Letter Tracks Terrorist's Footsteps," *Weekend Australian,* February 2, 2002; Barry Grey, "U.S. Oversees Abduction, Torture, Execution of Alleged Terrorists," *World Socialist,* March 20, 2002, <www.wsws.org/articles/2002/mar2002/cia-m20_prn.shtml>; and Rajiv Chandrasekaran and Peter Finn, "U.S. Behind Secret Transfer of Terror Suspects," *Washington Post,* February 11, 2002.

UPDATE BY COREY CLAPP: Although for the past year, the media has not covered the issue of rights for terrorist suspects on the front pages, the *Washington Post* did publish a followup article to its original story that was covered in *Censored 2003*. According to her *Post* article on December 26, 2002, Dana Priest reported U.S. officials claim approximately 3,000 suspected Al Qaeda members and their supporters have been detained worldwide since September 11. Thousands of these suspects have already been sent by the U.S. to countries that are known for human rights violations such as torturing prisoners.

As of late December 2002, some 625 of the captives still remained at the U.S. detainment facilities in Guantanamo Bay where military lawyers, media personnel, and the Red Cross have recently been granted some access to monitor conditions. Though a small, token number of professionals have been allowed to visit with detained suspects, prisoners are kept in tiny cells, exposed to the elements, and bombarded with arc lighting when it is dark.

Dana Priest described the conditions of one of several other secret interrogation centers located overseas inside Bagram Air Base in Afghanistan. In the cluster of shipping containers at one end of this air base, captured Al Qaeda suspects are kept standing or kneeling for hours, blinded with black hoods or painted goggles, forced into painful positions, and deprived of rest with a constant bombardment of light. These techniques are a trademark of CIA "stress and duress" interrogation methods. Priest describes how suspects are often taken by force and are often shot or wounded during their capture. The apprehension teams, made up of members of special-forces, FBI agents, and CIA case officers, as well as local allies, intentionally disorient and intimidate the suspects on their way to detention facilities. These practices are common not only at Bagram and Guantanamo Bay, but throughout U.S. detainment centers around the world.

There is a major contradiction in this push for such "alternative" interrogation and imprisonment methods. On one hand, in public, the U.S. government denounces and condemns human rights violations and torture of any kind. On the other hand, according to the *Post* article, our current national security officials defend the use of violence against terrorist suspects as just and necessary. Advocates of such harsh interrogation tactics include CIA director George J. Tenet, who claimed, in a speech on December 11, 2002, that much of the successful apprehension of the Al Qaeda leadership would not even be possible without the world wide efforts against terrorism. Tenet claims that the information obtained during these inhumane interrogations was instrumental in apprehending Al Qaeda members.

On May 6, *The Guardian* reported the intent of the White House to release a dozen or more prisoners held at Guantanamo Bay, Cuba. On the surface this can be seen as a progression towards human rights and justice, but the fact that these terrorist suspects have been held in questionable conditions in some cases for almost two years without being charged or given legal representation can not be overlooked.

The May 6 *Guardian* article placed some 660 suspects from 42 different countries still at the Guantanamo Bay facilities. While the exact number of suspects imprisoned throughout the world is unknown, the number is estimated at somewhere between 2,000 and 3,000.

In another related story reported by *Truth Out* on May 27 tells of U.S. plans to build permanent holding cells and an execution chamber at Guantanamo Bay. Prisoners could then be tried, convicted, and executed without having to leave the boundaries of the facilities.

Amnesty International released their annual report for 2002 on May 28, 2003, charging the U.S. with maintaining inhumane conditions for terrorist suspects. CNN, published a story with the headline "U.S. Rejects Amnesty Charge," though the piece went on to present much of the actual situation. Amnesty's report makes clear that the U.S. is in violation of numerous international human rights and war laws. Many suspects in the "War on Terror" are imprisoned without charges or access to council, for unlimited time, under harsh treatment and intense interrogations.

Ari Fleischer claimed that the treatment terrorist suspects receive at Guantanamo Bay is better than that which they received prior to detention. This does little to explain the more than 30 suicide attempts by detainees at Guantanamo Bay.

In late March 2003, Eyal Press wrote an article for *the Nation* called, "In Torture We Trust," a story that on a more philosophical level reiterates the questions surrounding torture and the U.S. governments' recent involvement. The biggest issue surrounding this situation seems to be one of ethics: Once we begin to dismantle human rights and international law, where will we stop? Taking a path in this direction could lead to the undermining of what "democratic norms" our society has left. Professor and expert on the Middle East Shibley Telhami claims that "we cannot defend what we stand for by subverting our own values in the process."

SOURCES: Amnesty International, "Report 2003-USA: Covering Events from January to December 2002," <web.amnesty.org/web/web.nsf/print/usa-summary-eng>; U.S. Prepared to Free a Dozen Prisoners from Guantanamo: Who is Responsible for their Agony?" *Balochistan Post-News*, May 30, 2003; Truth Out Organization, "U.S. Plans Death Camp" *The Courier Mail*, May 26, 2003, <truthout.org/docs_03/052703B.shtml>; CNN.com, "U.S. Rejects Amnesty charge," May 29, 2003, <www.cnn.com/ 2003/WORLD/europe/05/29/amnesty.report/>; *The Guardian Unlimited,* "U.S. Tries to Sort Out Terror Suspects," May 6, 2003, <web.amnesty.org/web/web. nsf/print/usa-summary-eng>; Eunice Moscoso, *The Atlanta Journal-Constitution,* May 28, 2003, <www.ajc.com/news/content/news/ 0503/28scotus.

html>; Eyal Press, "In Torture We Trust?" *The Nation*, March 31, 2003; Dana Priest and Barton Gellman, "U.S. Decries Abuse but Defends Interrogations; 'Stress and Duress' Tactics Used on Terrorism Suspects Held in Secret Overseas Facilities," *Washington Post*, December 26, 2002.

CENSORED # 19 2003

AMERICAN COMPANIES EXPLOIT THE CONGO

Western multinational corporations' attempts to cash in on the wealth of Congo's resources have resulted in what many have called "Africa's first world war," claiming the lives of over 3 million people. The Democratic Republic of Congo (DRC) has been labeled "the richest patch of earth on the planet." The valuable abundance of minerals and resources in the DRC has made it the target of attacks from U.S.-supported neighboring African countries Uganda and Rwanda.

The DRC is mineral-rich with millions of tons of diamonds, copper, cobalt, zinc, manganese, uranium, niobium, and tantalum also known as coltan. Coltan has become an increasingly valuable resource to American corporations. Coltan is used to make mobile phones, night vision goggles, fiber optics, and capacitators used to maintain the electrical charge in computer chips. In December 2000, the shortage of coltan was the main reason that the popular sale of the Sony PlayStation 2 video game came to an abrupt halt.

The DRC holds 80 percent of the world's coltan reserves, more than 60 percent of the world's cobalt and is the world's largest supplier of high-grade copper. With these minerals playing a major part in maintaining US military dominance and economic growth, minerals in the Congo are deemed vital U.S. interests.

Historically, the U.S. government identified sources of materials in Third World countries, and then encouraged U.S. corporations to invest in and facilitate their production. In 1998, U.S. military-trained leaders of Rwanda and Uganda invaded the mineral-rich areas of the Congo. The invaders installed illegal colonial-style governments which continue to receive millions of dollars in arms and military training from the United States. Our government and a $5 million Citibank loan maintains the rebel presence in the Congo. Their control of mineral rich areas allows Western corporations, such as American Mineral Fields, to illegally mine. Rwandan and Ugandan control over this area is beneficial for both governments and for the corporations that continue to exploit the Congo's natural wealth.

American Mineral Fields (AMF) landed exclusive exploration rights to an estimated 1.4 million tons of copper and 270,000 tons of cobalt. San Francisco-based engineering firm Bechtel established strong ties in the rebel zones as well. Bechtel drew up an inventory of the Congo's mineral resources free of charge and also paid for NASA satellite studies of the country for infrared maps of its minerals. Bechtel estimates that the DRC's mineral ores alone are worth $157 billion. Through coltan production, the Rwandans and their allies are bringing in $20 million revenue a month. Rwanda's diamond exports went from 166 carats in 1998 to 30,500 in 2000. Uganda's diamond exports jumped from approximately 1,500 carats to about 11,300. The final destination for many of these minerals is the U.S.

SOURCES: Dena Montague and Frida Berrigan, "The Business of War in the Democratic Republic Of Congo: Who Benefits?" *Dollars and Sense*, July/August 2001; keith harmon snow, "Depopulation and Perception Management (Part 2: Central Africa)," *Voice* (Pioneer Valley, MA), March/April 2001; and Ellen Ray, "U. S. Military and Corporate Recolonization of the Congo", *CovertAction Quarterly*, summer 2000.

UPDATE ON THE CONGO BY JOURNALIST KEITH HARMON SNOW: An appropriate subtitle for this update on war and propaganda: "How the despair and death of millions in Africa is daily determined by the lifestyle of ordinary Americans in small-town USA, and why most of us know nothing about it, and do nothing to stop it when we do know."

Dissent is intolerable to those who have something to hide and so the discussion about terrorism in Africa remains proscribed by academia, the media, and other institutions of American empire. Africa is off the agenda. People are getting away with murder because they know they can, and the media doesn't report it. Indeed, they cover it up.

Since 1998, the number of dead in Democratic Republic of Congo (DRC) has exceeds *four million* people. No one in the international community is talking about it. No one is listening. Torture is commonplace. Refugees have been massacred. Innocent men, women, and children have been slaughtered. Civil society is under attack. Children have been forcibly recruited as soldiers. Government is sowing terror. Government is getting away with murder, mutilation, and rape.

In 1990, Maj. Gen. Paul Kagame, now president of Rwanda, returned from training at the U.S. Army's Command and General Staff College, Fort Leavenworth, Kansas, to lead the first U.S. supported invasion of Rwanda by the army of the Rwanda Patriotic Front (RPF). Kagame is identified with the Tutsi tribe, but this is a meaningless social construction serving the Western media theme of "African conflicts by African people" (a.k.a. tribalism, yet again).

When the plane carrying the Hutu president of Rwanda and Burundi was shot down over the Rwandan capital on April 6, 1994, all hell broke loose. Under cover of "the genocide"—and a total U.S. media propaganda blitz—Kagame and the RPF invaded and secured Rwanda. Hundreds of thousands of killings attributed to "the genocide" were committed by RPF forces in 1994. The killings spread to DRC. With total U.S. military support, the RPF has committed countless crimes against humanity.

The second U.S.-supported invasion of DRC began in 1998. The International Rescue Committee and the National Academy of Sciences independently determined that some 3.5 million people died in DRC between August 1998 and June 2001. The counting stopped there, but the killing didn't.

The U.S. is the leading arms dealer in central Africa. By 1995, Halliburton subsidiary KBR was setting up military bases in Rwanda. Back in the U.S., Jean Raymond Bouelle was setting up America Mineral Fields Corporation in Hope, Arkansas, signing mining contracts in DRC and Sierra Leone. U.S. Special Forces assisted the RPF and UPDF and their Congolese allies in the U.S. proxy wars for the Congo. The Bouelle companies continue to pillage Africa under cover of war and executive privilege. The U.S. provided military support and training for all sides under International Military Education and Training, Joint Combined Exchange Training, and the Africa Crisis Response Initiative. These programs involve psychological operations, tortures, massacres, and disappearance as standard operating procedure.

The contre-genocide continues. In April 2003, the eastern DRC city of Bunia was devastated by RPF military operations. RPF, UPDF, and U.S. Special Forces have inflamed tribal tensions. Massacres of hundreds of people have lasted days at a time. Civilians have been herded into houses and set on fire.

Paul Kagame was received at the White House on March 3, 2003. He later spoke at the James Baker Institute in Houston, where he met with George H.W. Bush.

The DRC people die daily due to the complete breakdown of everything—while organized crime, sexual slavery and extortion proliferate. Eastern Congo has been absolutely, and unfathomably, ravaged. Malnutrition affects some 16 million people in DRC where, on average, some 2,600 people have died every day.

The American way of life is intimately connected with war-as-cover for Africa's petroleum, copper, manganese, uranium, gold, tin, bauxite, timber and water.

Even the peace and justice community has dismissed the DRC and Africa more broadly. People don't hesitate to take action to try to stop war in Iraq. We struggle with the Palestinians. Our Witnesses for Peace frequent Latin America. Our conferences and workshops proliferate and, more often than not, Africa is entirely off the agenda. Meanwhile Africa suffers in silence. It is the legacy of our lifestyle and the intention of empire. It is de facto depopulation.

LARGE U.S. TEMP COMPANY UNDERMINES
UNION JOBS AND MISTREATS WORKERS

Labor Ready Inc. is a national temporary employment agency that employed over 700,000 people in the year 2000. Labor Ready has 839 offices in 49 states and in Canada, and stands ready to place temporary workers as strikebreakers in union labor disputes. During the Northwest steel strike, it was Labor Ready who provided hundreds of strikebreakers to Kaiser Aluminum in Spokane, Washington.

According to a General Accounting Office study, temp jobs in all their various forms rose 577 percent between 1982 and 1998. Even though the largest rise in jobs has been temp work, the federal government has done very little to regulate or protect temp workers.

Labor Ready targets a vulnerable labor pool. Over half of Labor Ready's work force is homeless and nearly every Labor Ready branch office in the United States is within 2.5 miles of major urban areas where more than one-third of the population are people of color and nearly 15 percent live in poverty.

The company maintains an extremely high rate of injuries and illnesses at 31 percent. The average rate within the entire construction industry is only 8 percent. Workers for Labor Ready also receive no health benefits.

SOURCE: Harry Kelber, "Temps are Ready for Organizing If AFL-CIO Provides the Muscle," *The Progressive Populist*, June 1, 2001.

UPDATE BY DONALD YOON: There have been a number of lawsuits filed against Labor Ready in the past year. In California, Bay Area workers report that Labor Ready requires them to check in at the office an hour before they go out to work, even if they are returning to a job they worked the day before. They don't receive pay for the time they wait in the office or the time it takes them to get from their offices to the work site. This violates California's labor code according to a class-action lawsuit filed in Alameda County. Five company laborers are arguing that California law requires employers such as Labor Ready to pay workers for all the hours they spend under the employer's control.

Oregon Labor Commissioner Jack Roberts proposed imposing a $49,500 fine against Labor Ready Inc. for repeatedly failing to pay prevailing wages to workers it dispatched to publicly financed job sites. For example, they dispatched Aaron Wadsworth to a job site paying him $6.75 an hour when he should have been paid $43.83 per hour, classified as a carpenter working overtime.

There have also been a number of lawsuits regarding the check cashing machines that charge for the transaction.

David A. Lang, president of HFW, a software development company, submitted a shareholder proposal calling on Labor Ready, Inc. to adopt more labor-friendly policies. Lang is a registered stockbroker and a shareholder of LRW. The issues addressed by Lang's proposal include fair pay policies, adequacy of worker's compensation reporting, and job site safety standards. When shareholders start to complain, it implies that the disputes with the AFL-CIO are shutting the company out of certain markets, thereby limiting growth and shareholder value. While Labor Ready has made lots of profit by cutting corners, there is definitely a backlash.

SOURCES: Karina Ioffee, "Day Laborers Pay Price for Work," *Arizona Daily Star*, November 5, 2002; Gordon Hurd, "One Company's Exploits In Day Labor Reveal What's Wrong With The Temp Industry," *Hard Labor*; Sara Zaske, "Waiting for Good Dough," *ColorLines*, Fall 2002, Vol. 5, No. 3; U.S. Newswire, "Community Group Sued for Speaking Out Against Temp Firm," *Industrial Worker*, January 14, 2003.

THIS MODERN WORLD

by TOM TOMORROW

ONCE AGAIN, IT'S TIME TO CHECK IN ON...

PARALLEL EARTH!

AS YOU MAY RECALL, A QUIRK IN THEIR ELECTION LAWS LED OUR INTERDIMENSIONAL COUNTERPARTS ON *PARALLEL EARTH* TO ELECT A *SMALL CUTE DOG* AS *THEIR* PRESIDENT TWO YEARS AGO.

ARF!

THEY'VE BEEN THROUGH A LOT IN PARALLEL AMERICA OVER THE LAST COUPLE OF YEARS...THEIR LATEST CRISIS BEGAN ONE DAY WHEN NO ONE REMEMBERED TO TAKE THE PRESIDENT OUT FOR HIS AFTERNOON *WALK*...

WHO LEFT THIS *MAP* LYING ON THE FLOOR? THE PRESIDENT HAS URINATED ON *LIECHTENSTEIN!*

HE'S CLEARLY MADE AN IMPORTANT *FOREIGN POLICY DECISION!*

THE PARALLEL ADMINISTRATION SOON TOOK ITS CASE TO THE *PUBLIC*...

THE PRESIDENT HAS DRAMATICALLY EXPRESSED HIS CONVICTION THAT LIECHTENSTEIN *MUST BE DEALT WITH!*

WHAT ARE THEY *HIDING* IN THEIR 62 *SQUARE MILES OF EVIL?*

BEFORE LONG, THE PARALLEL PUBLIC WAS *OBSESSED* BY A COUNTRY TO WHICH THEY'D GIVEN *LITTLE THOUGHT* IN THE RECENT PAST...

THOSE MORAL DEGENERATES REMAINED *NEUTRAL* DURING WORLD WAR TWO!

AND WHO *KNOWS* HOW MANY TERRORISTS LURK AMONG THEIR POPULATION OF 33,000 CITIZENS?

OTHER NATIONS OF PARALLEL EARTH WERE LESS ENTHUSIASTIC ABOUT THE WAR--AND WERE TREATED WITH APPROPRIATE *DERISION*...

I'D LIKE BELGIAN WAFFLES WITH CANADIAN BACON, PLEASE.

YOU MEAN *FREEDOM* WAFFLES WITH *LIBERTY* BACON?

UH-- SURE.

Menu

AND AS THE WAR BEGAN, THE PRESIDENT WAS ALREADY LOOKING AHEAD TO THE *NEXT* CHALLENGE.

THE PRESIDENT HAS *VOMITED* ON A MAP OF *AMERICAN SAMOA!* YOU KNOW WHAT *THAT* MEANS!

BUT--THAT'S A U.S. TERRITORY!

ARE YOU *QUESTIONING* THE *PRESIDENT?*

ER--NO, OF COURSE NOT! I'LL DRAW UP BATTLE PLANS RIGHT AWAY!

CHAPTER 3

Junk Food News and News Abuse

BY JASON SPENCER AND CHRISTINA CUTAIA

Junk Food News

The "Junk Food News and News Abuse" Chapter shifts the focus of the
Censored *yearbook. Each year, we take the time to evaluate the frivolous stories that dominated our television screens and media spotlights.
With celebrity gossip and reality TV once again dominating our top
10 Junk Food News picks, a discussion of American culture may be
warranted. Are occurrences in celebrity personal lives justified and newsworthy cultural events?*

Last year's Junk Food News stories included the Tom Cruise and Nicole
Kidman breakup as well as Pamela Anderson's breast-reduction surgery.
The criticism was mild, but the question was asked, does Project Censored
have something against American popular culture and the necessary discussion of sexuality in the modern era? The answer to those questions by
the people within the project is obviously, no. Nobody at the project would
be averse to the media having a healthy, educational public discussion of
the evolution of human sexuality within our culture. Likewise, the larger
problem here is not that news organizations cover the cultural aspects of
art, music, and movies. The problem arises when the personal lives of the
performers become the primary filler of the limited time and space available for keeping the American people informed on critical issues.

As the brainstorming for this year's list began, it was obvious that the dominant irrelevant and overplayed news stories of the year would once again be laden with voyeuristic celebrity gossip. Here are the top 10 Junk Food News stories of the year:

1. *Joe Millionaire* and Reality TV
2. Michael Jackson: from his plastic surgery to his baby-dangling
3. Winona Ryder and her kleptomaniacal tendencies
4. *American Idol* in all its glory
5. J. Lo
6. Martha Stewart and her insider trading
7. *The Osbournes*: from the show to Kelly's burgeoning career
8. The antimarijuana campaign
9. SUV mania
10. Anna Nicole: The show, the lady, the inanity

Number 10 is yet another celebrity gossip extravaganza. With Anna Nicole Smith having two hours a week to grace the airwaves with her wit and beauty, you would think the mainstream media wouldn't need to waste our time analyzing the content and validity of the show. It seems the American people didn't get enough of Ms. Smith during her scheduled time on E! Television. We had to be subjected to the media hype that surrounded the show and the idiosyncrasies of its star. Necessary cultural dialogue or irrelevant celebrity hype clogging our media airwaves? You decide.

Next on the list, SUV Mania found its way into the national media spotlight over and over again this past year. While our nation was contemplating going to war in the Middle East and drilling in the Arctic, the media found it necessary to draw the public's attention to the inefficient gas-guzzling SUV as an ideal form of transportation. The technology for hybrid cars has been evolving at breakneck speed, but the media has not found that a significant news story. Instead of discussions about conservation and fuel efficiency, SUV mania has been the name of the transportation game for the mainstream.

Next, the list shifts to a national ad campaign that received mention in the media more times than one might expect. With state after state working to legalize the long prohibited hemp plant, the Office of National Drug Control Policy (ONDCP), the American Medical Association and 16 other organizations are working to keep America's youth from falling prey to marijuana. The ONDCP campaign focuses on scaring parents and not on evoking a significant parent-child dialogue.

While underage drinking is still the leading cause of indiscretion at teenage parties and problems at high school events, no discussion of manipulative beer commercials and other ads targeting young adults has ensued. The misguided antimarijuana ads, however, have received much fanfare in the mainstream press. This disconnect begs the question, why have the media jumped behind the ONDCP agenda instead of focusing on the consistent danger of readily accessible alcohol?

And now onto the celebrity reality-TV family that has swept the American media scene like a tidal wave. The Osbournes have been interviewed to death and we've heard everything we care to hear about Kelly and her zany outfits and her singles.

While the multibillion dollar debacle of Kenneth Lay and his Enron executives has faded into the shadows of the media spotlight, Martha Stewart and her profits from insider trading has been thrust into the mainstream debate. The issue here is one of emphasis. As celebrity ethics are now of major concern to the national networks, the still reverberating repercussions of the Enron catastrophe are of little concern anymore. Was what Martha Stewart is accused of doing illegal? Yes. Does it compare to the corrupt demise of one of the largest companies in America? We think not.

As Americans are once again distracted by the life choices of a well-known celebrity, the real corporate criminals, like WorldCom, Enron, Tyco, and Rite-Aid, and their misdeeds—billions of dollars of fraud contributing to thousands of lost jobs and furthering a national recession—quickly fade away into obscurity. Martha Stewart capitalizing on less than $225,000 of stock sales from the knowledge of a friend inside a biotech company—now *that* is news. We doubt reforms from corporate misdeeds will come from the Martha Stewart case. So why is she receiving the attention? We guess that is what the American people want to focus on. Or is it what the ever-shrinking oligopoly of media megacorporations would prefer we focus on?

From her movie releases and music award-show outfits to her stormy relationship with rapper/producer P. Diddy and then her eventual engagement to heartthrob Ben Affleck, Latin queen Jennifer Lopez has crowded real news stories off the airwaves and out of the print media. While not negating the cultural importance of movie/music stars, did Diane Sawyer really need to interview J. Lo to ask her all the sultry questions about her relationship and eventual engagement to Affleck? That is a decision for the masses, but here at the Project Censored headquarters, it appears that mid-November of last year could have yielded a more informative interview for Ms. Sawyer. As a perfume purveyor, restaurateur, and pop culture icon,

Lopez is second to none. As an interviewee for one of the countries most respected media personnel, J. Lo doesn't appear to be the most informative of choices for the American primetime media discussion.

Coming in at number 4, *American Idol* is the first reality-TV culprit of undeserving media dominance. Again, a show with a weekly time slot was awarded extra time in the lives of the American people—with newspaper column inches being consumed by the hundreds, asking who would win, delving into the pasts of the top contenders, and discussing the latest witty remarks of the infamous judges. It is obvious the voyeuristic new *Star Search* is also a cultural phenomenon. But we don't recall the weekly guests and judges on the original *Star Search* making headlines and dominating the news. Apparently, times have changed and there is less news to inform the citizens of our democracy about, or at the very least, there is apparently more time available in the mainstream media for the discussion of frivolous TV hype.

Number 3 on the list is reserved for Winona Ryder and her possible kleptomaniacal tendencies. As the media frenzy surrounded a shoplifting case that normally wouldn't even have gone to trial, the discussion ranged from how she plotted the scheme to the possibility of kleptomania. Whether Ms. Ryder is a kleptomaniac may be a valid question for the *National Enquirer*, but we hardly think it warrants the time and attention the national news networks and papers contributed to the discussion. From the day of the arrest to the dramatic coverage of the trial, the BBC all the way to the *Boston Globe*, we saw the media spotlight dance all around an issue that really had no importance to the average American.

At number 2 on this year's Junk Food News list is Michael Jackson. Where do we begin? The latest plastic surgery? The dangling baby? Or the hype surrounding the prime-time special and then the rebuttal prime-time special? With 27 million televisions tuning in to the British interview that aired on ABC, was a lengthy national media discussion necessary after the event was over? Apparently so; in fact, the media attention was so great and the discussion so widespread, FOX deemed it necessary to air a special of its own, giving Jackson the opportunity to discuss what had happened during the ABC interview and afterward during the media blitz. In addition, *Dateline NBC* drew 14 million viewers to a special about the changing of Jackson's face.

The media hype that led up to each of these events was ridiculous, but the vast coverage that followed each time was even worse. For nearly an entire month, the national news networks spent at least a portion of the evening news cast discussing what might and then what did happen during each of the aforementioned specials. And all of this was just months after every news organization imaginable had spent time and energy telling us that Jacko had dangled a baby from a balcony and that absolutely nothing significant had happened. No charges were filed by police, there was no arrest, no trial, nothing, but it made every major newspaper and newscast in the country.

If you're wondering how Jacko couldn't be number 1, you must have missed the world's most popular dating game and the million-dollar phony-turned-heartthrob. The honor of this year's number 1 Junk Food News story goes to *Joe Millionaire*.

The Dating Game and *Love Connection* have been a part of the American television landscape for decades, but when you raise the stakes, they seem to become a media event. Reality TV has taken America by storm and *Joe Millionaire* is no exception. The show was the talk of the town, water-cooler gossip for many Americans during the weeks it was on the air. Again, the question remains: does a dating game/reality TV phenomenon warrant national media coverage and a constant discussion of the winners, the losers, and the what-ifs? Given all the news that doesn't find its way into the mainstream media, Project Censored would dispute the necessity and relevance of this type of news coverage by the national networks. Much of the coverage is nothing more than hype that amounts to advertising for the next episode. Additionally, the newsprint and aftermath coverage of the personal lives of the participants is rubbish and absolutely deserves the dubious distinction of the number 1 Junk Food News story of the year. Thanks to all the voters and inane news coverage for making this year's list as titillating and gratuitous as it is.

News Abuse

News Abuse highlights stories that most would consider legitimate news and out of respect for the parties involved, we do not refer to them as "Junk Food News." These are the stories of heart-wrenching tragedy and unending fear that the mainstream media outlets glom onto and run with for as long as possible. Out of respect for those involved, one would expect the media organizations to make mention of these stories, somberly report the events, and then move on. That is rarely happens with the juicy, gory, or heart-wrenching cases of News Abuse. These are stories whose footage is often run over and over, exploit the fear of the average American and often the pain of the individual families. These stories of personal tragedy and sensationalized fear are repeatedly reported without the release of any new information. This is done for no reason other than attracting the rubbernecking viewer or reader to the sensationalized tragedy or fear-laden story of the day. With that in mind, here is the News Abuse top 5 for 2003.

1. The War on Terror and the Color Coded Alert System
2. Laci Peterson Abduction
3. Saddam's Cruelty and the War on Iraq
4. DC Sniper
5. Where's Osama?

The list this year starts and ends with the same theme: the unknown whereabouts of the invisible enemy. Coming in at number 5 is Osama Bin Laden and the hunt for the September 11 bandit. New video footage—possibly real or possibly fake, most of it poorly translated—has been used by the media without really telling the American people anything specific about their safety and national security. The incessant discussions of the validity of the tapes, the unknown whereabouts and health of the Al Qaeda leader, and the possible, but still unidentified, threat to the American populace all crowded the airwaves. Yet nothing ever came of any of it. Americans were told to be scared of what they couldn't see and cautious of those who looked like bin Laden. Now Osama is nowhere to be found, the focus of our post-9/11 aggression has shifted to Iraq, and Osama quietly slipped into the shadows.

Why the relentless coverage when even the experts seemed to know nothing? The same questions were being asked and the same nonanswers were being given. The American people were afraid to get on airplanes, and we were hearing about troops securing bridges and planes flying constant patrols. How much danger were we actually in? What were the real reasons we had been attacked? The tough questions about terrorism were not being asked, but the Hollywood drama that was the "Where's Osama?" extravaganza, filled our minds and fed our fears for months.

Next up on the News Abuse list is the DC Sniper. This was surely a newsworthy event and one that obviously portrayed some of the problems with our society, but the tug on your heartstrings was excessive the reenactments were truly unnecessary. What was the point of the constant stream of news conferences and print interviews that consistently told us nothing? Excess is the problem in stories like this. They are true tragedies and horribly painful for the families involved. That alone is reason enough for media companies not to exploit these kinds of stories to attract viewers, readers, and most importantly, advertisers.

As media consolidation continues and newsrooms become smaller pieces of large corporations, news budgets are becoming consistently leaner. In turn, true investigative journalism is disappearing as less expensive, "canned news" is being used. An event like the sniper case is "canned news." The news organization knows where the story is; they are guaranteed press conferences and soundbites without doing any research or sending anyone into the field searching for news. All the stations are at the same place showing the same thing at the same time; each trying to do it a little flashier than the next, attempting to retain the viewers attention. This is one of the ways a newsworthy event can be abused at the expense of other legitimate stories that are often more important to the civic life of a democracy.

Coming in at number 3 on the News Abuse list is Saddam Hussein and his evil empire that forced us into war. "Showdown with Saddam" was the catchy slogan. The horrors of his regime were the favorite topics of discussion and the investigative reporting consisted of regurgitated Pentagon and State Department announcements. The continuous reminders of what had happened in the past, without any justification of what it meant for the present, was all too consistent in the mainstream coverage. We would have been far better served by an honest discussion of the true potential dangers to the average American and the long-term implications of an aggressive "preemptive strike" policy. With all of the hours of television and radio airtime and miles of newsprint concerning Saddam and the War with Iraq, the American people never really got the straightforward discourse that included all the facts and realities that war would bring.

We heard soundbites alluding to the stupidity of the French and German opposition to the war, but we never heard the honest discussion of the concerns that they, and many within the British House of Commons, our staunchest ally, shared. Without being afforded the whole picture of the darkness of war and the reliability of the intelligence that was driving our country toward war, the American people were asked to accept a decision that will affect each and every one of us for generations. With all of the time and media attention spent focusing on the overpowering might of our weaponry and the fear mongering of Saddam Hussein, the lack of the revelation of the whole picture is the fault of the mainstream media. That, by our definition, is News Abuse.

At number 2 on the News Abuse list is the Laci Peterson murder. As if the family involved has not suffered enough, the mainstream media turned this tragedy into a full-fledged media circus. A LexisNexis news database search of Ms. Peterson's name returns over 500 hits in just Associated Press newswire releases. That number increases exponentially when you consider how many newspapers, television, and radio news organizations picked up on each one of those AP releases. Pennsylvania regional papers—we chose a region far from the small Californian town where the Petersons' lived to illustrate our point—had over 40 hits returned on the Peterson search. The reverberation of this murder has shocked the nation and absorbed the national media scene.

Rounding out the News Abuse chart is the War on Terror and our new color-coded terror alert system. Without ever telling the American public anything significant that will make them safer, the mainstream media managed to keep us scared of the invisible enemy for nearly an entire year. The coverage of the changing of the color for Tom Ridge's new terror warning system has been wasteful at best. With no substantial information regarding what the average American should be afraid of or looking out for, what good does it do us to have a constant reminder that we are under attack? It works to undermine the confidence and daily activities of Americans and supports the culture of fear we now seem to share.

The intelligence community may very well need to know when we are in a heightened state of alert, but ordinary citizens, given the ambiguous information provided, have no ability to make themselves safer. The constant reminders feed fear and nothing else. Apparently, we have come to the point where the purchase of duct tape and plastic are being touted as the first steps to American safety and security.

As Saddam Hussein and Iraq were thrust into the public mind, terrorism took a backseat, as Americans were riled up into the fearful frenzy of an aggressor. With that excursion summarily handled and out of the way, one can only imagine that useless updates on the War on Terror will once again become a top candidate for prime-time news coverage in this country. When there is a legitimate update or warning to be levied, go ahead. But if the purpose is to constantly subject the population to ambiguous fear-laden updates for the purpose of ratings, please spare us and spend a little more time keeping an eye on our elected leaders and the corporate swindlers, who may well be as serious a threat to American people.

CHAPTER 4

The Big Five Media Giants

BY MARK CRISPIN MILLER

The media giantism here depicted has, of course, been worsening for years. Such concentration poses an enormous threat to our democracy and culture, and, therefore, to democracy and culture all throughout the world. And yet, despite the scope and likely consequences of this crisis, too few Americans have even known exactly how and why it has occurred—a lack of knowledge that itself is powerful evidence of the destructive impact of the media cartel, which keeps us in the dark about itself and all its mighty allies in the business world and the political establishment. (The U.S. education system also bears some blame.)

But most of us are not the beery idiots that TV and the White House hopefully insists we are. The problem here is not one of collective brains, in other words, but of the massive blackout that the media cartel has long imposed on millions of Americans—despite the press's Constitutional obligation to keep every one of us informed. Yet people somehow know that something's wrong and, in startlingly high numbers, have recently begun to make it clear that they're unhappy with the giants' status quo.

As this book goes to press, such mass self-assertion is, miraculously, interfering with the cartel's plans to grow still larger, dumber, emptier and less competitive—an anti-democratic program long encouraged by the Bush Administration, whose FCC, under the "free-market" zealot Michael Powell, had tried to bring out about the Last Deregulation of our media. Amazingly—and yet predictably—the U.S. right and left joined forces to say no to any further media consolidation, thereby indicating a great national desire for more and smaller media owners, more diversity, more choice, more points of view: a media landscape less like Italy's, and more like what this nation's founders had in mind.

Whether next year's charts depict a media system even more distended than today's, or one that tends back toward democracy, will to a great extent depend on who wins, and who loses, in the sudden struggle raging now between the people and the Busheviks. We the people have the numbers, and the Constitution, on our side. The Busheviks have nothing but their money. Through broad circulation of these charts, and by proposing viable alternatives, we can help decide the outcome of this all-important fight.

AOL TIME WARNER

MAGAZINES

Time, Time for Kids, People, People en Espanol, Teen People, Who Weekly (Australian version of People), Sports Illustrated, Sports Illustrated for Kids, Entertainment Weekly, Southern Living, Sunset, Health, In Style, Fortune, Money, Business 2.0, Parenting, This Old House (also produces related TV series), Essence (49%), Travel & Leisure, Food & Wine, Departures, Golf, Ski, Skiing, Field & Stream, Yachting, Popular Science, DC Comics (publishes over 50 comics magazines, including Superman, Batman, Wonder Woman), E.C. Publications Inc. (publishes MAD Magazine), 19, 25 Beautiful Homes, Aeroplane, Amateur Gardening, Amateur Photographer, Angler's Mail, Bird Keeper, Cage & Aviary Birds, Cars & Car Conversions, Caravan, Chat, Classic Boat, Country Homes & Interiors, Country Life, Cycle Sport, Cycling Weekly, Decanter, essentials, Eventing, Family Circle, Farm Holiday Guides, Golf Monthly, The Guitar Magazine, Hair, Hi-Fi News, Homes & Gardens, Horse, Horse & Hound, Ideal Home, International Boat Industry, Land Rover World, Livingetc, Loaded, Marie Claire, MiniWorld, Mizz, Model Collector, Motor Boats Monthly, Motor Boat & Yachting, Motor Caravan Magazine, Mountain Bike RiderMuzik, NME, Now, 4x4, Park Home & Holiday Caravan, Practical Boat Owner, Practical Parenting, Prediction, Racecar Engineering, The Railway Magazine, Rugby World, Ships Monthly, Shoot Monthly, Shooting Times, Soaplife, Sporting Gun, Stamp Magazine, SuperBike, The Field, The Golf, TVTimes, TV & Satellite Week, Uncut, VolksWorld, Wallpaper*, Webuser, Wedding & Home, What Digital Camera, What's on TV, Woman, Woman & Home, Woman's Own, Woman's Weekly, Women & Golf, World Soccer, Yachting Monthly, Yachting World, Yachting & Boating World

BOOKS

AOL Time Warner Book Group (56 books on *NYT* best-seller lists in 2002), Warner Books, Inc., Time Warner AudioBooks, Little, Brown and Co.Time Warner Books U.K, Oxmoor House, Inc., Leisure Arts, Inc., Bulfinch Press, Warner Faith, Sunset Books/Sunset Publishing Corp., Book-of-the-Month Club (50% w/ Bertelsmann's Doubleday Books), Warner Publisher Services, Time Life Inc.

MUSIC

Warner Bros. Records Inc., Atlantic Recording Corp., Elektra Entertainment Group, Word Entertainment (Christian music company), London-Sire Records, WEA Inc., Ivy Hill Corp., Code Blue, Warner-Elektra-Atlantic Corp., Time Life Music, Rhino Entertainment Company, Columbia House (WMG 7.5%), Maverick Records, Lava Records (joint venture), Nonesuch, Reprise Records, CPP/Belwin Music, New Chappell Inc.

Subscription service licenses:
Echo Networks, MusicNet, OD2, Listen.com, FullAudio, Streamwaves.com, Pressplay

FILM

Warner Bros. Pictures, Warner Home Video Castle Rock, Village Roadshow Pictures (joint venture), Gaylord Entertainment (co-financing), Pandora Investments SARL, Morgan Creek Productions (distribution), Franchise Entertainment (distribution), Alcon Entertainment (distribution), Shangri-La Entertainment (distribution), New Line Cinema, Fine Line Features, Hanna-Barbera Entertainment Co.

AOL TIME WARNER

INTERNET/NEW MEDIA

AOL Music Channel, Winamp, Shoutcast (streaming audio and Internet music directory), Spinner Networks, Inc., MusicNet (owned by WMG, RealNetworks, Bertelsmann and EMI), AOL Call Alert, AOL by Phone, AOL Voicemail, AOL Instant Messenger, ICQ Ltd., MovieFone, MapQuest.com, Inc., Road Runner (high speed data service), Netscape Communications Corporation, Digital City, Inc., Quack.com, Inc., Tegic Communications Corp., Digital Marketing Services, Inc., EVoice, Inc., InfoInterActive Corp., AOL International (8.7 million members outside U.S.), AMSE France SAS, AOL Strategic Business Solutions, CompuServe Interactive Services France SNC, Netscape Communications India Private Ltd., Allpolitics.com, CNN.com, CNNMoney.com, NASCAR.com, PGA.com (operated by TBS), CartoonNetwork.com

BROADCAST AND CABLE

Turner Broadcasting System (TBS), TBS Superstation, TNT, Cartoon Network, Cartoon Network Japan, Turner Classic Movies, Turner South, Boomerang, CNN, CNN International, CNNfn, CNN en espanol, CNN+ (Spanish network), VIVA Media AG (Germany, Scandinavia, Eastern Europe), n-tv (German news network), CETV (China Entertainment Television), HBO (*The Sopranos*, *Sex and the City*, *Six Feet Under*), Cinemax, WB Television Network, Kids WB!, Court TV

Time Warner Cable (79% AOL TW, 21% Comcast), Time Warner Entertainment-Advance/Newhouse Partnership, Texas Cable Partners (50% Comcast, 50% TWE), Kansas City Cable Partners (50% Comcast, 50% TWE), Time Warner Telecom Inc. (44% AOL TW), Paragon Communications, TWI Cable, Inc., Erie Telecommunications Inc., Century Venture Corporation

NY1 News, News 9 Albany, R/News (Rochester, NY), Carolina News 14, News 8 Austin, News 24 Houston, Bay News 9 (Tampa, FL)

Production
Warner Bros.Television (*Smallville*, *Gilmore Girls*, *ER*, *Friends*, *The West Wing*, *The Drew Carey Show*, *George Lopez*, *3rd Watch*, *Without a Trace*), Castle Rock Entertainment, Telepictures Productions (*The Bachelor/Bachelorette*, *Extra*)

SPORTS

Atlanta Braves, Atlanta Hockey Club, Atlanta National League Baseball Club, Atlanta Hawks Basketball, Inc., Turner Arena Productions and Sales, Turner Sports, Inc., Philips Arena, Turner Field

MERCHANDIZING

Licenses rights to the names, likenesses, images, logos and other representations of characters and copyrighted material from film and TV series produced by Warner Bros., including: DC Comics superheroes, Hanna-Barbera characters, Classic films, Harry Potter

Credits: Project on Media Ownership,
Executive Director: Mark Crispin Miller, Director: Ted Magder,
Research Director: Aurora Wallace, with research assistance
by Melissa Aronczyk, Michael O'Neil and Adam Walker.

NEWS CORPORATION

TELEVISION

Broadcast, Cable and Satellite

FOX Channel, Fox Movie Channel, Fox News Channel (80 million U.S. cable and DBS households), Fox Sports International (85%), Fox Sports Australia (50%), FX Channel, Fox Regional Sports Networks (13 owned and operated), Regional Programming Partners (40%), Fox Pan American Sports (37.9%), Rogers Sports Net (20%), Speed Channel (100%), Sunshine Network (93.7%), Television Games Network, TV Guide Channel (43%), TV Guide Interactive, TV Sneak Prevue, Outdoor Life Network (100%), Nickelodeon U.K. (50% w/Viacom), History Channel U.K. (50%), Paramount U.K (25%), Australian News Channel (33.3%), Granada Sky Broadcasting (49.5%), MUTV (33.3%), National Geographic Channel (50%), National Geographic Channel (U.K.) (50%), Music Choice Europe (35.9), Attheraces (33.3%), Sky Network Television (30%), British Sky Broadcasting (36%) (11 wholly-owned television channels in digital, as well as DTH retailing of 82 digital channels owned by third parties), BiB (British Interactive Broadcasting), DirecTV (34%), Stream (50%), Balkan News Corporation (75%), Star TV (Asia), Channel V (87.5%), Phoenix Satellite Television, Star Plus (India), Star News, ESPN Star Sports (50%), Vijay Television (51%), Viva Cinema (50%), Zee Telefilms (3.9%), Space Shower Networks (10%), Sky PerfecTV! (8%), News Broadcasting Japan (80%), JSkySports (14.3%), Sky Movies Corporation (50%), Nihon Eiga Satellite Broadcasting (15%), Cine Canal (22.5%), Innova (30%), Sky Brasil (36%), Telecine (12.5%), Sky Italia (80%), FOXTEL (25%), Hathway Cable and Datacom (26%), Taiwan Cable Systems (20%), WAP TV, SiG (Sports Internet Group), KirchPayTV (24%), VCR+ programming guide

Stations

34 owned and operated stations, 9 duopolies including New York, Los Angeles, Chicago, and Dallas; 188 affiliated stations

Production

Twentieth Century Fox Television, Regency Television (50%), Greenblatt Jonollari (85%), XYZ Entertainment (50% Foxtel), Main Event Television (33%)

The Fox Television library contains *Batman*; *The Mary Tyler Moore Show*; *M*A*S*H*; *Hill Street Blues*; *Doogie Howser, M.D.*; *L.A. Law*; *The Wonder Years*; *Picket Fences*; *Room 222*; *Trapper John, M.D.*; *Daniel Boone;* and *The X-Files*; as well as such current hits as *The Simpsons*; *NYPD Blue*; *The Practice*; *King of the Hill*; *Buffy the Vampire Slayer*; *Judging Amy* (together with CBS Worldwide, Inc.); *Malcolm in the Middle*; *The Bernie Mac Show*; *24*; *and The Shield.*

MUSIC

Alberts, Asian Music Corporation, Best Boy, Compass Brothers, Echo, Embrace the Future, Festival Records, Fantasy, Flying Nun, Freskanova, Gut, Hollywood Records, Infectious Records, Lyric Street, Melodian Records, Mushroom U.K, Nettwerk, Palm Pictures, Perfecto, Picture This Records, PIAS, Rajon, Rapido, Rewind Music, Rosella Music, RYKO, Spin, Sprocket Music, Sputnik, Squint, Stax, Tommy Boy, Trifekta, TVT Records, V2, Vagrant, Vicious, Victory, ZTT

NEWS CORPORATION

BOOKS

HarperCollins, Harper Tempest, Access Press, Amistad Press, Avon, Bartholomew, Dolphin Bookclub, Ecco, Eos, Festival, Fourth Estate, Golden Press, Greenwillow Books, HarperAudio, HarperBusiness, Harper Design International, Harper Entertainment, HarperLargePrint, HarperResource, HarperSanFrancisco, HarperTorch, Julie Andrews Collection, Perennial, PerfectBound, Quill, Rayo, ReganBooks, Thorsons Publishers, Trophy, Unwin Hyman, William Collins & Sons, William Morrow, Zondervan (largest commercial Bible imprint)

NEWSPAPERS

New York Post, *Daily Telegraph*, *Fiji Times*, *Gold Coast Bulletin*, *Herald Sun*, *Independent Newspapers* (45.3%), Newsphotos, Newspix, *NT News*, *Post-Courier* (63%), Sunday *Herald Sun*, *Sunday Mail* (41.7%), *Sunday Tasmanian*, *Sunday Territorian*, *Sunday Times*, *Nai Lalakai*, *Shanti Dut*, *The Advertiser*, *The Australian*, *The Courier Mail* (41.7%), *The Mercury*, *The Sunday Telegraph*, *Weekly Times*, *News International*, *News of the World*, *The Sun*, *The Times*, *Times Educational Supplement*, *Times Higher Education Supplement*, *Times Literary Supplement*, TSL Education

MAGAZINES

Inside Out, *donna hay*, *Smart Source Magazine*, *In-Store*, *Nursery World*, *TV Guide* (38.5%), *SkyMall Magazine* (34%)

FILM

Fox Entertainment Group (80.6%), Twentieth Century Fox, Twentieth Century Fox Home Entertainment, Fox 2000 Pictures, Fox Searchlight, Fox Animation Studios, Fox Studios Australia, Premium Movie Partnership (20%), Fox Studios Baja, New Regency (20%), Fox Film Library (rights to more than 3,250 previously released films, including *The Sound of Music* and *Miracle on 34th Street*, and eight of the top 16 domestic box-office grossing films of all time), Drive-in Cinemas Limited (Kenya)(85%)

SPORTS

New York Knicks (40%), New York Rangers (40%), New York Liberty (40%), New England Seawolves, Hartford Wolfpack, Los Angeles Dodgers (100%), National Rugby League (50%)

OTHER

Hughes Electronics Corporation (34%), Staples Center (40%), L.A. Sports and Entertainment District (40%), HealthSouth Training Center (40%), Radio City Music Hall (40%), Madison Square Garden (40%), Hartford Civic Center (40%), Dodger Stadium (100%), Dodgertown, NDS (79%), National Advertising Partners (50%), Broadsystem, The Wireless Group (19%), Convoys Group, Sky Radio (71.5%), Radio 538 (42%), News Outdoor Group (75%), Newspoll (50%), Beijing PDN Xinren Information Technology (69.6%), UTV Software Communications (19.9%), Digiwave Infrastructure Services (50%), Yesky.com (20%)

VIVENDI UNIVERSAL

INTERNET

allocine.fr (movie ticketing), ad2-one.co.uk, downbeat.com, education.com, Emusic.com, flipside.com, globalmusic.com, ifrance.com, i(belgique), i(espana), i(france), i(italia), i(suisse), i(quebec), itelevision.fr, iwin.com, Movielink.com (20% w/MGM, Paramount, Sony and WB), mp3.com, mp4.com, rollingstone.com, totalaxess.com, trafficmarketplace.com, uproar.com, virtualvegas.com, VUnet (50 million registered users worldwide), yourmobile.com, Zidane.fr (soccer Web site)

BROADCAST, CABLE, AND SATELLITE

Universal Studios Television (92%), Universal Network Television (*Law and Order*, *Jerry Springer*, *Blind Date*), USA Network (*Monk*, *Dead Zone*, *Walker*, *Texas Ranger*), USA Network Brazil, USA Network Latin America, Reveille, SCI-FI Channel, SCI-FI U.K, Trio, Newsworld International, Sundance Channel (49% w/Viacom and Robert Redford), 13eme Rue (France), Calle 13 (Spain), Studios Universal Italy, Studio Expand (52%, largest TV producer in France), Studio Canal Espana (51% w/Sogepaq), 13th Street Germany, Working Title Television, Legende Enterprises (49%), Canal+ (40 theme channels in Europe), Canal+ Pay TV, Canal Club home shopping channel, CanalNumedia, Canal+ Horizons, Canal+ Horizons Cote D`ivoire, Canal+ Horizons Senegal, Canal Jimmy, Canal Satellite (67%), CanalSat Jeux, CanalSatellite digital Spain, CanalSatellite Horizons, Canalsatellite Antilles, Canalsatellite Reunion, Canalsatellite Caledonie, Cinecinemas, Multitv Afrique, NC Numericable, Planete, PlayJam games, PMU Direct (home betting for horse races), SFR La Carte (recharges cellphone accounts), Sport+ (60%), SogeCable (21.6% w/Prisa), Sogepaq (45%)

THEME PARKS AND RESORTS

Universal Studios Hollywood, City Walk in Universal City, Universal Studios Florida, Universal Islands of Adventure, Portofino Bay Hotel, Hard Rock Hotel, Royal Pacific Resort, Citywalk Osaka, Wet'n'Wild, Universal Studios Port Aventura, Costa Caribe, Hotel Port Aventura, Hotel El Paso

RETAIL AND GAMES

Spencer Gifts, Sega Gameworks, GameCube, Black Label Games, Coktel, Andiboo, Knowledge Adventure, Blizzard Entertainment (Hulk, warcraft, starcraft, Diablo II), Sierra Entertainment, Papyrus Racing Games, Impression Games

PUBLISHING

Partner Publishing Group, Atica (Brazil, 50%), Scipione (Brazil, 50%)

VIVENDI UNIVERSAL

MUSIC LABELS

A&M Records, American Records, Attica, Decca, Def Jam Records, Def Jam South, Def Soul, Deutsche Grammophon, ECM, Geffen, Interscope Records, island DefJam, Koch Universal, Lost Highway Records, MCA, MCA Nashville, Mercury Nashville, Motor Urban Defjam, Motown Records, Murder, Inc., Musik Fur Dich, Phillips, Polydor, Polygram, Roc-a-Fella Records, Roadrunner Records, Universal Classics, Universal Music Latino, Universal South, Verve

MUSIC PRODUCTION

Universal Mastering Studios

MUSIC PUBLISHING

Universal Music Publishing Group (1 million copyrights), Universal Music Chronicles (world's largest catalogue), Hip-O-Records, UTV Records (music used in advertising), Universal Music Enterprises (music for film and tv)

MUSIC CLUBS

Bitannia U.K, Dial in France

FILM

Universal Pictures (*Bruce Almighty*, *2Fast 2Furious*, *Cat in the Hat*), Focus Features (*Far From Heaven*, *Possession*), Hypnotic, Jersey Films (*Erin Brockovich*, *Man on the Moon*, *Out of Sight*), Universal Home Entertainment (*Shrek*, best-selling DVD of all time), Universal Studios International Video, Universal Cartoon Studios, Canal+ and StudioCanal (finance 80% of French films), Universal Cinemas International (50% w/Paramount), Warner Sogefilms, Sogecinema film production

TELECOM

Cogetel Groupe (70%), SFR (56%), Maroc Telecom (35%), Mauritel (54%), Kencell—Kenya mobile service (60%), Monaco Telecom (55%), Xfera—Spanish mobile service (26%), Universal Music Mobile

NONMEDIA

Veolia Water (20%), Sanepar, CGEA Brasil, Compan~aded Aguas de Puerto Rico, Generale des Eaux Guadeloupe, Martiniquaise Des Eaux, Guyanaise Des Eaux, Southern Water Capital (19.9%), Southern Water in U.K., Onyx waste management, Dalkia-cogeneration and heating and cooling, Generale des Eaux, Connex (bus, light rail, rail transport), Viventures (30%, venture capital fund)

WALT DISNEY COMPANY

BROADCAST AND CABLE

ABC Family, A&E Television Networks (37.5% w/Hearst, owns History Channel, Biography Channel, History International), Disney Channel, E! Entertainment Television and Style Channel (39.6%), ESPN (80%), ESPN2, ESPN Classic Europe (70%, France and Italy), Sports-i ESPN in Japan (19.99%), Fox Kids Europe (76%), Fox Kids Channel Latin America, Lifetime Channel (50%), NetStar (29.92% - The Sports Network, Le Reseau des Sports, ESPN Classic Canada, Discovery Canada and WTSN) SOAPnet, Toon Disney

10 stations, (226 local affiliates) including WABC-TV (New York, NY), KABC-TV (Los Angeles, CA), WLS-TV (Chicago, IL), WPVI-TV (Philadelphia, PA), KGO-TV (San Francisco, CA), KTRK-TV (Houston, TX), WTVD-TV (Raleigh-Durham, NC), KFSN-TV (Fresno, CA), WJRT-TV (Flint, MI), WTVG-TV (Toledo, OH)

TELEVISION PRODUCTION

Buena Vista Television, Saban, Touchstone Television, Walt Disney Television

INTERNET

ABC.com, ABCAuctions.com, ABCNews.com, Disney.com, DisneyAuctions.com, Eonline.com, ESPN.com, ESPNAuctions.com FamilyFun.com, Lifetime.com, Movies.com

PARKS AND RESORTS AND LIFESTYLE

560 retail disney stores (429 domestic, 131 international)

Disneyworld, Disneyland, Disneyland Tokyo, Disneyland Paris, Disney Cruiselines, ESPN Zone (8 Locations)

Disneyland Hotel, Paradise Pier Hotel, Grand Californian Hotel, Old Key West Resort, BoardWalk Resort, Wilderness Lodge, Beach Club, Celebration Hotel, resort in Vero Beach, Florida, and a resort on Hilton Head Island, South Carolina

Downtown Disney entertainment retail complex, Celebration, Florida, a town of 6,000 population

RADIO

62 stations (4,600 affiliates), including 6 in Minneapolis-St. Paul, 5 in Dallas-Ft. Worth, 4 in Los Angeles and Chicago, 3 each in San Francisco, Washington, Detroit, and Atlanta, and 2 in New York

PUBLISHING

Discover, Disney Adventures, Disney Publishing Worldwide, *ESPN: The Magazine*, *Family Fun*, Hyperion, Lifetime Books, *Lifetime Magazine*, *US Weekly* (50%)

MUSIC

Buena Vista Music Group, Hollywood Records, Lyric Street Records, Walt Disney Records

FILM

Buena Vista Home Entertainment, Buena Vista International, Dimension Films, Hollywood Pictures, Miramax, Touchstone Pictures, Walt Disney Pictures (940 titles in total)

THEATER

Buena Vista Theatrical Group, *Aida*, *Beauty and the Beast*, *The Hunchback of Notre Dame*, *The Lion King*, New Amsterdam Theater on Broadway, Disney On Ice

VIACOM

OUTDOOR ADVERTISING

Viacom Outdoor (outdoor advertising in 90 markets in North America, all 50 of the largest metropolitan markets in US, exclusive rights to London Underground, public transit advertising in Ireland, and displays in Netherlands, France, Italy, Spain, Finland, and Puerto Rico), BET Event Productions

BROADCAST AND CABLE

BET, BET Jazz, CBS, CMT, Comedy Central, CTN, FLIX, GAME ONE (50% w/Atari) GULF DTH LDC (Satellite direct to home in the Middle East), KinderNet (Netherlands), The Movie Channel, TMC xtra, MTV, (377.3 million households in 166 territories), MTV2, Nickelodeon (273 million subscribers), Nickelodeon Asia, Nick at Nite, Noggin, The N, Showtime, Sundance Channel (50% w/Robert Redford and Universal Studios), TNN (will be renamed Spike TV June 16, 2003), TV Land, UPN, VH1

39 Television Stations in 15 of the top 20 markets, including two each in Los Angeles, Philadelphia, San Francisco, Boston, Dallas, Detroit, Miami, and Pittsburgh

PRODUCTION

Big Ticket Television, CBS News (*60 Minutes*, *The Early Show*, *Face the Nation*, *48 Hours Investigates*), CBS Radio News (supplies 500 radio stations with newscasts)CBS News Productions (original nonfiction programming for cable, video, CD-ROM, audio books, in flight, schools and libraries), CBS Sports (NFL Regular Season, NCAA, PGA, U.S. Open Tennis), CBS Entertainment (*CSI*, *Everybody Loves Raymond*, *Judging Amy*, *Survivor*, *Grammy Awards*, *Country Music Association Awards*, *Late Show with David Letterman*, *Young and the Restless*), King World, Paramount Television, Spelling Television, Viacom Productions

PUBLISHING

Simon & Schuster (85 titles on *NYT* bestseller list in 2002), Simon & Schuster audio, Pimsleur (language instruction), Pocket Books, Scribner, The Free Press, *Nickelodeon Magazine*, BET Books, Arabesque

MUSIC

Famous Music (copyrights to more than 125,000 songs), Addax Music Co. Inc. (TV theme songs), Beverlyfax Music

INTERNET

bet.com, cbs.com, cbsbews.com, MarketWatch.com, Inc. (33% owned), mtv.com, SportsLine.com, Inc. (39.9% owned), vh1.com

THEME PARKS

Carowinds (Charlotte, NC), Paramounts Great America (Santa Clara, CA), King's Dominion (Richmond, VA), King's Island (Cincinnati, OH), Canada's Wonderland (Toronto, Canada), Star Trek: The Experience (Las Vegas Hilton), Terra Mitica (Valencia, Spain), Bonfante Gardens (Gilroy, CA -mgnt only), Nickelodeon Studios at Universal Studios Florida

RADIO

Infinity Radio (183 Radio Stations in 41 markets, including 7 stations each in Los Angeles, Chicago, San Francisco, and Baltimore, and 6 stations each in New York, Dallas, Tampa, Portland, and 5 each in Philadelphia, Washington, Boston, and Seattle) Westwood One, Inc. (15%)

FILM AND VIDEO

Blockbuster Video (81% - 8,500 stores throughout the Americas, Europe, Asia and Australia), Famous Players Theaters (822 screens in 97 theaters in Canada), Grauman's Theaters (50%), Mann Theaters (148 screens in 24 theaters - 50%), MTV Films, National Amusements Inc. (1,400 movie screens in U.S., U.K., and South America), Nickelodeon Movies, Paramount Pictures (2,500 titles in library), Paramount Classics, Paramount Home Entertainment, Quetzal (34%), Republic Pictures, United Cinemas International (50% w/Universal Studios- 1,120 screens in 121 theaters around the world), United International Pictures (33%), WF Cinema Holding (50%)

THIS MODERN WORLD

by TOM TOMORROW

CHAPTER 5

Media Democracy in Action

BY PETER PHILLIPS, DAVEYD, MARC SAPIR, AND
THE PROJECT CENSORED WRITING TEAM: Kagiso Molefhe,
Michael Kaufman, Matt Hamburg, Donald Yoon, and Josh Sisco

Media Democracy in Action is a report on the everyday activism of grassroots
media groups all across the nation. Media from the bottom up is a sharp contrast to the top-down corporate media being offered in the mainsteam. Expanding and growing, the media democracy movement is beginning to meet
the needs for alternative/independent news and information. Included in this
chapter are sections on: hip-hop and political action, Pacifica News, *Flashpoints, Democracy Now!*, Free Speech TV (FSTV), *North Bay Progressive*, independent media in the Middle East, American Coalition for Media
Education (ACME), and Retro Poll.

Project Censored Interviews DaveyD

DaveyD is a hip-hop historian, journalist deejay, and community activist. He
writes for numerous publications and magazines and puts out a popular online newsletter call *The FNV*, which has a subscriber base of 100,000 people. He is the host of *Hard Knock Radio* and *Friday Night Vibe* on Pacifica
Station KPFA in the San Francisco Bay Area.

PC: How do you define hip-hop culture?

DAVEYD: There are a couple of ways to answer this question. First, the term
"hip-hop" means many things for many people. In fact, back in the early days

of the 1970s, when this cultural phenomenon came to be, we never even called it hip-hop. It was a term that came about when a popular deejay named DJ Lovebug Starski incorporated scatting in his raps. Hence he would say something like, "You hip hop hippity-hip hop ya don't stop." Hip-hop pioneer Afrika Bambaataa heard Lovebug do this and decided to use the phrase to describe this emerging dance/music scene that had captivated most of the young people in the Bronx.

The other thing to keep in mind is that the term hip-hop is often used interchangeably with the term rap, which unfortunately doesn't speak to all that hip-hop encompasses. To put it simply, hip-hop is a set of cultural expressions that encompasses b-boying (break dancing), deejaying, writing, graffiti, and emceeing (rap). Hip-hop is the larger culture and lifestyle, while rap is just one aspect that happens to be commodified to the point that it has become the face of hip-hop. It's important to keep this in mind, especially if we see ourselves as media-savvy progressives.

I always find it a bit ironic when I'm around people who will suggest that we not take what is written and depicted in the media at face value because it is often done so to further a particular political or social agenda. Yet those same people will draw their opinions and assessments about something like hip-hop based upon what they have seen, read, and heard in those very same media they asked us to be wary of. So, in short, hip-hop is much more than the materialistic, misogynistic images that are routinely marketed and disseminated on the airwaves and throughout our community. Even more important is the fact that there are many within hip-hop who bemoan the fact that this vibrant culture, which is embraced in damn near every country on the planet, has been reduced to this one sliver and conversation.

We, who are reading a book like this annual text by Project Censored, can sometimes feel like we are spitting in the wind—or that we are all alone because of the overwhelming onslaught of corporate propaganda, slick public relations spins, and outright lies regarding issues concerning the environment, our government's foreign policy, or human rights. But there are many within hip-hop who feel just as frustrated when they flip on the TV and see a video being aired on MTV or BET during primetime hours with a scantily clad woman mindlessly gyrating to a gangsta rap tune from the latest flavor of the month rap star. In the words of rap star Chuck D of Public Enemy's, "Don't Believe the Hype," or more concretely, "don't selectively not believe the hype." If the Bill O'Reillys and Fox News networks of the world are distorting news stories about issues important to the progressive community, then they are definitely distorting stories and images about hip-hop music and culture.

With all that being said, let's build upon the initial definition of this thing we call hip-hop. It's important to note that hip-hop did not show up in a vacuum. Pioneers like Kingston, Jamaican-born deejay Kool Herc, Afrika Bambaataa, and Grandmaster Flash did not wake up one day, decide to go to a library and develop a blueprint for these activities. They personified and became a catalyst to the reaction an entire generation of disenfranchised, marginalized, oppressed Black and Latino youth had to certain social, economic, and political conditions that were impacting them in the early 1970s.

Those early expressions that we find within hip-hop, for the most part, were a continuation of the cultural aesthetics from past generations; in particular, those expressions that we can find within the African-American and various Latino communities that allowed one to cope while enduring troubled times.

While I'm aware that there are somewhat unique ways in which hip-hop expressions manifested themselves in New York during the early 1970s, if you look at what was going on throughout the country at the same time, you will find similar parallel expressions. For example, when I was in the Bronx running with a hip-hop crew, making pause button cassette tapes and trying to get known at local community centers for my emcee skills, 3,000 miles away in Oakland, California, where I live now, there were hundreds of garage bands. Now, on the surface someone would say that the garage bands in the Bay Area were different than the early hip-hop crews in New York. I say only to a certain degree. While their specific activities were different, what inspired folks to express themselves in the manner that they did was pretty much the same. Garage bands in the Bay Area were reacting to oppressive social, economic, and political conditions in the Bay Area and the formation of early hip-hop crews in the Bronx were reacting to oppressive conditions.

The city of New York, at the time I was coming up, had turned its back on Black youth. They were suppressing gang activity. They fired 15,000 schoolteachers to avoid a fiscal crisis, radio was shoving disco down our throats, etc. In Oakland, the same thing was happening. Both groups found themselves on the outs and being ignored. This left the doors wide open for the emergence of coping expressions that were part of a larger dance and music scene. In New York, we called it hip-hop. In California, it was the funk scene. In Washington, DC, we called it go-go. In Chicago, we called it house, etc. All these expressions were built upon expressions of the past generations, like doo-wop in the 1950s, or the be-bop scene in the 1940s, or the Lindy Hop scene in the 1930s. This means that, as we look at hip-hop carefully, the question that should arise is not, "When did hip-hop culture emerge?" but instead, "Where was hip-hop expression in each generation or geographical part of the country?"

PC: Why should Project Censored cover hip-hop when there are so many other pressing issues to cover?

DAVEYD: There are a couple of ways to answer this question. First, we have to take into account that over the years Project Censored has established itself as a watchdog group of sorts and a vanguard over mass media. It has done an excellent job alerting the public about some of the huge stories that have been covered up or omitted by the mainstream press. Project Censored has also done an excellent job of pointing out how there seems to be a systematic attempt by many who are in power to manipulate and distort information disseminated via popular means.

It's been my understanding that usually when such things happen, folks start to create alternative means to communicate. Hence, alternative weeklies have been established and the Internet has become increasingly popular, as has community radio. As those media become more popular, you start to notice increasing attempts to either corrupt, discredit, and marginalize or outright take over these alternative means of communication. For example, over the years we have seen a diluting of alternative weekly newspapers. There are many progressives who see them as no longer being as hard-hitting or viable alternatives to the mainstream papers that they initially sought to replace.

While the Internet has grown by leaps and bounds, we have also found that more and more big companies are getting into the act, and buying up and controlling important infrastructure that holds the Internet together. Suddenly, you find that popular sites like Yahoo or Hotmail will shut down your listserv and e-mail without warning based upon what they arbitrarily consider inappropriate content. Many ISPs will limit the number of e-mails you can send out unless you're on a special white list and even then they will limit you. In many neighborhoods throughout the country, DSL and other high-speed connections are either not available or overpriced. So the point that I'm making is that those who wish to control the flow of information have, and continue to find ways, to stifle the full potential of these alternative means and prevent one from seriously communicating to the masses.

Now, secondly, this brings us to hip-hop and why it's important to be covered by Project Censored. A lot of people often forget that, in addition to broadcast and print media, there are cultural media, many of which have proven to have as much if not more impact than the traditional media and forms of communication that Project Censored has monitored. We often forget that songs, dance, spoken word, and various forms of art and cultural expression are media. What makes these cultural and artistic media so important, and have potentially more impact, is the fact that they oftentimes allow for greater participation and interaction by those who embrace them, as opposed to the traditional media that we have been taught to socialize around.

So, now, if we understand that TV, radio, and newspapers have been co-opted, so much that they now serve as middle men or filters that limit and distort the communication that we should ideally have with one another, we should not be surprised when similar attempts are made to shut down, discredit, distort, or take over cultural expressions and media. It's all about who controls the flow of information. And he who controls the flow of information sets the societal tone and agenda.

PC: What do you mean when you say shutting down cultural media?

DAVEYD: Historically, one of the most glaring examples of cultural media shut-downs was the banning of the drum used by slaves in Louisiana's Congo Square and other places in the 1700s. The slave masters sensed that the African dances the slaves were doing had deeper meaning. In fact, they did: the slaves were parodying and making fun of the stiff aristocratic mannerisms and movements of whites. In Brazil, the dances were used to mask the fighting techniques (we now call it *capoeira*), which the slaves eventually used when they revolted and liberated themselves. We should also note that many of the movements used in *capoeira* are similar to the ones used by today's b-boys, or break dancers, although the early break dancers weren't aware or even trying to pattern their movements after this Brazilian slave dance/fighting style.

As for the drum, it set the tone and provided the rhythm, and continued to be a major source of communication. Fearing both a slave revolt and the African slaves becoming sinful, white slave owners shut down the medium and banned the use of the drum. The name of the game back during slavery was the same as it is today: control the flow of information. He who controls the flow controls the game.

Now, let's fast forward to the 1970s, when these African-based cultural expressions manifested themselves in what we now call hip-hop. It was around this time that radio was undergoing change. There was a move afoot to start toning down and silencing what was known as the personality jock. For those who don't understand how the personality jock presented himself, think back to Spike Lee's movie, *Do The Right Thing*, in which he depicted a deejay, named Mister Señor Love Daddy, on a fictional neighborhood radio station. The colorful mannerisms and chatterbox style of Love Daddy exemplified the pioneering style that was heralded by Black radio deejays in years past. These personality jocks went on to influence their white counterparts like Alan Freed and, later, Wolfman Jack.

These radio jocks were more than just announcers. They were historians and community bulletin boards, who not only provided cultural and entertaining information, but would often rhyme on the mic while introducing songs. Sadly, many people overlook the fact that these Black radio jocks were the precursors to today's rap stars. They even influenced the toasting style of Jamaican deejays, who would hear the rhyming chatterbox styles of jocks like Jocko Henderson, whose radio show, *Ace of Rockets*, could be heard off the coast of Florida. This Jamaican style was later brought to New York City and inspired today's rappers.

So important was the Black radio deejay that on August 11, 1967, Dr. Martin Luther King Jr. gave a speech to The National Association of Television and Radio Announcers, in which he spoke at length about how radio was the primary means of communication for Black people and how significant a role the Black radio personality jock was in the community. He talked about landmark figures like Daddy O, Magnificent Montague, and others who used radio as a powerful tool to enhance their communication to the community and further the civil rights struggle and other liberation movements. In fact, King's Atlanta SCLC (Southern Christian Leadership Coalition) headquarters sat right above the nation's first Black-owned radio station WERD. Here, King would frequently hook up with legendary radio personality Jack the Rapper and communicate where folks should assemble for the next march, what to expect, how to execute the plan of action, etc.

PC: How does all this relate to hip-hop?

DAVEYD: Whenever we look at cultural expression, we should ideally be able to establish some sort of historical context. I mention all this about Black radio because as the personality jocks were being silenced and the music was being compromised and diluted, you had the systematic shut down of the Black power movement. It was in this vacuum that the social, economic, and political conditions of that time period gave birth to hip-hop.

In the 1970s, many Black radio stations began to adapt a mode of operation, which was accompanied by a slogan of "More music, less talk" in order to appeal to white advertisers. They even stopped calling themselves Black and adapted the term "Urban Contemporary" to make themselves sound more diverse and mainstream. Even more disturbing was the fact that many of these deejays were being restricted from playing the music they liked, as it was now being dictated to them by the program directors of these radio stations. Nelson George chronicles a lot of this information in the book *Death of Rhythm and Blues.*

Sadly, as much of the inspirational message/protest music of the 1970s, which had inspired the civil rights and Black power movements and was personified by artists like Curtis Mayfield, Sly Stone, James Brown, Edwin Starr, and others, was being phased out on these Black radio stations, it was replaced with formulaic disco music. Interestingly, a lot of the disco music that was starting to be played on the Black radio stations in New York City was done by white rock artists like Mick Jagger, Rod Stewart, and others. Nelson George talks about how popular Black stations like WBLS would have huge advertising posters of a white woman with the station's call letters and the slogan "World's Best Looking Sound."

This is significant because, as I mentioned before, prior to the 1970s, radio was the primary means of communication within the Black community. The personality jocks reflected the cultural mannerisms, language, and modes of communication that were completely relatable to the larger community, thus making radio even more powerful. I don't believe it was coincidence that, as all these mediums were being compromised, we suddenly found our community in the crosshairs of an overzealous FBI, which was on a mission to derail the Black power movement and many of the youth organizations that stirred it.

During this time there were a lot of leaders, in particular Black Panthers, SNCC members,and other militants who got killed or sent to jail for long periods of time for what many believed to be trumped-up charges. This was accomplished under a program called COINTELPRO [an acronym for counterintelligence program] that was started by FBI director J. Edgar Hoover.

One of the main goals, which was spelled out in the FBI's internal documents from 1968, was goal number five which was to prevent the long-range growth of Black militant organizations especially among youth. Specific tactics to prevent these young people from converting other young people need to be developed. Former Congresswoman Cynthia McKinney recently pointed out that in 2003, based upon all that has happened in the past, if you look at what has been happening with various sectors of hip-hop, it appears that goal number five from the FBI's 1968 memo is still being carried out. In short, there seems to be an all out effort to destabilize today's youth movement and distort and control aspects of hip-hop through the use of traditional media.

PC: So what are some of the biggest obstacles facing the hip-hop community?

DAVEYD: There are myriad challenges facing the hip-hop community. Ranging from internal beefs to generational divide to the media selectively focusing on one aspect of hip-hop and making it seem like it's the whole thing. Additionally there is the co-opting and corporatization of the culture and ongoing harassment by law enforcement including the DEA and FBI. Several police municipalities have formed task forces that are investigating artists and labels. There have even been attempts to connect hip-hop to terrorism and the Beltway snipers. In many respects the problems hip-hop faces mirror the problems that we face as Black folks, communities of color and young people in America. We help set trends, make lots of businesses lots of money, and we're also the convenient scapegoats for many of societies ills.

In order to answer this question, there are a few points people need to keep in mind. First, hip-hop always reflects the values, sentiments, and mindset of the people and communities who embrace it. Second, a tool is only as good as the people who use it. Third, within hip-hop, there are a multitude of conversations taking place.

Let's deal with the first two points. Mos Def who is a well-respected "conscious" artist starts off his landmark album *Black on Both Sides* by answering the question: "Where is hip-hop going?" He states that hip-hop is going where the people are going. If the people are smoked out, hip-hop will be smoked out. If the people are uplifted, hip-hop will be uplifted.

Today within hip-hop, we have an interesting dichotomy. We have a tremendous amount of activism with tons of folks and hip-hop organizations doing some incredible things. On the other hand we have people who seemingly everyday are running afoul of the law, getting investigated by the federal government, getting arrested, shot or killed.

It's puzzling how in hip-hop we can have two or three hip-hop political action committees, including one set up by music mogul Russell Simmons, another one spearheaded by Ras Baraka, deputy mayor of Newark New Jersey, and one set up by Afeni Shakur, who is the mother to the late Tupac.

We have a couple of hip-hop think tanks, the most prominent being the Urban Think Tank, which is headed by long time hip-hop fixture Yvonne Bynoe. They put out a quarterly publication called *Doula*. They're about to publish a book of essays and white papers addressing all sorts of issues impacting the hip-hop community and they regularly hold workshops to train people to do political organizing.

The other hip-hop think tanks are the Hip-Hop Archives, which is housed on Harvard's Campus, and another one that is supposed to be starting up on Columbia's campus under the leadership of Manning Marable.

As we speak there are several hip-hop museums and cultural centers being built, have been built or are in the planning stages in several cities around the world including Seattle; Cleveland; Oakland; Mount Vernon, New York; Harlem, New York; and [a city in] Germany.

We have political organizations like Hip-Hop Congress, which is on several college campuses throughout the country and have just held their third national convention in Los Angeles. We even have a newly formed hip-hop Republican chapter that just set up on the campus of Howard University.

We have hip-hop organizations that have been knee-deep in the fight to stop the prison industrial complex. We have hip-hop organizations that have been on the front line fighting AIDS. Hip-hop played a major role in sparking gang truces. We have lots of people who are deeply involved in the fight to improve education and they have been developing hip-hop–oriented curriculum that is working. We had a lot of hip-hoppers, who organized, developed songs, and came out in full force against the war in Iraq. We have all these great and positive things going on. This is what Project Censored is doing. This is what the hip-hop community is struggling with as well. We are trying to expose those other conversations, so folks will know there is more to us than violence, misogyny, and mayhem.

I often remind progressives and activists that over the years corporate media, along with the help of folks pushing a conservative agenda, have successfully mounted a campaign that has resulted in the discrediting of their community. In many circles, the progressive community is depicted as a body of out-of-touch '60s leftovers, who wear Birkenstocks, eat granola, and have no real sense of reality. Those of us who see ourselves as progressive know that this the furthest thing from the truth. Sure, there are some folks who can fall into some of those categories. But being progressive is a lot more than wearing Birkenstocks and eating granola.

Within hip-hop, a similar thing has happened. We have been depicted as violent criminals who have no political savvy or understanding. That is also a far cry from the truth. With that in mind, it's up to us to take steps to learn about communities outside our own, to bridge the gap. If we remember how the corporate media is falsely depicting progressives, then it is pretty likely that they are falsely potraying other communities including hip-hop. It's up to all of us to know and do better.

Now within the hip-hop community there has been a lot of activism around the issues of media and media reform. Artist like Chuck D of Public Enemy has been at the forefront, both in terms of writing about it as well as speaking before Congress and the FCC on numerous occasions. He, like others, has recognized that the ongoing unbalanced presentation of images and information is having dire effects within the hip-hop and larger African-American community.

Chuck decided to spearhead a campaign of encouraging artists to create their own media. He uses the Internet and digital technology as the tool. His <rapstation.com> Web site, where artists can upload and distribute their music as well as design their own album covers, has been a huge success. In fact, it's been so effective that major media conglomerates like Clear Channel have resurrected similar models within their own online ventures.

Chuck recently released a video/documentary called *Digitize or Die,* in which he is shown dealing with media giants and explaining how we should be using technology to our advantage.

Another thing about Chuck D we should mention is that he was also among the first major recording artists to record and distribute his albums via the Net, thus showing folks that they can bypass corporate media middlemen. Some groups like Hieroglyphics out of Oakland have generated a million dollars worth of album sales online, while other popular acts like the Living Legends Crew have been able to tour the world two or three times via their online ventures.

Another artist, Paris, decided that putting out records that received little if any airtime was not enough, so he launched an incredible Web site called <guerillafunk.com>, which features all his political musings. He also teamed up with a news agency called the Guerilla News Network and produced an incredible film called *The Aftermath: Unanswered Questions About 9/11.* Everytime the film has been shown, it's been standing room only.

On an editorial tip, dozens of hip-hop artists have set up well-heeled Web sites that have effectively replaced newspapers and many other outlets as primary sources for political and entertainment information. One prominent site, <blackelectorate.com>, is run and conceived by Cedric Muhammed, who is the former general manger for the popular multiplatinum group Wu-Tang Clan. His day-to-day articles and insightful political analysis have been so much on point that many elected officials around the country actually purchase his services. He's launched an online political university and has become frequent commentator on radio and TV stations around the country. That's not bad for a hip-hopper who is under 30.

<Popandpolitics.com> is another landmark site run by author and former CNN/ABC news commentator Ferai Chideya, who is also well established and known throughout the hip-hop community.

Sites like <sohh.com>, <allhiphop.com>, <hiphopactivist.com>, <okay player.com>, <playahata.com>, <eurweb.com>, <daveyd.com>, and <guerilla

funk.com> are online destinations that easily reach more then 5 million visitors a month. These are places I would highly encourage the progressive community to check out.

I would also encourage people to applaud the efforts that were launched by Bay Area based hip-hop organizations like the Mindz Eye Collective, Lets Get Free, and the Touth Media Council, which lead a two-year campaign against Clear Channel's number one radio station KMEL to hold them accountable. The campaign included taping and monitoring the radio station, issuing a report that went on record with the FCC, and setting up a series of meetings with the station in which they issued three demands including more community access, more airplay for local artists, and more airtime for the station to address social justice issues being championed by many within the hip-hop community. On June 2, KMEL bowed and agreed to let the consortium of organizations do a live broadcast from the BlackBox community center in downtown Oakland to address the issues of violence. The event was well received and had standing room only.

It was a testament to the strength and power of the hip-hop community that other radio shows that have made noise and been seen as beacons in this ever consolidating media landscape include Dominque Diprima's show *Street Science*, which is heard every Sunday on KKBT in L.A., and *Hard Knock Radio,* which is heard daily on KPFA 94.1 here in the Bay Area, and *Radio X* up in Seattle.

Another hip-hop–inspired campaign that has been picking up steam by demanding media reform is the Turn Off the Radio campaign, which was started by long time community activist and radio vet Bob Law. He's teamed up with hip-hop pioneers like Afrika Bambaataa, Chuck D, dead prez, and Daddy O of the group Stetsasonic to call into account the harmful impact commercial radio in New York, along with Viacom's popular video shows on BET and MTV, is having on the Black community. Law has been relentless in speaking out and bringing the community up to speed on what is taking place in the media. This past January he held a tribunal that included more than 1,000 people as well as New York City council members who spoke for more than six hours about this important issue. The mainstream media has tried to ignore the Turn Off The Radio campaign, but it's been picking up steam and has been spreading to other cities including Detroit and Kansas City.

Lastly, we would be remiss if we did not mention the ongoing uncompromising efforts of hip-hop activist Najee Ali, who was recently appointed to be West Coast chair of Al Sharpton's presidential campaign. Najee has an organization called Project Islamic Hope that has gone head-to-head with everyone from Clear Channel to Russell Simmons to Snoop Dogg about misogynist, negative imagery. Ali, a former gangbanger who served time in prison, has been a key player in helping forge peace and understanding amongst L.A.'s gangs.

His most recent campaign helped in forcing the offensive hip-hop TV show *Platinum*, which depicted hip-hoppers as gangs and thugs, to be taken off the air. Ali had written a series of articles calling for a boycott of the show. His next move was to rally the troops to the streets and start targeting advertisers. He even had a public verbal tangle with Russell Simmons over this show. Ali eventually won out.

Simmons recently teamed up with grassroots activists in New York to combat the Rockefeller Drug Laws as it celebrated its thirtieth anniversary. They had a countdown to fairness in which they demanded the laws be repealed or the hip-hop community would march on City Hall. When this didn't happen 50,000 people showed up along with many of hip-hop's biggest stars—50 cent, Jay-Z, Fat Joe, Sean "P-Diddy" Combs, dead prez, Rosa Clemente, and many others—to speak out against the drug laws. Russell got a two-hour private meeting with the governor of New York, George Pataki.

Here in the Bay Area, a two-year campaign spearheaded by hip-hop groups like Books Not Bars, Lets Get Free, Ella Baker Center, Youth Force, and others curtailed the building of a juvenile super prison in Dublin. These groups effectively negotiated with Alameda County supervisors, did demonstrations, and got arrested for civil disobedience. In the end, they got the county to yield. It was a major victory and again it underscored the power of hip-hop.

There is also a league of hip-hop voters being formed by a number of hip-hop activists, Active Elements Foundation, who recently published a book called *Future 500* <future500.org>, which spotlights all the prominent youth and hip-hop organizations in the country. The purpose of this organization is the inform the hip-hop community about politics.

We had a lot of hip-hoppers who have organized, put out songs, and come out in full force against the war in Iraq. In fact, it was the hip-hop community that was among the first to put on any sort of rally protesting the war on terrorism. Groups like Lets Get Free and Mindz Eye Collective along with artists like Michael Franti and the late June Jordan held a well-attended rally at Snow Park in Oakland the day after 9/11 to bring attention to racially motivated attacks upon Muslims.

Congresswoman Barbara Lee gave her first interview explaining her historic "No" vote against Bush's war on a hip-hop show, *Street Knowledge*.

Since 9/11, there have been close to 40 songs released by hip-hop artists addressing the war in Iraq and the War on Terrorism. Many of these songs have been done by popular artists like Nas, Public Enemy, Black Eyed Peas, Black-alicious, Dilated Peoples, The Coup, dead prez, Beastie Boys, and Michael Franti and Spearhead, to name a few. Sadly, many of these songs have not been played on the radio or MTV and BET with any sort of consistency.

There's even a posse cut that features many of the country's so-called gangsta rappers who are part of Snoop Dogg's camp—including producer Fredwreck, an outspoken Palestinian hip-hopper; WC; Daz; RBX; Soopafly; and Trey Dee, to name a few—who speak out against the war and how it relates to domestic problems faced by everyday people living in the hood. Radio stations all around the country have refused to play this record, which is called *Down With U.S.* and is under the name S.T.O.P.

Fredwreck pointed out very clearly that at any given moment you can turn on your radio and hear any of the artists—many whom are former gang members and who have sold millions of records on commercial radio—glamorizing street life and other negative things. Yet when they come together and try and do something positive or release positive material, the radio stations don't wanna touch it.

The best thing that folks can do is start to look beyond the headlines and include members of the hip-hop community in all these important conversations. Help support the efforts that are already being undertaken to combat some of the problems they are facing. Start the important process of dialoging so we can share resources, learn from one another, and have a true cultural exchange. There is no one answer. Listed below are some organizations and resources that you may find useful:

<allhiphop.com>: Great information on hip-hop day-to-day happenings.
<blackelectorate.com>
<daveyd.com.>: Tons of articles on media, hip-hop, and politics.
<future500.org>
<guerillafunk.com>: Paris hip-hop political Web site.
<hiphopactivist.com>: Information on hip-hop activism and activists.
<hiphopsummitactionnetwork.org>
<okayplayer.com>: Check their political message board.
<playahata.com>: Get their great political newsletter.
<popandpolitics.com>
<rapstation.com>
<urbanthinktank.org>

Pacifica Networks

BY KAGISO MOLEFHE

Pacifica Foundation was founded in 1949 by Lewis Hill, who pioneered the idea of listener sponsored radio. The goal of this foundation was "to promote cultural diversity and pluralistic community expression; to contribute to a lasting understanding between individuals of nations, races, creeds, and colors; to promote freedom of the press; to serve as a forum for various viewpoints; and to maintain an independent base" <www.pacifica.org>. Pacifica started with KPFA in Berkeley, and later added KPFK in Los Angeles, KPFT in Houston, WBAI in New York, and WPFW in Washington, DC. Today, Pacifica has over 50 affiliates in the nation. The Pacifica affiliates are both community radio stations and college stations nationwide. The Pacifica network has broadened and is not only on radio, but also online at <www.pacifica.org>, and on television. Popular programs like *Democracy Now!*, *Peace Watch*, and *Flashpoints* are being broadcast throughout the nation.

DEMOCRACY NOW!

Democracy Now! is a national listener sponsored public radio and TV show. Hosted by Amy Goodman and Juan Gonzalez, it was launched in 1997 as the only source of daily election coverage in public broadcasting. The show met with so much success that it broadened its focus and became a national news show. This program is currently aired on about 120 stations nationwide, including the Pacifica radio stations, Pacifica affiliates, <WBXI.org>, public access television stations, Free Speech TV (Dish Network channel 9415), and short-wave radio (Radio for Peace Intention).

Democracy Now! focuses on a range of issues that demand attention, highlighting grassroots efforts to enhance and ignite democracy. According to <democracynow.org>, some call this kind of programming "public journalism" or "civic journalism," but *Democracy Now!* likes to think of their program as "Radio in the Pacifica Tradition."

This show exposes important and timely issues ranging from global to local in scope. For instance, in 1998, *Democracy Now!* went to Nigeria, Africa, to document the activities of U.S. oil companies in the Niger Delta. The program was titled "Drilling and Killing: Chevron and Nigeria's Military Dictatorship." It was one of Project Censored's top ten news stories that year and won the 1998 George Polk Award for best radio documentary. In 1999, the program headed to Seattle, Washington, for an eight-day special on the "Battle for Seattle," to document the street action and the explosion of anticorporate-globalization activists onto the world stage.

In 2000, *Democracy Now!* started a unique multimedia collaboration involving non-profit community radio, the Internet, and satellite and cable television. During Republican and Democratic national conventions, *Democracy Now!* broadcasts a two-hour daily show from Independent Media Centers in Los Angeles and Philadelphia. This program increased the audience of Pacifica radio and expanded its potential audience to 25 million households.

FLASHPOINTS

Flashpoints is KPFA's award-winning news magazine, whose staff includes investigative reporter, radio host, and producer Dennis Bernstein; associate producer Leslie Kean; contributing producer Robert Knight; and technical director Mary Bishop. This show airs on KPFA 94.1 in Berkeley, California, from 5 P.M. to 6 P.M., and online at <www.flashpoints.net>. According to KPFA's Web site, *Flashpoints* "became the third-most popular program on the station in 1992." This show evolved from daily reportage of Persian Gulf news and is now known for its hard-hitting international investigative journalism, covering censored issues around the world. "We take the hardest issues and hit them head on," Dennis Bernstein explained to Project Censored during a phone interview. The highly esteemed investigative journalist also spoke of the two-year struggle at KPFA that started in July 1999. Bernstein told Project Censored that San Francisco's Media Alliance came across an e-mail discussing the selling and consequent reprogramming of KPFA. "I was under the impression," wrote Palmer—a Pacifica board member and real estate entrepreneur, "that there was support in the proper quarters, and definite majority, for shutting down that unit and re-programming immediately. Has that changed?"

Bernstein said he decided to break the story on his regular show—a show he didn't get a chance to finish that day of July 13, 1999: "I was arrested while on air during my show; thousands of listeners heard the arrest." Bernstein said he was dragged from the station, for which he had worked for over 20 years. He was held until midnight for trespassing—at his place of work, doing his job. Bernstein was just the first of the many arrests among the KPFA staff as well as the public who protested the takeover. The station manager, Nicole Sawaya, was also fired without explanation just before KPFA was seized. "The door code security was replaced by armed guards with CIA/ FBI training," Bernstein explained. He stated that these new guards were from

IPSA International, hired by Pacifica's new human resource manager, Gene Edwards. "IPSA specializes in providing security for 'hostile terminations,' or firings. Workers who tried to enter the building were treated as strangers."

KPFA survived the turmoil with the help of its loyal listeners who took to the streets of Berkeley protesting the takeover. Bernstein told Project Censored that there were three people particularly responsible for saving KPFA: Barbara Lubin, involved in <savepacifica.net> ; Robbie Osman, host of folk music show *The Great Divine* for 22 years; and Sherry Gendelman of the Local Advisory Board at KPFA (LAD)." He said these people put up a truly heroic fight for the station.

Today, with all that behind it, KPFA continues to grow, with *Flashpoints* reaching about 2 million listeners nationwide.

Free Speech TV (FSTV)—Real Reality TV

BY MICHAEL KAUFMAN AND MATT HAMBURG

Though they might not have as many hot babes prancing around on desert islands as FOX or ABC, Free Speech TV (FSTV) has the real "reality TV." "FSTV is a service to people who understand we basically have a censored media. We are here to present viewpoints that are ignored by the mainstream press and encourage people to get involved politically," said John Schwartz, president of FSTV. As a 501-c-3 non-profit organization, FSTV became a full-time channel on DISH Network in January of 2000 as part of a federally mandated public interest obligation. With an annual budget of $1.9 million, 17 full-time paid staffers and about 20 volunteers, FSTV currently reaches more than 7 million U.S. homes via its full-time broadcasts. It is also received part time through a cross-country network of community access cable stations. FSTV also offers lost-cost Web hosting to activists as well as boasting the Internet's largest archive of progressive audio and video content.

FSTV's stated mission is "working with activists and artists to cultivate an informed and active citizenry in order to advance progressive social change." In most circumstances TV seems antithetical to social change. But anyone who has checked out FSTV's programming knows these activists are on the cutting edge. Their programs serve not only as education for the casual viewer, but in creating these programs FSTV is establishing a network of collaborative progressive groups. Long-time Green Party activist and organizer Nancy Harvey is the director of FSTV's outreach program. "By partnering with grassroots organizations to create TV programming, we make ties in the activist community," says Harvey. The outreach program is one of the central new features of FSTV's infrastructure and was explicitly designed to "cultivate movement-building collaborations." FSTV hopes that the programming that comes out of their collaborative efforts in turn mobilizes people to participate in campaigns to "revitalize democracy and build a more compassionate world."

In January of 2002, FSTV hired five full-time employees and started its own production department. The result was a program called *World in Crisis*, which began on a part-time basis to help voice critical analysis of post 9/11 events. *World in Crisis* was designed "to fill the void of critical coverage in the country's drumbeat to war, the threats to civil liberties, and racist hate crimes." The program was initially a top-of-the-hour news update, but was transformed into a weekly half-hour news and analysis program. The *World in Crisis* program has since transformed into the *Mobile Eyes* organizing/media campaigns, which began in the summer of 2002.

Seeking to connect issues with media activists and audiences, FSTV pre-empted their regular weekend broadcasting in order to provide programs and documentaries from independent producers. FSTV likens the *Mobile Eyes* programming to a "teach-in" that combines original productions, acquired programs, and supplemental Web content in thematic weeks or weekends. In each episode of *Mobile Eyes*, FSTV focuses on a single issue and partners with other social justice groups. Emphasis is placed on working with organizations whose constituencies are under-represented by the corporate media. "With the *Mobile Eyes* program the idea is to use the mobile camera lens to mobilize people to get involved and active in their community," said Nancy Harvey. *Mobile Eyes* supplies the viewer with the facts and contacts they need to get active politically. "Our objective is to score concrete public policy victories, while building a broad-based, multi-issue movement for systemic social change."

In addition to its connections with indymedia groups, FSTV airs such staples of alternative media as *Democracy Now!*, featuring award winning journalist Amy Goodman and Juan Gonzalez. Also, in an effort to link up with community activist groups and go directly to where the action is, FSTV, in partnership with Downtown Community Television of New York City, has instituted its "Sybercar," the Free Speech TV Bus that serves as a state-of-the-art TV production studio with a satellite uplink. The Bus travels throughout the county locating grassroots activists whom it provides with broadcast capabilities. Recent *Mobile Eyes* productions have included programs dealing with sustainable development, Palestine, military interventions, and indigenous rights.

FSTV's Web site is a professional compliment to the organization's other media functions. In addition to advertising FSTV's programming, the site features articles related to civil liberties issues, such as the reduction in personal freedoms that come as a result of the Patriot Acts (I and II) and links to other articles that treat subjects of current interests like the ongoing FCC hearings regarding plans to increase levels of media consolidation (a subject that directly touches on the future and importance of alternative news outlets like FSTV). In the present atmosphere, in which civil liberties are being eroded and the media is being consolidated, we are thankful for FSTV.

North Bay Progressive

BY MATT HAMBURG

At a time when corporate media chains are gobbling up local newspapers like candy and then spitting out censored, canned news-speak, California's North Coast has generated a grassroots newspaper, the *North Bay Progressive*, committed to independent free speech media.

It is not an easy task to put out a monthly newspaper. Volunteer journalists, donations, grants, advertisers, and a slowly growing subscription base keep the paper afloat. It was in December of 2000 that Peter Phillips, director of Project Censored, and his friend Will Shonbrun decided to launch the *North Bay Progressive*, which is based in Santa Rosa, California. The duo enlisted Suzanne Regalado, former director of the Santa Rosa Peace and Justice Center, and a core group of people associated with the center.

"The idea was to cover local and regional, national and international news that was not getting out to people by means of the mainstream, corporate media," Shonbrun said. "In a sense, it would be like Pacifica Radio's KPFA, except in print. We would publish news, commentaries, and op-eds covering stories and issues that were being ignored, censored, or buried on the back pages."

Before the paper hit the street, however, there was the issue of scraping together the cash to make it happen. The core team decided they needed a nest egg to cover the first year of printing. So they set about raising money by selling subscriptions to the yet unpublished paper for $30 a year. The fact that they were able to raise $30,000 from a group of 600 subscribers who pledged money before they even had an issue in hand is a testament to how hungry readers are for progressive news.

The hope was to raise even more money before launching the paper, but the post-9/11 need to get the paper out was greater than expected, said Marcus Borgman, the paper's general manager and only paid employee. "The political events of the 2000 election and the continuing fictional character of what was happening nationally made the paper happen earlier," he said. "We couldn't wait any longer to move in with real news and real media."

And so the *Progressive* was born March 4, 2002, the day Michael Moore came to town. Papers were handed out for the first time at the Moore event, giving subscriptions an added boost.

The paper began by operating with two volunteer editors and a team of volunteer writers, who produced issues every two weeks. The idea was to increase subscriptions by about 100 a month, with the ultimate goal of having a total of 2,500 subscribers supporting the paper. That would just about cover the $3,000 basic rent and general overhead expenses including printing, which is done by Howard Quinn of San Francisco, a union shop.

By September 2002, the paper was getting close to the target of attracting 100 new subscribers a month—but not close enough. With about 60 new subscriptions coming in monthly, the decision was made to go from a biweekly to a monthly.

Still, subscriptions continued to rise. A series of political events with people like Congressman Dennis Kucinich of Ohio, rallies, and the Michael Moore event helped bump subscriptions up to about 1,200, which covers about 75 percent of the paper's expenses. The rest comes from advertisements, donations, and fundraising. So far, the paper has been awarded $2,500 from the Tides Foundation and other grants are pending.

In terms of advertising, the paper accepts ads from "...non-profit organizations, labor unions, and local/regionally owned businesses that support sustainable environments, social justice, and pay their employees a living wage within the capabilities of their operation."

For content, the economic reality mandates a nearly all-volunteer team of writers, editors, and photographers to crank out the 16-page paper each month. Regular contributors include Norman Solomon and Jim Hightower. "I think the quality of work we're producing is pretty impressive, especially considering that for most of those involved in the production of the paper, it's pro bono, and purely a labor of love," said Shonbrun. "The volunteers who make the *North Bay Progressive* happen are dedicated people, committed to bringing real and important information to the public so that we may have an aware and informed society."

With an editorial motto of "All the news that didn't fit," the paper includes investigative reporting, local commentary, analysis, local and national news stories, a calendar of local progressive events, environmental reporting, labor news, world news, and a roundup of news items from Project Censored, which provides an inside look at independent news.

Stories have run the gamut from a local feature on the group Food Not Bombs, which provides meals for the hungry and homeless, to a look at how the California budget crisis affects the state. There are stories on how the government shunts irradiated foods off to the state's school districts, an exposé on U.S. biological weapons, and environmental reporting on water tussles and attempts by out-of-state corporations to hijack local water sources.

Skaidra Smith-Heisters, a member of the *Progressive*'s North Bay Media Collective has found that being involved in the paper has also helped her cultivate her skills as an activist. "At 23 years old, I'm the youngest member of the collective. Being involved in the paper gives me good perspective on how groups coordinate and the different strategies activists use to operate. I've also had the privilege of being involved with a great group of people."

While there is no shortage of news to cover, it's often a challenge to publish the right mix of stories using all-volunteer journalists, said Al Schmeder, the papers regional editor. "The challenge now is to cover more local news stories and local government like the supervisors or city council meetings. But it's often tough to assign volunteer reporters to late-night planning commission meetings. The reality is volunteers are often more jazzed about reviewing speeches, attending rallies and demonstrations, or writing opinion pieces."

Peter Phillips has also been training some of his Sonoma State University sociology students as reporters and the paper is building a pool of investigative journalists whose work is published in the paper.

"Hard news and investigative stories are hard nuts to crack with unpaid journalists," Schmeder said. Still, most of the stories meet Schmeder's editorial criteria: "To me, the value of a well-done news story is that it gives readers tools to make their own decisions."

Stories are chosen and edited during group editing sessions and decisions are made on a consensus basis by the nine person collective that manages the paper. "From our perspective, there's a dire need for alternative news and commentary and for publications not dependent on advertising or beholden to corporations or boards of directors," Shonbrun said. "The need for free and independent speech is more crucial now than ever," he said.

As subscriptions continue to come in, the *Progressive* still has some goals to achieve. Said Helen Kochenderfer, the paper's treasurer, "Down the road I would like to see a weekly paper with paid staff, maybe three full time employees, and still connected to volunteers and community based reporters that make our paper unique."

North Bay Progressive
2525 Cleveland Avenue, Suite D
Santa Rosa, CA 95401
Tel: (707) 525-1422
Fax: (707) 578-5964
Web site: <www.northbayprogressive.org>

Subscriptions are $17.50 for six months, $30 for a year. To subscribe send check or credit card information to: *North Bay Progressive*, P.O. Box 14384, Santa Rosa, CA 95402.

Alternative and Independent Media in the Middle East

BY MICHAEL KAUFMANN

Although I am writing these lines just as Operation "Iraqi Freedom" enters its moment of truth, i.e., the invasion of Baghdad, most of the Web sites and magazines that I have surveyed continue to focus on the two-and-a-half-year-old Palestinian Intifada against Israeli's occupation of the West Bank and Gaza Strip, as well as the deteriorating political situation in that part of the world in general.

I have divided my findings into a couple of different categories:

A) Newer media organizations that are primarily Web-based and see their main focus as media itself—in other words, media activists who are opening up a "space" for alternative portrayals of current events in the Middle East, while at the same time taking advantage of the technology of the Web to democratize the process of news reporting.

B) More "traditional" groups that are primarily political activist in nature, who see themselves as involved in day to day political activities such as organizing demonstrations, publishing "appeals to conscience" in the mainstream press, and in some cases, even running political campaigns. These groups, although they make heavy use of the Web for publicizing their positions and updating their constituencies, also publish, and in most cases, have been publishing since before the advent of the Web, monthly or bimonthly magazines in English.

WEB SITES

Al Jazeera: <english.aljazeera.net>
The Alternative Information Center (AIC): <www.alternativenews.org>

Between the Lines (BTL): <www.between-lines.org>
Challenge: <www.hanitzotz.com/challenge>
Electronic Intifada (EI): <electronicintifada.net>
Electronic Iraq: <electroniciraq.net>
Independent Media Center–Palestine (IMC–Palestine):
    <jerusalem.indymedia. org>
Indymedia Israel: <www.indymedia.org.il>
Islam Online: <www.islam-online.net>
The Other Israel: <israelipalestinianpeace.org>

WEB-BASED MEDIA ACTIVIST GROUPS

AL JAZEERA: As in Afghanistan, during the present war on Iraq, Al Jazeera, the fiercely independent satellite station based in Doha, Qatar, and financed by the moderate Emir of Qatar, has again been a model of journalistic integrity, embodying in its coverage of the war on Iraq everything that the U.S. corporate media, in its own blatantly jingoistic coverage of the war, does not. Reviled by both Arab governments and the White House alike, and twice attacked by U.S. forces, first in Afghanistan and then again in Iraq, Al Jazeera must be doing something right. AlJazeera.net, the English Web site of the satellite channel at <English.aljazeera.net>, has also met with its share of disruptions from hacking and other attacks, and was shut down on March 25, 2003, only to resurface on April 9, 2003. Although the main banner declares that "this site is temporarily on hold" to be fully restored at the end of April, AlJazeera.net still continues to post breaking news from Iraq. For all those concerned about objective reporting on events in the Middle East, Al Jazeera's complete return to the Web cannot come too soon.

THE ALTERNATIVE INFORMATION CENTER (AIC): The AIC is a Palestinian-Israeli organization that disseminates information, research, and analysis on the Israeli-Palestinian conflict. Connie Hackbarth, advocacy officer for the AIC, says the group's Web site reflects the organization's "progressive values and the joint Palestinian-Israeli struggle for a just peace in the Middle East." Even though the site is currently only in English, it receives upwards of 10,000 hits a day, mostly from Europe, but with almost 20 percent coming from Israel, as well as a few hundred hits a day from the Occupied Territories. The AIC, which is linked to Indymedia Israel (see below), is supported mainly by foundations and churches in Europe, but even with this support, it still experiences periodic financial problems. And although according to

Hackbarth, because of its radical politics the AIC has so far had limited interest from North America, some of its current efforts will be focused in that direction.

ELECTRONIC INTIFADA (EI): The first thing one notices upon pulling up this Chicago-based Web site, which recently celebrated its second anniversary, are the eye-catching graphics and striking attention to professionalism and detail in evidence throughout. In contrast to some of the other sites reviewed for this article, whose main focus seems to be on an unadorned "getting the message out," EI combines both form and content to produce a superior Web site whose purpose is to combat corporate media distortions in relation to the Israel-Palestine conflict. According to Ali Abunimah, one of EI's founders, in an area such as mass media where image is so important, attention to the visual cannot be neglected. And in order to increase credibility, it is necessary to duplicate the same standards of professionalism in areas held to by mainstream media (such as graphics). But in the case of EI, this attention to detail in the area of form does not—as is so often the case with the corporate media—come at the expense of content. In addition to information demystifying the background to the Israeli-Palestinian conflict, updates on EI's own media activism, and the latest on the activities of the pro-Israel lobby, the site also contains a "Breaking News" section that allows readers to sample articles on the Middle East from a variety of perspectives. Since the beginning of the U.S.-led war on Iraq, EI has also started a sister site, Electronic Iraq.

INDEPENDENT MEDIA CENTER–PALESTINE (IMC–PALESTINE): This group, like Indymedia Israel, is affiliated with the IMC (Independent Media Center) network. The Center was founded "to record and explore the current practices of the Israeli occupation" and states its mission as helping Palestinian activists to organize, motivate, and inform within the constantly changing realities of the current Intifada. Additionally, the IMC hopes to make the case for Palestine through humanistic, rather than simply journalistic, writing which reflects the intricate picture that is Palestinian life under the occupation. In line with this philosophy, the group consists of mainly Palestinian refugees from areas now under Israeli occupation, and the goal of the Web site is to develop tools that help the latter "tell their story."

INDYMEDIA ISRAEL: This organization bills itself as a grassroots group of journalists providing non-corporate coverage of news. The trilingual site (English/Arabic/Hebrew) provides up-to-the-minute coverage of important events related to the Israeli-Palestinian conflict, as well as other news affecting the region that tends to get downplayed or ignored by mainstream media. According to Bryan Atinsky, English editorial coordinator for the site, although Indymedia Israel's audience consists of a wide range of readers and writers from left to right, the target audience is mainly various leftists and radicals including Greens, Marxists, and Palestinians as well as European and American Jewish progressives. Indymedia Israel is financed through donations from individuals and a couple of grant foundations, as well as, Atinsky adds, by contributions "out of our own pockets."

ISLAM ONLINE (IOL): In a category of its own is the Cairo-based Islam Online. Like Electronic Intifada, this site is graced with impressive production values, but unlike EI, whose focus is secular and political, IOL, while also dealing with political issues and current events, sees itself as primarily religious in orientation. According to its mission statement, IOL wishes to create a "unique, global Islamic site on the Internet that provides services to Muslims and non-Muslims," and indeed the site appears to serve as a sort of clearinghouse for information about Islam, both in providing answers to religious issues by clerics, as well as being a source for the growing number of non-Muslims who, especially since 9/11, have expressed an interest in and curiosity about the religion. Arwa Salah Mahmoud, views and analyses editor for the English edition, stresses the unaffiliated nature of the site, which prefers to be considered an inclusive platform for everyone interested in Islam. With September 11, IOL's hits boomed to a high of 3 million, the average since having dropped back to a still impressive 200,000 per day.

PRINT-BASED POLITICAL ACTIVIST GROUPS

In additional to their more overtly "hands-on" political activities, the three political activist groups surveyed here all publish either monthly or bimonthly magazines in English. They also serve an important function in translating controversial articles from the Hebrew press that would otherwise be ignored.

BETWEEN THE LINES: *Between the Lines* is a monthly independent political magazine published in Jerusalem by Dr. Tikva Honig-Parnass and Toufic Haddad. The magazine categorically "opposes the Oslo Process and the Apartheid reality which has been established in its wake in the '67 Occupied Territories and strengthened within Israel."

Along with original articles dealing with the second (Al-Aksa) Intifada, coverage and analysis of the recent Israeli elections from a critical left non-Zionist perspective, *Between the Lines* also keeps its readers abreast of the latest developments in the growing campaign of "refuseniks," or Israeli soldiers who refuse to serve in the Occupied Territories. Another vital function provided by the magazine is the translation of articles from the Hebrew press. Many of these articles reflect a little-known side to the Israeli media which is often more critical of its own government's policies than Western media or specifically, the American-Jewish press. In addition to the above, *Between the Lines* has recently published articles on the "Separation Fence" being built along the West Bank, "The Architecture of Apartheid," and an exposé translated from the Egyptian *Al Ahram Weekly* dealing with "Israeli Biological and Chemical Weapons—Past and Present."

With its firm commitment to full equality between Arabs and Jews, something the editors feel is impossible both within the contexts of Zionism and Islamic fundamentalism, *Between the Lines* makes a valuable contribution to the opening up of new horizons and ways of thinking concerning what many regard as the intractable problems of the Israeli-Palestinian conflict.

CHALLENGE: *Challenge*, a bimonthly leftist magazine published in Jaffa, Israel, is a joint project of Arab and Jewish activists organized around the Organization for Democratic Action (ODA). The ODA is a Marxist political party that, in addition to its political activities against the Israeli occupation of the West Bank and its vigorous defense of the rights of Arab citizens within 1967 Israel, also stands for election to the Israeli Parliament (Knesset). Also associated with the ODA is the Worker's Advice Center (WAC), which advocates for improved working conditions for Israeli-Arab workers.

Although also publishing magazines in Hebrew and Arabic, the organization's main vehicle for getting its message out to America and Europe has been its bimonthly English magazine, *Challenge*. *Challenge*, which bills itself as a journal "for all those who seek a just solution to the Palestinian-Israeli conflict," was founded in the wake of the first Intifada (1987) and has continued to publish through the Oslo Process and on into its collapse with the start of the second Intifada (2000). The magazine, published by Shimon Tzabar, features articles and analyses from such well-known peace activists as Roni Ben Efrat and Michal Schwartz. *Challenge* has been consistently critical of both what they feel are the repressive policies of the Israeli-Zionist establishment in dealing with the prolonged occupation, as well as equally with what they feel is a corrupt Palestinian leadership under Yassir Arafat. In short, *Challenge* spares no one, and in the process gives voice to a much-needed alternative in Middle East reporting which is all too often ignored by the mainstream press.

THE OTHER ISRAEL: *The Other Israel* is a bimonthly newsletter published since 1983 by the Israeli Council for Israeli-Palestinian Peace. The newsletter, which began publication during the initial days of the highly divisive Israeli invasion of Lebanon, became more influential as a result of its association with Gush Shalom (Israeli Peace Bloc), which was founded by veteran peace activist Uri Avneri in 1993. Gush Shalom defines itself as "peacer than *Peace Now*" and as the "hard core" of the Israeli peace movement. In its advocacy of a two-state solution—Israel alongside a Palestinian state—Gush Shalom has been able to attract members from the Zionist left who feel that they have been abandoned by the drift toward the right of political parties such as Meretz and the Israeli Labor Party.

According to coeditor Beate Zilversmidt, *The Other Israel*'s audience consists of Jews, Palestinians, and the international peace movement. Recent articles have included reports on the destruction of Palestinian homes as well as Israeli army/settler harassment of Palestinian farmers during their olive harvest. The newsletter is able to survive financially by maintaining modest production costs and more importantly, through the labor of a dedicated core of volunteers.

The Other Israel, which is based in Holon, Israel, also seeks to expand its influence outside of the immediate area of the conflict by means of its affiliate, the America-Israel Council for Israel-Palestinian Peace, the U.S. representative of *The Other Israel*.

CONCLUSION: NEEDED: MORE LIGHT, LESS HEAT

Few geopolitical hot spots are capable of stirring up the amount of emotion and passion as the Middle East, the Israeli-Palestinian conflict in particular. And since for many people, especially those in the United States, the Middle East, with its seemingly interminable conflicts, remains one of the most difficult regions to decipher, dispassionate, objective media coverage is a crucial prerequisite for understanding this area of the world. Unfortunately, in contrast to the situation in Europe, consumers of U.S. corporate media are invariably subjected to anything but levelheaded reporting concerning the Middle East. Pro-Israel interest groups and the recently created unsettling alliance between neoconservative American Jews and right-wing fundamentalist Christians that makes up a large part of the Zionist lobby must share much of the responsibility for media distortions in this area. Using a combination of tactics ranging from subtle manipulation to outright threats of boycotts against media outlets that aspire to present evenhanded coverage, these pressure groups have succeeded in exercising a stranglehold over discourse surrounding the Israeli-Palestinian conflict and America's imperial aims in the region.

American Coalition for Media Education (ACME)

BY DONALD YOON AND JOSH SISCO

For our current business-friendly administration, deregulation is the number one priority. Loosening the rules for virtually every industry is restricting the power of the electorate in making the decisions that affect our lives on a daily basis. The mass media and telecommunications industries are one area in which our government's deregulatory policies can be clearly seen.

Print, radio, television, and the Internet have brought a vast diversity of information into our homes and workplaces. As the technological potential expands, however, the media that shapes our culture is largely controlled by a just a few corporate players. Even when one may have 100 channels on digital cable, the majority of them are owned by the same oligopoly of corporations. The current media system is dominated by advertising revenue and entertainment values. In such a system, important news may get trivialized while the superficial is at the forefront of the media. This is how issues like privatization largely get ignored in comparison to stories that saturate the media such as the disappearance of Chandra Levy, to cite one example. In the interest of preserving the integrity and diversity of the major media outlets, the Action Coalition for Media Education (ACME) is taking a three-step approach to create a more democratic media by expanding the range of perspectives in our media environment: by promoting media literacy, supporting independent media, and supporting legislative reform. Rob Williams, president of ACME, says that, "ACME seeks to change democracy and media that buy the people to a democracy and media by the people."

ACME seeks to develop, distribute, and promote media literacy curricula that encourage critical thinking and free expression, examine the corporate media system, and inspire active participation in society. This translates to media education that gives people better skills to access, analyze, interpret, and create media; in other words, to become "media literate." The goal is for people to think critically about what they see, hear, and read. Media education is often associated only with the classroom environment, but should be used in a broader context to encompass the community, political, and outreach education spheres as well. This applies to newspapers as well as radio, television, film, Internet, and any other way information source.

ACME, which is free of corporate media funding, is a strategic network that links media educators, health advocates, media reformers, independent media makers, community organizers, and others. It connects members to crucial resources. The Media Education Foundation (MEF), largely known for putting out the *Killing Us Softly* series with Jeane Kilbourne, gives 20 percent discounts on all 24 of their videos exclusively to ACME members. There are plans to start production on a video that teaches people how to watch television news critically. Teachers involved in ACME tend to teach media literacy in their courses. The idea is that when we are more critical media consumers, we will be more active in our communities with regard to media and other important social issues.

There is a nine-standard set of criteria that has been formed to be utilized by the coalition to endorse independent media. Media Literacy Curricula that receive ACME's stamp of approval from the evaluating committee will then be promoted via Web and monthly e-bulletins to all members. Williams informed us, "Currently, large media corporations are rubber-stamping Media Literacy curricula with their own pro-corporate agenda in mind; as a non-profit media organization that takes no big media money, ACME is in a unique position to evaluate and promote truly independent media and literacy curricula."

The coalition involves and will serve the interests of educators, youth leaders, community organizers, parents, researchers, students, children, teens, schools/school districts, community and non-profit organizations, and anyone else who feels it's time to advocate for media literacy education that inspires citizens to action about important issues. This is where educators and media reformers come together. ACME is the organization that links people to the cause of media democracy and education. The second approach ACME supports is the advocacy of independent media. Independent media is a critical part of a democratic society. ACME supports the diversity of as many different opinions and perspectives as possible. Parallel to Project Censored's media guide is ACME's *Essential Resources Guide*, which covers more than just Web sites. It also encompasses books, film, zines, and anything else that ACME find to be essential to understanding our media culture. ACME has made donations to a number of independent media organizations like Prometheus Radio and the Schmio Awards. The Web site is always expanding for the promotion of indymedia. ACME's Indy Media Action Group is currently building a list of indy producers who have media they wish to make available. Williams stated that ACME is also exploring the possibility of producing its own line of films.

The third approach is to support local, state, and national media reform efforts. ACME has already played a major role in promoting grassroots media reform by encouraging members and all concerned citizens to write, call, and fax both elected officials in Congress and appointed FCC members in current debates about media deregulation. ACME has also worked together with like-minded organizations (The Future of Music Coalition, Free Press, Media Tank, Consumer's Union, etc.) to build political support for media reform. Williams said that they are currently exploring ways to work with supportive policymakers to endorse media reform as part of a larger political platform.

The more educated a population, the greater the potential for social action. Progressive education and education reform agendas should incorporate media education and have it firmly in place as curriculum.

The critical consciousness, however, incorporates more than production of independent media. It is understanding the policies and decision-making processed that have led to the current state of media homogeneity.

The Federal Communications Commission (FCC) is the government organization that oversees the regulation of the media. However, instead of ensuring the general public's access to a diversity of ideas, which is a foundation of the democratic process, they have gone in the opposite direction. Michael Powell, the son of Colin Powell and the head of the FCC, has made it a priority to stay in the background and allow the media conglomerates to police themselves. Williams spoke out strongly against the FCC's penchant for deregulation: "The FCC exists in part to stimulate debate. Powell has shown little interest in such debate." This debate can only occur if there is a diversity of ideas in the marketplace.

While the antitrust legislation that has been in effect for roughly 100 years still directly opposes monopolies and there is no single company that owns all mass media, the current state of affairs places control in the hands of a few. In *Censored 2003*, there are a number of diagrams that illustrate the 10 major companies that control virtually every idea that Americans are exposed to. Contrary to popular belief, this is not the working of the "invisible hand" that supposedly controls the marketplace. Williams states that elected officials are there to make laws that prevent the negative effects of deregulation. However, campaign contributions prevent this from happening. The National Association of Broadcasters and the telecommunications industry are two of the main lobbyists on Capitol Hill. The telecommunications industry is among the top five organizations that finance politicians' campaigns.

FCC regulations used to prohibited one company from owning television stations that serve more than 35 percent of an audience in a single market. There were also regulations that prohibited ownership of both television stations and newspapers in a single market. Powell and the FCC recently changed that. On June 2, 2003, the FCC announced new regulations on the ownership of media in individual markets. Among these is an increase from the 35 percent audience limit to 45 percent. For a complete list of all the new deregulations as well as comments from Chairman Powell and the five commissioners, including dissenting opinions from Democrats Michael J. Copps and Jonathan S. Adelstein, go to <www.fcc.gov>. According to Williams, when television was in its infancy, there was spectrum scarcity, or limited channels, and "the regulation of the spectrum was absolutely necessary." Now with the digital spectrum providing literally thousands of channels Powell maintains that there will always be avenues for different ideas. However the 1996 Telecommunications Act allowed media companies to carve up the digital spectrum as they desired and provided for cross-ownership in multiple markets. As a result a majority of the programming is the same across the nation, sacrificing much-needed diversity.

We asked Williams if he feels that media companies are consciously promoting an agenda with homogenous programming or if it is merely the result of the profit motive. He feels that the two cannot be discussed separately. Using the same program in all markets makes it much easier to turn a profit. The companies rely on "tried and true" formulas that have worked in the past. If diversity is lost, then so be it. When Powell stated, "It's hard to see how a complete ban on newspapers owning TV stations serves the public interest," the battle for media literacy and diversity looks to be long an arduous.

The most fundamental starting point for media literacy will be in the classroom. ACME will provide resources for teachers that give students an understanding of the importance of media diversity. They will explain the current corporate hold on mass media and how it affects every person in this country. These resources will include examples of independent media used for both informative and entertainment purposes. Students will also be provided with tools necessary to create their own media. Posted on the ACME Web site is information regarding their stance on media literacy education: "Ideally, ACME will promote synergy in the media reform movement and will help to prevent media education from becoming watered down by profit-driven or appreciationist agendas. Progressive education and education reform agendas *must* incorporate media education as a fundamental literacy for the twenty-first century; we believe ACME can help make this connection." Children, our nations largest group of consumers, must be taught from an early age to reject the corporate consumer attitude that is so rampant in our society. Media literacy is a vital part of critical thinking skills that must be ingrained from the beginning.

One idea that Rob Williams says must be stressed in the classroom is that "truth is not completely objective. There is not one magic source that will provide the complete truth. One must synthesize a variety of sources and determine truth for one's self." In the first years of journalism, there were large numbers of newspapers. While each one was openly biased in promoting its own ideas as the truth, there were enough sources for an individual to use in developing his or her own ideas. Now with just a few companies owning numerous radio and television stations, as well as newspapers in markets around the country, the same information is disseminated everywhere with the same handful of viewpoints. The result is individuals not having the necessary variety of information to make informed decisions.

All of these issues fit into ACME's three main goals: developing a progressive media literacy curricula free from corporate and political influence; helping individuals to create their own independent media; and supporting local, state, and national political reform efforts. The most important catalyst for a true democracy is access to a diverse and free-flowing range of ideas and information. In order to have a government by the people, we must be accurately informed of the issues that are affecting our daily lives. If the information is not there to make informed decisions, that responsibility falls into the hands of a small powerful and wealthy group of people. Contrary to the belief of those in power, the American public is capable of controlling their own lives. We are not here to consume what someone 3,000 miles away says is good for us. Once we lose the belief that we are intelligent and willing to make our own decisions, there is no hope for democracy. For more information on ACME and related organizations, please visit <www.acmecoalition.org>.

Deception and Public Opinion Polling
BY MARC SAPIR, DIRECTOR, RETRO POLL, <WWW.RETROPOLL.ORG>

From presidential popularity to support for war, from the death penalty to abortion, from O.J. Simpson to Homer Simpson, polls are seen, heard, and read trumpeting what we, the public, think about it all. Polls have become a key instrument in the battle for public attention. Yet opinion polls are generally misleading. Even the best polls, those that use reliable methods, usually conceal vital truths from the public either by omitting, hiding, or oversimplifying important information. By choice, polls validate the media's filtered view of the world.

During September 2002 and April 2003, Retro Poll, an alternative polling organization, made thousands of phone calls to people all over the U.S. regarding the War on Terrorism, Palestine and Israel, War in Iraq, the USA Patriot Act, the Bill of Rights, and the removal of civil liberties in the U.S. Retro Poll uses a unique methodology that investigates people's background knowledge in addition to asking their opinions. This allows an assessment of the extent to which background knowledge or its absence contributes to particular political views. We also compare answers to general questions with those to highly specific questions on the same subject.

One of our most important findings (seen in both polls) was that people who supported war against Iraq were overwhelmingly those who believed the media-promoted lies about Saddam Hussein being involved with Al Qaeda and the 9/11 terrorist attacks. By failing to look at such issues, major polls validate disinformation and create the sense that public opinion is based on values and belief rather than manipulated by false claims.

In April 2003, more than 30 volunteers, mainly college students in the San Francisco area, polled a random sample of the U.S. population on their knowledge and views concerning Constitutional rights, the USA Patriot Act, and the War on Terrorism. Of more than 1,000 people contacted, 215 from 46 states agreed to participate. The results, showing revulsion toward the infringements of the Patriot Act, were ignored by the corporate media. Here's why: opinion research is not just error prone, but actually fraudulent.

Like the big polls the public hears about, Retro Poll buys phone lists from a reputable company that randomly generates and sells these lists for surveys and marketing purposes. Only about one in four of the people we reached agreed to answer the questions. The others either declined or hung up. This isn't surprising. It is commonly accepted in public opinion research that 70 percent or more of those contacted will refuse to participate in polls. With that single act, the refusers destroy the claim that a poll sampled people randomly because the results of any poll can honestly reflect the views of the general population only if the 70 percent who refuse to talk have near identical views with the 30 percent who agree to participate. If there are significant differences, the smaller group is not a random sample and the results cannot be said to equate to public opinion.

Polls usually report out a statistical "margin of error" for their results. The margin of error that polls report depends not upon the number of people called but upon the number who responded, the sample size. They usually report a margin of error of about 3 percent for a sample size of 1,000. But this margin of error statistic that makes polls look highly accurate is, in essence, a cover to hide the 70 percent who refused to participate. Even if 99 percent refused to participate and we had to speak to 100,000 people to find 1,000 who would talk with us, the margin of error statistic would still be reported as the same 3 percent. That's a fraud.

While it is always possible that those refusing have similar views to those agreeing to be polled, Retro Poll has found evidence to the contrary. When we asked over 1,000 people, "Would you take a few minutes to respond to a poll on the impact of the war on terrorism on the rights of the American people," one woman responded, "You wouldn't want to hear our view on that. People wouldn't like what we think."

"That's okay," I said. "Your views are important; they should be counted and reported as part of the democratic process. We want your opinion to count." "No," the woman answered insistently. "We're against the war the way they did it. We think they should just bomb all of them, not send our troops over there. . . ." I didn't ask whether she meant bomb everyone in Iraq or some larger group of people, but the woman's self-awareness that her views were outside the "norm" caused her to refuse to participate. Undoubtedly others have different specific reasons for non-participation that we don't know because most won't talk about them.

If the "bomb them all" woman may seem the exception among nonrespondents, consider this: Fewer African Americans and Latinos agree to be polled in most national samples (in the current poll, 5.7 percent were African Americans and in the prior poll, 4 percent; for Latinos, the corresponding figures were 6.2 percent and 8 percent. Each of these groups make up about 12 percent of the U.S. population, actually 12.5 percent for Latinos). As a result, our poll sample ended up being 79.4 percent European American, but the actual white/non-Hispanic European American proportion of the population is 69.1 percent according to the 2000 Census.

It is possible to improve the participation of underrepresented groups in a poll. Gallup reports on their Web site that after completing a poll, they weight the demographics to assure correct proportions are represented. Weighting means that you multiply the results of an underrepresented group by a factor that will bring their input up to intended and expected levels. Another thing that can be done is to simply oversample in a population that is expected to self-select out of the poll. If, for example, you want to double the number of African-American responses you just begin with a sample that has 24 percent African Americans instead of 12 percent. These tricks of the trade work on paper and in statistical analysis, but they both fail to address the important question: "Why would any particular group be less likely or more likely to participate?"

If that question sounds familiar, it should. It is just a more specific and powerful example of the pesky problem of the 70 percent refusers who won't participate in polls—the problem that won't go away. When we take it to the level of the underrepresentation of ethnic groups, however, it is easier to see that there are probably specific sociopolitical and/or economic reasons why some people are more likely to participate than others. These can include issues like English language skills, fear of being monitored by race, lack of self-confidence, or poor educational background. Any of these factors or dozens of others that may have an impact on a person's decision would invalidate the principle of a random poll sample that can be used to approximate the general public. If those African Americans who agreed to participate were more middle class or better educated than those that refused, then adjusting their input upward by a multiplier (weighting them) to provide a bigger contribution would be a charade because their views might not represent those of less educated lower socioeconomic classes of African Americans. You might, for example, be inappropriately magnifying the views of a tiny group of African-American Republicans. But the pretense of random samples and low margin of error is only part of the problem.

WHY ARE SO MANY POLLS DONE?

In a recent investigative article on the Field Poll, a group at the Poor News Network was able to tease out a key part of the polling fraud. When directly interviewed, Field Poll leaders claimed that poll publishers in the media and other big-dollar poll funders have no influence on poll subject, content, or interpretation. They claimed that Field researchers choose their own survey topics and the media financially supports them mainly by subscriptions. But when Poor News investigators called and pretended to be interested in purchasing (i.e. commissioning) a particular poll, they were told by a Field director that they would have to come up with six figures in big bucks to get what they wanted. The caller was given the example of a $100,000 poll funded by the *San Francisco Chronicle* and other unnamed sponsors, which found renewed strong public support for nuclear power. Who funded that poll besides the *Chronicle*? The Field director didn't say, but we might guess it was the energy industry.

The weak attempt to deny these practices actually conceals more ominous and detrimental purposes and impacts of these polls. Our April 2003 poll on public views concerning the Patriot Act, the War on Terrorism, civil rights, and Iraq revealed a public totally confounded by the disinformation they receive from the media and government, something that major polls almost never explore. For instance, when Americans hear specific provisions of the USA Patriot Act, they oppose the intrusions of this law into their civil rights by a wide margin (average 77 percent). Yet when asked generally what impact the War on Terrorism is having upon civil rights, many of the same people say it is "strengthening" or having "no impact" upon their rights (57 percent).

This inner confusion and conflicting loyalties was exemplified by a 37-year-old woman from Udora, Kansas, who rejected each of three provisions of the Patriot Act mentioned in the poll and also opposed the use of torture, other outlawed forms of coercion, and lengthy prison detention without trial; she also supported a requirement that the U.S. prove accusations against other nations before attacking them. However, when asked each of the following two questions: "Should the U.S. support international efforts to prosecute war crimes?" and "Should the U.S. make war against Iraq or other countries the government accuses of supporting terrorism when they are not attacking anyone?", this same Kansan hesitated and replied: "I'm confused. What is Bush for? I want to do whatever Bush wants. I want to support the president."

One might think that the media would be fascinated with and want to study this contradictory phenomenon. But there are strong financial incentives for polls to provide a simpler picture, one which validates the sponsors and the government. Because most major polls are generated by the mass media and other corporate forces (including foundations that depend upon money from their parent corporations), they will aim to show public views to be consistent with the funders' needs and wishes. As a source of embarrassment to the media, the contradictions and confusion in the public outlook, which often derive from media disinformation and government-media collaboration, will tend to be suppressed, even when they are seen in results.

Likewise, key questions are kept general to create emotional mass responses rather than to challenge people's abililty to reason. Questions like: "Do you like the president?", "Is he doing a good job?", "Do you support the troops overseas?", and "Is the war on terrorism protecting your rights?" are actually a test of what people have absorbed from the media. To say "no" to any of these implies aberrance. Such questions require a person with a different perspective to risk identifying themselves as outside the norm.

People are so used to having such hidden assumptions placed into mass media and polling discourse that some (regardless of political ideology) inevitably find Retro Poll's attempts to neutralize such assumptions and bias to reflect "bias." For instance, the September 2002 Retro Poll contained this obscure factual question from <www.IfAmericansKnew>:

"In the Palestinian uprising of the past two years, 84 children were killed by one side before the other side killed a child. Were these 84 children killed by:

> the Israeli Army
> Palestinian militants
> neither
> don't know?"

Obviously, this factual question was chosen to investigate the impact of disinformation around the Palestinian-Israeli conflict, but it is nevertheless a *factual* question, with a factual answer. Someone who knows the correct answer but prefers that such bitter and suppressed truths not be highlighted in public may rankle at this question and may call it biased, for it challenges the media purveyed disinformation that the Palestinians have been the main source of the terror against civilians. But the question itself is not biased, as those who do not know the answer will simply say so. The results measured bias in the mass media coverage when 13 percent of respondents (more than those who correctly gave "the Israeli Army" as his or her answer), assumed it had to be the Palestinians rather than answering "don't know." (Retro Pollsters tell people it is better to answer "don't know" than to guess the answers to the factual questions.)

Because major polls before the invasion consistently showed at least two-thirds of Americans opposed to attacking Iraq without U.N. approval, one might ask how it became important to ask people so frequently whether they support the invasion once war had begun. The media editors certainly know that, historically, at the initiation of any war, the public view will always appear to shift to support of government policies. This is a well-studied mass "loyalty" effect. By making it look like a surprising shift in public belief rather than an inevitable by-product of government action, the media polls helped generate a "pro-war" movement for the government. Clear Channel went so far as to organize pro-war demonstrations. In actuality, the revulsion at what the U.S. government was doing remained widespread, though somewhat muted and demoralized. Such media behavior empowers right-wing extremism, potentiates attacks on democratic dissent, and weakens the general public perception of the peace movement.

The eagerness with which media conduct polls is a measure of the extent to which relevant news and critical thinking are supplanted by the business of news marketing. Even the more "professional" and "reputable" polling outfits end up as prostitutes to all-powerful government, corporate and market-ing forces and, as in the case of the Field Poll, dare not admit that most of what they do is designed to insure the success of their organizations by pleasing their corporate funders and government leaders with beneficial results.

CHAPTER 6

FROM SAVING PRIVATE LYNCH TO THE "TOP GUN" PRESIDENT

The Made-for-TV "Reality" War On Iraq

BY ROBIN ANDERSEN

The final scenes providing the concluding shots for Bush's war on Iraq featured the triumphant president dressed in a military flight suit in the cockpit of a fighter jet, making what Jim Hightower (*AlterNet*, May 20, 2003) referred to as "a dramatic, made-for-TV, tail hook landing" onto the U.S.S. Lincoln, an aircraft carrier that was returning to San Diego from military action in Iraq. The million-dollar photo opportunity was so blatant a political stunt that the administration felt compelled to say that Bush needed to take the jet because the carrier was too far out to sea to be reached by helicopter. In fact, the carrier was so close that it had to be turned around to prevent cameras from catching the San Diego coastline in the background. Nevertheless, Hightower predicts that the American public will see repeated snippets of the "Top Gun" images in campaign ads during the upcoming 2004 election cycle. If so, Bush W. will capitalize on a popular war during an election in a way his father failed to do in 1992.

If the first Gulf War allowed CNN to be a contender, just as TV had brought the Vietnam War into America's living rooms, the Iraq War has given birth to a new media genre—call it militainment—that has done more to transform combat news into fictional entertainment than any previous war reporting combined. As we will see, at every phase along the way, war's reality was systematically shaped and understood through set fictional frameworks that rendered the images more convincing and compelling than the unpleasant truths they sought to hide. Successful as entertainment, the war coverage of Iraq, especially on TV, has obscured more than illuminated a complicated conflict, and taken great strides in creating a public unwilling and incapable of understanding the policies, practices, and motivations of the American government. Consider this: though it is widely known that President Bush used his family connections to keep from fighting in Vietnam, the power of such "Top Gun" imagery all but erases that fact. In the words of Jim Hightower, "Imagine Eisenhower, or Kennedy, or even Bush the Elder—all of whom were real war heroes—resorting to such a political stunt." In this new age of militainment, seemingly any image can be made credible with enough production expertise. And with the war in Iraq, the battle for public opinion has never been fought with such high-powered weaponry.

WAITING FOR WAR

The media buildup to war presented a military attack on Iraq as an overwhelming natural force whose momentum could not be stopped. "The clock is ticking," NPR reported in early March (March 8, 2003), with soldiers in Kuwait complaining that there was "too much waiting around." Military preparations were like a "huge gun and every day you cock the hammer back a little more."

February 15, 2003 marked the first time in history that millions of people around the world demonstrated against a war before it started. But Dan Rather and Tom Brokaw were already wearing khakis in the desert, driving humvees, profiling soldiers, hitching rides on helicopters and previewing high-tech weaponry. "With all this firepower and all these forces primed and ready to go, how long can they stay in peak condition?" worried Brokaw (NBC, February 18, 2003), reporting with a "band of brothers" on the northern border of Kuwait.

The "waiting for war" stories that dominated coverage were the result of what was being heralded a new era of military openness. The Pentagon promised access to the battlefield unseen since Vietnam. Embedding was the brainchild of Assistant Defense Secretary Victoria Clarke, formerly with Hill & Knowlton, the PR firm infamous for promoting the false baby-incubator story from the first Gulf War. "We want robust coverage," she claimed (CNBC, February 19, 2003). Hundreds of journalists were "embedding" with military units waiting for close-up views of combat. A spate of stories followed showing "embeds" training at media boot camps, learning about gas masks and running with heavy backpacks pointing their cameras at soldiers.

One reporter waiting to embed told me over the phone from Bahrain: "They're not crapping around this time. Journalists could die." ABC's Peter Jennings (March 11, 2003) told viewers the military wanted Americans to "see war as it really is." It was the best PR the Pentagon had seen in decades.

"A MEMBER OF THE TEAM"

The military did not hide its desire to shape positive coverage. The media-friendly war used a Hollywood set design created as the backdrop for official briefings in Qatar. Gen. Wesley Clark, now a CNN analyst, admitted that restricting the press during the 1991 Gulf War was a "huge mistake" (Carol Brightman, *AlterNet*, February 20, 2003): It was "perhaps the biggest armored battle ever, but not a single image was reported or documented." The military understood the need to enlist the vast resources of the media, in what White House chief of staff Andrew Card referred to as the war's extensive "product-marketing campaign" (*The New York Times*, March 23, 2003).

At briefings in Kuwait City, journalists were told, "The idea is by making you a part of the unit, you'll be a member of the team" (*Washington Post*, March 7, 2003). Veteran war correspondent Chris Hedges called embedding insidious and predicted that it would produce a "further loss of distance" and a "false sense of loyalty" (*Democracy Now!*, February 27, 2003). "The level of trust is staggering." But just in case, they would also have escorts.

In Vietnam, journalists understood the nature of official escorts and military briefings, referred to as "five o'clock follies." Some photojournalists and "renegades" found their own units, buddied up with soldiers and officers alike, covered them for a time, then moved on. "Embeds" in Iraq had no independence, no vehicles, and were required to stay with the assigned unit for the duration of the war. Assignments were centrally organized by the Pentagon, and there was no "cutting deals" in the field.

The Center for Constitutional Rights filed a lawsuit against the Pentagon for press censorship during the first Gulf War. The suit documented the ways public affairs "escorts engaged in arbitrary censorship of interviews, photography and altered the activities of the soldiers when reporters came into their presence, not for security reasons, but to ensure favorable coverage of the military presence."

Military minders made their intentions clear to would-be embeds, even as they promised battlefield access to Iraq: "Reporters shouldn't be . . . independently probing for facts," Lt. Col. Rick Long told the *Washington Post* (March 7, 2003). "If something bad happens, it's the military's job to investigate."

In Afghanistan, American troops showed their displeasure with a *Washington Post* reporter trying to investigate civilian casualties from the aerial bombing. They explained that he shouldn't be there for his own security, as they threatened to shoot him "That's always the line they are going to feed you," Chris Hedges said (*Democracy Now!*, February 27, 2003). "If things go wrong the press won't be anywhere in sight." The idea that they will have "unfettered access is ludicrous."

A HOST OF MYTHIC WARRIORS

One way military strategists shaped positive coverage of the first Gulf War was by favoring local TV crews over national and print journalists. "Hometowners" were given much freer access to the field because the Information Bureau chief in Saudi Arabia admitted he favored human-interest news (*The Progressive*, March 1991). Local TV excelled in morale-boosting stories by sending words and pictures of the boys to the folks back home.

Network anchors learned the lesson well. Twelve years later, NBC's Tom Brokaw promised his TV audience (February 18, 2003), "I'll be back later in the broadcast with a touching story of a sergeant with the 3rd Infantry Division who is here, his family back in America, and how we managed to connect them via videotape." Sgt. Charles Weaver waved to his wife and children, who gazed back at him from the screen of Brokaw's digital video camera—all for the benefit of national TV audiences.

"I want to be battle-tested, but the idea of going and destroying someone else's family…. There's nothing good about that," the soldier told Brokaw. But there was something good about it for Anthony Swofford, the Desert Storm veteran who's acclaimed memoir *Jarhead* came out just in time to contradict TV's mythic profiles. Swofford and his Marine sniper unit celebrated being deployed for combat by getting drunk and watching war movies. They loved the "magic brutality" that celebrated the "terrible and despicable beauty of their fighting skills. Filmic images of death and carnage are pornographic for the military man." When journalists visited Swofford's platoon in the Saudi desert, his sergeant told the troops to take off their shirts, show their muscles, and say they believed in the mission.

ENTERTAINMENT FROM THE FRONT LINE

Now Rather and Brokaw profile only camera-ready soldiers and such stage-managed heroes have become the mythic stereotype at the center of the militainment genre. The news media was taking cues from movie producer Jerry Bruckheimer and ABC's entertainment division. As the press begged for access to the war in Afghanistan, Bruckheimer filmed *Profiles From the Front Line* with full cooperation from the U.S. military.

Much of the media coverage of the invasion of Iraq was foreshadowed by *Profiles*. Initial scenes establish the war's noble cause as an officer preps his soldiers: "How dare they" come to the U.S. and attack American citizens?

There was no attempt to set the record straight on the civilians killed in the bombing of Afghanistan, and certainly no pictures.

Profiles offers a wholesome, sanitized version of war in which young men are mothered by a surrogate, tough-talking African-American woman who whips her staff into line to prepare the daily meals. The disproportionate number of nurturing women enlisted on *Profiles* makes war fun for the whole family, such as the female nurse who gloats that she was called for duty, not her husband.

Viewers ride along with the bearded Special Forces troops who bully Afghans they claim are Al Qaeda, but look just like villagers. We have no way of knowing, but information is not the point. This is entertainment that primes viewers to be receptive to the messages of war through powerful production qualities, film montages, and the pounding drums of conflict.

An American soldier dies, but we see only grainy, muted-green night-vision images (repeated and slowed down) of a stretcher being carried into the surgical unit and long sequences of the wife and mother who smile nobly at the camera. Similarly grieving family members of dead or captured fighters became familiar TV images during the invasion of Iraq. Such media treatment gives war a dignified purpose, making it appear honorable and virtuous. It justifies the loss of life in its wake.

Amid all the excitement, patriotism, and glory before the war, one tended to forget that war is about killing people unnecessarily, as Chris Hedges told Bill Moyers. "We've lost touch with war's essence. And that essence is death" (*Now*, March 7, 2003). No wonder viewers were not prepared after the war started to see an American soldier face down on the ground, his hands behind his back, subdued after throwing grenades into the tent of his comrades, killing his commander and wounding 15 others. The media-friendly war provided no context for understanding the complexities of a real war and the effects it has on human beings.

Best-selling investigative reporter Greg Palast told me, "We've forgotten about the Iraqis. Who will document the effects of the bombing?" When I asked a journalist if the military would allow embeds to take pictures of Iraqi civilian casualties, the response was, "We're telling the U.S. military's story, that will be up to other journalists." Chris Hedges predicted that reporters who tried to break free and give an accurate picture would "come under great pressure" (*Democracy Now!*, February 27, 2003). But embeds were not likely to investigate, as one from *U.S. News and World Report* told CNBC (February 19, 2003), the Taliban lied about civilian casualties "so we'll be a kind of truth brigade" for the American military. Days before the war (March 13,

2003), the BBC reported that the U.S. military had threatened to target the satellite uplinks of independent journalists covering the war in Iraq. Under such circumstances, the killing of non-embedded veteran ITN reporter Terry Lloyd and other crew members by American forces in Southern Iraq at the start of the war remains suspicious. Journalists continue to refute U.S. claims that troops were being fired upon when they fired into the hotel in Baghdad where the journalists were staying, killing and wounding a number of independent reporters.

WAR AS ADRENALINE RUSH

When the "Final Hour" finally came on March 19, the war was picture perfect. Initial coverage blended excitement and anticipation with firepower and the photogenic bombing of Baghdad. Images of incredible devastation registered as painterly pink clouds when on March 21, 300 cruise missiles destroyed two dozen buildings in a matter of minutes. In the city once again, NBC journalist Peter Arnett exclaimed, "An amazing sight, just like out of an action movie, but this is real."

As U.S. troops pressed into southern Iraq, TV images merged cinematic references with reality-style camera perspectives. Viewers gazed across the sand from inside army vehicles, a fantasy ride with Lawrence of Arabia as the tanks and armored convoys sped "virtually unopposed deep into the Iraqi desert" (CNN, March 21, 2003).

Empowered by riding shotgun with these road warriors, journalists barely contained their excitement. They wore goggles, flack jackets, and even reported through gas masks as they adopted military jargon ("There are boots on the ground"). They interviewed Top Gun pilots and crawled along the ground with gunfire in the distance, pressing microphones into soldier's faces as they pointed their weapons. So surreal was the experience that newscasters felt compelled to repeatedly tell viewers that the images they were seeing were live, not a movie.

Tom Brokaw (*The New York Times*, March 23, 2003) understood the effects of such visual and narrative representations: "Television cannot ever adequately convey the sheer brute force of war, the noise and utter violence." This is certainly true when the violence and brutality are edited out, while the excitement and heroics are sensationalized. But Brokaw passed blame to the medium itself. "It somehow gets filtered through the TV screen and that's probably just as well," he said.

Few unpleasant images disrupted the flow, certainly nothing horrific, gruesome, or in "bad taste." This was war as adrenaline rush with no responsibility.

Americans interested in the effects on the Iraqi population flocked to Web sites for news and pictures of wounded civilians, the war's consequences. One diary of a young man from Baghdad, written under the pseudonym Salam Pax read, "Why does this have to happen to Baghdad? As one of the buildings I really love went up in a huge explosion, I was close to tears."

SHATTERED ILLUSIONS

But by the afternoon of March 23, unmanaged images from Iraqi state TV shattered the grand illusion. As the whole world was watching, Al Jazeera aired video footage of the bloodied bodies of dead American soldiers sprawled carelessly on a slab floor. Iraqi interrogators interviewed the POWs. The war that couldn't wait had suddenly become a problem. Alternative information finally rendered the war real, horrible. Though networks censored the footage initially, they showed clips.

Almost overnight, the tone of media coverage flipped from what CNN's Aaron Brown (*New York Times*, March 25, 2003) admitted was a "gee whiz" attitude to a tempered anxiety about "another messy, frustrating combat situation" (CNN, March 24, 2003). The mix of sentimentality and visual sensationalism was wildly successful as long as it remained unchallenged. By Tuesday, March 24, *The New York Times* noted, "An image of awesome American firepower had been replaced by pictures of vulnerability." The thrilling momentum of the Iraq reality war slammed into a different set of cultural references and memories. An overmatched enemy was engaging in guerrilla tactics resulting in American casualties: quagmires, body counts, and body bags.

A Web site displaying images of Iraqi civilian casualties, <Yellow-Times.org>, was shut down on March 24. That night, embedded journalist Phil Ittner (CBS, March 24, 2003) showed pictures of wounded children, but provided the acceptable context that justified the war. The videophone story from south-central Iraq showed a soldier rocking a little girl in his arms and another stroking her face. They came "streaming out to give what aid they could. They are here to take down the leadership in Baghdad, which they see as a threat to their families back home.... They wish they didn't have to do it."

As the Pentagon scrambled to control the meaning of its now unpredictable war, it knocked out the Iraqi TV signal. "War as it really is" was far too harsh for the Pentagon. On Tuesday, Dan Rather announced approvingly that the U.S. military had "pulled the plug" on what CBS called Saddam's "propaganda" channel.

Ironically, those most critical of the Pentagon as the war stalled were not media professionals themselves, but their retired military consultants. At such moments, the importance of "reliable" embeds became clear. Fox's Sean Hannity (April 1, 2003) fawned over Oliver North embedded with a marine unit, as he dispelled criticism of the war. "There's a lot of negative reporting out there, Ollie." But the marines have gone "so far, so fast, with so few casualties, all the munitions you need, all the supplies you ever wanted, all the gasoline. When people hear it from you, because you're there, it means more than anything I can tell them."

SAVING PRIVATE LYNCH

What the war needed was a stunning plot reversal to propel the narrative forward. On April 2, the military provided the much-needed heroic device (with middle-of-the-night footage): the rescue of Private Jessica Lynch from a Nasiriyah hospital, in what was ubiquitously described as a "daring raid" (CNN, April 8, 2003; NBC, April 6, 2003; ABC, April 7, 2003).

The gripping story of a crack commando operation that plucked the wounded private from danger was fed to reporters at CentCom and eagerly repeated. For CBS (April 11, 2003), it was "a story for history, Jessica comes home." CNN (April 11, 2003) declared, "it was such a lift"; as *Time* magazine put it (April 14, 2003), the story "buoyed a nation wondering what had happened to the short, neat liberation of Iraq." "Hollywood," the magazine asserted, "could not have dreamed up a more singular tale."

But an eyewitness account published in *The Times* (London) (April 16, 2003) undermined the fantasy. Lynch's rescue, the paper reported, "was not the heroic Hollywood story told by the U.S. military, but a staged operation that terrified patients and victimized the doctors who had struggled to save her life." Based on interviews with hospital personnel, including Dr. Harith al-Houssona, the doctor who attended Lynch, *The Times* account described a terrifying assault in which soldiers handcuffed and interrogated doctors and patients, one of whom was paralyzed and on an intravenous drip.

The British Broadcasting Corporation (BBC2, May 18, 2003) has thoroughly investigated the incident and concluded that, "Her story is one of the most stunning pieces of news management ever conceived." Though the assault met no resistance, as Iraqi and Baath leadership forces had fled the city the day before, the action was staged by the U.S. military. "It was like a Hollywood film. They cried 'go, go, go,' with guns without bullets, blanks, and the sound of explosions. They made a show for the American attack on the hospital—action movies like Sylvester Stallone or Jackie Chan" (BBC2, May 18, 2003) No embedded journalists accompanied the raid, and the green night footage was shot by the military. As Robert Scheer (*AlterNet*, May 20, 2003) noted, "The video was artfully edited by the Pentagon and released as proof that a battle to free Lynch had occurred when it had not."

When the footage of the rescue was released in Doha, the words of Gen. Vincent Brooks sounded familiar, similar to the lines delivered in the movie *Black Hawk Down*, "Some brave souls put their lives on the line to make this happen, loyal to a creed that they know that they'll never leave a fallen comrade." Such adherence to fictional texts led the BBC (May 18, 2003) to observe, "The Pentagon had been influenced by Hollywood producers of reality TV and action movies, notably the man behind *Black Hawk Down*, Jerry Bruckheimer." Indeed, it seems more than a coincidence that military spokesman refer to the movie, as one officer quoted in *Time* (April 14, 2003) claimed the rescue, "worked perfectly. It was like *Black Hawk Down* except nothing went wrong."

The sad irony is that the Iraqi doctors worked hard to save her life, but when they attempted to deliver Jessica to a U.S. outpost the day before the raid, the Americans fired on the ambulance driver, making it impossible to proceed. Following the CentCom briefing, the *Washington Post* (April 3, 2003) headlined that "She was Fighting to the Death" and had sustained multiple gunshot wounds, adding that Jessica was later stabbed by Iraqi forces. "It has since emerged that Lynch was neither shot nor stabbed, but rather suffered accident injuries when her vehicle overturned. A medical checkup by U.S. doctors confirmed that account of the Iraqi doctors, who said they had carefully tended her injuries, a broken arm and thigh and a dislocated ankle, in contrast to the U.S. media reports that doctors had ignored Lynch" (*AlterNet*, May 20, 2003).

This incident demonstrates how propaganda, in its reincarnation as militainment, has been reinvented for the wars of the twenty-first century. As the war became problematic, it looked as if the brutal realities might overtake the fictions. The rescue of Jessica, a classic damsel in distress story of mythic proportions, is already culturally compelling. With an overlay of more recent war-hero texts and expert timing, the fictional story buoyed the broader war narrative, providing the heroism, patriotism, and indignation needed for boosting morale and public support for the war.

The ongoing made for TV "reality" war was ready for the next and last plot sequence. It needed an ending.

"NOT CHOREOGRAPHED, NOT STAGE-MANAGED"

If Lynch's rescue provided the symbol of America's sacrifice and heroism, the downed statue of Saddam Hussein in Baghdad's Firdos Square became the icon of its triumph over Iraq. In an interview before the war, publisher and author John MacArthur told me that the military wanted embeds with the troops "for the victory pictures, waving flags and cheering Iraqis." Later, MacArthur told *Democracy Now!* (April 17, 2003), the idea of "irrational exuberance" was preposterous. Upending the statue "is Torry Clark's great media moment."

This is precisely what the statue-toppling provided and networks ran the footage countless times, with breathless commentary about its meaning. "It's a time for rejoicing particularly because of what television cameras clearly revealed—that many Iraqis support the coalition's mission and see the U.S. and its allies not as enemies but as friends and liberators," the *Indianapolis Star* (April 10, 2003) spelled out.

"The picture says something about us as Americans," pronounced *USA Today* (April 10, 2003), "about our can-do spirit, our belief in lending a hand." The *Washington Post's* Ceci Connelly, interviewed on Fox News Channel (April 9, 2003), was one of many to compare it to the tearing down of the Berlin Wall: "Just sort of that pure emotional expression, not choreographed, not stage-managed, the way so many things these days seem to be. Really breathtaking."

A few reporters indicated that the event was not as straightforward as U.S. media usually presented it. "Whenever the cameras pulled back, they revealed a relatively small crowd at the statue," the *Boston Globe* noted (April 10, 2003); others were struck by the fortuitous appearance on the scene of a pre–Gulf War-era Iraqi flag, as well as crowd members who had been spotted at Nasiriyah just the previous day, suggesting their appearance in Firdos Square might be something other than spontaneous.

This use of the power of images to mold perceptions of Iraq was stunningly effective, and at times, as we have seen, quite at odds with what was real. As Ron Martz, a print journalist for *The Atlanta Journal-Constitution* and a former marine, wrote in *Editor and Publisher* online (May 15, 2003), "When I wrote in one story about 'bloody street fighting in Baghdad,' it appeared the morning TV viewers were seeing jubilant marines and Iraqi civilians tearing down statues of Saddam Hussein on the eastern side of the Tigris River. Some readers, believing all of Baghdad was like that, were livid. They did not grasp the fact that, on the western side of the river, pitched battles were still taking place. Because they did not see it on TV, it was not happening. And it did not fit their view of the war."

With the media's overwhelming rush to lift the image of the tumbling statue to iconic status, reality was once again overtly ignored. By the end of the day, noted *Chicago Tribune* television critic Steve Johnson (April 10, 2003), "the symbol's power had overtaken the hard facts."

Indeed, 23 days after the war started, CBS's *48 Hours* (April 11, 2003) opened its celebratory segment, "After the Fall," with footage of the toppling statue. As Dan Rather observed with evident approval, "Remnants of the regime still stand, but surrounded now by a conquering power." Rather encountered burnt-out vehicles and intoned, "In this one, there is a body. What happened, who shot him, who knows?" In the world of militainment, the "conquering power" bears no responsibility for the death left in its wake. In the chaos that was Baghdad, where soldiers served as "police and social workers," no phrase was too hackneyed for Rather: "Theirs is not to reason why, theirs is but to do or die."

The actual quotation, from Tennyson's "Charge of the Light Brigade," is the less melodramatic "theirs but to do *and* die." In either case, an ominous quotation at a time of endless war, when democracy's critical dialogue is replaced with militainment.

A MODEL WAR?

Before the war, with the promise of covering combat, the press corps was all abuzz with World War II heroics and "band of brothers" camaraderie, evoking the memory of Ernie Pyle, the correspondent famous for his grunt's-eye view of the infantrymen he followed. "Pyle embedded himself among the troops, taking terrific risks to report on 'the boys' on the front lines," the *Washington Post* recalled (March 7, 2003). But Pyle's assuring words always passed army censors even, for example, after the terrible defeat at the Kasserine Gap in Tunisia. "I have seen them in battle… and there is nothing wrong with the common American soldier. His fighting spirit is good. His morale is okay."

It is less widely known that Ernie Pyle grew weary of battle. He had burned out and gone home but returned to the Pacific theater to boost the men's morale at the request of the military. When he was shot and killed by the Japanese, more disturbing words were found in his pocket: "You at home need not even try to understand. You don't see him lying so grotesque and pasty beside the gravel road in France. We saw him, saw him by the multiple thousands, that's the difference." His editor would not publish these words after his death.

Veteran and critic Paul Fussell knows the grand narratives of the Second World War are always invoked for a reason: "The Allied war has been sanitized and romanticized almost beyond recognition by the sentimental, the loony patriotic, the ignorant, and the bloodthirsty."

The media would be better served by remembering the First Great War, World War I, "the war to end all wars" instead of trying to model the new wars of the twenty-first century through the mythic lens of World War II. Journalist John Keegan says, "The First World War was a tragic and unnecessary conflict" (*The First World War*, Knopf, New York, 1999, p. 3). Yet it wasn't stopped and raged on to kill 20 million people. Phillip Knightley places a major portion of the blame on the public's ignorance, and the failure of the war correspondents: "They identified themselves absolutely with the armies in the field; they protected the high command from criticism, wrote jauntily about life in the trenches, kept an inspired silence about the slaughter, and allowed themselves to be absorbed by the propaganda machine" (*The First Casualty: The War Correspondent as Hero and Myth-Maker from the Crimea to Kosovo*, Johns Hopkins University Press, Baltimore, 2000, pp. 84–85).

Historians have not been kind to the brutal generals of World War I or to the war correspondents that helped create the hysteria that propelled the war. A kind of war hysteria was promoted during the Iraq conflict, creating intolerance common to a propaganda environment. The few print journalists who rejected the militainment spin came under fire from their readers. As Martz (*Editor and Publisher* online, May 15, 2003) noted, "Criticism was not limited to me. They even criticized soldiers for doing what all soldiers do—complain. When I voiced complaints from soldiers about the lack of mail, water, and spare parts, they were called "whiners" and "crybabies." And when I quoted one soldier, who had been under fire almost daily for four weeks, complaining about faulty intelligence, one reader suggested he be stripped of his uniform and sent home in disgrace." Such were the effects of propaganda on the target public.

Unarguably influential is shaping public opinion in the short term, the true consequences of any new form of propaganda are not always apparent, even to those who propagate it. The demonization of the Germans as "Barbaric Huns" propelled World War I, but led to untold misery. And as Jim Hightower (*AlterNet*, May 20, 2003) points out, in addition to the million dollars spent on the "Top Gun" episode, Bush also spent "the integrity of the American presidency" as he used "our brave soldiers as his political props." For Robert Scheer (*AlterNet*, May 20, 2003), one of the disturbing aspects of the Jessica Lynch story is that "the premeditated manufacture of the rescue... stains those who have performed real acts of bravery, whether in war or peacetime." The president may have experienced a "Top Gun" moment of fame, but history will not be kind to the propagandistic creation of the Private Lynch story, to militainment in general, and surely not to the entire web of fabrications that are the stated rationales for the invasion itself.

CHAPTER 7

Weapons of Mass Deception

BY SHELDON RAMPTON AND JOHN STAUBER, *PR WATCH*

Led into war by U.S. president George W. Bush, more than 300,000 U.S. and British soldiers—many of whom no doubt sincerely believe that they are helping to make the world a better, safer place for themselves and their loved ones— are risking their lives. Outside the United States, however, most nations have refused to support the Bush Administration's plans, and there is strong popular opposition to war against Iraq. The absence of broad domestic and international support for U.S. actions is especially striking in light of the aggressive public relations campaign that the Bush Administration has waged to win the "hearts and minds" of the world. International opinion remains strongly opposed to the war, and although a majority of Americans now say they support the invasion of Iraq, polls report "wide disparities among demographic groups."

Experts warn that the war in Iraq violates international law and will increase the likelihood of domestic and international terrorism, making the world *more* dangerous. In spite of these warnings, few antiwar viewpoints penetrate the major U.S. media or other institutions responsible for informing public opinion. Indeed, the media appear to have adopted President Bush's philosophy: "Either you are with us, or you are with the terrorists." This binary worldview of "good" and "evil" nations has come to form the basis of the Bush Administration's foreign policy communication strategy, with potentially dangerous consequences.

The Bush Administration and its multinational corporate sponsors have already squandered the worldwide sympathy that the United States government enjoyed following the terrorist attacks of September 11, 2001. Unilateral U.S.

military actions around the world, coupled with the administration's refusal to cooperate on many international issues such as global warming, land mine proliferation, and resource conservation have contributed to rising anti-U.S., or more likely anti-Bush, sentiments throughout the world. These sentiments are especially strong in countries that are likely recruiting grounds for Al Qaeda and other terrorist organizations. Moreover, it is precisely because the U.S. military seems so invulnerable that America's adversaries have chosen to turn its citizens into targets.

SELF-FULFILLING PROPHECIES

The first example of the Bush mentality in practice came in his January 2002 State of the Union address, in which he described Iran, Iraq, and North Korea as an "axis of evil." In reality, not a shred of evidence suggested any alliance, practical or otherwise, among them. Moreover, Iran and Iraq have been bitter enemies for decades. Indeed, the Bush Administration has produced no evidence linking any of the three countries to the terrorists of September 11. The main thing each country had in common was that the Bush Administration hated them.

Nevertheless, the Bush equation has acquired the characteristics of a self-fulfilling prophecy. As the U.S. Administration fans the flames of war, Iraq and North Korea have found themselves thrust for the first time into an alliance of convenience, as North Korea opportunistically uses the administration's preoccupation with Iraq to push forward its effort to develop nuclear weapons, convinced it is on Washington's next hit list. The Iranians also realize that they are next on the administration's list of nations to invade, and they too have begun to respond in kind.

THIS MODERN WORLD

by TOM TOMORROW

The Bush Administration's attempt to link Iraq with Al Qaeda has also become a self-fulfilling prophecy. On the eve of war with Iraq, Osama bin Laden emerged briefly from his fortress of solitude to call for *jihad* against Jews and the United States. Bin Laden's hatred for Saddam Hussein is long-standing and well-known, but thanks to the Bush Administration, they now see a need to fight against a common enemy—namely, the people of the United States.

Even traditional U.S. allies in Europe are rapidly becoming enemies, thanks to the Bush doctrine. Even as the administration attempted, through PR gestures, to dispel the world's growing perception of the United States as an arrogant superpower, Donald Rumsfeld helped *reinforce* that perception by publicly dismissing the antiwar positions of France and Germany as fuzzy-minded thinking from "old Europe." As if that weren't enough to anger Europeans, Rumsfeld went further a few days later and equated Germany with long-time U.S. adversaries Libya and Cuba. If Germany is not "with the United States," in other words, it too must be "with the terrorists."

These kind of statements contradict the beneficial role Germany has played in the War on Terrorism. For example, U.S. officials currently fail to mention how German soldiers helped protect U.S. military personnel and families at U.S. bases in Germany after September 11, along with the investigative and intelligence assistance Germany has provided. The German news magazine *Der Spiegel* reveals that Donald Rumsfeld, who is of German descent, had for a long time—until September of last year—strong relations with and a very positive view of Germany. It is uncertain if and when the American-German relations will be reconciled.

For supporters of the current U.S. policy, the Bush doctrine has the emotional appeal of all simplistic equations. As a solution to the problems we face, however, it is dangerously misguided. Perhaps the most dangerous as-

pect of the Bush doctrine is its circular reasoning. If you *agree* with us, the doctrine says, you are a friend and your views are worth hearing. If you *disagree*, you are an enemy and your views are suspect. This has made it impossible for the Bush Administration to listen to the views of its critics.

ENSURING CONSISTENCY

In January 2003, the Bush Administration signed an executive order creating an Office of Global Communications (OGC), whose mission is to "ensure consistency in messages that will promote the interests of the United States abroad, prevent misunderstanding, build support for and among coalition partners of the United States, and inform international audiences." To achieve this goal, the OGC is sponsoring a "Global Messenger" e-mail of talking points sent almost daily to administration officials, U.S. embassies, Congress, and others. It is also organizing daily telephone conference calls to coordinate foreign policy messages among U.S. government agencies and representatives of British Prime Minister Tony Blair.

These activities may sound rather innocuous. The idea of "ensuring consistency" is a cardinal rule of PR crisis communications, whose practitioners try whenever possible to make sure that all messages flow through a single, controlling channel. In practice, however, ensuring consistency leads to a concerted effort to enforce a "party line" on all messages emanating from the U.S. government, effectively silencing anyone whose point of view contradicts the official institutional message.

The Bush executive order also says that the OGC will "coordinate the creation of temporary teams of communicators for short-term placement in areas of high global interest and media attention." Here, what they are contemplating is the deployment of crisis teams to respond quickly to controversies. The State Department is creating an Islamic media center in London to manage U.S. communications with the Al Jazeera satellite television network. The State Department is also dispatching U.S. teams abroad to counter statements issued by the government of Iraq or other critics of U.S. policy.

The administration's obsession with "staying on message" is also reflected in Bush's reluctance to hold press conferences and its insistence on tightly scripting those few conferences it does allow. Activist and journalist Russell Mokhiber says the administration's March 6, 2003 news conference "might have been the most controlled presidential news conference in recent memory. Even the president admitted during the press conference that 'this is a scripted' press conference. The president had a list of 17 reporters who he was going to call on. He didn't take any questions from reporters raising their hands. And he refused to call on Helen Thomas, the dean of the White House press corps, who traditionally asks the first question."

White House communications director Dan Bartlett explained, "If you have a message you're trying to deliver, a news conference can go in a different direction." However, "In this case, we know what the questions are going to be, and those are the ones we want to answer."

All of these tactics fall within the framework of a "propaganda model" of communication, whose strategies and assumptions are fundamentally contrary to a democratic model. Propaganda consists of attempts to manipulate or coerce the thinking of an enemy or captive population. Some scholars refer to propaganda as a "hypodermic approach" to communication, in which the communicator's objective is to "inject" his ideas into the minds of a "target population." This is quite different from the democratic model, which views communications as a *dialogue* between presumed equals. The goal of the propaganda model is simply to achieve efficient indoctrination, and it therefore tends to regard the assumptions of the democratic model as inconvenient obstacles to efficient communication.

This may seem like merely a theoretical point, but it has serious practical consequences. The Bush Administration's approach to communication through the Office of Global Communications is bound to fail, and it is failing already. In reality, it is impossible to "ensure consistency" and control the channels of communications on an international scale, and glaring contradictions are already evident in the Bush Administration's message strategy.

THE WORLD'S BIGGEST FOCUS GROUP

The first contradiction comes when the Bush Administration tries to counter the growing worldwide perception of the United States as an arrogant nation while simultaneously refusing to listen to its critics. Rumsfeld's dismissal of France and Germany as "old Europe" is only one example of the administration's inability to listen to other points of view. The same pattern was also evident following February 15, 2003, when more than 11 million people protested in cities throughout the world to oppose an invasion of Iraq. Conservative pundits disingenuously characterized the protesters as "treasonous" and as "giving comfort to Saddam Hussein." Bush himself airily dismissed the protests, saying that he doesn't "decide policy based upon a focus group."

Bush's statement speaks volumes, both about his disregard for real opinion and about his inability to think outside the framework of a propaganda model of communication. There is a world of difference between a focus group and a mass citizen protest (which attracted 500,000 people in New York alone, as well as more than a million in London). Marketers use opinion polls and focus groups to design strategies for selling products and policies to the public, but their purpose is simply to facilitate the delivery of propaganda. Polls are not intended to influence *what* to do but simply *how to sell it*. It is inconceivable that Pepsi would let a focus group tell it whether to sell fizzy brown soda. All it wants to know is whether the Britney Spears ads are working better than the Ozzy Osbourne ads. The people who show up at political rallies, however, are trying to send a message about *what* to do.

Bush's claim that he doesn't rely on focus groups is also spin. U.S. politicians routinely use focus groups, and the Bush Administration has been using them both in the United States and abroad. Writing in the *Washington Monthly* in April 2002, Joshua Green noted that "the Bush Administration is a frequent consumer of polls, though it takes extraordinary measures to appear that it isn't." In 2001, the administration spent close to $1 million for polling, using political advisors like Jan van Lohuizen and his focus-group guru, Fred Steeper. "Policies are chosen beforehand, and polls are used to spin them," Green wrote. "Because many of Bush's policies aren't necessarily popular with a majority of voters, Steeper and van Lohuizen's job essentially consists of finding words to sell them to the public."

Polling is also being used to sell the United States abroad. In May 2002, Franklin Foer reported in *The New Republic* that the Rendon Group, one of the Pentagon's PR firms, "monitors Muslim opinion with polls and focus groups, and then it generates plans for influencing it."

Charlotte Beers, the former advertising executive who recently resigned her position as U.S. Undersecretary of State for Public Diplomacy, also used focus groups in her work. Testifying before Congress in April 2002, Beers promised to "increase polling… in Muslim countries and communities to provide policymakers with information on foreign publics' attitudes, perceptions, and opinions so public diplomacy messages can be more effectively targeted…. These surveys will include regular polls in Afghanistan and in Muslim-majority countries to track public opinion over time…. Other enhancements include increased polling in sub-Saharan Africa on HIV/AIDS, democracy, and the economy; focused polling in Indonesia, Thailand, and the Philippines; research into Western Hemisphere countries, especially Mexico, Brazil, Venezuela, and the Caribbean;… regular focus groups and polls in Russia and the former Soviet republics; studies in Europe on missile defense and anti-Americanism; and targeted polling in the Middle East on a variety of issues."

The real problem with the Bush Administration is that it doesn't consider anything *but* focus groups and opinion polls. It never thinks of public opinion as worth considering in its own right and instead merely uses it to refine the message points that go out each day in its "Global Messenger" e-mails.

BELIEVING THEIR OWN PROPAGANDA

As the editors of PR Watch, we have frequently reported on manipulative and deceptive propaganda practices of governments and corporations. One of PR's dirtiest little secrets, however, is that it often fails to influence the "hearts and minds" of its "target audiences." The Bush Administration has failed at persuading the Arab world to support its policies toward Iraq. It has also failed in Europe and throughout the rest of the world, and its hold on public opinion in the United States is shaky at best.

In fact, propaganda is often more successful at indoctrinating the propagandists themselves than it is at influencing the thinking of others. The discipline of "ensuring message consistency" cannot hope to succeed at controlling the world's perceptions of something as broad, sprawling, and contradictory as the Bush Administration's foreign policy. However, it may be successful at enabling people like George W. Bush and Donald Rumsfeld to ignore the warnings coming from Europe and other quarters. As our leaders lose their ability to listen to critics, we face the danger that they will underestimate the risks and costs involved in going to war.

One indication of the administration's credulity regarding its own propaganda is its reliance on information coming from the Iraqi National Congress (INC). The INC was created in the early 1990s with support from the Rendon Group. At the time, the first Bush Administration hoped that by sponsoring a political opposition group, it might prompt Iraqi military leaders to overthrow Saddam Hussein in a "zipless coup." This never happened, but the INC remains active today. Its head, Ahmed Chalabi, openly dreams that the United States will install him as the country's next ruler.

Writing in *The American Prospect*, journalist Robert Dreyfuss noted in December 2002 that the Bush Administration prefers the INC's analysis of conditions inside Iraq over the analysis coming from scholars and even from intelligence agencies like the CIA. "But most Iraq hands with long experience in dealing with that country's tumultuous politics consider the INC's intelligence-gathering abilities to be nearly nil," Dreyfuss wrote. "The Pentagon's critics are appalled that intelligence provided by the INC might shape U.S. decisions about going to war against Baghdad. At the CIA and at the State Department, Ahmed Chalabi, the INC's leader, is viewed as the ineffectual head of a self-inflated and corrupt organization skilled at lobbying and public relations, but not much else."

Other indications of the Bush Administration's success at self-indoctrination became evident shortly after the commencement of war. At the onset, several administration officials predicted a quick, easy victory. "Support for Saddam... will collapse at the first whiff of gunpowder," predicted Richard Perle. The war will be "a cakewalk," said Ken Adelman. According to Donald Rumsfeld, "it will not be long." And Dick Cheney said the Iraqi people "will welcome as liberators the United States." When those predictions failed to materialize, journalists began to hear leaks from the Pentagon saying that Rumsfeld and others had gravely underestimated the strength of Iraqi resistance and the resulting risks and costs of the war. "Intelligence officials say Rumsfeld, his deputy Paul Wolfowitz, and other Pentagon civilians ignored much of the advice of the CIA and the Defense Intelligence Agency in favor of reports from the Iraqi opposition and from Israeli sources that predicted an immediate uprising against Hussein once the Americans attacked," reported Joseph L. Galloway, the military affairs correspondent for Knight Ridder.

Following World War I, Austrian journalist Karl Wiegand made an interesting observation: "How are nations ruled and led into war?" he asked. "Politicians lie to journalists and then believe those lies when they see them in print." This may seem cynical, but it was true then, and it is true today.

No one with any knowledge of history or politics would expect today's leaders to behave in a perfectly moral fashion. Few politicians have ever done that, and perhaps they never will. However, we should expect them at the very least to know what they are doing, and as the Bush Administration traps itself within the mirrored echo chamber of its own propaganda, the danger increases that it will miscalculate, with catastrophic consequences for the United States and the world. If Bush's invasion of Iraq triggers a pan-Islamic *jihad* against the United States, the religious fundamentalists close to the Bush Administration may see their apocalyptic vision of the future of the Middle East become yet another self-fulfilling prophecy. The bullet points in the Bush Administration's message on Iraq are easy to summarize. Each point has been carefully "focused" to appeal in a misleading fashion to legitimate public aspirations for peace, safety, freedom, human rights, and democracy:

"IRAQ IS IN CAHOOTS WITH INTERNATIONAL TERRORISM."

The Bush Administration has not hesitated to use outright disinformation to deliver this message. In December, *60 Minutes* debunked an often-mentioned report that Al Qaeda hijacker Mohammed Atta met with Iraqi intelligence officials in Prague prior to the deadly attacks on September 11. Despite the absence of evidence that the meeting took place, administration officials as senior as Vice President Dick Cheney continue to repeat it. The very idea of such an alliance is far-fetched because Osama bin Laden has called for the destruction of the "infidel" Saddam Hussein's regime.

Still, the Bush and Blair Administrations seem to feel the need to attempt to fabricate links between Iraq and Al Qaeda. This lay at the heart of the scandal in England in February following the disclosure that much of its published dossier on Iraq was actually plagiarized from the Internet. Touted as an analysis by the British MI6 spy agency, the document was actually cobbled together by junior aides to Alastair Campbell, Tony Blair's top spin doctor. Several pages had been cut and pasted, right down to the typographical errors, from the Internet version of an article by a postdoctorate student.

The dossier was "obviously part of the prime minister's propaganda campaign," said Charles Heyman, editor of *Jane's World Armies*. "The intelligence services were not involved—I've had two people phoning me today to say, 'Look, we had nothing to do with it.'" In fact, a leaked report from British intelligence explicitly contradicts the government's official position, saying there "are no known links between the Iraqi regime and the Al Qaeda network."

"IRAQ HAS WEAPONS OF MASS DESTRUCTION."

Iraq did possess weapons of mass destruction at the time of Operation Desert Storm (many of them supplied by the United States and other western nations). International sanctions forced the destruction of many weapons in the Iraqi arsenal, and it is true that the regime has failed to document their complete destruction, so it is possible that some such weapons remain. However, the Bush Administration's paranoid warnings of imminent danger are contradicted by prominent analysts within the Western intelligence community. The main reason that this claim continues to circulate is that the U.S. Administration has been relentless about demanding "message consistency" from government officials.

"Even as it prepares for war against Iraq, the Pentagon is already engaged on a second front: its war against the Central Intelligence Agency," reported Robert Dreyfuss in the December 16, 2002 issue of *The American Prospect*. "Morale inside the U.S. national-security apparatus is said to be low, with career staffers feeling intimidated and pressured to justify the push for war."

In July, Senator Bob Graham (D–Florida), who houses the Senate Intelligence Committee, was so baffled by the contradictory assessments of Iraq coming from different agencies that he asked the CIA to come up with a report on the likelihood that Saddam Hussein would use weapons of mass destruction (WMD). The CIA concluded that the likelihood of Hussein using such weapons was "low" for the "foreseeable future." However, the CIA analysis added, "Should Saddam conclude that a U.S.-led attack could no longer be deterred, he probably would become much less constrained in adopting terrorist actions.... Saddam might decide that the extreme step of assisting Islamist terrorists in conducting a WMD attack against the United States would be his last chance to exact vengeance by taking a large number of victims with him."

The gap between rhetoric and reality about Iraq's weaponry became evident with the launch of war in March 2003. As U.S. forces stormed into Iraq, U.S. and Kuwaiti officials talked ominously about reports that Iraq had allegedly fired two banned Scud missiles at U.S. positions inside Kuwait. Neither missile produced any casualties, but hundreds of newspapers and other media reported ominously on the alleged Scud attack. "The very missiles Saddam Hussein fired at U.S. forces in Kuwait appear to have been the same weapons he either claimed not to possess or agreed to destroy," reported the Associated Press on March 21. "The first salvos were both a telling sign of Iraq's hidden weapons and a reminder that Saddam still has the capability of delivering chemical or biological warheads." This triumphant line ended when Kuwaiti and U.S. officials had to withdraw their claim that Scuds had been used.

As late as September 2002, a British report said that Iraq might have as many as 20 banned Scud missiles, about one-fourth of the 88 Scuds that Iraq actually fired during Desert Storm. And even if Hussein still possesses Scuds, weapons specialist John Clearwater said it was doubtful that they still function, noting that Iraqis have not been able to fire and test the missiles or obtain replacement parts for them for more than a decade. "These missiles have a short shelf life," said Clearwater, who has written three books on nuclear weapons and cruise missiles. "The longer you go without testing, the lower confidence you have in them."

A hypothetical arsenal of 20 Scuds also pales in comparison with the hundreds of real Tomahawk cruise missiles that the United States launched directly into Baghdad on the first day of its "Shock and Awe" bombing campaign.

"IRAQ HAS A NUCLEAR WEAPONS PROGRAM."

No one disputes that Saddam desires to have nuclear weapons and made active attempts to develop them before the first Gulf War. However, the 1991 Gulf War led to the destruction of whatever facilities he did have, with subsequent weapons inspections making it difficult for Saddam to restart the program.

In the push for the 2003 war with Iraq, Bush Administration officials, including the president himself in his spring 2003 State of the Union speech, cited evidence that Saddam attempted to buy 500 tons of uranium from Niger. However, officials of the International Atomic Energy Agency (IAEA) looked at the evidence and stated that it was obviously forged. Also, a year earlier the CIA found the evidence to be unreliable.

Congressmen Henry Waxman, who approved Bush's war initiative, is concerned that such a mishap could have occurred. "It is hard to imagine how this situation could have developed," he stated in a letter to the president. The two most obvious explanations—knowing deception or unfathomable incompetence—both have immediate and serious implications." Waxman added, "These facts raise troubling questions. It appears that at the same time you, Secretary Rumsfeld, and State Department officials were citing Iraq's efforts to obtain uranium from Africa as a crucial part of the case against Iraq, U.S. intelligence officials regarded this very same evidence as unreliable. If true, this is deeply disturbing: It would mean that your administration asked the U.N. Security Council, the Congress, and the American people to rely on information that your own experts knew was not credible."

The Bush Administration has failed to provide adequate explanation for this situation, and the national media has failed to pursue the matter.

"IRAQ BRUTALIZES ITS OWN PEOPLE."

There is no question that this is true, but nevertheless, the administration has resorted to lying about Iraqi atrocities. During the buildup to Operation Desert Storm in 1990, the first Bush Administration, working closely with the Hill & Knowlton PR firm, circulated false claims that Iraqi soldiers had bayoneted pregnant women and pulled newborn infants from hospital incubators, leaving the babies to die on the cold hospital floor.

Why tell lies about Iraqi atrocities when there are so many true stories to showcase? One reason is that many of Saddam Hussein's *worst* crimes were committed with U.S. support, both before and after Operation Desert Storm. In the 1980s, Donald Rumsfeld and other officials in the first Bush Administration treated Hussein as a valued ally while he gassed Kurds and launched human wave assaults against Iran. Rather than face these realities about Iraqi human rights violations, the White House prefers to dwell on false stories or on stories that are selectively told to omit mention of the U.S. role.

The National Security Archive, a non-profit research institute on international affairs, recently published a series of declassified U.S. documents detailing the U.S. embrace of Saddam Hussein in the early 1980s, including a photo and video footage of Donald Rumsfeld personally shaking Hussein's hand. More important than the handshake, the documents show that the United States supported Saddam even though he had invaded neighboring Iran and even though the United States knew that Iraq had long-range nuclear aspirations, abused the human rights of its citizens, and used chemical weapons on Iranians and Kurds. As the *Washington Post* reported in December 2002, "The administrations of Ronald Reagan and George H.W. Bush authorized the sale to Iraq of numerous items that had both military and civilian applications, including poisonous chemicals and deadly biological viruses, such as anthrax and bubonic plague."

"THIS WAR IS NOT ABOUT OIL."

The Bush Administration constantly repeats that war with Iraq is not about oil. U.S. Secretary of Defense Donald Rumsfeld proclaimed on a 2002 Infinity Radio call-in program, "It has nothing to do with oil, literally nothing to do with oil." However, this goes contrary to history and Rumsfeld's own involvement with Iraq during the Reagan Administration.

As shown in declassified documents published by the National Security Archive, the embrace of Saddam Hussein by the Reagan and Bush Administrations in the 1980s was motivated by oil. The Institute for Policy Studies (IPS) has produced an investigative report, *Crude Vision,* showing connections between the Aqaba pipeline project and then–Secretary of State George Schultz's former company Bechtel. Many of the officials involved with the failed deal—including Donald Rumsfeld, Ed Meese, George Shultz, James Schlesinger, Robert McFarlane, Lawrence Eagleburger, and Judge William Clark—have subsequently helped craft current president George W. Bush's policy towards Iraq. According to the IPS report, "The break in U.S.-Iraq relations occurred not after Iraq used chemical weapons on the Iranians, nor after Iraq gassed its own Kurdish people, nor even after Iraq invaded Kuwait, but rather, followed Saddam's rejection of the Aqaba pipeline deal."

"THIS IS NOT A WAR AT ALL; IT'S A 'LIBERATION' MOVEMENT."

This message is embodied in the very name of the latest White House PR front group, the "Committee for the Liberation of Iraq." However, this message too is a mixed bag.

The Kurdish population of Iraq has learned through bitter experience not to trust U.S. promises of "liberation." In fact, U.S. policies have historically aligned it more closely with the Sunni Muslims who comprise the power base for Saddam Hussein's Baath party than with the Shiite Muslims and Kurds who comprise 80 percent of the country's population.

During Desert Storm, the Bush Administration called on the Kurds to rise up and rebel, but when they did, realpolitik took precedence over morality. The United States may hate Saddam Hussein, but it has no desire to see Kurdish aspirations realized, particularly when Turkey, an important U.S. ally, regards the Kurds as terrorists. The Kurds, who made the mistake of taking the Bush Administration at its word, were shocked when it pulled back and allowed Hussein's regime to brutally crush their uprising. Is there any reason to expect a different result this time? As preparations for war neared completion in January 2003, reported Patrick Cockburn, "American officials angered representatives of the Iraqi opposition, much of which is Shia and Kurdish, at a meeting in Ankara, Turkey by revealing that America planned a military government for Iraq but would keep in place most of the Sunni establishment that had served President Hussein." Reports of Turkish troop movements into Kurdish north Iraq on March 22 suggest that this war may again trap the Kurds between Iraq and a hard place. On the one hand, "There is deep concern in Turkey that the Kurds in northern Iraq may use the war to set up an independent Kurdistan, which Turkish officials fear would inflame their own large Kurdish minority." On the other, Kurds fear new Turkish military atrocities.

Iraq's Shiite Muslims, who make up a majority of the country's total population, also distrust the United States. Mohammed Baqir Hakim heads the Supreme Assembly of the Islamic Revolution in Iraq (SAIRI), the main Shiite opposition movement in Iraq's south. On March 22, 2003, he pledged that SAIRI would not join the United States in its war to topple Saddam Hussein. Moreover, SAIRI, which looks to Iran for leadership, is likely to fight against any plans for U.S. military occupation after Saddam is toppled. "Even a lightning quick blitzkrieg victory in this war could be complicated and soured by a far more massive guerrilla campaign in oil-rich, majority Shiite areas," reported UPI's Martin Sieff. "Its refusal to raise a finger to topple Saddam, despite his ruthless crushing of a Shiite popular uprising after his 1991 Gulf War defeat, confirms trends United Press International Iran Media Watch columnist Mojdeh Sionit has been tracking that the Tehran government now looks upon a confident, aggressive United States newly victorious in Iraq as a far more dangerous and immediate threat than Saddam, even though he killed close to a million Iranians in the 1980–88 Iran-Iraq War."

Many U.S. citizens, including soldiers currently at war, genuinely believe that they are helping lead the Iraqi people into a better, more democratic regime where civil rights are respected. The people who live in the Middle East, however, are well aware of the long and contradiction-filled history of U.S. government support for undemocratic regimes in the region and elsewhere. For the people in Arab nations, therefore, the attitude of this war slogan is seen as naiveté at best and at worst, as arrogance and malign indifference.

"WE'RE NOT AGAINST MUSLIMS."

Officially, the Bush Administration has taken pains to insist that it regards Islam as a "religion of peace." The Council of American Muslims for Understanding, an organization created by the U.S. State Department, has been trying to impress Muslims abroad. It has a Web site and a glossy brochure titled "Muslim Life in America." However, these words belie the anti-Muslim vitriol coming from Bush's strongest supporters in the ultra-conservative Christian movement. On February 1, 2003, the Conservative Political Action Committee held its annual meeting in Washington while vendors at exhibition booths sold Islamaphobic paraphernalia such as a bumper sticker that said, "No Muslims—No Terrorism."

During the Islamic holy month of Ramadan, Bush was forced to issue a statement disavowing anti-Islamic comments by prominent conservative Christian leaders. Yet key supporters of the president, including some of his advisors, regard Muslims as "worse than the Nazis" because "what the Muslims want to do to the Jews is worse" (to use the words of Pat Robertson, whose Christian Coalition was a key source of voters that got Bush elected). A prominent book in their circles is *Islam Unveiled* by Robert Spencer, which purports to prove that violence is taught at the root of the Qur'an.

A February 15, 2003 conference of the Christian Coalition of America (CCA) was dubbed an "Islamaphobic hate-fest" by the Council on American-Islamic Relations. Speakers included Daniel Pipes, who said "increased stature, and affluence, and enfranchisement of American Muslims will present true dangers to American Jews," along with Joseph Farah, editor of <WorldNetDaily.com>, who said "Islam has been at war with the West, with Christianity, with Judaism... ever since the days of Muhammad." Another speaker at the forum, *Boston Herald* columnist Don Feder, characterized Islam as a religion which, "throughout its 1,400-year history, has lent itself well to fanaticism, terrorism, mass murder, oppression, and conversion by the sword."

Many Christian fundamentalists also see conflict in the Middle East as a fulfillment of Biblical prophecies of Armageddon that predict war and mass slaughters of Jews and Muslims. Others speak of the need for converting Muslims to Christianity to end their "problem with violence"—talk that reminds Muslims of the Christian crusades and other past attempts at forcible conversion.

It is hardly surprising, therefore, that Muslims are skeptical when the Bush Administration talks of peace, love, and understanding. In December, Charlotte Beers launched an advertising campaign in Arab countries. Titled "Shared Values," the campaign tried to showcase the religious tolerance and friendly treatment of Muslims in the United States. The campaign was abruptly terminated after a month, however, when several Arab governments refused to run the ads and focus groups said the ads left them cold.

A frequently-updated version of this article has been posted to the Disinfopedia, a collaboratively-produced Internet database and "encyclopedia of propaganda" that collects information on government and industry propaganda campaigns. If you would like to contribute to the Disinfopedia or read the latest update of this article, visit <www.disinfopedia.org/wiki. phtml? title=Weapons_of_mass_deception>.

CHAPTER 8

Iraq War: Before and Beyond

BY NORMAN SOLOMON, PETER PHILLIPS, MARCUS BORGMAN, AND TOM LOUGH

Media Fog Of War

BY NORMAN SOLOMON

By a two-to-one margin, Americans "use clearly positive words in their descriptions of the president," a polling outfit reported in early May of 2003. The Pew Research Center concluded that "there is little doubt... the war in Iraq has improved the president's image" in the United States.

Such assessments stood in sharp contrast to views overseas. Earlier in the same spring, the Pew center released survey results showing that "U.S. favorability ratings have plummeted in the past six months"—not only in "countries actively opposing war," but also in "countries that are part of the 'coalition of the willing.'" The poll numbers indicating a "favorable view of the U.S." were low in one country after another—only 48 percent in Great Britain, 31 percent in France, 28 percent in Russia, 25 percent in Germany, 14 percent in Spain, and 12 percent in Turkey.

To a large extent, the disparity between public opinion in the USA and elsewhere in the world can be explained with one word: media. Overall, the American news media do a great job of cheerleading Uncle Sam's stride across the planet.

Soon after Gulf War II ended, meticulous researchers at the media watch group Fairness and Accuracy in Reporting (FAIR), where I'm an associate, pointed out that U.S. news outlets "have been quick to declare the U.S. war against Iraq a success, but in-depth investigative reporting about the war's likely health and environmental consequences has been scarce." As reported by the London-based *Guardian*, during the war the Pentagon dropped 1,500 cluster bombs—horrific weaponry designed to fire small pieces of metal that slice through human bodies. Unexploded cluster bombs continued to detonate, sometimes in the hands of Iraqi children. In addition, as had occurred during the first Gulf War, the U.S. government again fortified some munitions with depleted uranium (DU), leaving behind fine-particle radioactive dust of the sort that has been linked to cancer and birth defects.

Those important stories—about cluster bombs and depleted uranium—became known to many news watchers on several continents. But not in the United States. Searching the comprehensive Nexis media database through May 5, 2003, the FAIR researchers found that "there have been no in-depth reports about cluster bombs on ABC, CBS, or NBC's nightly news programs since the start of the war" on March 20. Those news shows provided just "a few passing mentions of cluster bombs." And the network evening news programs did even worse on DU reportage. "Since the beginning of the year," FAIR discovered, "the words 'depleted uranium' have not been uttered once on *ABC World News Tonight*, *CBS Evening News*, or *NBC Nightly News*, according to Nexis."

Meanwhile, the deck of cards featuring 52 Iraqi villains (with Saddam Hussein as the Ace of Spades) became one of the great PR innovations of the war on Iraq. By coincidence, on the same day that FAIR completed its research, five "Army intelligence specialists"—who designed the cards—stepped forward to take a bow in Washington. Although a spokesperson for Central Command conceded that there was "no word on the cards helping find anyone," the Pentagon's deck had turned out to be a stroke of media genius. It tapped into the American public's appetite for fun ways to identify bad guys to be hunted down.

By mid-spring 2003, the tables had turned on Iraq's Deputy Prime Minister Tariq Aziz, suddenly a prisoner of the U.S. government. The previous fall and winter, I had participated in three meetings with Aziz at his office in Baghdad. Up close, he made me think of a bantam rooster with a foghorn voice. Tough and articulate, he seemed equally comfortable in a military uniform or a business suit. Serving a tyrannical dictator, Aziz used his eloquence the way a cosmetician might apply makeup to a corpse. With the urbanity of evil, he glibly represented Saddam Hussein's regime as it tortured and murdered Iraqi people.

In the United States, news media have encouraged us to believe that U.S. leaders are cut from entirely different cloth than the thugs on the "most-wanted" cards. But I don't think so. In some respects, the terrible choices made by those men and women are more explainable than ones that are routine in U.S. politics. Many of the Baath Party operatives had good reason to fear for their lives—and the lives of their loved ones—if they ran afoul of Saddam. In contrast, many politicians and appointed officials in Washington have gone along with lethal policies merely because of fear that dissent might cost them prestige or power. Why denounce the use of cluster bombs or depleted uranium and risk losing a top post in Washington? Why take a moral position against a war after it starts and risk losing the next election?

I thought of such matters in late 2002 during visits to Baghdad's Al-Mansour Pediatric Hospital, where mothers sat on bare mattresses next to children who were languishing with leukemia and cancer. The young patients were not getting adequate chemotherapy because U.S.-led sanctions continued against Iraq. Walking through the cancer ward, I remembered a response from Madeleine Albright, when she was the U.S. ambassador to the United Nations, during a *60 Minutes* interview that aired on May 12, 1996. CBS correspondent Lesley Stahl said, "We have heard that a half a million children have died." She then asked, "Is the price worth it?" Albright replied: "I think this is a very hard choice, but the price—we think the price is worth it."

During the war on Iraq in spring 2003, American media consumers caught only glimpses of the carnage, but most of them were led to believe that the price—to be paid by others—was worth it.

For the most part, major U.S. networks sanitized their war coverage. As always, the enthusiasm for war was rabid on Fox News Channel. After a prewar makeover, the fashion was the same for MSNBC. At the other end of the narrow cable-news spectrum, CNN cranked up its own militaristic fervor.

There were instances of exceptional journalism in the mainstream U.S. press. Some news magazines provided a number of grisly pictures. A few reporters, notably Anthony Shadid of the *Washington Post* and Ian Fisher of *The New York Times*, wrote vivid accounts of what the Pentagon's firepower did to Iraqi people on the ground; only a closed heart could be unmoved by those stories. But our country remained largely numb.

Media depictions of human tragedies may have momentary impact, but the nation's anesthetic flood of nonstop media leads us to sense that we're somehow above or beyond the human fray: Some lives, including ours of course, matter a great deal. Others, while perhaps touching, are decidedly secondary. The official directives needn't be explicit to be well understood: Do not let too much empathy move in unauthorized directions.

Millions of Americans tune into NPR News. During the war, that public radio network carried the reporting of correspondent Anne Garrels, who provided some outstanding eyewitness accounts from Baghdad—but her exceptional reports were hardly indicative of NPR's overall coverage, heavily dominated by reliance on an array of U.S. government sources, claims, and assumptions. (Day by day, the contrast to the audibly more independent approach of the BBC World Service was striking.) NPR has its own style of numbing.

Consider the spirit of discourse, in the midst of the war, as two of the network's mainstays held forth on Saturday morning's *Weekend Edition*. During an April 5 discussion with host Scott Simon, the NPR news analyst Daniel Schorr exclaimed: "It really is quite amazing, whether one likes the plan of the Pentagon or not, it certainly, as of now, has been a most roaring success."

Simon replied: "And let's remind ourselves today, of course, there have been casualties. So far, according to NPR's estimate, 67 U.S. troops have died, 16 are missing, 7 captured; 27 British troops dead, none missing or captured. Recognizing that these are all sacred souls that have been lost, at the same time the casualties seem to be standing a good deal lower than some people had projected."

The response from Schorr: "That's right. And, you know, an interesting thing is one of the great successes of the week is what has not happened. One is that there have not been very major casualties. Another is they have not been able to devastate the oil fields. Another is that they have not been able to cow the American Marines and the troops by sending in suicide bombers. They've managed to cope with that. There've been some unfortunate deaths of civilians there. But whatever was the strategy of resistance has not worked, and whatever is the strategy for marching to Baghdad seems to be working pretty well."

The back-and-forth between Schorr and Simon embodied the dominant tenor of the war coverage provided by NPR News—the kind of media assessments that seem to be tacitly guided by the overarching PC sensibilities of Pentagon Correctness. The homage is to victory. Americans and their allies are the sacred people. And accolades go to iron fists in the White House.

"If real leadership means leading people where they don't want to go," Michael Kinsley wrote in the April 21, 2003 edition of *Time* magazine, "George W. Bush has shown himself to be a real leader." Militarism in America had become a runaway train on a death track. Kinsley observed: "The president's ability to decide when and where to use America's military power is now absolute. Congress cannot stop him. That's not what the Constitution says, and it's not what the War Powers Act says, but that's how it works in practice."

Mostly, it works that way in practice because countless journalists— whether they're flag-wavers at Fox News or liberal sophisticates at NPR

News—keep letting authorities define the bounds of appropriate empathy and moral concern. I know of very few prominent American journalists who pointed out that President Bush had the blood of many Iraqi children on his hands after launching an aggressive war in violation of the U.N. Charter and the Nuremberg principles established more than half a century ago.

The avoidance certainly extended to NPR News. On April 21, 2003, I did a search to find out how often the word "Nuremberg" had been mentioned on NPR during the year. On Nexis, in the National Public Radio category, from January 1 through April 21, the word came up a total of four times—and none of the references had anything to do with raising any question about the U.S. government's war on Iraq.

Despite such deafening media silences, the judgments at Nuremberg and precepts of international law forbid launching an aggressive war—an apt description of what the U.S. government inflicted on Iraqi people in the spring of 2003. "We must make clear to the Germans that the wrong for which their fallen leaders are on trial is not that they lost the war, but that they started it," said Supreme Court Justice Robert L. Jackson, a U.S. representative to the International Conference on Military Trials at the close of World War II. He added that "no grievances or policies will justify resort to aggressive war. It is utterly renounced and condemned as an instrument of policy."

When a country—particularly "a democracy"—goes to war, the passive consent of the governed lubricates the machinery of slaughter. Silence is a key form of cooperation, but the war-making system does not insist on quietude or agreement. Mere passivity or self-restraint will suffice to keep the missiles flying, the bombs exploding and the faraway people dying.

Norman Solomon, a syndicated columnist on media and politics, is coauthor of *Target Iraq: What the News Media Didn't Tell You* (Context Books, 2003). He is executive director of the Institute for Public Accuracy.

The Humanitarian Impacts of the Iraq Wars
BY PETER PHILLIPS

In 1998, Project Censored gave a top ten rating to a story about how U.S. weapons of mass destruction were linked to the death of a half-million children in Iraq. By then it was clear that the U.N. sanctions advanced by the United States against Iraq had taken the lives of more Iraqi citizens than did the military actions of the first Gulf War itself. The sanctions imposed on Iraq are causing shortages of food, medical supplies, and medicine.

In May 1996, then-U.N. Ambassador Madeleine Albright acknowledged on *60 Minutes* that more than half a million children under the age of five had died since the war ended. UNICEF reported in 1998 that child mortality continued at 150 per day. The United States, up to Gulf War II, held the position that sanctions against Iraq must continue until it can be proven that the country is unable to build biological or chemical weapons. Of these deaths, many are attributed to depleted uranium (DU) weapons. Additionally, severe birth defects are known to be caused by radiation exposure. The rate of cancer in Iraqi children has increased dramatically.

Few Americans were ever fully aware of the enormous human toll caused by the continuing war on Iraq. The corporate media characterized the deaths, disease, and hardships of Iraq as 'claims,' while misunderstanding and grossly understating the damage and potential health hazards caused by the sanctions and the use of depleted uranium.

The historical context of the U.S. being the original supplier of the weapons of mass destruction in Iraq was rarely mentioned in corporate media. Little media attention was paid to 1994 Senate panel reports that between 1985 and 1989, U.S. firms supplied microorganisms needed for the production of Iraq's chemical and biological warfare. U.N. inspectors found and removed chemical and biological components identical to those previously furnished by the United States to Iraq. The Simon Wiesenthal Center in Los Angeles reported that in 1990 more than 207 companies from 21 Western countries, including at least 18 from the United States, contributed to the buildup of Saddam Hussein's biological and chemical arsenal.

By the year 2000, over one million Iraqi children had either starved to death from U.N.-imposed sanctions or become the victims of cancer and other maladies from exposure to chemical and biological weapons. In the *San Francisco Chronicle* on September 19, 1999, UNICEF was reported to have claimed that an average 4,500 Iraqi children under the age of five die each month and that the number of Iraqi children with cancer has increased sevenfold. When asked about the effects of the sanctions on the plight of Iraq's children, U.S. Secretary of State Madeleine Albright said, "I think this is a very hard choice, but the price—we think the price is worth it." The *Houston Chronicle* expounded on Albright's position, stating that Washington refuses to take responsibility for the human toll from economic sanctions.

Denis Halliday, a former U.N. assistant secretary general and coordinator of the U.N.'s humanitarian program in Iraq, resigned his post in protest in

1998. Halliday stated he no longer wanted to be a part of the devastating effects of the sanctions on the children: "Sanctions are starving to death 6,000 Iraqi infants every month, ignoring the human rights of ordinary Iraqis, and turning a whole generation against the West," Halliday stated. Halliday's successor, Dr. Hans Von Sponeck, also resigned rather than carry out what he called "information cleansing." Von Sponeck described in December of 2002 how the Iraqi people were expected to live on only $174 per person per year under the embargo. "Infant mortality has risen 150 percent since 1990," he stated.

CIVILIAN DEATHS: GULF WAR II

A postwar survey of hospitals by the *Los Angeles Times* disclosed that during Gulf War II over 1,700 civilians died and more than 8,000 were injured in Baghdad alone. Nationwide, the number probably reached tens of thousands, but these are numbers that the Pentagon chooses not to collect. Undocumented burials were common during the war, making it impossible to get accurate data on total civilian deaths. Given that the estimates are that some 3,500 Iraqi civilians died in Gulf War I, almost all by air attacks, it seams likely that the numbers for 2003 are much higher.

Rohan Pearce, writing in the *Green Left Weekly* on April 16, 2003, stated:

According to the International Committee of the Red Cross, on April 7, the Al Kindi hospital in Baghdad—the only hospital ICRC representatives could visit because of continuing clashes between U.S. troops and Iraqi resistance forces—was admitting around 10 patients per hour. Hospital staff had already been working nonstop for three days.

An April 7 report by the BBC put the average number of admissions to the hospital at 100 per hour. It noted that even before the first incursion of U.S. troops in Baghdad on April 5, all five major hospitals in the city were overflowing with wounded—so many that the ICRC has given up trying to calculate the number.

Journalists from the British *Independent* reported that stocks of anesthetics at Al Kindi had run so low that when surgery was performed patients were being provided with 800 mg of ibuprofen—"the equivalent of two headache pills"—and even the ICRC has only been able to provide medical supplies for 100 operations, falling short of enough for even one day's injured. "Clean towels cannot be supplied because the hospital washing machines overload the emergency generators," *The Independent* reported.

In Umm Qasr, under British occupation, the situation is much the same. Its clinic is overflowing, reported Radio Free Europe on April 7: "The helpless staff includes two doctors and 25 nurses, all working 12-hour shifts, who have long ago run out of medicines, including simple antibiotics."

UNICEF has warned that 100,000 Iraqi children under the age of five are in danger of serious illness after the war. On April 2, the head of the U.N. agency's Iraq operations, Carel de Rooy, said that more Iraqi children had died from drinking unsanitary water than any other cause last year. Marc Vergara, a UNICEF worker trying to ensure a sanitary water supply to the country, told the April 9 *Baltimore Sun*: "What we're doing is symbolic. It does not even come close to meeting the need." Iraq's humanitarian crisis is exacerbated by the fact that 41 percent of the population is 14 years old or younger. An April 6 press statement by UNICEF noted that even for those children who are saved from death, "there are other profound and debilitating consequences that last for years to come." The statement added: "The scars of war do not easily fade. Physical and psychological trauma, fear and the loss of loved ones continue to plague the lives of those who have endured such horrors."

HEALTH IMPACTS OF DEPLETED URANIUM

Gregory Elich reported in *Global Outlook* (Winter 2003) of the impacts depleted uranium (DU) munitions from the first Gulf War were having on the people of Iraq. DU munitions (800 tons used during Gulf War I) leave thousands of alpha radioactive particles in the environment with a half-life of 4.5 billion years. People or animals ingesting even a single particle of DU suffer grave consequences to their health. Leukemia and other cancers have soared in Iraq in the past decade.

DU dust, when inhaled or ingested, creates flu-like symptoms within a few days. Severe exposure may result in respiratory problems vomiting and internal bleeding. The Royal Society (2002) reported that DU contamination may lead to death within a few days because of its toxic effects on the renal system. Long-term impacts include cancer and compromised immune systems.

Christian Science Monitor's Scott Peterson visited four randomly chosen sites hit by depleted uranium shell in Baghdad and reports that local people haven't been warned of the radiation danger, but U.S. troops have orders to avoid the sites.

The May 15, 2003 *Christian Science Monitor* reported:

At a roadside produce stand on the outskirts of Baghdad, business is brisk for Latifa Khalaf Hamid. Iraqi drivers pull up and snap up fresh bunches of parsley, mint leaves, dill, and onion stalks. But Ms. Hamid's stand is just four paces away from a burnt-out Iraqi tank, destroyed by —and contaminated with—controversial American depleted uranium bullets. Local children play throughout the day on the tank, Hamid says, and on another one across the road.

No one has warned the vendor in the faded, threadbare black gown to keep the toxic and radioactive dust off her produce. The children haven't been told not to play with the radioactive debris. They gather around as a Geiger counter carried by a visiting reporter starts singing when it nears a DU bullet fragment no bigger than a pencil eraser. It registers nearly 1,000 times normal background radiation levels on the digital readout.

Alex Kirby reported on BBC News on April 15 that the U.S. rejected proposals for cleanup of DU sites in Iraq—even though both U.N. and U.S. reports acknowledge the dust can be dangerous if inhaled.

HUMANITARIAN IMPACTS AT HOME

In addition to the impact on the families of U.S. solders who are killed or wounded in the Iraq war, Jon Elliston and Catherine Lutz reported in the Spring 2003 issue of *Southern Exposure* that after war, there are sharp increases in domestic violence when the solders come home. "We could literally tell what units were being deployed from where, based on the volume of calls we received from given bases," says Christine Hansen, executive director of the Connecticut-based Miles Foundation, which has assisted more than 10,000 victims of military-related domestic violence since 1997. The calls were from women who were facing threats and physical abuse from their partners—the same men who were supposedly being deployed on a mission to make America safer. "Then the same thing happened on the other end, when they came back," Hansen adds.

Elliston and Lutz wrote:

It took the rapid-fire deaths of four women to turn national attention to this oft-overlooked form of domestic terror. The problem forced its way into the headlines last July [2002], following a spate of murders by soldiers stationed at Fort Bragg in Fayetteville, North Carolina. In the space of just five weeks, four women married to soldiers were killed by their spouses, according to the authorities. Marilyn Griffin was stabbed 70 times and her trailer set on fire, Teresa Nieves and Andrea Floyd were shot in the head, and Jennifer Wright was strangled. All four couples had children, several now orphaned as two of the men shot themselves after killing their wives.

The murders garnered wide attention because they were clustered over such a short period and because three of the soldiers had served in special operations units that fought in Afghanistan.

The murders have raised a host of questions—about the effects of war on the people who wage it, the spillover on civilians from training military personnel to kill, the role of military institutional values, and even the possible psychiatric side effects of an antimalarial drug the army gives its soldiers. On the epidemic of violence against women throughout the United States and on the role of gender in both military and civilian domestic violence, however, there has been a deafening silence."

SOURCES: Dennis Bernstein, "Made in America," *San Francisco Bay Guardian*, February 25, 1998; Bill Blum, "Punishing Saddam or the Iraqis," *I.F. Magazine*, March/April 1998; Most Rev. Dr. Robert M. Bowman, Lt. Col., USAF (Ret.), "Our Continuing War Against Iraq," *Space And Security News*, May 1999; *The New York Times*, January 3, 1999 and August 24, 1999; *Houston Chronicle*; March 4, 1999; *Christian Science Monitor*, April 29, 1999 and October 5, 1999; *Chicago Sun-Times*, August 13, 1999; *San Francisco Chronicle*, September 19, 1999; *Southern Exposure*, Spring 2003; *Christian*

Science Monitor, May 15, 2003; The Royal Society, "The Health Hazards of Depleted Uranium, 2002"; "U.S. War Creates Humanitarian Crisis," *Green Left Weekly,* April 16, 2003.

Witness to War

BY MARCUS BORGMAN

Santa Rosa California family doctor April Hurley was outraged and desperate to do something about the war against Iraq.

"We were just flailing here. I couldn't stay. Whatever danger there was didn't amount to much in my mind. I had no reason to not go. I wanted to see the truth because I knew we would be lied to. And I wanted to see the Iraqi people and tell them that we didn't support this, that we were trying to stop it. I thought we could get the word out about what was happening. And we did," she said.

Hurley saw bombing victims and bombed-out homes and shops. Hurley saw soldiers drive triumphantly into Baghdad. She saw families care for their injured because there was a shortage of nurses in the five hospitals open in Baghdad.

She joined the Iraq Peace Team, part of the Chicago-based Voices in the Wilderness group that sends medical supplies and drugs to Iraq in purposeful violation of the U.N. sanctions. She arrived in Baghdad March 13 and returned April 13.

"We heard from incoming patients coming from farms, where they thought they would be safe because it was not a military target. They said the airplanes would circle around and then attack the farm buildings. There were tons of dead. Families would group together, sometimes 30 people, includ-

ing extended members. They needed to do that because of the threat of 'Shock and Awe' and they wanted to be together during the danger. They couldn't afford to leave and they thought the farms would be safe. They got blasted," she remembered. Hurley relayed a story she got from five injured men in a hospital: "There was a civilian bus with Red Crescent [Red Cross for the Middle East] workers. The bus was followed by an Apache attack helicopter and fired on. Sixteen were killed. The Apache helicopter stayed and watched the area. The injured waited to be rescued by a bus from Baghdad for three hours. After they were rescued and the bus was pulling away, the Apache incinerated the disabled bus. Whatever dead were in the bus were incinerated."

Another time, Hurley said one little boy, probably seven or eight years old, "told me he was sitting with two friends at the market, and then they were gone. Exploded." Most people died from blood loss before transportation could be found to bring them to a hospital. But not all died. One such case, which became internationally known, was a 12-year-old boy named Ali Ismaeel Abbas. Hurley saw little Ali after he first came in. The bones in his arms were sticking out, scorched from a bomb blast. He had third-degree burns over 30 percent of his body. He arrived March 30. The rest of his family, 16 people in all, was killed. One uncle survived.

"We tried to get the word out about Ali, but only the European media got the story and showed pictures of him injured. We weren't going to see survivors like this because there wasn't intensive care available. This kid was a miracle." When the U.S. did get to know about Ali, 11 days later when the bombing was over and soldiers were shown victorious in Baghdad, amputations has already occurred. The U.S. military evacuated him to Kuwait where he had three skin grafts at the Saud A. Albabtain Centre for Burns and Plastic Surgery. The story had changed from a casualty of U.S. bombing to a Western-style rescue and care for the injured.

Not everyone Hurley talked to was Iraqi. After U.S. troops arrived, she spoke with them too. "The soldiers were very conflicted about what was going on. 'I'm here to get school benefits. I'm not interested in being here.' That's what they'd tell you." One sergeant in particular was upset with his deeds and seriously questioned his place there. "He told me he had been losing sleep over some of the decisions he had made, but not to blame his boys because they were just taking orders from him. He said 'I don't want to be here. I don't want to kill. I want to get out and I don't know how. How do I do it?' We didn't know what to tell him. Some members of our group prayed with him.

"One of his soldiers I talked to said he had not fired his weapon once. He kept saying it was jammed." U.S. soldiers appeared confused by confrontations from nonuniformed attackers. "One U.S. soldier was upset civilians would attack with machine guns and thought that wasn't playing fair. I said, 'This is a militia army just like the Revolutionary War in the U.S.! These guys are wearing the clothing they have because they are defending their city and their homes.' I told them we were using cluster bombs, depleted uranium weapons. It's sad. They are very much in the dark. But they walked up to talk to us."

Hurley said Iraqi children displayed various stress symptons. "During the day the kids would function pretty well. We heard about children at night screaming and unable to sleep. Some kids stopped talking. Some started stuttering. They had problems with chronic skin problems like eczema, psoriasis; any such condition would get worse with stress." Others with chronic conditions suffered too. "I saw people with high blood pressure and diabetes who were not being managed because the hospital was busy taking care of war victims."

Hurley arrived in Amman, Jordan, on March 6. It took seven days for Iraq to decide she was not a U.S. spy and give her a visa. On her team "were two retired CIA people, a couple, one expert in the Middle East, the other in Russian nuclear arms. Both were pacifists and actively writing for *Counter-Punch*. However, they never got visas. They were letting in so many human shields, Christian Peacekeepers, and folks like us. Every time they let people in there was a risk of CIA operatives coming in, which I think was a very real risk. We were under a lot of surveillance." That included a government "minder," who took them around until the war was over.

And the Winners Are!

BY TOM LOUGH

GEN. JERRY BATES—will lead logistical and support operations in postwar Iraq. Bates took part in the military intervention in Haiti. He is senior vice president of the National Group, an arm of MPRI (Military Professionals Resources Inc.).

JOHN BOLTON—a prime architect of Bush's Iraq policy, who served Bush Sr. and Reagan in the State Department, Justice Department, USAID, and now undersecretary for arms control and international security. He is part of the Jewish Institute for National Security Affairs (JINSA), a right-wing think tank that puts Israel and its security at the heart of U.S. foreign policy, and the Project for the New American Century (PNAC). He is also vice president of the American Enterprise Institute (AEI). His financial interests include oil and arms firms and JP Morgan Chase, like George Shultz. It's said he believes in the inevitability of Armageddon.

AHMED CHALABI—leader of the London-based Iraqi National Congress. He is supported by Paul Wolfowitz, Donald Rumsfeld, Richard Perle, Douglas Feith, and JINSA, and is linked to the American Enterprise Institute (AEI). Wolfowitz and Rumsfeld are pushing for Chalabi to be interim leader of the postwar Iraq. Convicted in absentia in Jordan for his part in a massive embezzlement scandal, Chalabi received $12 million from Washington after the first Gulf War. In Iraq he will be working with Robert Reilly, a close friend and business partner.

DICK CHENEY—secretary of defense under George H.W. Bush, ending early 1993. Now vice president, Cheney is a founding member of PNAC and was on the JINSA board of advisors; he has been calling for a regime change in Iraq for over a decade. He was chairman and CEO of Halliburton oil company. Halliburton's subsidiary, Kellogg Brown & Root (KBR), has secured contracts worth up to $7 billion from the U.S. Army's Corp of Engineers to put out oil well fires in Iraq. He is a trustee of the American Enterprise Institute and has links to Chevron, for whom he negotiated the building of an oil pipeline from the Caspian Sea.

LYNNE CHENEY—wife of the vice president. Cheney sits on the board of Lockheed Martin, which manufactures cruise missiles and now has a $800-million military satellite system that will help troops in Iraq.

DOUGLAS J. FEITH—undersecretary for Pentagon policy. Feith selects members of the Defense Policy Board and is on the board of JINSA. As a lawyer, he represented Northrop Grumman. Feith is zealously pro-Israeli and is a keen supporter of Chalabi.

ZALMAY KHALILZAD—Afghanistan-born Khalilzad is George W. Bush's special envoy to Afghanistan and Iraq and has a wide variety of oil interests. He co wrote an article on Saddam Hussein, entitled "Overthrow Him" with Paul Wolfowitz, his former boss. A consultant with the oil company Unocal, he was pushing for a natural gas pipeline in Afghanistan during the Taliban regime and worked under Condoleezza Rice when she served as director of Chevron. He is also a close associate of George Shultz. He is a former RAND Corporation employee and a charter member of the PNAC.

LEWIS LIBBY—Cheney's chief of staff. Libby was in George H.W. Bush's Defense Department; a friend and confidant of Paul Wolfowitz; a founding member of PNAC; and a board member of the RAND Corporation, which has a huge number of contracts with the Pentagon. Libby owns shares in armament companies and has various oil interests; consultant to Northrop Grumman, which has his influential voice on the Defense Policy Board (DPB), the so-called brains of the Pentagon. Rand Corporation has $83 million in defense contracts.

ANDREW NATSIOS—head of USAID, the department that hands out Iraqi reconstruction contracts, which only U.S. companies can bid on. Natsios is a retired lieutenant colonel from Gulf War I. As CEO of the Massachusetts Turnpike Authority, he oversaw a three-mile highway construction project in Boston, undertaken by Bechtel cost, which has a overrun of $10 billion over the projected cost, with the largest budget rises occurring during Natsios's tenure.

RICHARD PERLE—key member of JINSA and a prominent member of the American Enterprise Institute (AEI). Perle sits on the Foundation for the Defense of Democracies, along with James Woolsey. Perle was chair of the Defense Policy Board and resigned the chair following a scandal over a conflict of interest relating to his business connections, but still sits on the board. Perle advised clients of Goldman Sachs, the investment house, on postwar investment opportunities in Iraq. He is also a director of Autonomy Corp., a software company with many Pentagon clients. Autonomy says it expects its profits will increase dramatically after the war in Iraq ends.

ROBERT REILLY—former director of Voice of America, the pro-U.S. radio service. Reilly has been entrusted with overhauling Iraqi radio, television, and newspapers. He's already setting up Radio Free Iraq, using transmitters that have been sent to the Middle East for the military's psychological operations. He is also involved in setting up a media network in the Middle East. A $62-million satellite TV station is scheduled to begin at the end of the year. He is a close friend and business partner of Ahmed Chalabi.

CONDOLEEZZA RICE—Cheney's national security advisor. Rice was the director of Chevron until 2001 and had an oil tanker named after her. During her tenure, Chevron's CEO Kenneth Derr once said, "Iraq possesses huge reserves of oil and gas reserves I'd love Chevron to have access to."

DONALD RUMSFELD—secretary of defense under George W. Bush. Rumsfeld is a founding member of PNAC, one of the best-connected men in American politics, and designer of the Iraqi invasion plan. Every detail of the postwar reconstruction has to be cleared with Rumsfeld. As Ronald Reagan's special envoy to Iraq in the 1980s, during the Iran-Iraq war, he spent time with Saddam Hussein discussing the building of an oil pipeline on behalf of Bechtel, while both Iraq and Iran were using poison gas on each other. Rumsfeld was then working for Reagan's secretary of state, George Shultz, who became vice chairman of Bechtel, now one of the front-runners in the bid to secure U.S. government contracts to rebuild Iraq.

GEORGE SHULTZ—secretary of state under Richard Nixon, George W. Bush's presidential campaign advisor, and a member of the Bechtel board of directors. Shultz is one of the administration's key thinkers on running postwar Iraq and chairman of the International Council of JP Morgan Chase, the banking syndicate in which Lewis Libby has heavy investments. Morgan Chase lent Saddam's regime $500 million in 1983. Shultz is a member of the Committee for the Liberation of Iraq and a patron of the American Enterprise Institute (AEI).

PAUL WOLFOWITZ—deputy secretary of defense under Donald Rumsfeld. Wolfowitz is the arch-ideologue of the Bush Administration and the key architect in the Pentagon of the postwar reconstruction of Iraq. He is a ranking member of the leading neoconservative think tank PNAC, which advocated regime change in Iraq before George W. Bush took office. Wolfowitz is also a key member of the ultra-right-wing JINSA.

R. JAMES WOOLSEY—a long-time supporter of war on Iraq, a PNAC and JINSA member, and former director of the CIA under Bill Clinton (1993–95). Woolsey may become the information minister in the postwar Iraqi interim government. He sits on the Foundation for the Defense of Democracies, along with Richard Perle. His business interests include British Aerospace, Titan Corporation, DynCorp. He has said, "Only fear will reestablish [Arab] respect for us... we need a little Machiavelli."

BECHTEL INC.—almost certain to win $900 million in contracts. The total amount of business from Iraqi construction could total $100 billion. Bechtel has donated $1.3 million to political campaign funds since 1999, the majority going to the Republican Party. George Shultz is Bechtel's former CEO and is still on their board of directors. Other Republicans linked to the company include former Reagan defense secretary Caspar Weinberger.

Jack Sheehan, retired Marine Corp general, is its senior vice president, and also sits on the Pentagon's influential Defense Policy Board. In 1980, Bechtel proposed building an oil pipeline through Iraq with Donald Rumsfeld as an intermediary. Also, Rumsfeld, while working with Reagan's State Department (secretary of state George Shultz, later vice director of Bechtel), negotiated with Iraq's Saddam Hussein on behalf of a pipeline to be built by Bechtel. Bechtel built Camp X-Ray in Guantanamo Bay for the indefinite detention of Al Qaeda suspects for $16 million.

BOOZ ALLEN HAMILTON—a corporate consultant firm, which won a contract to develop a computer model of postwar Iraq society after the first Gulf War I. Booz Allen is also linked to James Woolsey and to the Defense Policy Board.

DYNCORP—linked to former CIA director James Woolsey. It provides security in world trouble spots where America has had to act as the policeman. DynCorp offers a tally of Woolsey's intellectual inclinations: both he and Richard Perle sit on the Foundation for the Defense of Democracy, a promilitary think tank. DynCorp provides bodyguards for Hamid Kharzai, the Afghani president, and has installed a police force monitoring service in Bosnia. DynCorp is being sued for human rights violations in Bosnia, environmental health disasters in Ecuador, and fraud in America.

FLUOR CORP.—donated $275,000 to the Republicans and $3,500 personally to George W. Bush. Fluor Corp. has ties to a number of intelligence and defense procurement officials, including Kenneth J. Oscar, former acting assistant secretary of the army and Bobby R. Inman, a retired admiral, former NSA director, and CIA deputy director.

HALLIBURTON—the oil giant once run by Dick Cheney. Cheney walked out the door with a payoff worth about $30 million. There have been deferred payments of $180,000 a year while he has been vice president. Halliburton's subsidiary, Kellogg Brown & Root (KBR), was the first company to be awarded an Iraqi reconstruction contract by the Pentagon to cap burning oil wells. The deal is reportedly worth $500 million and was awarded by the Army Corps of Engineers without any competitive bidding process. KBR is also one of two contractors chosen by the Defense Threat Reduction Agency to undertake the disposal of weapons of mass destruction (WMD)—if they are ever found. Since 1999, Halliburton has given 95 percent, or just under $700,000, of its political donations to the Republican party; it also gave George W. Bush nearly $18,000.

INTERNATIONAL RESOURCES GROUP (IRG)—Washington-based company that has won a $70-million contract to establish the humanitarian aid program in Iraq. Obviously, this involves an exceptionally close working relationship with USAID, which awards the contracts. Four of IRG's vice presidents have held senior posts with USAID and 24 of the firm's 48 technical staff have worked for USAID.

LUCENT TECHNOLOGIES—California congressman Darell Issa wants firms such as Lucent Technologies and Qualcomm to rebuild Iraq's decrepit telecoms system—a deal worth about $1 billion. Pentagon undersecretary Douglas Feith has up to $500,000 invested in Lucent, and Dick Cheney's chief of staff, Lewis Libby, has shares in Qualcomm.

NORTHROP GRUMMAN—one of the biggest winners under Bush's increases in defense spending. It won $8.5 billion in contracts during 2002. It has links with the AEI and key Bush Administration hawks. The company planned a merger with Lockheed Martin, another defense giant, which has Dick Cheney's wife Lynne on the board.

PARSONS CORP.—donated $152,000 to the Republican Party and to George W. Bush. It has helped reconstruct Kosovo and Bosnia and built the Saudi "military city" of Yanbu. Bush's secretary of labor, Elaine Chao, served on its board before joining the cabinet. It has a chance of $900 million of reconstruction contracts and works closely with Halliburton. Chao's husband, assistant majority leader and majority whip Mitch McConnell, has links to defense contractor Northrop Grumman. He has also received donations from Halliburton and arms firm Lockheed Martin, among others.

RAYTHEON CORP.—chosen by the Defense Threat Reduction Agency, along with Halliburton's KBR, to undertake the disposal of weapons of mass destruction (WMD)—if they are ever found. Raytheon, along with Lockheed Martin, is also involved in producing the Patriot missiles.

STEVE DORING SERVICES OF AMERICA (SSA)—world-leading Seattle port company that won the first USAID contract for Iraqi reconstruction—a $4.8-million deal to manage Iraq's strategic port, Umm Qasr. Known for its union-busting activities, it turns about $1 billion a year, and its president, John Hemmingway, has made personal donations to Republican Party candidates.

CHAPTER 9

The USA Patriot Act: Uncensored

PART I BY HERBERT FOERSTEL AND PART II BY NANCY KRANICH

The September 11, 2001, attacks on New York's World Trade Center set in motion an intense political conflict within the United States over the proper balance between governmental power and personal privacy. Only days after the attacks, the FBI reportedly began installing its "Carnivore" system at some Internet providers to monitor electronic communications. The government also wanted unfettered access to telephone records, e-mail, library records, and the ocean of data assembled by corporations each day about individuals' personal lives, all to assist in the hunt for potential terrorists. To accomplish this task, the White House, the Department of Justice, and their allies in Congress wanted to remove the restraints on governmental power that had been imposed in the wake of scandals like Watergate, COIN-TELPRO, and the shocking revelations of the earlier Church Committee.

A particular focus of the new "antiterrorist" coalition was to rewrite the law regarding the Foreign Intelligence Surveillance Act (FISA), originally created to restrain government authority to conduct domestic surveillance. This original purpose of FISA now seemed to be an impediment to the Bush Administration's desire to expand domestic surveillance, secretly detain terrorism suspects, control charities and bank accounts, and examine business databases containing virtually unlimited information about the private lives of ordinary citizens.

"It's the beginning of a different epoch," explained award-winning journalist Scott Armstrong. "It's a conceptual shift in the way government and First Amendment freedoms interact. We are now in a period where civil liberties get put to the side while we fight this war against terrorism. And since it is a war of ideas, it has all of the problems one would associate with a war against ideas."

The morning after the 9/11 attacks, Assistant District Attorney Viet Dinh, Attorney General John Ashcroft's "take-charge-guy," convened a meeting with Justice Department policy specialists in Dinh's suite of offices. Ashcroft did not attend. He was in hiding, along with other top government officials, but he had conveyed all of his desires to Dinh. The attorney general's wish list of expanded police powers was codified and transmitted to Congress in a bill that included new authority to obtain sensitive personal information about individuals, eavesdrop on conversations, monitor computer use, and detain suspects without probable cause, all with minimal judicial oversight. To make matters worse, Ashcroft demanded that his proposal be enacted within three days, and he suggested publicly that Congress would be responsible for any subsequent terrorist attacks if it did not meet his deadline.

Under growing public pressure and strident demands from Ashcroft, Senate Judiciary Committee Chairman Patrick Leahy agreed to negotiate Ashcroft's bill directly with the Bush Administration, bypassing the normal committee approval process. Leahy believed he had reached a final agreement that would provide a degree of oversight of domestic surveillance, and on October 2, he met with Ashcroft, Orrin Hatch, Michael Chertoff, chief of the Justice Department's criminal division, and Alberto Gonzales, the White House counsel, to sign off on the deal. But Ashcroft quickly made clear that he would abide by none of the negotiated agreements.

A shocked Leahy told Ashcroft, "John, when I make an agreement, I make an agreement. I can't believe you're going back on your commitment."

Ashcroft would not budge. After he left Leahy's office, he held a press conference at which he declared, "Talk won't prevent terrorism."

Leahy remained concerned about the Justice Department's bill, particularly Section 215, which would greatly expand the power of FISA to gain access to business records from libraries, bookstores, Internet providers, grocery stores—virtually anybody. On October 11, the Senate convened to vote on the what was now being called the USA Patriot Act. Leahy warned, "I have deep concerns that we may be increasing surveillance powers and the sharing of criminal justice information without adequate checks on how information may be handled and without adequate accountability in the form of judicial review." Nonetheless, Leahy and Senate Majority Leader Tom Daschle had decided that since every Republican senator had committed to support the Act, they would pressure their fellow Democrats to vote unanimously for it as well.

Only Russ Feingold (D–Wisconsin) refused to accede to his party's demands. When he expressed a desire to introduce amendments to protect personal privacy, Daschle cornered him in the back of the Senate floor, insisting that the bill would only become worse if it were opened up to debate and amendments. That evening, a disconsolate Feingold spoke on the Senate floor:

If we lived in a country where the police were allowed to search your home at any time for any reason; if we lived in a country where the government was entitled to open your mail, eavesdrop on your phone conversations, or intercept your e-mail communications; if we lived in a country where people could be held in jail indefinitely based on what they write or think, or based on mere suspicion that they were up to no good, the government would probably discover and arrest more terrorists.... But that would not be a country in which we would want to live.... Preserving our freedom is the reason we are

now engaged in this new war on terrorism. We will lose that war without a shot being fired if we sacrifice the liberties of the American people in the belief that by doing so we will stop the terrorists.

Feingold attempted three times to introduce amendments to moderate the Patriot Act's assault on civil liberties, but each time, Majority Leader Tom Daschle rose to oppose them. In fact, Daschle opposed Feingold's right to introduce *any* amendments, and he urged his colleagues to ignore the merits of the amendments. "[M]y argument is not substantive, it is procedural," said Daschle. "We have a job to do. The clock is ticking. The work needs to get done.… I hope my colleagues will join me tonight in tabling this amendment and tabling every other amendment that is offered, should he choose to offer them tonight. Let's move on and finish this bill."

Needless to say, the Patriot Act was overwhelmingly passed by the Senate, without debate or amendments. Feingold cast the only "nay" vote.

Now it was up to the House to face the stampede. The Republican-controlled House would soon show itself to be much more responsible and collegial in addressing the delicate issues of security and civil liberties than had been the Democratic-controlled Senate. When the Judiciary Committee's Republican chairman, F. James Sensenbrenner, Jr. (R–Wisconsin), indicated his intention to follow normal committee procedure in approving the Patriot Act, he came under immediate attack by the Bush Administration. John Conyers (D–Michigan), the ranking Democrat on the House Judiciary Committee, congratulated Chairman Sensenbrenner for preserving the regular committee process in considering the Patriot Act and joined him in praising the final bill.

Indeed, the bill approved by a 36–0 vote in the House Judiciary Committee was too constitutionally sound to be acceptable to the Bush Administration. It had to be headed off at the pass before it reached the House floor. The arm-twisting used by the Senate leadership to pass the Patriot Act there would not work in the House. A more devious strategy would be required. The Justice Department persuaded the House leadership to rewrite the bill in the middle of the night before the floor debate, making it conform to Ashcroft's specifications.

In a discussion with myself and National Public Radio host Marc Steiner on August 21, 2002, Conyers explained the bizarre procedure followed to ensure that the government's wish list would prevail in the House bill:

"What you need to know is that the Patriot Act that I sponsored is not the Patriot Act that was passed. After the chairman of the Judiciary Committee and I had worked to get a unanimous Committee vote in favor of original version of the act, it went before the leadership on the way to the Rules Committee.

At that point, the bill was scrapped and replaced by a bill written by the staff of the Attorney General's office. So it was a bill that was foreign to all of us on the committee. It was quite different, and it was a bill that I voted against . . . Nobody had read it, nobody knew about it, but we had to vote out the administration's bill. It was a usurpation of the congressional prerogative."

On October 12, the House passed Ashcroft's rewrite of the Patriot Act, but Conyers explained: "Nearly everybody in both houses voted for the Patriot Act. But they voted for it not knowing what was in it and under a great fear of being considered unpatriotic if they didn't vote for it. Were there hearings held today and the bill brought to a vote, the Patriot Act would be defeated."

Only after the bill became law did a modicum of debate surface among members of Congress, many of whom felt demeaned by the bizarre process of its passage. Representative Ron Paul of Texas, one of three Republicans to stand up to the House leadership and vote against the Patriot Act, said, "It's my understanding the bill wasn't printed before the vote—at least I couldn't get it. They played all kinds of games, kept the House in session all night.... [T]he bill definitely was not available to members before the vote."

When asked what the nation's founding fathers would have thought of the Patriot Act, Paul responded, "Our forefathers would think it's time for a revolution.... They revolted against much more mild oppression."

GENERAL PROVISIONS

The 342-page bill that became law on October 26, 2001 had an elaborate title and a self-righteous acronym: the Uniting and Strengthening America by Providing Appropriate Tools to Intercept and Obstruct Terrorism Act (USA Patriot Act). The massive act is among the most wide-ranging laws ever passed by Congress, creating new federal offices and new crimes, substantially amending at least 12 federal statutes, mandating dozens of new reports and regulations in four cabinet departments, and directly appropriating $2.6 billion while frequently "authorizing" unspecified additional amounts.

The act has had three fundamental effects on American government and society: 1) It introduced unprecedented government secrecy; 2) It removed checks and balances within our governing system, specifically weakening the judicial oversight of the executive branch; 3) It eroded the civil liberties of citizens and noncitizens alike, allowing secret arrests and detention of persons based solely on their country of origin, race, religion, or ethnicity.

Within its ten titles are numerous sections, the more prominent of them being:

SECTION 101: Establishes a new counterterrorism fund without fiscal year limitation and of unnamed amount, to be administered by the Justice Department.

SECTION 105: Establishes a "national network of electronic crimes task forces" to be set up by the Secret Service throughout the country to prevent, detect, and investigate various electronic crimes.

SECTION 203: Mandates the sharing of "foreign intelligence" information between numerous federal agencies. The broad definition of "foreign intelligence" includes virtually anything related to national defense, national security, or foreign affairs.

SECTION 206: Provides "roving wire tap" authority to FISA.

SECTIONS 207 AND 208: Increases the duration of FISA warrants and increases the number of FISA court judges.

SECTIONS 209, 212, 215, AND 216: Enacts numerous technical changes and enhancements to standard surveillance techniques, including the authorization of the government's controversial "Carnivore" electronic surveillance programs.

SECTION 213: Allows delayed notification of "nonphysical search warrants," known as "sneak and peek warrants."

SECTION 214: Allows pen/trap orders concerning foreign intelligence information.

SECTION 215: Allows federal investigators to seize "any tangible thing" from libraries and other institutions in FISA type investigations.

SECTION 216: Explicitly places access to Internet information, including e-mail and Web browsing information, within the reach of pen/trap orders, without need to show probably cause.

SECTION 217: Allows any government employee to conduct electronic content surveillance of U.S. persons.

SECTION 218: Lowers the standard for obtaining FISA warrants.

SECTIONS 219 AND 220: Establishes single jurisdiction search warrants and nationwide service of warrants.

SECTIONS 311, 312, 316, AND 319: Allows federal investigators to impose "special measures" upon any domestic bank or financial institution and imposes new due diligence requirements upon such institutions as a way of revealing terrorist financing.

SECTION 326: Establishes new or expanded requirements to track identities of persons opening new bank accounts.

SECTION 358: Allows government investigators access to consumer records without a court order.

SECTION 411: Creates a new definition of terrorism, with wide latitude for federal investigators to identify "terrorist groups."

SECTION 412: Provides for mandatory detention of suspected aliens, allowing a person to be held for seven days without charge and possible indefinite detention for aliens deemed not removable.

SECTION 504: Links the investigation of any crime with the search for foreign intelligence, including information sharing.

SECTIONS 507 AND 508: Allows government investigators access to educational records without a court order.

SECTION 802: Creates a new crime called "domestic terrorism," defined as "activity that involves acts dangerous to human life that violate the laws of the United States or any state and appear to be intended: (i) to intimidate or coerce a civilian population; (ii) to influence the policy of a government by intimidation or coercion; or (iii) to affect the conduct of a government by mass destruction, assassination, or kidnapping."

SECTION 803: Expands the crimes of harboring, concealing, or providing material support for terrorists.

SECTIONS 809–812: Allows increased penalties for certain terrorist crimes, with no statute of limitations.

SECTION 901 AND 905: Mandates information sharing by the CIA with the Justice Department and by the Justice Department with the CIA.

SECTION 903: Deputizes all "officers and employees" of the "intelligence community," authorizes them to investigate terrorism.

Most of the provisions of the Patriot Act go well beyond terrorism offenses, applying to all federal investigations. The loss of judicial oversight of executive power is one of the more troubling effects of the Patriot Act. Under many of the act's provisions, the court exercises no review function whatsoever. For example, the court is often required to grant government access to sensitive personal information upon the mere request by a government official. The act also provides only a minimal standard of review for Internet communications, allowing law enforcement agents to acquire such information by merely certifying that it is "relevant" to an investigation. The court must accept such a claim, and the judge must issue the order even if he or she finds the certification unpersuasive.

PROVISIONS DIRECTLY AFFECTING LIBRARIES AND BOOKSTORES

The sweeping new surveillance procedures embodied in the Patriot Act represent a major challenge to privacy and confidentiality in libraries and bookstores. Sections 214 and 216 concern pen register and "trap and trace" telephone devices, and new authority in this regard can have implications for privacy and confidentiality. Section 216 extends telephone monitoring laws ("pen register" and "trap and trace") to include routing and addressing information for all Internet traffic, including e-mail addresses, IP addresses, and URLs of Web pages. Since virtually all libraries now provide public Internet terminals, they will become targets of these new surveillance powers and will be required to cooperate in the monitoring of a user's electronic communications sent through the library's computers.

Section 214 is similar to Section 216, applying to "pen register" and "trap and trace" authority under the Foreign Intelligence Surveillance Act (FISA). Because Section 214 concerns the secret FISA court, an agent acting under that section need only claim that the records he seeks may be related to an ongoing investigation related to terrorism or intelligence activities, a very low legal standard.

Perhaps the greatest potential danger to libraries, publishers, and booksellers in the Patriot Act comes from Section 215: Access to Records Under Foreign Intelligence Security Act (FISA). This section allows an FBI agent to obtain a search warrant for "any tangible thing," which can obviously include books, circulation records and other data, floppy disks, data tapes, and computer hard drives. The generality of "any tangible thing" allows the FBI to compel the library or bookstore to release virtually any personal information it has maintained, including Internet records and registration information stored in any medium.

The Freedom to Read Committee of the Association of American Publishers complains that the Patriot Act "contains provisions that threaten the First Amendment–protected activities of book publishers, booksellers, librarians, and readers." In its statement on "The Patriot Act and the First Amendment," the organization warns, "Section 215... threatens the privacy and First Amendment rights of library patrons and bookstore customers whose readings choices and Internet usage patterns may be subject to disclosure despite existing protections for the confidentiality of library readership records and customer records in bookstores."

Attached to the Freedom to Read Committee's statement was a form letter that supporters could send to Senator Patrick Leahy (D–Vermont) and Representative James Sensenbrenner Jr. (R–Wisconsin) urging them to hold hearings on the Patriot Act. The letter concluded with the warning: "If people come to believe that the government can readily obtain access to their library and bookstore records, they will no longer feel free to request the books and other materials they want and need out of a fear that they might become a target of government surveillance."

There are a number of aspects of this new government surveillance of libraries and bookstores under Section 215 that make it far more dangerous than what was endured in the past. As with Section 214, the FBI agent does not need to demonstrate "probable cause," that is, facts to support the belief that a crime has been committed or that the data sought are evidence of a crime. Instead, the agent only needs to claim that the records sought are "relevant" to an ongoing investigation related to terrorism or intelligence activities.

Past FBI requests for library records have required a court-ordered subpoena, which can be challenged in open court by the library. Under the Patriot Act, a "warrant" issued by a secret FISA court is sufficient to require the immediate release of library records, and no court review or adversarial hearing is available to challenge the process. To make matters worse, libraries or librarians served with such a warrant may not disclose, under penalty of law, the existence of the warrant or the fact that records were produced in response to it.

Another discouraging aspect of library surveillance under Section 215 of the Patriot Act is the fact that state library confidentiality laws, passed in 48 of our 50 states, are overridden by these new FBI warrants. Thus, years of hard work by librarians and state legislators throughout the land to protect the privacy of library patrons has been undone by a single federal law.

Section 217 adds a new form of government surveillance, allowing *any* government employee, not just a law enforcement officer, to conduct content surveillance of U.S. persons. This can occur whenever a computer owner and operator "authorizes" surveillance and a law enforcement officer "has reasonable grounds to believe contents of a communication will be relevant" to an investigation of computer trespass. The section allows interception of messages sent through a computer without "authorization," a term that is not defined, thus leaving the owner/operator and government agent dangerous discretion in determining a violation.

EXECUTIVE ORDERS, REGULATIONS, AND ADMINISTRATIVE GUIDELINES

Shortly after the passage of the Patriot Act, Justice Department spokesperson Mindy Tucker warned, "This is just the first step. There will be additional items to come." Since then, there have been numerous nonlegislative extensions of executive power inspired by the Patriot Act, most of them related to government secrecy and surveillance. Of all the nonlegislative federal initiatives since 9/11, the new Attorney General Guidelines on the FBI have most directly threatened library privacy and confidentiality. The revisions, issued on May 30, 2002, by Attorney General Ashcroft, removed a host of restraints on FBI surveillance.

The deceptively simple statement that FBI agents will now have clear authority to visit public places that are open to all Americans was prominent in the new guidelines. It will open a Pandora's box of new surveillance because this new authority specifically includes visits to libraries and places of worship. The bureau has always reserved the right to pursue their investigations wherever they may lead, including libraries, but Ashcroft's new guidelines allow the bureau to go beyond the intrusive inquiries of the ill-fated Library Awareness Program by routinely posting undercover agents in libraries to observe and record the behavior of patrons. Previous FBI guidelines prohibited agents from secretly frequenting libraries, churches, mosques, and temples for purposes of surveillance. The FBI can now enter libraries or bookstores, not in the search for books, but for terrorists. Undercover agents will "hang out" in libraries to secretly spy on other patrons, and a library inhabited by plain-clothed snoops quickly becomes a chilling place.

In his May 30 press conference, Ashcroft complained that the old guidelines frequently barred FBI field agents from taking the initiative to detect and prevent future terrorist acts unless the FBI was aware of possible criminal activity. The new guidelines, said Ashcroft, expand the scope of FBI investigations "to the full range of terrorist activities under the USA Patriot Act."

Ashcroft concluded by reading from the new guidelines: "For the purpose of detecting or preventing terrorist activities, the FBI is authorized to visit any place and attend any event that is open to the public, on the same terms and conditions as members of the public generally."

But of course, the general public does not go to libraries in order to spy on their neighbors. Those are not the "terms and conditions" under which we attend libraries. Were ordinary citizens found to be surreptitiously monitoring the conversations and reading habits of fellow library patrons, they would likely be asked to leave the library, and one hopes that undercover FBI agents will be similarly regarded as unwelcome intruders on library confidentiality.

The new guidelines expressly state that FBI agents may engage in online research on individuals and may use commercial "data-mining" services, such as those companies that track commercial transactions, including book purchases. The Center for Democracy and Technology (CDT) warns: "The FBI will now be conducting fishing expeditions using the services of people who decide what catalogs to send you or what spam e-mail you will be interested in. The problem is, the direct marketers can only... mail you another credit card offer based on that information—the FBI can arrest you."

Under the heading, "Protecting Constitutional Rights," the new guidelines offer what is intended to be a reassurance to the civil liberties community: "It is important that... investigations not be based solely on activities protected by the First Amendment or on the lawful exercise of any other rights secured by the Constitution or laws of the United States."

Note the prominent inclusion of the word "solely" in describing First Amendment rights. Thus, the new guidelines would allow FBI surveillance directed primarily or overwhelmingly against activities protected by the First Amendment. This is hollow assurance indeed.

The above is excerpted from Herbert Foerstel's forthcoming book, Refuge of a Scoundrel: The USA Patriot Act in Libraries (Greenwood Publishing Group/Libraries Unlimited).

Part II: The USA Patriot Act Impacts Free Expression in the U.S.

BY NANCY KRANICH

Hours after the terrorist attacks on September 11, 2001, people rushed to libraries to read about the Taliban, Islam, Afghanistan, and terrorism. Americans sought background materials to foster understanding and cope with this horrific event. They turned to a place with reliable answers—to a trustworthy public space where they are free to inquire and where their privacy is respected.

Since 9/11, libraries remain more important than ever in ensuring the right of every individual to hold and express opinions and to seek and receive information, the essence of a thriving democracy. But just as the public is exercising its right to receive information and ideas—a necessary aspect of free expression—in order to understand the events of the day, government is threatening these very liberties, claiming it must do so in the name of national security.

While the public turned to libraries for answers, the Bush Administration turned to the intelligence community for techniques to secure U.S. borders and reduce the possibility of more terrorism. The result was new legislation and administrative actions that the government says will strengthen security. Most notably, Congress passed into law the Uniting and Strengthening America by Providing Appropriate Tools Required to Intercept and Obstruct Terrorism Act (USA Patriot Act) just six weeks after the events of September 11. This legislation broadly expands the powers of federal law enforcement agencies to gather intelligence and investigate anyone it suspects of terrorism.

The USA Patriot Act contains more than 150 sections and amends over 15 federal statutes, including laws governing criminal procedure, computer fraud, foreign intelligence, wiretapping, and immigration. Particularly troubling to free speech and privacy advocates are four provisions: Section 206, which permits the use of "roving wiretaps" and secret court orders to monitor electronic communications to investigate terrorists; Sections 214 and 216, which extend telephone monitoring authority to include routing and addressing information for Internet traffic relevant to any criminal investigation; and, finally, Section 215, which grants unprecedented authority to the Federal Bureau of Investigation (FBI) and other law enforcement agencies to obtain search warrants for business, medical, educational, library, and bookstore records merely by claiming that the desired records may be related to an ongoing terrorism investigation or intelligence activities—a very relaxed legal standard that does not require any actual proof or even reasonable suspicion of terrorist activity.[1]

Equally troubling, Section 215 includes a "gag order" provision prohibiting any person or institution served with a search warrant from disclosing what has taken place. In conjunction with the passage of the USA Patriot Act, the U.S. Justice Department issued revised FBI guidelines in May 2002 that greatly increase the bureau's surveillance and data collection authority to access such information as an individual's Web surfing habits and search terms.[2]

These enhanced surveillance powers license law enforcement officials to peer into Americans' most private reading, research, and communications. Several of the act's hastily passed provisions not only violate the privacy and confidentiality rights of those using public libraries and bookstores, but sweep aside constitutional checks and balances by authorizing intelligence agencies (which are within the executive branch of government) to gather information in situations that may be completely unconnected to a potential criminal proceeding (which is part of the judicial branch of government). The constitutional requirement of search warrants, to be issued by judges, is one such check on unbridled executive power. In addition to the dangers to democracy from such unbridled executive power, it is not clear that these enhanced investigative capabilities will make us safer, for under the new provisions, far more information is going to the same intelligence agencies that were failing to manage the ocean of information they collected prior to September 11.

We do not know how the USA Patriot Act and related measures have been applied in libraries, bookstores, and other venues because the gag order bars individuals from making that information public. The executive branch has refused to answer inquiries from members of the House and Senate Judiciary Committees, and from civil liberties groups under the Freedom of Information Act (FOIA), regarding the incidence of surveillance activities, except an admission of snooping in libraries by FBI agents.[3]

Officially, librarians are not allowed to comment on FBI visits to examine library users' Internet surfing and book-borrowing habits. Unofficially, though, some details have surfaced. Two nationwide surveys conducted at the University of Illinois after September 11 found that more than 200 out of 1,500 libraries surveyed had turned over information to law enforcement officials.[4] A March 2003 article in the *Hartford Courant* revealed that librarians in Fairfield and Hartford, Connecticut, were visited by the FBI, but only one case involved a search warrant.[5] And an *FW Weekly* article on April 17, 2003, cited a case in New Mexico where a former public defender was arrested by federal agents and interrogated for five hours after using a computer at a Santa Fe academic library, apparently as a result of a chat room statement that President Bush was out of control.[6] It is unclear whether any of these incidents involved secret search warrants as authorized under Section 215 of the USA Patriot Act.

Federal officials claim that the USA Patriot Act and related measures have helped quash terrorist attacks. Mark Corallo, a Justice Department spokesman, has assured the public that, "We're not going after the average American. . . . If you're not a terrorist or a spy, you have nothing to worry about."[7] Nevertheless, many Americans are uncomfortable relying on government officials for assurances that they will protect both civil liberties and national security effectively.

The USA Patriot Act is just one of several troubling policies that compromise the public's privacy rights. Another is the Enhanced Computer Assisted Passenger Pre-screening System (CAPPS-II), which profiles airline passengers and provides "No-Fly" watch lists to the Transportation Security Administration.[8] The danger here is that all airline passengers are assigned a risk assessment "score" without recourse. As a result, innocent people could be branded security risks on the basis of flawed data and without any meaningful way to challenge the government's determination.

A third example is the Department of Defense Total Information Awareness program that seeks to scan billions of personal electronic, financial, medical, communication, education, housing, and travel transactions, analyze them utilizing both computer algorithms and human analysis, and then flag suspicious activity.[9] Americans innocent of any wrongdoing could be targeted by this system because it will collect information (and misinformation) on everyone, much of which can be misused. Furthermore, a planned identity tracking system could follow individuals wherever.

And finally, not to be overlooked, is the proposed Domestic Security Enhancement Act of 2003, a more extreme version of the USA Patriot Act, which could be introduced in Congress at any time. This proposed legislation, leaked by a Justice Department official to the Center for Public Integrity, would make it easier for the government to initiate surveillance and wiretapping of U.S. citizens, repeal current court limits on local police gathering information on religious and political activity, allow the government to obtain credit and library records without a warrant, restrict release of information about health or safety hazards posed by chemical and other plants, expand the definition of terrorist actions to include civil disobedience, permit certain warrantless wiretaps and searches, loosen the standards for electronic eavesdropping of entirely domestic activity, and strip even native-born Americans of all of the rights of United States citizenship if they provide support to unpopular organizations labeled as terrorist by our government.[10]

Citizens and organizations around the country are standing up and passing resolutions opposing the USA P Patriot Act and related measures,[11] and are urging local officials contacted by federal investigators to refuse requests that they believe violate civil liberties—whether Fourth Amendment rights guaranteeing freedom from unreasonable searches and seizures, First Amendment intellectual freedom and privacy rights, Fifth Amendment protections of due process, Sixth Amendment rights to a public trial by an impartial jury, Fourteenth Amendment equal protection guarantees, and the constitutional assurance of the writ of habeas corpus.[12]

In addition, some in Congress are now leading legislative efforts to counter some of the more egregious provisions of the law. For instance, an alliance of librarians, booksellers, and citizen groups is working with Representative Bernie Sanders and more than 70 additional sponsors on the Freedom to Read Protection Act of 2003. If passed, this act would exempt libraries and bookstores from Section 215 and would require a higher standard of proof than mere suspicion for search warrants presented at libraries and bookstores.[13] Similarly, Senators Leahy, Grassley, and Specter have introduced the Domestic Surveillance Act of 2003 to improve the administration and oversight of foreign intelligence surveillance.[14]

Librarians and booksellers are counting on these efforts, along with public outcry, to stem federal actions that threaten Americans' most valued freedoms without necessarily improving national security. Until the protection of civil liberties reaches a balance with the protection of national security, libraries must affirm their responsibility to safeguard patron privacy by avoiding unnecessary creation and maintenance of personally identifiable information (PII) and developing up-to-date privacy policies that cover the scope of collection and retention of PII in data-related logs, digital records, vendor-collected data, and system backups, as well as more traditional circulation information. In short, if information is not collected, it cannot be released.

If libraries are to continue to flourish as centers for uninhibited access to information, librarians must stand behind their users' right to privacy and freedom of inquiry. Just as people who borrow murder mysteries are unlikely to be murderers, so those seeking information about Osama bin Laden are not likely to be terrorists. Assuming a sinister motive based on library users' reading choices makes no sense and leads to fishing expeditions that both waste precious law enforcement resources and have the potential to chill Americans' inquiry into current events and public affairs.

The millions of American who sought information from their libraries in the wake of September 11 reaffirm an enduring truth: a free and open society needs libraries more than ever. Americans depend on libraries to promote the free flow of information for individuals, institutions, and communities, especially in uncertain times. In the words of Supreme Court Justice William O. Douglas, "Restriction of free thought and free speech is the most dangerous of all subversions. It is the one un-American act that could most easily defeat us."[15]

Nancy Kranich is a Senior Fellow with the Free Expression Policy Project Senior Research Fellow, recent past-president of the American Library Association (ALA) and a Project Censored national judge. She can be reached at <nancy.kranich@nyu.edu>.

NOTES

1. USA Patriot Act, October 26, 2001, P. L.107-056; 115 STAT. 272, <frwebgate.access. gpo.gov/cgi-bin/useftp.cgi?IPaddress=162.140.64.21&filename=publ056.pdf&directory=/diskb/wais/data/107_cong_public_laws>. Analyses are available at: Center for Democracy and Technology, <www.cdt.org/security/usapatriot/analysis.shtml>; Congressional Research Service, April 15, 2002, <www.fas.org/irp/crs/RL31377.pdf>.

2. U.S. Department of Justice, Attorney General's Guidelines on Federal Bureau of Investigation Undercover Operations, May 30, 2002, <www.usdoj.gov/olp/fbiundercover.pdf>. For analyses of the Guidelines, see Electronic Privacy Information Center, <www.epic.org/privacy/fbi>; ACLU, <archive.aclu.org/congress/l060602c.html>; and the Center for Democracy and Technology, <www.cdt.org/wiretap/020530guidelines.shtml>. See also: "In Defense of Freedom—Statement of Principles," and Letters to Congress on the Attorney General's Guidelines, June 4, 2002; www.indefenseoffreedom.org.

3. House Judiciary Committee, "Letter from F. James Sensenbrenner (Committee Chair) to Attorney General John Ashcroft regarding the USA Patriot Act," June 13, 2002, <www.house. gov/judiciary/ashcroft061302.htm>. "Response from Ashcroft," July 26, 2002, <www.house.gov/judiciary/patriotresponses101702.pdf>. "Letter from F. James Sensenbrenner (Committee Chair) to Attorney General John Ashcroft regarding the USA Patriot Act," April 1, 2003, <www.house.gov/judiciary/patriot 040103.htm>. For more information about the FOIA request, filed August 22, 2002, and subsequent legal actions, see the ACLU's Web pages on Government Surveillance After the Patriot Act: <www.aclu.org/patriot_foia/index.html>; <www.aclu.org/patriot_foia/foia2.html>; and <www.aclu.org/patriot_foia/foia3.html>. See also the ACLU Press Release, January 17, 2003, <www.aclu.org/SafeandFree/SafeandFree.cfm?ID=11638&c=206>.

4. Leigh Estabrook, "Public Libraries and Civil Liberties: A Profession Divided." (Urbana, IL: U. of Illinois Library Research Center, January 2003), <www.lis.uiuc.edu/gslis/research/civil_liberties.html> (narrative) and <www.lis.uiuc.edu/gslis/research/finalresults.pdf> (questionnaire with summary of responses); and "Public Libraries' Response to the Events of 9/11." (Urbana, IL: U. of Illinois Library Research Center, Summer 2002), <www.lis.uiuc.edu/gslis/research/national.pdf>. See also, Leigh Estabrook, "Response Disappointing," *American Libraries*, September 2002: 37–38.

5. Diane Struzzi, "Legality of Patriot Act Questioned: Some Worry The Law Infringes On Civil Liberties," *Hartford Courant*, March 23, 2003: B1.

6. Dan Malone, "Spies in the Stacks: Is Uncle Sam Watching What You Read? We're Not Allowed to Tell," *FW Weekly*, April 17, 2003, <www.fwweekly.com/issues/2003-04-17/feature.html/page1.html>.

7. Rene Sanchez, "Librarians Make Some Noise Over Patriot Act: Concerns About Privacy Prompt Some to Warn Patrons, Destroy Records of Book and Computer Use," *Washington Post*, April 10, 2003: A20, <www.washingtonpost.com/wp-dyn/articles/A1481-2003Apr9.html>.

8. "Proposed (CAPPS II) Rules," *Federal Register*,Vol. 68, No. 10, January 15, 2003. For an overview and analysis of CAPPS II, see: Electronic Privacy Information Center, "Passenger Profiling," <www.epic.org/privacy/airtravel/profiling.html>.

9. U.S. Department of Defense, Defense Advanced Research Projects Agency, Information Awareness Office, "Total Information Awareness," <www.darpa.mil/iao/TIASystems.htm>. For background and analyses, see: Electronic Privacy Information Center, "Total Information Awareness," <www.epic.org/privacy/profiling/tia/>.

10. For a copy of the January 9, 2003 document leaked on February 7, 2003, see: <www.publicintegrity.org/dtaweb/downloads/Story_01_020703_Doc_1.pdf>. For analyses, see David Cole, "What Patriot II Proposes to Do," February 10, 2003, <www.cdt.org/security/usapatriot/030210cole.pdf>; ACLU, Interested Persons Memo: Section-by-Section Analysis of Justice Department draft "Domestic Security Enhancement Act of 2003," also known as "Patriot Act II," February 14, 2003, <www.aclu.org/SafeandFree/Safeand Free.cfm?ID= 11835&c=206>. See also: Jason Kuiper, "Organizations, Lawmakers Question Proposed Patriot Act II legislation," *Daily Nonpareil*, April 3, 2003, <www.zwire.com/site/news.cfm?newsid=7594285&BRD=2554&PAG= 461&dept_id= 507134&rfi=6>.

11. For a list of communities passing resolutions or assistance in drafting one for your town, see: The Bill of Rights Defense Committee, "Make Your City or Town a Civil Liberties Safe Zone," <www.bordc.org/index.html>. See also: American Library Association, "Resolution on the USA Patriot Act and Related Measures That Infringe on the Rights of Library Users." (Chicago, IL: American Library Association, January 23, 2003); <www.ala.org/Content/ NavigationMenu/Our_Association/Offices/Intellectual_ Freedom 3/ Statements _and_Policies/IF_Resolutions/Resolution_on_the_USA_Patriot_Act_ and_ Related_Measures_That_Infringe_on_ the_Rights_of_Library_Users.htm>; and USA PATRIOT Act Resolutions of State Library Associations, www.ala.org/Content/Navigation Menu/Our_Association/Offices/Intellectual_Freedom3/IF_Groups_and_Committees/State _IFC_Chairs State_IFC_in_Action/USA_Patriot_Act_ Resolutions.htm>.

12. For an analysis of civil liberties threats, see: Nancy Chang, *Silencing Political Dissent: How Post-September 11 Anti-Terrorism Measures Threaten our Civil Liberties* (New York: Seven Stories Press, 2002); Nancy Chang, "The State of Civil Liberties: One Year Later—Erosion of Civil Liberties in the Post 9/11 Era," (New York: Center for Constitutional Rights, 2002), <www.ccr-ny.org/v2/whatsnew/report.asp?ObjID =nQdbIRkDgG& Content=153>; and Stephen J. Schulhofer, *The Enemy Within: Intelligence Gathering, Law Enforcement, and Civil Liberties in the Wake of September 11* (New York: Century Foundation Press, 2002).

13. "Freedom to Read Protection Act of 2003" (introduced in House), H.R.1157, March 6, 2003.

14. "Domestic Surveillance Oversight Act of 2003" (introduced in Senate), S. 436, February 25, 2003.

15. William O. Douglas, "The One Un-American Act" (from a speech by Justice Douglas to the Authors Guild Council in New York, December 3, 1952, on receiving the 1951 Lauterbach Award), *Nieman Reports*, Vol. 7, No. 1, January 1953: 20.

CHAPTER 10

FAIR'S THIRD ANNUAL "FEAR & FAVOR" REPORT, 2002

How Power Shapes the News

BY JANINE JACKSON, PETER HART, AND RACHEL COEN

It would be hard to overstate the impact of news media in shaping public opinion, on issues ranging from health care to plans for war. With media as such an influence on us, it's crucial that we understand who's influencing media.

The annual Fear & Favor report by Fairness and Accuracy in Reporting (FAIR) is an attempt to chart some of the pressures that push and pull mainstream journalists away from their fundamental work of telling the truth and letting the chips fall where they may. These include pressures from advertisers, well aware of their key role in fueling the media business; from media owners, who frequently use their journalistic outlets to draw attention to, or away from, their other corporate interests; and from the state, as the last year has made especially clear, with the Bush Administration doing its best to promote its own spin on events and to tamp down dissent.

While by no means exhaustive, Fear & Favor offers specific illustrations of these broad phenomena, in the belief that an understanding of the forces at work and their concrete, day-to-day impact will help media consumers decode the news they get and recognize what news they do not get from the corporate press.

As always, this report is dedicated to journalists who continue to stand up for independent reporting—like Kathy Finn, former editor of New Orleans' *City Business*, who was fired in 2002 after objecting to a series of commercial encroachments including the introduction of "advertiser-sponsored news pages" (*Columbia Journalism Review,* September/October, 2002). One wonders: What are the odds the paper would hire someone who shared Finn's ideas to replace her? And how many outlets are left where she, and journalists like her, can work without such constraints? These questions should concern not just reporters who want to work without fear or favor, but the public that relies on that reporting.

IN ADVERTISERS WE TRUST

In a commercial media system, the advertiser is king. It's even better to be king during a recession, when the sponsors whose dollars media rely on are able to push for better deals: product placement, extensive promotional packages, etc. Outlets looking for corporate support come up with plans of their own that may be lucrative but hardly seem journalistic. For example, Seattle TV station KIRO has a Web site that includes a section called "kirotv.com Experts"; you wouldn't know by looking that the main qualification for being an "expert" is being able to pay the station as much as $1,000 a month (*Seattle Times,* June 7, 2002).

Media outlets routinely claim that such deals do not influence the content of their coverage, but they haven't shown themselves eager to spell out such relationships to an already skeptical audience.

The New York Times has a special fondness for Starbucks. The front page of its April 29 Metro section devoted over 1,300 words, with two big photographs, to chronicling the coffee chain's rapid growth in Manhattan, along with anecdotes about how New Yorkers "love to complain about Starbucks… yet they drink Starbucks coffee by the gallon." Part business story, part lifestyle piece, the article presented Starbucks as part of the New York way of life, explaining that "the coffee shops provide an environment for doing homework, writing screenplays, holding business meetings, socializing after work, or reading the newspaper."

But not just any newspaper. As the story eventually discloses, the *Times* happens to have a promotional agreement with Starbucks, requiring the chain to sell only the *Times* in its stores, excluding all other national newspapers. In return, the paper promotes Starbucks in national ad campaigns.

The agreement calls for ads, not favorable news stories, but readers may be forgiven a little confusion—especially since, just a few weeks later (June 1, 2002), the *Times'* main front page featured another Starbucks celebration. This time it was the company's European rise that was tracked admiringly; though many "sniff that their culture has been infected," the Viennese have nevertheless made Starbucks a "resounding success." One other difference:

This time the paper didn't bother disclosing that they have a promotional deal with the company.

Nor was the deal disclosed in the paper's July 9 installment, "In Japan, Make that Starbucks to Go," though readers did learn that "with a strong brand name in Japan, Starbucks now feels it can meet the competition by going into the stand-up fast-food business—and do so without cheapening its image." Had the deal been disclosed, readers still might not have seen a smoking gun in *The New York Times*' zealous coverage of their promotional partner—but it might have helped to explain the bad smell.

Charlie Rose is a correspondent for CBS's *60 Minutes II* and also hosts his own talk show on PBS. He also had another job last year: emceeing the Coca-Cola shareholders' meeting at Madison Square Garden in New York, where he gushed about the privilege of being associated with "the Coca-Cola family" (KCRW, *Le Show*, April 21, 2002).

CBS policy is that news correspondents may not do commercials or product endorsements, but a network official told the *Washington Post* (April 23, 2002) that the company was "comfortable" with Rose's role at the Coke meeting. For his part, Rose told the *Post* that he saw no ethics problem because, among other things, he was only paid a "minimal" sum for his appearance (as if conflicts of interest only kick in over a certain dollar amount).

In any case, Coca-Cola's agreement to become a leading underwriter of the *Charlie Rose* show is not minimal; the *Post* reported Coke will be funding the show "to the tune of six or possibly seven figures." This is also no problem, according to Rose, who told the *Post* that he "would never do a story on *60 Minutes II* about anybody who underwrites my PBS show." (A promise to avoid covering a sponsor, of course, is no less a conflict than a promise of favorable coverage.)

Attentive viewers may have noticed a mug at Rose's elbow sporting what appears to be the distinctive red-and-white Coke logo on one side, and the *Charlie Rose* show logo on the other. The *Orange County Weekly* (January 24, 2003) reported that "the mystery" of the mug was solved when guest Robin Williams "picked up the cup with the Rose logo facing viewers, then turned it around to expose the Coca-Cola logo." According to the *Weekly*, Rose responded to Williams' maneuver with "nervous chuckling."

Sometimes media favor their advertisers not with a story's content but with its placement. The *Wall Street Journal*'s October 3 edition carried an ad on page C3 for the Wall Street firm Bear Stearns. On the same page, readers learned from a news report that Bear Stearns had just made a tremendous error—accidentally ordering a sale of $4 billion worth of stock, instead of $4 million. The juxtaposition of that news with an ad hawking the company's ability to "execute complex transactions—flawlessly" was striking, to say the least; such coincidences are not unprecedented, however, and a usual reaction would be for the paper to move the ad to mitigate the problem. But this time, according to a report from <thestreet. com> (October 11, 2002), the *Journal* chose to sacrifice the news instead: Later editions of the paper carried the ad in its original place, while the bad news about Bear Stearns had been reduced to a subsection of another story on a different page.

The *Chicago Sun-Times* wanted to improve its coverage of the city's theater scene. But according to an account in *The New York Times* (June 3, 2002), "in meetings with theater owners to find a solution to their problem, the executives may have sent an unintended message: that if the theaters wanted more coverage, they should take out more ads." Marj Halperin, executive director of The League of Chicago Theatres, told *The New York Times* that *Sun-Times* executives suggested to her that theaters advertising in the paper might get preferential treatment on the news pages. The *Sun-Times* denied that such a link exists, though the paper has a history of tying coverage to advertising (*Chicago Reader*, January 17, 1997).

It's hard to deny the link between ads and news at the *Washington Times*, where an ad salesperson actually called a group that had been criticized in the paper to suggest that it buy an ad to air its side of the story. The Unification Church–backed paper had been attacking the advocacy group Forest Service Employees for Environmental Ethics, publishing more than a dozen stories and editorials in a year suggesting that forest service employees planted false evidence of a rare Canadian lynx in forests in Washington. Subsequent investigations showed that the *Times'* reports were erroneous (*Extra!*, May/June 2002).

Perhaps the *Times* ad rep thought he'd have an easy sell, therefore, when he suggested to the group that they consider buying a $9,450 ad to counter the negative coverage. The group, however, was simply appalled. And when the story got out (*Washington Post*, February 4, 2002), *Times* general manager Richard Amberg said the whole thing was "just a mistake that shouldn't have happened." Indeed.

THE BOSS'S BUSINESS

Media owners, whether powerful families, individuals or corporations, seek to influence news content in many ways. Some seem almost quaintly overt, as when *San Francisco Examiner* publisher James Fang reportedly told then-editor David Burgin (*Washington Post*, March 18, 2002): "We bought the paper for two reasons, business and politics. I see 5 percent of the stories having to do with what the Fangs need, promoting the Fangs and our interests." (Days after Burgin made clear he defined the editor's role rather differently, he was fired.)

Corporate boasts of "synergy" are less direct but amount to the same thing: owners using media they control to promote their "interests," as when AOL Time Warner's *Time* magazine declared AOL Time Warner's movie *The Lord of the Rings: The Two Towers* a resounding hit before it was released, with the cover line, "Good Lord! *The Two Towers* is Even Better Than the First Movie" (December 2, 2002).

Such cross-promotion is ubiquitous, but no less unethical than a small-town newspaper owner who uses the outlet to promote the used-car business he runs on the side.

And journalists who resist pressure from upstairs—whether that means a pushy publisher's office or a megacorporate headquarters—face consequences up to and including the loss of their jobs. Readers and viewers may never learn that a reporter was fired or demoted or moved off the beat, nor will they be aware of the stories that go untold as a result.

"I love Push, Nevada!" exclaimed *Good Morning America* weather reporter Tony Perkins (September 4, 2002), surrounded by what appeared to be teenage athletes. "Because the guys from the Push, Nevada, high school hockey team have given me this jersey!" Perkins gave details about the team's record and their chances for the season before going back to the weather.

Good Morning America claimed they had no idea that "Push, Nevada" was not a real town, but the name of a new prime-time drama airing, like *Good Morning America*, on ABC. The drama program's producers did acknowledge that they'd hired actors to pose as real people on a news show, but instead of calling it a misleading hoax or a journalistic transgression, they called it an edgy promotional technique suggested by their marketing company.

If the network is to be believed, the *Push, Nevada* stunt was so "under the radar" that no one at ABC's news or entertainment divisions knew about it. They don't appear to have been too upset, though: As Lisa de Moraes pointed out in the September 6, 2002, *Washington Post*, the network hadn't edited out what turned out to be a lengthy plug for the series by the time *Good Morning America* aired on the West Coast.

In the novel *Divine Secrets of the Ya-Ya Sisterhood*, the main character, New York playwright Siddalee Walker, is interviewed by *The New York Times*. But in the movie, Siddalee, played by Sandra Bullock, sits down with a reporter from *Time* magazine instead. As the *Washington Post's* Howard Kurtz noted (June 17, 2002), "The *Time* interview is mentioned repeatedly in the film, and toward the end Bullock is inducted into the sisterhood and presented with a hat bearing a big fat *Time* logo."

Accounting for the change is not only the fact that the movie was from Warner Brothers, another AOL Time Warner unit, but that *The New York Times* would not allow the depiction in the film of events that never took place. *Time*, on the other hand, was happy to cooperate. "Product placement is a good thing," *Time* spokesperson Diana Pearson told the *Post.*

Coverage of the Olympics is a perennial case of corporate self-promotion overtaking news judgment. The 2002 Winter Olympics were broadcast on NBC and its affiliated cable channels, and as previous experience would have predicted, *NBC Nightly News* found the event far more newsworthy than other networks (69 minutes of coverage, compared with 30 minutes at ABC and 10 at CBS). According to ADT Research, publisher of the *Tyndall Report*, NBC's *Today* show devoted 544 minutes to the Olympics—more than any other news story for the entire year.

The use of morning news shows, in particular as promotional vehicles for network fare is not restricted to NBC, of course. As J. Max Robins noted in *TV Guide*, (January 18, 2003), "CBS's *Early Show* provided slavish coverage of *Survivor* (432 minutes) and the low-rated *Amazing Race* (129 minutes)." The following data gives some indication of what all that "synergistic" coverage was replacing: The 79 minutes *Good Morning America* devoted to *The Bachelor* was "more time than was spent on the midterm congressional elections."

Media bosses' business interests extend beyond their own corporate parents, of course. In July, the *Washington Post* gave extensive attention to the Cadillac Grand Prix, a Washington, DC, road race. But it wasn't until days into their coverage that the paper acknowledged that they had a business relationship with the event. The *Post* signed on as an "exclusive print and online advertiser," DC's *City Paper* revealed (July 18, 2002), which meant that the paper got ad dollars from the grand prix, along with other "considerations," like signs at the race site.

The *Post's* reporting wasn't uncritical. For example, some coverage detailed stonewalling by the Sports Commission on event financing. But the paper's failure to disclose its interests without prodding raised eyebrows even within its own ranks. In his July 28 ombudsman report, the *Post's* Michael Getler reminded editors that no matter how plausible their claims of editorial independence, "this is a tricky business in which credibility, which can't be bought, can be squandered."

Some outlets seem to think disclosing a conflict of interest is the same thing as avoiding it. According to *Columbia Journalism Review* (March/April 2002), the *Las Vegas Sun* didn't attempt to hide that its sole owner, the Greenspun family, also owned half of the newly opened Green Valley Ranch Station Casino. But neither did it explain whether that economic link had anything to do with the 400 column inches it devoted over two days to the casino's opening, with 13 photos and three maps.

Roy Brown, CEO of the Brown Publishing Company chain of Ohio newspapers, apparently suffers from a similar lack of embarrassment. Brown, who was running for Congress, sent editors at some of those papers a series of "must-run" press releases from the campaign, followed by "stacks of Brown-for-Congress flyers" (*Columbia Journalism Review,* March/April 2002). One of the editors, Kevin O'Boyle of the *Vandalia Drummer News*, complained, telling the *Dayton Daily News* (April 6, 2002) that the company's actions broke every rule in the book. O'Boyle was fired two months later.

Among the most high-profile tales of an owner's heavy hand is that of former *New York Post* entertainment reporter Nikki Finke. Finke was fired after writing critically about the Walt Disney Company and their legal wrangling over the licensing rights to Winnie-the-Pooh. It seems that *Post* parent news corporation and Disney had an online business deal in the works, and after Disney complained to its new partner about Finke's reporting, threatening to pull its advertising as a consequence, she was history. *Post* editor Col Allan claimed the firing was due to "inaccuracies" in her work, yet the paper never ran any corrections (*Village Voice*, April 30, 2002). Finke, now a columnist at *L.A. Weekly*, filed a $10 million suit against the *Post* and Disney. As *Extra!* went to press, her case remained unsettled.

POWERFUL PLAYERS AND PR

A powerful individual, lobby or institution need not own a media outlet outright or fuel it with ad dollars in order to exercise influence. Sometimes the pressure comes from a store that sells the medium in question, whose disapproval might affect distribution. Or a powerful corporation makes it known that its displeasure with local media might cost a town jobs and resources.

And some influence, like that of Wall Street, appears to be so widespread and so internalized by media decision-makers that no overt exertion of power is necessary. Such influence can be harder to pin down, but its effects are nonetheless palpable. Finally, some journalists are themselves walking, talking conflicts of interest. Nancy Snyderman was one of those: The *ABC News* medical correspondent was suspended without pay for a week by the network last year after she appeared in a radio commercial for Tylenol (New York *Daily News*, April 30, 2002). Snyderman found a way out of her journalistic conflict, though; she left ABC in December to become vice president of medical affairs at Johnson & Johnson—the company that makes Tylenol.

CNBC, the financial news cable channel owned by General Electric, had a novel response to the business troubles of 2002: As reported in a *Dow Jones Newswire* column by Brian Steinberg (January 26, 2002), CNBC began airing a series of promotional spots that featured network reporters and anchors making can-do declarations about the economy.

"People are battling back.... Business is coming back, slowly but surely," declared Maria Bartiromo in one spot. In another, Ron Insana assured viewers that "most people don't realize that by the time you figure out you're in a recession, it's almost over." Reporter David Faber went even further, saying, "We know who our enemies are. We've identified them, and we're going after them." According to *Dow Jones*, Faber went on to suggest that as a result of this new resolve, the post–September 11 world is "less risky."

Setting aside the unsettling image of CNBC staffers "going after" the nation's "enemies," it's ethically suspect to place journalists whose job is reporting economic developments in the role of predicting them. And, as Steinberg suggests, the network may be motivated by something other than faith in the U.S. economy: CNBC's ratings tend to rise—and fall—with the market.

Lou Dobbs, anchor of CNN's *Moneyline*, stayed cheerful in the face of a year of conflicts of interest. According to <MSNBC.com> (April 4, 2002), Dobbs has been doing radio ads for financial services companies—an industry he covers on CNN. Though Dobbs isn't identified by name in the voice-overs, they air after the financial news spots he does on United Radio Networks and NBC. When asked if he might be compromising his integrity, Dobbs told <MSNBC.com>, "That is a silly, silly question. Would I do it if I thought I were compromising anything? I've got to run now."

CNN couldn't see the problem either, telling <MSNBC.com> that it was "standard practice" for radio journalists to read ad copy, adding, "Howard Stern does it." The network also stood by its man when critics questioned Dobbs' vigorous defense of the accounting firm Arthur Andersen in the face of federal prosecution over its role in the Enron scandal. As a scathing *USA Today* editorial (April 8, 2002) explained it, Dobbs regularly featured "a one-sided array of pro-Andersen guests" on *Moneyline* and behaved "fawningly" during an interview with Andersen's CEO. The problem, said *USA Today*, wasn't Dobbs' polemics, but his failure to disclose that Andersen had for years paid him "substantial fees for speaking engagements," sponsored an old CNN show of his, *Business Unusual,* and served as the auditor for Space Holdings, the company that runs Space.com Inc., "of which Dobbs is part owner and 'nonexecutive chairman.'"

After mainstream articles appeared suggesting a conflict of interest, Dobbs disclosed his ties to Andersen on *Moneyline,* but maintained that such disclosure was unnecessary since "Space Holdings pays Andersen, not the other way around" (*The New York Times,* April 4, 2002).

New York Post columnist Neal Travis (January 11, 2002) cited "widespread" rumors that *Time* magazine's original choice for their 2001 person-of-the-year cover was Osama bin Laden—until Wal-Mart intervened. "I'm told by very reliable sources," wrote Travis, that when Wal-Mart executives heard of the bin Laden choice, they "decided to flex their red-white-and-blue muscles" and "told *Time* honchos that if bin Laden was on the cover in any kind of laudatory position, their stores would refuse to stock that edition." (*Time*'s person-of-the-year pick is not necessarily "laudatory"; it's meant to highlight the year's biggest newsmaker—as with Adolf Hitler in 1938.) In the end, *Time* featured Rudy Giuliani. Travis noted that some *Time* staffers suggested that "in the days before AOL and the days before Warner, anyone trying such coercion on Time-Life would have been tossed out the window."

Wal-Mart gave contradictory answers when asked for comment; spokesperson Tom Williams told the *Arkansas Democrat-Gazette* (January 17, 2002) that the rumors were untrue, while spokesperson Jay Allen refused to confirm or deny them, saying that "you could read that [silence] as you choose." Allen did, however, acknowledge that "if Osama bin Laden had been on the cover of that magazine, we would not have liked it and would have evaluated how our customers feel before selling it."

The *San Antonio Express-News* reported (May 10, 2002) that the nightly news on San Antonio TV station KENS aired what was essentially an infomercial for a brand of wrinkle cream sold locally by a KENS employee. The spot, which was also re-aired during sweeps week as part of a "special" on beauty, reportedly featured "a half-dozen or more funny, likeable women" gathered in a living room extolling the virtues of the new cream and trying it out. The segment closed with KENS anchorwoman Sarah Lucero assuring viewers of the product's safety and giving the phone number for purchasing it.

All the information about the cream was provided by Jennifer McCabe, the salesperson on the segment who was identified only as a "distributor." As the *Express-News* pointed out, however, McCabe is also a "producer/director in commercial production" for KENS and the fiancée of KENS news executive producer, Ian Monroe.

Remarkably, none of the KENS staffers quoted by the *Express-News* exhibited discomfort with the arrangement. The affianced executive producer, Monroe, said that he had recused himself from the story, and the station's news director, Tom Doerr, told the paper that he saw no ethical problem with using a news segment to push a station employee's business, nor with the segment's unabashed promotion of the cream. "It's just one of the gimmicky things out there that appeal to the desire to look better," he said.

In perhaps the most depressing editorial of the year, the Alabama *Selma Times-Journal* (March 7, 2002) affirmed that because "there is no greater goal for the management of the *Times-Journal* than to see Selma and Dallas County succeed," the paper would not report details of a proposed Hyundai manufacturing plant that might come to town. The plant could bring jobs, said the paper, so stories about the venture should remain vague, lest they frighten off the corporate benefactor.

"Big companies do not like pressure... and they sure don't like ordinary citizens like us telling them they better move to our community," wrote the *Times-Journal*. "When media get involved, when members of the press ask questions and get pushy about details, big companies get angry. They ask media to leave them alone. They ask state officials to stay quiet. And if state officials know what's best, they do stay quiet." Arguing that an excess of press coverage had stopped Hyundai from opening a plant in Mississippi, the paper concluded, "we can't let that happen to us. So for now, we'll remain quiet on Hyundai, just like every other media organization in Alabama should do."

GOVERNMENT AND OTHER "OFFICIAL" PRESSURE

Like any government rallying a country for war, the Bush Administration is engaged in a massive propaganda campaign. That the war is a vaguely defined, open-ended "War on Terror" creates holes that images and "messages" must fill. In such circumstances, the press corps have a special duty to maintain independence, to question official pronouncements, and to inform the public as thoroughly as possible about policies being carried out in their name. With some notable exceptions, U.S. corporate media have not taken up the charge, appearing to see their role as supporting the government at the expense of wide debate and fair treatment of dissent.

In January, a few months after the September 11 attacks, NBC's Tom Brokaw got special access to the White House for a news special called "Inside the Real West Wing" (which aired, neatly, just before NBC's fictional *West Wing* drama). Although the presidential schedule was tailored for the taping for maximum PR value, Brokaw insisted that the special was "not an infomercial for the White House" (*New York Times*, January 23, 2002). Yet he told the *Washington Post* (January 21, 2002) that part of the reason NBC got such extensive access was that the administration was "concerned about the public drifting away from the mission of the war," and "this was an opportunity for them to kick-start it, to keep the country refocused." Apparently, Bush agreed: The *Post* reported that at one point during the day, the president remarked that "while he has to keep the country's attention on the war against terrorism, it's also 'part of Mr. Brokaw's job.'"

The Voice of America (VOA) is a broadcasting agency that, until a few years ago, was managed by the U.S. State Department. Though the VOA is now overseen by a board of directors, the government's control over the operation was made clear in February.

In September of 2001, VOA reporter Spozhmai Maiwandi landed what many would consider a real scoop: an interview with Taliban leader Mullah Mohammed Omar. The interview was one of the last conducted with Omar. Though his comments were included in a report with an official from the U.S.-backed Northern Alliance and an academic from Georgetown University, the report was "put on hold amid criticism from State Department officials" (*Chicago Tribune*, February 6, 2002).

The report eventually aired. Maiwandi, meanwhile, was reassigned to what VOA's news director Andre de Nesnera told the *Tribune* is a "useless job."

In his book *Fallout*, New York *Daily News* reporter Juan González recounts the difficulties he encountered at the paper while investigating the environmental consequences of the World Trade Center disaster. While most mainstream media were uncritically repeating the assurances of officials, Gonzalez was breaking stories about toxins in lower Manhattan that far exceeded safety levels. The backlash was intense; complaints about Gonzalez came rolling in from one of Rudolph Giuliani's deputy mayors, the head of the New York City Partnership and Chamber of Commerce, and EPA administrator Christine Whitman.

Subsequently, *Daily News* editors "showed a marked reluctance" to pursue the story. "One courageous editor at the *News*, however, refused to buckle under the pressure," writes Gonzalez. Metropolitan editor Richard T. Pienciak encouraged his reporting and "assigned a special four-person team of reporters to take a closer look" at the health impact in lower Manhattan. But "within days of forming the team," Pienciak "was removed from his post without explanation" and the new team was dissolved. Though Pienciak was not fired, he was essentially demoted from editor to an enterprise reporter for the paper's Sunday edition.

While we like to think of journalists and media outlets as independent truthseekers, there are times when specific information is withheld from the public because of government pressure. Boston TV station WBZ-TV had been investigating local software company Ptech, which is said to be financed by a Saudi man who allegedly donated money to Al Qaeda.

Before federal authorities raided Ptech's Quincy, Massachusetts, offices in early December, they requested that journalists looking into the matter refrain from reporting about the investigation until after they had conducted the raid. WBZ complied with the request, along with eight other media outlets, according to the *Washington Post* (December 7, 2002). WBZ news director Peter Brown explained to the *Boston Globe* (December 7, 2002) that the station was happy to comply: "Frankly, there wasn't a great deal of internal debate. I'm very conservative. I believe we have a role to play as citizens."

WBZ appeared to think that it was getting some kind of quid pro quo from the government by holding back on the story. As station reporter Joe Bergantino told the *Post*, "We were promised that because we agreed to hold off, we would be told before the raid was held." He added: "In the end that didn't happen. We certainly were disappointed. We were lied to. It was an unsettling and disturbing development."

An article appearing in the November 10 *Washington Post* provided readers with a fleeting insight into the real relations between the media and the military. Headlined "War Plan For Iraq Is Ready, Say Officials; Quick Strikes, Huge Force Envisioned by Pentagon," the *Post* report laid out what some government officials considered a likely battle plan for Iraq. The article relied almost exclusively on White House spin, noting that "the emerging U.S. approach tries to take into account regional sensitivities by attempting to inflict the minimum amount of damage deemed necessary to achieve the U.S. goals in a war."

While the *Post's* uncritical reliance on the official line is troubling enough, the paper adds this disclaimer: "This article was discussed extensively in recent days with several senior civilian and military Defense Department officials. At their request, several aspects of the plan are being withheld from publication. Those aspects include the timing of certain military actions, the trigger points for other moves, some of the tactics being contemplated, and the units that would execute some of the tactics."

The story is almost entirely based on Pentagon officials, so it's hard to imagine their objections. In fact, the propaganda value of the piece is not hidden: One unnamed official comments, "Discussing [the plan's] broad outline would help inform the Arab world that the United States is making a determined effort to avoid attacking the Iraqi people." The *Post* seemed content to provide that platform.

"Until last year," wrote Gwen Shaffer (*Columbia Journalism Review*, November/December 2002), "I would have insisted public radio stations were immune from quid pro quos." Shaffer was disabused of this notion by her experience as a reporter for Philadelphia public radio station WHYY, which during her tenure entered into a "partnership" with a non-profit media company called GreenWorks. GreenWorks, as she eventually discovered, received money from ICF Consulting, a PR firm working for Pennsylvania's Department of Environmental Protection (DEP); the group in turn gave money to WHYY, to pay the salaries of two reporters and a researcher who would work on environmental stories. Though originally assured that all editorial decisions would be made by the station, Shaffer soon learned otherwise, as GreenWorks' executive producer took part in weekly story meetings. The producer urged her and her colleague to "cover 'positive' stories of dubious merit," she says, including reports on specific DEP-funded projects, and chastised them for covering controversial issues like oil drilling in the Allegheny National Forest. Shaffer was fired after six months at the station.

WHYY news director Bill Fantini insisted (*Columbia Journalism Review*, November/December 2002) that there was a "firewall" between GreenWorks and the station, but he nonetheless resigned after Shaffer's allegations came to light, and WHYY ended its arrangement with the company.

In a troubling coda to the story, WHYY aired a discussion on the problems of "grant-funded journalism" on the show *Radio Times* on December 17, but it didn't discuss the station's own controversy, and callers were not allowed to bring it up (*Philadelphia Inquirer*, December 19, 2002). Explained *Radio Times* host Marty Moss-Coane, "We decided the show we would do would be slightly at arm's length." (FAIR was asked to participate in the program, but was not contacted again after a lengthy pre-interview.)

While voters benefit from substantive questioning of those running for public office, the candidates themselves aren't always so keen on it. Alaskan Republican state senator David Donley apparently bridled at questions from Rhonda McBride, moderator for a series of pre-election candidate debates called "Running" on Alaska public TV station KAKM. In a discussion of Donley's record on education, McBride referred to concerns of inequity in the funding of Alaska's rural schools (*Columbia Journalism Review*, November/December 2002). Donley complained to the station's general manager and—perhaps because he is co-chair of the finance committee that determines KAKM's funding—his complaints were heard. McBride was told to "tone down her questions," and a few days later the station removed her as moderator, citing disagreements "about the direction the program would take." She subsequently resigned.

Officials' involvement in journalism is a problem at all levels of government. In July, two of the three full-time employees of the *Northport* (Alabama) *Gazette* resigned in protest over the paper's hiring of a town councilmember to cover town council meetings. According to the *Tuscaloosa News* (July 5, 2002), the councilmember, David Allison, was hired to write for both the *Northport Gazette* and its parent paper, the *West Alabama Gazette*, by publisher Barbara Bobo, who is also mayor of a local town, Millport. Bobo brushed away conflict-of-interest concerns, asserting that overlap between newsmakers and news reporters is a "fact of small-town life." She cited herself as an example. Apparently, Bobo covers the town that she is mayor of for the newspapers she publishes: "I write [Millport's] news. I don't have a reporter there" (*Tuscaloosa News*, July 9, 2002). Not to worry—Mayor/Publisher Bobo told the *Tuscaloosa News* that managing her various jobs isn't so tough because "it's not like there's a whole lot going on."

Janine Jackson is FAIR's program director, and Peter Hart is a FAIR media analyst; they co-host FAIR's radio show, *CounterSpin*. Rachel Coen is a freelance writer and former FAIR media analyst. This article originally appeared in the April 2003 issue of FAIR's magazine, *Extra!*.

Fairness and Accuracy In Reporting (FAIR) is a national media watch group that offers well-documented criticism of media bias and censorship. FAIR monitors mainstream news media—newspapers, magazines, television, and radio—and exposes pro-establishment, pro-corporate spin. Visit <www.fair.org> for more information.

CHAPTER 11

Bearing Bad News

BY ROHAN JAYASEKERA, ASSOCIATE EDITOR, *INDEX ON CENSORSHIP*

In the realm of free expression, the world seems to send nothing but bad news to Index on Censorship. 2002 marked the thirtieth anniversary of the founding of the magazine in London and during that "celebratory" year, the situation for free speech did visibly improve in countries like Sri Lanka, Azerbaijan, Bosnia-Herzegovina, and Fiji. Freedom of Information laws were passed in several countries, including Taiwan, Jamaica, Peru, Mexico, Pakistan, and most notably, India.

But these small advances were swamped by setbacks in other countries. Russia, with Ukraine and Belarus trotting behind, turned back to the ways of the Soviet Union, jailing journalists, closing publications, banning books, and imposing ever more draconian media laws. Countries such as Jordan and Thailand, which had begun to build reputations for tolerating dissident opinion, changed their tune and slammed their jail doors on their critics. Supporters of politicians in crisis—notably Venezuelan president Hugo Chavez—turned violently on journalists as the bearers of bad news.

Has the magazine *Index on Censorship* seen anything as bad in the years since it was founded in 1972? Like most other advocates of free expression, we saw 2002 as the year when the changes wrought by September 11 seemed to be set in stone. One of the few briefly heartening sights that year were the meetings of communities and tribal groups across Afghanistan convened to consider candidates to the Loya Jirga, the tribal gathering called to pick an interim government for the country.

There, some people—including a few brave women—found the courage to speak out against the tyrannical warlords who took over from the Taliban. It was to be their only cheer. The tyrants are now well paid mercenaries of the U.S. government, meeting the Pentagon's policy targets in Afghanistan; the government of Hamid Kharzai that emerged from the Loya Jirga in 2002 was a marginalized agency barely able to extend its reach beyond the capital.

The war on terror became an excuse. Over the Afghan border in neighboring Uzbekistan, president Islam Karimov silenced independent news sources. The state controls the national print and broadcast services, as well as the media licensing system and runs a fierce official censorship regime that saw three Uzbek journalists jailed in 2002. In each case, the war against Islam and terrorism is invoked as justification. But as an essential U.S. ally, providing bases and intelligence for the war in Afghanistan, Karimov evaded serious censure from the West.

The effect of September 11 battered free speech rights in the U.S. in the year that followed. U.S. Attorney General John Ashcroft vigorously urged federal agencies to resist more Freedom of Information Act (FOIA) requests. "Offensive" political posters, newsletters, even T-shirts, were banned. Students and teachers were suspended. Groups went to court to ban optional college courses on "understanding Islam." In July 2002, country music artist Steve Earle was pilloried for his song, "John Walker's Blues," which some said romanticized John Walker Lindh, the American jailed for aiding the Taliban. The USA Patriot Act's powers to detain suspected terrorists indefinitely and secretly monitor political groups were widely supported by the public. One U.S. poll found nearly half of those surveyed felt the constitutional protection of free speech sometimes "goes too far." To question the prevailing

THIS MODERN WORLD

by TOM TOMORROW

view was to stand in a lonely place. "For critics of war a day at the office is rather like being a homosexual in a homophobic world," wrote New York legal clerk and Web "blogger" Michael Steinberg. "You search others for signs that it's safe to come out to them."

Others did not care to justify their actions. Holding tight to power and chasing private wealth, Zimbabwe's president Robert Mugabe made life difficult for white farmers and dangerous for independent journalists—but he made life for the ordinary people who democratically campaigned against him a living hell. His thugs employed murder, rape, and intimidation to silence his political grass roots opponents.

Iran's reactionary clergy sentenced history lecturer, journalist, disabled veteran of the Iran-Iraq war and active reformist Hashem Aghajari to death in November 2002 for blaspheming and insulting the Shiite Imams during a landmark speech on clerical reform made the previous June. His case is under appeal.

In Italy, media, man, and government were wrapped up in the single person of media magnate and Prime Minister Silvio Berlusconi, who used his business interests to secure unprecedented powers of censorship and stand within reach of controlling 90 percent of the country's television market. His critics were merely "politically motivated," he complained.

The consistent quality shared by the ordinary and extraordinary people who combat these tyrannies? A sense of simple duty. "We became dissidents without actually knowing how, and we found ourselves behind bars without really knowing how," wrote Václav Havel in the pages of *Index on Censorship* 24 years ago. "We simply did certain things we had to do and that seemed proper to do: nothing more nor less." A week after he was published in 1979,

he was in jail. In 2002 he was bringing his presidency of his homeland Czech Republic to a close. The voices are always heard in the end.

Index on Censorship magazine is published quarterly. Subscription details from <www.indexonline.org>.

INDEX INDEX

Index Index is a regularly updated chronicle of freedom of expression violations worldwide, logged by *Index on Censorship* and published online and in the magazine. Here are selections from just some of the entries for the more than 90 countries we tracked in 2002.

AFGHANISTAN: The Afghan Supreme Court dismissed Judge Marziya Basil after she was pictured without a headscarf in a photo taken with President George W. Bush during an official trip to Washington. The Kabul daily *Suhbat* described it as a "disgrace to the dignity of Afghanistan."

ALGERIA: Algerian security forces ordered civilian police to haul in independent journalists, starting with *Liberté* cartoonist Ali Dilem and journalist Salima Tlemçani of the daily *Al Watan*, then moving on to Mohamed Benchicou, editorial director of the daily *Le Matin* on January 30. On July 1, former Algerian defense minister General Khaled Nezzer sued ex-army officer Habib Souaidia, over his eyewitness account of how soldiers disguised as Islamic rebels massacred civilians. French courts refused the suit, citing Souaidia's right to free expression.

ARMENIA: Caucasus Media Institute deputy director Mark Grigorian was hospitalized in a hand grenade attack on October 22 in Yerevan. He was working on an article about the October 1999 attack on the Armenian parliament. The assailant was not identified.

BANGLADESH: On September 3, the authorities in Bangladesh banned a new novel by exiled feminist writer Taslima Nasreen, claiming that it was anti-Islamic and could foster religious tensions. It was a sequel to a 1999 work, also banned for blasphemy.

BELARUS: A court in Hrodna found Mikola Markevich, editor-in-chief of the local independent newspaper *Pahonya*, guilty of organizing an unauthorized rally in defense of his newspaper on November 19. The paper had investigated state links to the disappearance of opposition figures.

BOSNIA-HERZEGOVINA: On August 6, a British court vindicated U.S. police-woman Kathryn Bolkovac, fired by her employers, DynCorp, after she revealed the extent of U.N. personnel and aid workers' involvement in prostitution rings in Bosnia. A tribunal found she was unfairly dismissed.

BRAZIL: TV journalist Tim Lopes was reported tortured and killed by drug dealers in Rio de Janeiro on June 2 after having been missing for a week. Police blamed drug lord Elias Maluco for the killing of Lopes, who was investigating drug trafficking and sexual abuse of girls in Rio's slums.

BURMA: Nobel Peace prize winner and opposition leader Aung San Suu Kyi was freed from 20 months of house arrest on May 6. The Burmese junta held more than 1,000 political prisoners, including 17 elected members of parliament at the time.

CAMEROON: Cartoonist Paul Nyemb Ntoogue, pen name "Popoli," was stopped by police on November 30 and told by an officer that "all he was doing in the country was insulting people." Ntoogue, of the daily *Le Messager*, was then beaten for 10 minutes by the police.

CHINA: After the U.S. Internet search engine Google was blocked by Chinese authorities between August 31 and September 12, analysts estimated that the Chinese state employed 30,000 people to monitor and control information on the Internet. In the two months prior to the November 8–16 National Congress of the Chinese Communist Party in Beijing, dozens of publications, groups, and media deemed to threaten the image of the party were banned, and scores of potential dissidents detained.

COLOMBIA: The Foundation for Press Freedom reported three media workers killed, three kidnapped, four attacked, four forced into exile, and two threatened in July alone. They are victims of both sides in Colombia's long running civil conflict. Among them were Mario Prada Díaz, of the weekly *El Semanario Sabanero* in Santander, kidnapped on July 11 and found shot dead the following day, and radio journalist Dennis Segundo Sánchez of Radio 95.5 Estero in El Carmen de Bolivar, murdered on July 17 while at home with his wife. Elizabeth Obando, distribution manager for the regional newspaper *El Nuevo Día* in the municipality of Roncesvalles, died on July 13 from wounds sustained at a roadblock two days earlier. Angela Yesenia Bríñez, the municipality's spokesperson, died in the same attack.

CYPRUS: On August 8, editor-in-chief Sener Levent and Memduh Ener of the daily *Afrika* were jailed for six months for libelling Turkish Cypriot leader Rauf Denktash in a July 1999 article titled "Who is the Number One Traitor?" They were released early on October 6.

EGYPT: Professor Saad Eddin Ibrahim, director of the Ibn Khaldun Centre for Development Studies, had his seven-year jail sentence upheld on July 29. After investigating electoral corruption he was charged with receiving foreign funds from the European Union without authorization. Web designer Shohdy Surur faced jail on June 30 for posting a poem on the Internet written by his late father, Naguib Surur, more than 30 years ago. The court said the politically critical poem, notorious for its use of crude street Arabic, violated "public morality."

ERITREA: Nine journalists and a photographer began a hunger strike on March 31 to protest against their illegal detention. The journalists were arrested in September after all eight of Eritrea's independent newspapers were closed down.

ETHIOPIA: Academic Mesfin Wolde-Mariam, 71, returned to Ethiopia in late January to voluntarily face charges of inciting students at the University of Addis Ababa, widely regarded as a trumped-up response to his address to a seminar in May 2001 on human rights and academic freedom.

FRANCE: Novelist Michel Houellebecq was cleared on October 22 of incitement to racial hatred in his anti-Islamic outbursts in interviews and recent novel *Platform*. A Paris judge ruled that the comments did not constitute an incitement to discrimination against Muslims.

GERMANY: A court stopped German sales of U.S. historian Daniel Goldhagen's book, *A Moral Reckoning: The Role of the Catholic Church in the Holocaust and Its Unfulfilled Duty of Repair*, after complaints by church officials.

INDIA: On June 6, film censors demanded that director Anand Patwardhan make several cuts to his award-winning antinuclear documentary *Jang aur Aman* (*War and Peace*) before it could be released. Police held journalists Kumar Badal and Aniruddha Bahal from the Web site <tehelka.com> in July on charges relating to reports on illegal poaching of leopards and assaulting a policeman. The charges were linked to the Web site's earlier exposés of political and military corruption. Zafar Iqbal, a journalist for the Kashmir-based English-language daily *Kashmir Images*, was shot and seriously injured by three unidentified assailants on May 29. The assailants fled the scene and have not been caught.

INDONESIA: Indonesia delayed a decision on its new broadcast bill to limit the right of radio and TV stations to relay foreign programming, a proposal that media rights groups view as a bid to limit uncensored news coverage from the BBC, Voice of America, and CNN.

IRAN: Renowned Iranian journalist and film critic Siamak Pourzand, 72, was reported to have confessed to treason under ill treatment in jail. Pourzand was sentenced to 11 years of imprisonment in May 2002 on charges of links to monarchists and counter-revolutionaries. Tehran's Press Court suspended two newspapers in September, bringing the total number of publications banned since April 2000 to 54. The newly opened daily *Golestane-Iran* was accused of publishing lies and rumors and the weekly *Vaqt* of publishing immoral photos and articles.

IRAQ: The daily *Babel* newspaper was banned on November 20, despite the fact that it is owned by Saddam Hussein's eldest son, Uday Hussein. It had reprinted some foreign news reports including a British story alleging that Saddam was ready to pay Libya to guarantee political asylum for his family.

ISRAEL: Dr. Ilan Pappe, senior lecturer in political science at Haifa University and the academic director of the Research Institute for Peace at Givat Haviva, was threatened with dismissal, he said, for his support of a student who published research on Israeli massacres of Palestinians in 1948. In August, Prime Minister Ariel Sharon ordered an investigation into the peace group Gush Shalom after it issued warning letters to 15 senior Israeli army officers that their actions in the occupied West Bank constituted war crimes.

ITALY: State-owned RAI TV banned an edition of the satirical show *Blob* dedicated to Prime Minister Silvio Berlusconi, solely comprising video clips of his public mannerisms aired without comment. The channel director said too much focus on one person was "not good satire."

KAZAKHSTAN: Journalist Sergei Duganov, author of an online critique of Kazakh President Nursultan Nazarbayev, was attacked by an unknown assailant on August 28. He had previously been arrested on July 9 and charged with "insulting the honour and dignity of the president."

KENYA: On May 8, parliament imposed laws designed to muzzle the press ahead of presidential elections, increasing a libel bond required from every publication to a maximum of $12,800 and penalizing vendors and distributors who fail to check that their publications were legal.

LIBERIA: On April 26, police ransacked the offices of the independent *Analyst* newspaper, claiming that the paper had "incited the public to create chaos" during an ongoing state of emergency. It had published a human rights lawyer's criticism of President Charles Taylor a day before. Hassan Bility, editor of the private weekly *The Analyst*, was freed in November from four months' detention incommunicado. The release order came on the strict condition that he would be rearrested "in the event of any (unspecified) violations."

MAURITANIA: The August 19 edition of the Nouakchott daily *al-Qalem* was banned without official explanation. Editor-in-chief Riadh Ould Mohamed Elhadi said the government's action may have been related to an article that criticized political Islam.

MEXICO: Fernández García, editor of the weekly *Nueva* was shot dead on January 18 in the city of Miguel Alemán. He had recently published an article on alleged relations between the former city mayor and drug traffickers.

MOROCCO: Parliament approved a new press law on March 12. Article 29 retains the government's right to ban Moroccan or foreign newspapers if they "undermine Islam, the monarchy, national territorial integrity, or public order."

NETHERLANDS: Dutch legislators declared digitally created false images of child pornography illegal, with sentences up to six years. The ruling means that the physical involvement of a child is no longer needed for a child sex crime to be committed in the country.

NIGER: Sanoussi Jackou, opposition leader and owner of the weekly *La Roue de l'Histoire* and his publisher, Abarad Mouddour, were sentenced to suspended four-month prison terms and a fine of 100,000 CFA francs ($136) for defaming the prime minister in May.

NIGERIA: Fashion journalist Isioma Daniel of the newspaper *This Day*, whose November 16 article on the Miss World pageant sparked deadly riots across the country, sought refuge in the U.S. after Islamic authorities and local officials in the state of Zamfara endorsed a call for her murder.

PAKISTAN: Daniel Pearl, South Asia bureau chief for the *Wall Street Journal*, was kidnapped on January 23 and murdered while investigating Pakistani Islamist extremists. The man convicted for his murder was British-born militant Ahmed Omar Saeed Sheikh.

PALESTINE: On January 2, Dr. Mustafa Barghouti, director of the Union of Palestinian Medical Relief Committees, was arrested after meeting European parliamentarians and U.S. officials. Israeli authorities claimed Barghouti did not have permission to enter Jerusalem. *Voice of Palestine* radio journalist and presenter Esam al-Tellawe was fatally shot in the back of the head, apparently by an Israeli army sniper, as he was reporting on a Palestinian demonstration in Ramallah during the night of September 21–22.

POLAND: The state brought 12 lawsuits against *Rzeczpospolita* newspaper in a reported bid to bring the paper under the influence of the ruling party. Three members of the paper's board were deprived of their passports for four months and put under police surveillance.

QATAR: After participants on a August 6 talk show broadcast by Qatar-based Al Jazeera alleged that Jordan was allowing its territory to be used by U.S. covert operations against Iraq, Jordan lodged a diplomatic protest with Qatar and recalled its ambassador "for consultations."

RUSSIA: A January 2002 court decision liquidated the parent company of TV-6, Russia's last independent nationwide television channel. The suit was brought by interests backing President Vladimir Putin against his political foe, industrialist Boris Berezovskii, main owner of the station. Lawyers for jailed journalist Grigorii Pasko failed to overturn his treason conviction on June 25. Pasko, who worked for the Russian Pacific Fleet's own newspaper, was first arrested in November 1997 after exposing the fleet's nuclear pollution record. During the October 23–26 siege of a Moscow theatre held by Chechen rebels, information minister Mikhail Lesin clamped down on the media, threatening to shut down the radio station Moscow Echo's Web site after it posted an interview with the kidnappers. Offices of the weekly *Versia* were searched by FSB secret police on November 2; the head of Tatarstan TV said Moscow forced his resignation after he hosted a October 24 talk show which included calls for an end to the war in Chechnya.

SAUDI ARABIA: A Harvard Law School report found that the Saudi government blocked approximately 2,000 Web sites, mostly sex or religion sites, but also conventional sites about women, health, drugs, and pop culture.

SIERRA LEONE: In March, the private daily *Africa Champion* was banned for two months. The paper had published a story accusing the president's son of corruption. The managing editor of the publication defied the order and the newspaper was distributed on March 18.

SPAIN: Spain banned the Batasuna Party, which won 10 percent of the vote in 2001 regional elections as the political wing of the banned Basque nationalist group ETA. Spain's Supreme Court is empowered to ban any party it says is guilty of supporting racism, xenophobia, or terrorism.

SRI LANKA: On January 22, the government announced plans to abolish the law of criminal defamation, set up an independent press complaints commission, and introduce a freedom of information act, as part of a series of media reforms.

SUDAN: Editor Nhial Bol of the English-language daily *Khartoum Monitor* was fined five million pounds (approximtely $1,950) and the paper an extra 15 million pounds ($5,800) on January 16 over an article linking the state to the slave trade in the country. The fines threatened to bankrupt the paper.

TAJIKISTAN: The Prosecutor General's Office dropped a criminal case first opened in 1993 against Dododjon Atovulloev, editor of the opposition newspaper *Tcharoghi Ruz*. The charges were revived in 2001 in connection with his criticism of the country's present leadership.

TOGO: Publisher Julien Ayi of *Nouvel Echo* was jailed on September 13 for four months for "attacking the honor" of President Gnassingbé Eyadéma by alleging that he had a personal fortune of $4.5 billion. His editor, Alphonse Névamé Klu, went into hiding after the case.

TUNISIA: The editor of the online political magazine *TUNeZINE*, Zouhair Yahyaoui, was sentenced to 28 months in prison after being found guilty of spreading "false information" on June 20. He set up the Web site in 2001 to circulate news about democracy and freedom issues.

TURKEY: Hulya Avsar, one of Turkey's most famous singers, was charged in July with insulting the Turkish flag after she was seen playing with hundreds of balloons bearing the flag to celebrate the Turkish soccer team's first appearance in the World Cup since 1954. On October 7, Istanbul state security court opened the case of publisher Sanar Yurdatapan and Yilmaz Çamlibel, charged with publishing a book called *Freedom of Thought— 2001*. Only 2 of the 11 people who signed the book as publishers in a deliberate attempt to challenge the court, including U.S. writer Noam Chomsky and Turkish human rights activist, Eren Keskin, were prosecuted. Parliament legalized Kurdish radio and TV broadcasts, ending years of severe state restrictions. The country's estimated 12 million Kurds will also be allowed to have private Kurdish-language education.

UKRAINE: On September 14, tens of thousands of people marched in Kiev and around the country in defense of an independent media and in memory of investigative journalist Georgiy Gongadze, allegedly killed by associates of President Leonid Kuchma.

UNITED KINGDOM: On July 2, organizers defended giving a platform to Nick Griffin, leader of the far-right British National Party, and fundamentalist Muslim cleric Sheikh Abu Hamza al-Masri, at a debate at the Royal Academy. The two argued that they have the right to freedom of expression through the media.

UNITED STATES: Author and scientist Haluk Gerger was refused entry into the U.S. on arrival at New York; his 10-year visa was cancelled; he was photographed, fingerprinted and deported on the next flight. A founding member of the Human Rights Association of Turkey, his arrest in Turkey in 1994 and 1995 was once cited by the U.S. State Department as an example of how Ankara misused antiterror laws to violate the free speech rights of writers and academics. The FBI is visiting libraries and checking the reading records of people it suspects of having ties to terrorism, U.S. library officials said. The searches were legalized under the USA Patriot Act, which also made it a criminal offense for librarians to reveal details or the extent of searches.

ZIMBABWE: Between March and June 2002 alone, 36 journalists were arrested and 13 charged. In May Geoff Nyarota, editor of the *Daily News*, Lloyd Mudiwa, his journalist, and Andrew Meldrum, correspondent for the London *Guardian*, were charged after reporting allegations that government supporters hacked a mother to death in front of her children. On July 15, Meldrum was acquitted, but was ordered to leave the country within 24 hours. On June 16, three other *Daily News* staffers were arrested while covering a meeting of the opposition MDC Party and charged under the recently enacted Public Order and Security Act. Reporters from the *Standard* were also charged for stories on police harassment of journalists.

SOURCES: Agence France-Presse, *al-Ahram*, <Algeria-interface.com>, Amnesty International, Article 19, Associated Press, BBC, Bellona, Cartoonist Rights Network, Committee to Protect Journalists, *El País*, Freedom Forum,

Glasnost Media, *The Guardian*, *Gulf News Online*, *Ha'aretz*, Human Rights Watch, IFEX, *Index Online*, Info-Türk, International Federation of Journalists, *La Repubblica*, *LAW* (Jerusalem), *Liberté* (Algiers), *Middle East International*, NEAR, PEN–Writers in Prison Committee, *Periodistas*, Radio Echo Moscow, Radio Free Europe, Reporters sans Frontieres, SEAPA, *South China Morning Post*, *Sudan Online*, <Tehelka.com>, *The Independent* (London), *The Times* (London), *Times of India*, *Turkish Daily News*, *Washington Post*, *Wired*, World Association of Newspapers, *Xinhua*.

CHAPTER 12

Why Japan Remains a Threat to Peace and Democracy in Asia

THE PROBLEM OF LAP DOG JOURNALISM

BY KENICHI ASANO

Most people from this region, as well as other parts of the globe, would be quite surprised to hear the assertion that Japan is one of the most under-developed states when it comes to the development of democracy and healthy journalism in the Asia-Pacific region—and that politically, Japan is not yet a fully independent nation. And why shouldn't they be surprised? Most people assume that since Japan is a highly industrialized country with one of the highest standards of technology in the world, it must therefore be a democratic state as well.

In fact, this is not the case. I would even go so far as to say that Japan remains a threat to peace and prosperity in Asia.

MY EXPERIENCE AS A NEWS REPORTER

In examining the media situation and political governance in Japan, let me first introduce my experience as a correspondent in Southeast Asia. For 22 years, I worked as a news reporter for Kyodo News, Japan's representative wire service, including a stint as Kyodo's Jakarta Bureau Chief from February 1989 to July 1992. In 1992, I was deported by General Suharto's military regime.

I also covered the Cambodian conflict and democratization process in Thailand. I have been an independent journalist for eight years, having also taken a position as professor of mass communications at Doshisha University in April 1994.

I have a special interest in media ethics, mainly how the news media should cover crimes and criminal victims, as well as suspects, defendants, and convicts. I often compare media-accountability systems in various countries. I also try to monitor the "independence" of journalists from the political centers of local and national power that they cover.

Let me share with you my experience, in particular, in Indonesia. I was blacklisted by the Indonesian military and Japanese embassy in Jakarta for my critical reporting on the Indonesian human rights situation and for reporting on some shady ties with corrupt Japanese politicians.[1]

WHY JAPAN IS SO UNDEMOCRATIC

Let me now turn to why Japan is one of the most underdeveloped states when it comes to healthy journalism and democracy in the Asia-Pacific region.

Firstly, according to opinion polls in late September 2002, more than 55 percent of the Japanese public reportedly support Prime Minister Junichiro Koizumi's cabinet, even after he twice worshipped at Yasukuni Shrine near Tokyo, a Shinto shrine where Class-A war criminals from World War II (including Japan's then-prime minister Hideki Tojo) are enshrined as gods. Yasukuni Shrine was the center of state-sponsored Shintoism during the years of Japan's invasion of the Asia-Pacific region since 1895, when Japan annexed Taiwan by military force. To make a comparison, that would be like the current German president paying an official visit to Adolf Hitler's graveyard on the day that Nazi Germany surrendered to Allied forces.

Moreover, Shintaro Ishihara, the current governor of Tokyo—infamous for repeatedly denying Japanese atrocities in the Nanjing Massacre in China during the 1930s—ranks number one in Japanese public opinion polls as the politician most favored to be the next premier of Japan. It is safe to say that on the political spectrum, Ishihara is to the far right of Jean Le Pen of France.[2]

Most Japanese citizens, to this day, refuse to admit that Japan ever invaded any Asia-Pacific countries. They even go so far as to emphasize that Japanese military occupation in the region has helped these countries to gain independence from Western imperialism.

Japanese Emperor Hirohito was acquitted of wartime atrocities at the close of World War II, and since then, most Japanese people have closed the book on taking any responsibility for their government's own past crimes against humanity. From that time up to the present day, Japan's ruling party, the Liberal Democratic Party (LDP) has been dominated by ultra-right politicians and bureaucrats.

Herbert P. Bix's recent Pulitzer Prize-winning biography, *Hirohito and the Making of Modern Japan* shows in painstaking detail the many ways that the former Emperor led Japan's military wartime regime, and how he was later protected by Occupation forces after the war. The book, which has been out in English since 2000, was finally translated into Japanese mid-2002, the language that would expose it to its most important audience. Japanese publishers had been reluctant to publish Bix's book in fear that they will become targets of right-wing violence. Kodansha, leading publishing firm in Tokyo, published its translation. Most Japanese newspapers criticized the book in their book reviews. What makes Bix's book so threatening is the high quality of his scholarship, revealing the truth of the matter with indisputable facts.

Mr. Minoru Kitamura, one of several Japanese historians seeking to prove that the Nanjing Massacre in China never happened, has written a new book called "The Massacre Myth." Kitamura accused Mr. Harold Timperley, correspondent to China for the then-Manchester *Guardian* newspaper of Britain, of "creating" the story of the massacre.

Kitamura stresses that Timperley, author of the widely read book "The Japanese Terror in China," was an agent of the Chinese Kuomintang, the nationalist party then in government.[3] Mr. John Gittings, a *Guardian* correspondent to Shanghai, wrote an article about it titled "Japanese Rewrite *Guardian* History: Nanjing Massacre Reports Were False, Revisionists Claim" on October 4, 2002.

Gittings, by analyzing *Guardian* archives in London, found out that the reason for the misquoting of the numbers of massacred people was due to Timperley's references to the Yangtze River delta being omitted at the time by Japanese diplomats in China. I too firmly believe that the number of victims of the massacre committed by Japan is still not clear, simply because the Japanese government has burnt or otherwise nullified evidence of its crimes all over the world.

More recently North Korean leader Kim Jong-il has admitted that his country kidnapped Japanese citizens—and that at least four were still alive. "It is regretful and I want to frankly apologize," Kim said to Japanese Prime Minister Koizumi, as the two leaders held talks in Pyongyang during their first face-to-face meeting on September 17.

Eight Japanese nationals, who were abducted in the 1970s and 1980s, are confirmed as being dead. Mr. Kim reportedly said that those responsible for the kidnappings had been "sternly punished." Six out of 11 people, whom Tokyo has long claimed were abducted, were confirmed to have died in North Korea.

In a joint statement that followed the meeting between the two nations' leaders, North Korea said it would abandon compensation from Japan's 35-year imperial invasion of the Korean Peninsula. In turn, it demanded Japanese official development aid and expected private investment from Japan. Pyongyang has long held complete compensation from Japan's colonialism as a pre-condition for talks over normalizing relations between the two countries. But suddenly, North Korea let Japan's responsibility for wartime atrocities just fade away.

In this sense, the Japan-North Korea joint statement is worse than the 1965 so-called "peace treaty" between Japan and the military government of South Korea. Mr. Kim of North Korea now badly seems to need Japanese economic help as well as diplomatic support, at a time when he is under intense pressure from the United States. North Korea can no longer afford to make so many demands.

Revisionists and ultra-rightists in Japan have acquired renewed political power following North Korea's admission that it abducted Japanese citizens several decades ago. The Japanese media, and most Japanese citizens, are behaving as if they are innocent victims of some brand of devilish "outlaw state." It seems to me that they have all conveniently forgotten what their own Japanese Imperial Army had done to the people of *several* Asia-Pacific countries since 1895. Among many other things, Japan had abducted more than three million Koreans, forcing them to be soldiers, mine workers, and "sex slaves."

In this instance with North Korea, as with many other past issues, the major Japanese newspapers, magazines, and TV networks again showed their bad side: carrying out their reporting via the phenomenon known as "pack journalism."

In "pack journalism," the employees of news organizations throng to a single news source like a pack of animals, pursue the story almost as one herd, and report mass amounts of information that end up in stories nearly identical to one another. This is exactly the term the *New York Times* once used to describe Japanese news reporters, when the corrupt president of the Toyoda Shoji company was stabbed to death by a mobster in 1985, right in front of the reporters.

Mr. Kim Sok-pom, a Korean writer born in Japan, severely criticized the Japanese nation and its media recently during an October 26 citizen's group meeting on monitoring the media coverage of the North Korea abduction cases.

Kim stated publicly: "The mass media in Japan have been reporting the abduction cases without mentioning what Japan has done to Koreans. This kind of reporting by the Japanese mass media, which incites anti-Korean sentiment among the Japanese public, is a kind of violence against Koreans born in Japan. Japan has neglected to commemorate the massacre of Koreans born in Japan during the massive earthquake in the Kanto area [of Japan] on September 1, 1923, as well as all kinds of atrocities during Japanese colonial rule. Is there any country like Japan in the world?"

Kim Sok-pom added that "Japan is suffering from amnesia." He further accused the Kim Jong-il government of an "act of treachery and shameful diplomatic policy" when it recently gave up its right of any future claims to Japan's cruel occupation of the past.

Japanese revisionists have made great strides in erasing any written references to *ianfu*—former "sex slaves" of the Japanese Imperial Army—and the Nanjing Massacre in China from Japanese school textbooks. Very few Japanese citizens today know about Japanese modern history in any real depth.

Secondly, Japan is still under the military occupation of the United States of America. Following Japan's unconditional surrender to the U.S.-led Allied forces on August 15, 1945, and the subsequent end of World War II, Japan was placed under U.S. military control. The American military forces have never left Japan since then. More than 40,000 U.S. troops remain based in Japan today, as we speak. This is ostensibly to protect Japan from "enemies" like North Korea—and yet no U.S. military bases in the area, outside of those in South Korea, are facing imminent war with North Korea.

The Japanese news media and citizens are now criticizing North Korea's nuclear weapons plan. However, the Japanese have also totally forgotten that there are functioning nuclear reactors all over Japan, not to mention large numbers of nuclear weapons located on U.S. military bases in Japan.

Yet the Japanese government has confidently claimed that Japan's nuclear program will never be used for weapons and that U.S. armed forces are restricted under the antinuclear policies of the Japanese constitution from bringing nuclear weapons into Japan.

And this propaganda seems to be working well. One would be hard-pressed to find any large demonstrations against U.S. bases in Japan by Japanese students or Japanese workers. One can find an active anti-U.S. base movement only in the southern island of Okinawa, where most of the beautiful beaches are essentially occupied by the U.S. military.[4] Extremely weak trade unions and university student bodies in our country make it very easy for the ruling class to control people. The Japanese, I would say, have politically changed very little since 1868, when the shogun-ruled Edo period ended and the Western-leaning Meiji period began.

Thirdly, the Japanese people have never experienced any real social revolutions in their history, unlike nations in many other parts of the world that have fought hard to acquire democracy at the cost of enormous numbers of their own citizens.

JAPAN'S LAP DOG PRESS

I would like to assert one good reason why Japanese democracy is not yet matured, despite Japans enjoyment of a high technological standard of living: the problem known as "lap dog journalism."

The press in Japan is as free and open as that of any nation in the world, including the U.S. and European countries. Freedom of the press in Japan is absolutely and strongly protected by the constitution that Japan adopted after World War II. Any kind of censorship is strictly forbidden. Yet self-censorship runs rampant. Those who work in Japanese media circles do not use their constitutional right to carry out investigative reporting. The Japanese press, as a whole, lacks any skepticism toward authority.

Lack of diversity and variety is the cause of such weak journalism. There is only one local newspaper in most of the local prefectures of Japan. Major TV networks are owned by prominent newspaper companies, which enjoy high business profits. Japan has the highest number of newspaper readers per capita of any country in the world.

And still, ironically, journalists and the general public alike in our country do not realize that Japan's freedom of expression was a "gift" bestowed upon us by the Allied forces at the cost of 23 million victims throughout the Asia-Pacific region during World War II. Major newspapers throughout Japan since the 1950s have acted as if their highest duty were to help enforce the continuing rule of the LDP.

A healthy, tense atmosphere between news sources and journalists is indispensable for solid journalism to flourish.

In Japan, news sources try to curry favor with journalists only so they can obtain favorable coverage of the organizations they belong to. But this is not right. Journalists should be independent of any news source if they are to effectively carry out their duty of working for the citizens' right to know.

According to a survey taken in Japan in the late 1980s, 90 percent of news stories in the Japanese press originate from government officials and Big Business. This is because the majority of mainstream news reporters get their "facts" through a system known as the "kisha clubs," or press clubs—a system imposed on media outlets from above.[5] Under this system, the mass media serve merely as mouthpieces for those in power. The number of commentators and academics who appear daily on major television networks in Japan are overwhelmingly scholars whose work is patronized by the government.

A lack of objective, balanced reporting principles is another problem. The Japanese media as a whole pay little or no attention to clarifying news sources and attribution of those sources.

You may be surprised to know that very few professional journalists in Japan have ever studied journalism before entering their profession. Only a few universities—out of about 400 universities in all of Japan—even have a journalism department. A professional journalist is only regarded to be such when he or she becomes gainfully employed by any of the news organizations.

Generally speaking, Japan's concept of democracy is just like one that Professor Noam Chomsky of the United States defines as "an alternative conception of democracy."[6] That is, under this conception, citizens must be barred from managing their own affairs and the means of information must be kept narrowly and rigidly controlled.

CONCLUSION

In closing, I could see with my own eyes how the people of Thailand fought against the regime of General Sutchinda in May 1992 in seeking democratic reforms, and how the people and journalists of Indonesia waged a courageous struggle to oust General Suharto in the 1990s. Likewise, the people of the Philippines fought against the former dictator Ferdinand Marcos and contributed to the eventual withdrawal of U.S. armed forces from their country.

Journalists in those Asian nations were always to be found in public demonstrations, alongside laborers, students and activists of nongovernmental organizations.

If Japan is ever to attain the status of a truly democratic state in the modern world, then it is precisely this type of free and open journalism that Japanese journalists will need to vigorously practice and defend.

Kenichi Asano is a Professor of Communication Studies at Doshisha University, Kyoto, Japan.

FOOTNOTES:

1. Several years later, on September 5, 2002, nearly 3,861 Indonesian people went on to file a lawsuit in Tokyo, seeking 5 million yen each for the damages caused by the dam that Japan funded with ODA. The plaintiffs claim they were forcibly resettled after the Kotopanjang Dam was completed in 1997. The hydroelectric dam was built at a cost of some 31 billion yen and paid for with a yen-denominated government loan. Among those named as defendants in the suit, brought before the Tokyo District Court, were the Japanese government and its foreign assistance body, the Japan International Cooperation Agency, the state-run Japan Bank for International Cooperation, and Tokyo Electric Power Services Co., which is an affiliate of Tokyo Electric Power Co., Japan's largest utility.

    See: *The Japan Times*, September 6, 2002, </www.japantimes.co.jp/cgibin/getarticle. pl5?nn20020906a3.htm>.

2. Michiko Jitoku, a student of mine at Doshisha University, has written a dissertation on "Governor Shintaro Ishihara's Views and the Japanese Media" in March 2002, regarding the Nanjing Massacre.

3. Former Japanese emperor Hirohito and his followers, not Harold Timperley, should be the ones who stand accused. Japanese historians like Minoru Kitamura must be criticized by the international community. The only reason why these Japanese ultra-rightists can get away with writing such fiction is because their books are printed only in Japanese and therefore are not generally accessible to readers of other languages.

    John Gittings replied thus on October 12, 2002 to an earlier e-mail of mine: "The figures for the massacre generally given are too high, of course. The same is true of the Indonesian massacre in 1965–66, on which I have done some work (and for that matter, of the Tiananmen massacre). It is a natural tendency to inflate the figures, but it does not detract in any of these cases from the horrific nature of the deeds and the inhumanity of man to man."

4. In Okinawa, a 12-year-old schoolgirl was gang-raped by three U.S. Marine soldiers in September 1995. In June 2001, a U.S. Air Force sergeant sexually assaulted a Japanese woman, age 24, on the bonnet of a parked car outside a cluster of bars in the Okinawan town of Chatan. In March 2002, the soldier was jailed for two and a half years for rape. Incredibly, some Japanese bestselling weekly magazines blamed the Japanese rape victim, saying, "It is the fault of the young woman for being in a café in the middle of the night." There is still no concrete plan to remove or reduce the number of U.S. bases in Okinawa.

5. Concerning the Japanese "kisha clubs," there is a recent expose on the subject published in 2000 by Princeton University Press, *Closing the Shop: Information Cartels and Japan's Mass Media* by Laurie Freeman. The scholarly but highly readable book is an excellent introduction to the subject for any English reader. I also presented a paper titled "The Japanese Self-Imposed 'Kisha Club' System Decays Investigative Journalism" at Workshop #6, Democracy and Media in East Asia, Preconference of International Communication Association, Yonsei University, Seoul, Republic of Korea, July 14, 2002. The kisha club system still exists today in South Korea, one of the unfortunate remains of the former Japanese occupation of that land.

    Also, I have written about the kisha clubs in most of my books, all of which are in Japanese. These two books deal with more recent developments of the kisha clubs: "Musekin-na Mass Media" (Japan's Irresponsible Mass Media), Gendaijinbunsha, 1996 (edited with Masanori Yamaguchi), and "Imminent Statutory Regulations & Obstacles in Establishing a Press Council," Gendaijin Bunsha, 2002.

See also Kenichi Asano: "Kisha Clubs Should be Abolished," Tsukuru magazine [in Japan], March 2002, and Kazue Suzuki: "The Press Club System in Japan," a thesis submitted to the graduate faculty in partial fulfillment of the requirements for the degree of Master of Science, Iowa State University, Iowa, USA, 1982.

6. Noam Chomsky, *Media Control: The Spectacular Achievements of Propaganda,* Seven Stories Press, New York, 1997.

THIS MODERN WORLD

by TOM TOMORROW

HEY, LIBERALS! DOES THE CURRENT REPUBLICAN STRANGLEHOLD ON ALL THREE BRANCHES OF GOVERNMENT FILL YOU WITH *DESPAIR*? WELL, *CHEER UP!* AT LEAST YOU CAN ALWAYS COUNT ON...

THE UNCOMPROMISING LIBERAL MEDIA

THEY'VE BEEN ON GEORGE BUSH'S CASE FROM *DAY ONE!* THANKS TO THEIR TIRELESS EFFORTS, THERE'S NOT A MAN, WOMAN OR CHILD IN THIS *COUNTRY* WHO REGARDS HIS PRESIDENCY AS *LEGITIMATE!*

EVERYONE KNOWS GORE WOULD HAVE WON AN *HONEST* RECOUNT!

AND WHAT ABOUT ALL THOSE BLACK VOTERS WHO WERE "ACCIDENTALLY" DROPPED FROM THE ROLLS?

AND THEY'RE *STILL AT IT!* WHEN A WHITE HOUSE OFFICIAL OPENLY ACKNOWLEDGED THAT THE EVIDENCE FOR W.M.D.'S HAD BEEN OVERSTATED TO JUSTIFY WAR WITH IRAQ, THE MEDIA *COULD* HAVE BURIED THE STORY-- BUT OF *COURSE* THEY *DIDN'T!*

THE WHITE HOUSE TRIED TO MANI- PULATE PUBLIC OPINION THROUGH *BLATANT FEAR- MONGERING!*

DID THEY THINK THE UNCOMPRO- MISING LIBERAL MEDIA WOULD LET THEM GET *AWAY* WITH IT?

AND WHEN THE PRESIDENT STARTED PUSHING A DIVIDEND TAX CUT WHICH DISPROPORTIONATELY FAVORS THE RICH, THE UNCOMPROMISING LIBERAL MEDIA MADE *SURE* WE UNDER- STOOD THE DETAILS!

THE TOP ONE PERCENT WOULD RECEIVE AN AVERAGE OF ALMOST *TWELVE THOUSAND DOLLARS--*

--WHILE THE BOTTOM EIGHTY PERCENT GET ABOUT *THIRTY BUCKS!*

AND THE LIBERAL MEDIA *CERTAIN- LY* WEREN'T GOING TO LET BUSH FLY TO THAT AIRCRAFT CARRIER TO GIVE HIS SPEECH--WITHOUT REMINDING US OF THE QUESTIONS SURROUNDING HIS *OWN* SERVICE RECORD!

AT THE HEIGHT OF THE VIETNAM WAR, HIS FAMILY PULLED STRINGS TO GET HIM INTO THE TEXAS AIR NATIONAL GUARD--

--AND EVEN THEN, HE SEEMS TO HAVE GONE AWOL FOR A YEAR OR SO!

YES, THESE *ARE* HARD TIMES FOR LIBERALS...BUT REMEMBER: WITH- OUT THE *UNCOMPROMISING LIBERAL MEDIA*, THINGS COULD BE A *WHOLE LOT WORSE...*

WHERE WOULD WE *BE* WITHOUT THEIR TIRELESS EFFORTS TO EXPOSE BUSH'S CHICANERY AND DECEIT?

I SHUDDER TO EVEN *CONSIDER* IT!

THANKS, LIBERAL MEDIA!

TOM TOMORROW©2003 ... www.thismodernworld.com

APPENDIX A

Censored 2004 Resource Guide
SOURCES OF THE TOP 25 CENSORED STORIES

NATIONALS/INTERNATIONALS

THE AMERICAN PROSPECT
5 Broad Street
Boston, MA 02109
Tel: (888) MUST-READ
or (617) 547-2950
Fax: (617) 547-3896
E-mail: <letters@prospect.org>
Web site: <www.prospect.org>

A bimonthly publication covering
areas of concern such as political,
social, and cultural issues.

ASHEVILLE GLOBAL REPORT (AGR)
P.O. Box 1504
Asheville, NC 28802
Tel: (828) 236-3103
E-mail: <editors@agrnews.org>
Web site: <www.agrnews.org>/issues/
130/index.html>

We cover news underreported by
mainstream media, believing that a
free exchange of information is necessary to organize for social change.

BRIARPATCH
Saskatchewan's Independent News
Magazine
2138 McIntyre Street
Regina, SK S4P 2R7
Canada
Tel: (306) 525-2949
Fax: (306) 565-3430
Web site:
<www.briarpatchmagazine.com>

Alternative views on politics, labor,
and international events.

BULLETIN OF THE
ATOMIC SCIENTISTS
Education Foundation for
Nuclear Science
6042 S. Kimbark Avenue
Chicago, IL 60637
Tel: (773) 702-2555
Fax: (773) 702-0725
E-mail: <bulletin@thebulletin.org>
Web site: <www.bullatomsci.org>

Since 1947, the magazine of global
security news and analysis. Covers

international security, military affairs, nuclear issues. Bimonthly.

CENTER FOR PUBLIC INTEGRITY (CPI)
Publication: The Public I
910 17th Street, NW, 7th Floor
Washington, DC 20006
Tel: (202) 466-1300
Fax: (202) 466-1101
E-mail: <contact@publicintegrity.org>
Web site: <www.publicintegrity.org>

The CPI provides a mechanism through which important national issues can be analyzed by responsible journalists over time and the results can be published in full form without the traditional time and space limitations.

CHILDREN OF WAR
209 Iowa Avenue
Muscatine, IA 52761
Tel: (563) 264-1500
Fax: (563) 264-0864
E-mail: <info@stanleyfoundation.org>
Web site: <www.warchildren.org>

A documentary—produced by The Stanley Foundation in association with KQED, public television in San Francisco—about the effects of DU in Iraq by journalist and filmmaker Reese Erlich.

CORPWATCH
2288 Fulton Street #103
Berkeley, CA
Tel: (510) 849-2423
Fax: (510) 849-2423
E-mail: <corpwatch@corpwatch.org>
Web site: <www.corpwatch.org>

CorpWatch counters corporate-led globalization through education, network-building, and activism. We work to foster democratic control over corporations by building grassroots globalization, a diverse movement for human rights and dignity, labor rights, and environmental justice.

COUNTERPUNCH
P.O. Box 228
Petrolia, CA 95558
Tel: (800) 840-3683
E-mail: <counterpunch@counter-punch.org>
Web site:

Twice a month, CounterPunch brings its readers the stories that the corporate press never prints. Theirs is muckraking with a radical attitude.

COVERTACTION QUARTERLY
c/o Institute for Media Analysis, Inc.
143 W. 4th Street
New York, NY 10012
Tel: (212) 477-2977
Fax: (212) 477-2977
E-mail: <info@covertaction.org>
Web site: <www.covertaction.org>

Investigative journalism exposing malfeasance and covert activities in government, corporations, and other areas affecting the public.

DOLLARS AND SENSE: WHAT'S LEFT IN ECONOMICS
The Economic Affairs Bureau, Inc.
740 Cambridge Street
Cambridge, MA 02141-1401
Tel: (617) 876-2434
Fax: (617) 876-0008
E-mail: <dollars@dollarsandsense.org>
Web site:

Reports on issues of social justice and economic policy. Prints articles by journalists, activists, and scholars on a broad range of topics with an economic theme.

EARTH FIRST!
P.O. Box 3023
Tucson, AZ 85702-6900
Tel: (520) 620-6900
Fax: (413) 254-0057
E-mail: <collective@earthfirstjournal.org>
Web site: <www.earthfirstjournal.org>

Earth First! reports on the radical environmental movement. The journal publishes hard-to-find information about strategies to stop the destruction of the planet.

EXTRA!
Fairness and Accuracy in Reporting
112 W. 27th Street
New York, NY 10001
Tel: (212) 633-6700
Fax: (212) 727-7668
E-mail: <fair@fair.org>
Web site: <www.fair.org>

Provides media criticism featuring articles on biased reporting, censored news, media mergers, and more.

FEASTA
159 Lower Rathmines Road
Dublin 2
Ireland
Tel: 353(0)149-12773
E-mail: <feasta@anu.ie>
Web site: <www.feasta.org>

Feasta aims to explore and promote the characteristics—economic, cultural, environmental—that society must have in order to be fully sustainable.

FREE INQUIRY:
The International Secular Humanist Magazine
The Council for Secular Humanism
P.O. Box 664
Amherst, NY 14226
Tel: (716) 636-7571
Fax: (716) 636-1733
E-mail: <info@secularhumanism.org>
Web site: <www.secularhumanism.org>

A quarterly magazine that celebrates reason and humanity.

GLOBAL OUTLOOK
RR 2
Shanty Ray, L0L 2L0
Canada
Tel: (888) 713-8500
Fax: (888) 713-8883
E-mail: <editor@globaloutlook.ca>
Web site: <www.globalresearch.ca/globaloutlook/>

Global Outlook, based in Montreal, publishes news articles, commentary, background research, and analysis on a broad range of issues, focusing on the interrelationship between social, economic, strategic, geopolitical, and environmental processes.

THE GUARDIAN (London)
3-7 Ray Street
London, EC 1R 3DR
United Kingdom
Tel: (020) 7278-2332
E-mail: <editor@guardianunlimited.co.uk>
Web site: <www.guardian.co.uk>

Not-for-profit London daily newspaper.

HARPER'S
666 Broadway
New York, NY 10012
Tel: (212) 614-6500
E-mail: <letters@harpers.org>
Web site: <www.harpers.org>

Provides readers with unique perspectives on the world.

THE HIGHTOWER LOWDOWN
P.O. Box 20596
New York, NY 10011
Tel: (212) 741-2365
Fax: (212) 979-2055
E-mail: <lowdown@pipeline.com>
(subscription)
<lowdown@newslet.com> (editorial)
Web site: <www.Jimhightower.com>

A twice-monthly populist newsletter featuring Jim Hightower.

IN THESE TIMES
2040 N. Milwaukee Avenue, 2nd Floor
Chicago, IL 60647-4002
Tel: (773) 772-0100
Fax: (773) 772-4180
E-mail: <itt@inthesetimes.com>
Web site: <www.inthesetimes.com>

Provides independent news and views you won't find anywhere else.

LABOR NOTES
7435 Michigan Avenue
Detroit, MI 48210
Tel: (313) 842-6262
Fax: (313) 842-0227
E-mail: <labornotes@labornotes.org>
Web site: <www.labornotes.org/>

News and information for workplace activists. Aimed at rebuilding the labor movement through democracy and member activity.

LEFT TURN
P.O. Box 445
Seattle, WA 98112
E-mail: <left-turn@left-turn.org>
Web site: <www.leftturn.org>

Left Turn magazine focuses on the issues and debates within the growing anticapitalist movement.

MEDIAFILE
Media Alliance
814 Mission Street, Suite 205
San Francisco, CA 94103
Tel: (415) 546-6334
Fax: (415) 546-6218
E-mail: <ma@igc.org>
Web site: <www.media-alliance.org>

Includes independent reviews of Bay Area media issues including publications, broadcast outlets, and Internet publishing.

MOTHER JONES
731 Market Street, 6th Floor
San Francisco, CA 94103
Tel: (415) 665-6637
or (800) 438-6656
Fax: (415) 665-6696
E-mail:
<subscribe@motherjones.com>
Web site: <www.motherjones.com>

The magazine of investigative journalism; now with the online sister "mojowire."

NACLA REPORT
ON THE AMERICAS
475 Riverside Drive, Suite 454
New York, NY 10115
Tel: (212) 870-3146
Fax: (212) 870-3305
E-mail: <nacla@nacla.org>
Web site: <www.nacla.org>

NACLA has, for 30 years, been the best source for alternative information and analysis on Latin America, the Caribbean, and U.S. foreign policy in the region. NACLA analyzes the major political, social, and economic trends in Latin America, in an accessible format not seen anywhere else.

THE NATION
33 Irving Place, 8th Floor
New York, NY 10003
Tel: (212) 209-5400
Fax: (212) 982-9000
E-mail: <info@thenation.com>
Web site: <www.thenation.com>

Investigative journalism; a leading forum for leftist debate; home of Radio Nation and the Nation Institute.

NEW INTERNATIONALIST (NI) MAGAZINE
P.O. Box 1062
Niagara Falls, NY 14304
Tel: : (905) 946-0407
Fax: (905) 946-0410
E-mail: <magazines@indas.on.ca>
Web site: <www.newint.org>

NI exists to report on issues of world poverty and inequality; to focus attention on the unjust relationship between the powerful and the powerless; to debate and campaign for the radical changes necessary if the basic material and spiritual needs of all are to be met.

PEACEWORK
2161 Massachusetts Avenue
Cambridge, MA 02140
Tel: (617) 661-6130
Fax: (617) 354-2832
E-mail: <pwork@igc.org>
Web site:
<www.afsc.org/peacewrk.htm>

A monthly journal published since 1972, Peacework covers the full range of "Global Thought and Local Action for Nonviolent Social Change," with a special focus on the northeastern United States. It is meant to serve the movement as a trade journal, with minimal pretensions.

PEOPLE'S WEEKLY WORLD
3940 High Street, Suite B
Oakland, CA 94691
Tel: (510) 336-0617
Fax: (510) 336-0617
E-mail: <ncalview@ipc.org>
Web site: <www.pww.org>

Reports on and analyzes the pressing issues of the day: peace, social and economic justice, workers' rights, civil liberties, reproductive rights, protection of the environment, and more.

<Pilger.carlton.com>
The news writings of journalist-author John Pilger

POLITICAL AFFAIRS
235 W. 23rd Street
New York, NY 10011
Tel : (212) 989-4994, ext. 257
E-mail: <pa@politicalaffairs.net>

Web site: <www.politicalaffairs.net/>

Our mission is to go beyond events to provide analysis and investigate what is new and changing in our world. We do this from a working-class point of view.

THE PROGRESSIVE
409 E. Main Street
Madison, WI 53703
Tel: (608) 257-4626
Fax: (608) 257-3373
E-mail: <circ@progressive.org>
Web site: <www.progressive.org>

The Progressive discusses peace, politics, social justice, and environmental concerns from a liberal point of view.

PUBLIC CITIZEN
Trade Watch
1600 20th Street, NW
Washington, DC 20009
Tel: (202) 588-1000
E-mail: <member@citizen.org>
Web site: <www.citizen.org>

Public Citizen is a national, non-profit consumer advocacy organization founded by Ralph Nader in 1971 to represent consumer interests in Congress, the executive branch, and the courts.

<Rense.com>
Vast unedited information billboard covering topics ranging from politics to health.

THE SIERRA TIMES
1970 N. Leslie, Suite 204
Pahrump, NV 89060
Tel: (775) 751-3375

Fax: (775) 582-1323
E-mail: <editor@sierratimes.com>
Web site: <www.sierratimes.com>

An Internet publication for real Americans.

TASK FORCE CONNECTIONS
The National Task Force
on AIDS Prevention
973 Market Street, Suite 600
San Francisco, CA 94103
Tel: (415) 356-8110
Fax: (415) 356-8138
E-mail: <info@cdcnpin.org>
Web site: <www.cdcnpin.org/con-nect/start.htm>

Updates and reports on issues related to AIDS prevention and treatment.

THE TEXAS OBSERVER
307 W. 7th Street
Austin, TX 78701
Tel: (800) 939-6620
Fax: (512) 477-0746
E-mail: <business@texasobserver.org>
Web site: <TexasObserver.org/>

The Texas Observer writes about issues ignored or underreported in the mainstream press. Our goal is to cover stories crucial to the public interest and to provoke dialogue that promotes democratic participation and open government.

UTNE MAGAZINE
1624 Harmon Place, Suite 330
Minneapolis, MN 55403
Tel: (612) 338-5040
Fax: (612) 338-6043
E-mail: <info@utne.com>
Web site: <www.utne.com>

A digest of alternative ideas and material reprinted from alternative and independent media sources.

WAR TIMES
EBC/War Times
1230 Market Street
San Francisco, CA 94102
Tel: (510) 869-5156
E-mail: <distribution@war-times.org>
Web site:

The terrorist attacks of September 11 marked the beginning of a new and frightening period in our history. But the response of "permanent war against terrorism at home and abroad" has further endangered the lives and liberties of millions of people everywhere. War Times is a free, mass produced, biweekly, and nationally distributed tabloid-sized newspaper. It will be a valuable outreach and education tool for organizers on the ground and an entryway for new people into the peace and justice movement.

WASHINGTON FREE PRESS
PMB # 178
1463 East Republican
Seattle, WA 98112
Tel: (206) 860-5290
E-mail: <freepress@scn.org>
Web site:

It reports the underreported events of the Northwest. It specializes in labor and environmental topics, but is open to other topics as well. Bimonthly progressive news from Seattle and Washington State. Emphasis on labor and environment.

WILD MATTERS
Food & Water, Inc.
P.O. Box 543
Montpelier, VT 05601
Tel: (802) 229-6222
or (800) 328-7233
Fax: (802) 229-6751
E-mail: <info@foodandwater.org>
Web site: <www.wildmatters.org>
Formerly Food & Water Journal, Wild Matters is now published 10 times a year. A magazine that advocates for safe food and water, and a clean environment by educating the public on the health and environmental dangers of food irradiation, genetic engineering, and toxic pesticides.

YES! A JOURNAL
OF POSITIVE FUTURES
P.O. Box 10818
Bainbridge Island, WA 98110-0818
Tel: (206) 842-0216
or (800) 937-4451
Fax: (206) 842-5208
E-mail: <editors@futurenet.org>
Web site: <www.futurenet.org>

A journal that helps shape and support the evolution of sustainable cultures and communities. It highlights ways that people are working for a just, sustainable, and compassionate future.

Censored 2004 Resource Guide

OUR FAVORITE NATIONAL/INTERNATIONAL NEWS SOURCES

ADBUSTERS:
A MAGAZINE OF MEDIA AND
ENVIRONMENTAL STRATEGIES
The Media Foundation
1243 W. Seventh Avenue
Vancouver, BC V6H 1B7
Canada
Tel: (604) 736-9401
or (800) 663-1243
Web site: <www.adbusters.org>

Provides strategies for fighting mind
pollution from advertising.

AGAINST THE CURRENT
Published by Solidarity
7012 Michigan Avenue
Detroit, MI 48210-2872
Tel: (313) 841-0160
Web site: <www.igc.apc.org/
solidarity>

Promoting dialogue among activists,
organizers, and serious scholars of the
left, from the general perspective of
"socialism from below."

ALBION MONITOR(AM)
P.O. Box 1733
Sebastopol, CA 95473
Tel: (707) 823-0100
Web site: <www.monitor.net/moni-
tor/0106a/default.html>

AM is an online biweekly with a
nationwide readership. News and
commentary from both alternative
and mainstream sources, primarily
covering environmental, human rights,
and politics. Syndicated and other
copyrighted material available to
subscribers only.

ALTERNATIVE PRESS REVIEW
A.A.L. Press
P.O. Box 4710
Arlington, VA 22204
Tel: (573) 442-4352
Web site: <www.altpr.org>

Publishes a wide variety of the best
essays from radical zines, tabloids,
books, and magazines.

THE AMERICAN PROSPECT
5 Broad Street
Boston, MA 02109
Tel: (888) MUST-READ
or (617) 547-2950
Web site: <www.prospect.org>

A bimonthly publication covering areas of concern such as political, social, and cultural issues.

ANIMAL PEOPLE
P.O. Box 960
Clinton, WA 98236-0960
Tel: (360) 579-2505
Web site:
<www.animalpeoplenews.org>

Animal People is the leading independent newspaper and electronic information service providing original investigation of animal protection worldwide.

ARMS SALES MONITOR
The Federation of
American Scientists
1717 K Street, NW, Suite 209
Washington, DC 20036
Tel: (202) 546-3300, ext. 193
Web site: <www.fas.org/asmp/

U.S. government policies on arms exports and conventional weapons proliferation.

ASHEVILLE GLOBAL
REPORT (AGR)
P.O. Box 1504
Asheville, NC 28802
Tel: (828) 236-3103
Web site: <www.agrnews.org/issues/130/index.html>

We cover news underreported by mainstream media, believing that a free exchange of information is necessary to organize for social change.

BRIARPATCH
Saskatchewan's Independent News Magazine
2138 McIntyre Street
Regina, SK S4P 2R7
Canada
Tel: (306) 525-2949
Web site:
<www.briarpatchmagazine.com>

Alternative views on politics, labor, and international events.

BULLETIN OF THE
ATOMIC SCIENTISTS
Education Foundation
for Nuclear Science
6042 S. Kimbark Avenue
Chicago, IL 60637
Tel: (773) 702-2555
Web site: <www.bullatomsci.org>

Since 1947, the magazine of global security news and analysis. Covers international security, military affairs, nuclear issues. Bimonthly.

CHALLENGE
P.O. Box 41199
Jaffa 61411
Israel
Tel: (972) 3-6839145
Web site: <www.odaction.org/challenge/>

Our publication is directed to those members of the international community seeking a critical and accurate presentation of the dramatic events in our region.

CIVIL LIBERTIES

The American Civil Liberties
Union (ACLU)
125 Broad Street, 18th Floor
New York, NY 10004-2400
Tel: (888) 567-ACLU
or (212) 549-2585
Web site: <www.aclu.org>

Issues of civil liberties including
online information on Internet free
speech issues.

CLAMOR

Become The Media
P.O. Box 1225
Bowling Green, OH 43402
Tel: (419) 353-8266
Web site: <www.clamormagazine.org>

New bimonthly magazine, bringing the
depth of the human experience without the corporate filters, providing
new perspectives on politics, culture,
media, and life.

COUNTERPUNCH

P.O. Box 228
Petrolia, CA 95558
Tel: (800) 840-3683
Web site: <www.counterpunch.org/>

Twice a month, CounterPunch brings
its readers the stories that the corporate press never prints. Theirs is
muckraking with a radical attitude.

COVERTACTION QUARTERLY

c/o Institute for Media Analysis, Inc.
143 W. 4th Street
New York, NY 10012
Tel: (212) 477-2977
Fax: (212) 477-2977
Web site: <www.covertaction.org>

Investigative journalism exposing
malfeasance and covert activities in
government, corporations, and other
areas affecting the public.

CULTURAL SURVIVAL QUARTERLY (CSQ)

215 Prospect Street
Cambridge, MA 02139
Tel: (617) 441-5400
Web site: <www.cs.org>

The mission of this quarterly magazine
is based on the belief that the survival
of indigenous people and ethnic
minorities depends on the preservation of their rights in deciding how to
adapt traditional ways to a changing
world.

DARK NIGHT FIELD NOTES

Dark Night Press
P.O. Box 3629
Chicago, IL 60690-3629
Tel: (207) 839-5794
Web site: <www.darknightpress.org/>

A quarterly publication covering
issues related to the recognition and
liberation of indigenous peoples.

DEFENSE MONITOR

1779 Massachusetts Avenue, NW
6th Floor
Washington, DC 20036
Tel: (202) 332-0600
Web site: <www.cdi.org>

A journal that provides independent
research on the social, economic,
environmental, political, and military
components of global security.

DEMOCRATIC LEFT
The Democratic Socialists of America
180 Varick Street, 12th Floor
New York, NY 10014
Tel: (212) 727-8610
Web site:
<www.dsausa.org/dl/index.html>

A quarterly review of socialist issues
and activities.

DISSENT
310 Riverside Drive, Suite 1201
New York, NY 10025
Tel: (212) 316-3120
Web site: <www.dissentmagazine.org>

A quarterly magazine of politics,
culture, and ideas. Dissent covers
national and international politics
from a progressive perspective with
focus on providing forums for debate,
disagreement, and discussion on the
left.

DOLLARS AND SENSE:
WHAT'S LEFT IN ECONOMICS
The Economic Affairs Bureau, Inc.
740 Cambridge Street
Cambridge, MA 02141-1401
Tel: (617) 876-2434
Fax: (617) 876-0008
Web site:

Reports on issues of social justice and
economic policy. Prints articles by
journalists, activists, and scholars on
a broad range of topics with an economic theme.

E MAGAZINE
P.O. Box 5098
Westport, CT 06881
Tel: (203) 854-5559
Web site: <www.emagazine.com>

E is an independent newsstand-
quality publication that focuses on
environmental issues. E strives to
educate, inspire, and empower
Americans to make a difference
for the environment.

EARTH FIRST!
P.O. Box 3023
Tucson, AZ 85702-6900
Tel: (520) 620-6900
Fax: (413) 254-0057
Web site: <www.earthfirstjournal.org>

Earth First! reports on the radical
environmental movement. The journal
publishes hard-to-find information
about strategies to stop the destruction
of the planet.

EARTH ISLAND JOURNAL
300 Broadway, Suite 28
San Francisco, CA 94133-3312
Tel: (415) 788-3666
Web site:

International environmental news
magazine focusing on socioeconomic,
political issues affecting Earth's
ecosystems and on the work being
done to conserve, preserve, and
restore the Earth.

THE ECOLOGIST
c/o MIT Press Journals
1920 Martin Luther King Jr. Boulevard
Berkeley, CA 94704
Tel: (510) 548-2032
Web site: <www.theecologist.org>

Produced monthly, The Ecologist
is the world's longest running
environmental magazine. Thirty-third
year: Campaigns on the environment
and social issues facing this planet.

ECONOMIC JUSTICE NEWS
3628 12th Street, NE
Washington, DC 20017
Tel: (202) 463-2265
Web site: <www.50years.org>

Economic Justice News is the quarterly newsletter produced by the 50 Years Is Enough Network, a network of 200 social and economic justice organizations working to bring about radical reform of the World Bank and the International Monetary Fund.

EXTRA!
Fairness and Accuracy in Reporting
112 W. 27th Street
New York, NY 10001
Tel: (212) 633-6700
Fax: (212) 727-7668
E-mail: <fair@fair.org>
Web site: <www.fair.org>

Provides media criticism featuring articles on biased reporting, censored news, media mergers, and more.

FOOD FIRST NEWS
Institute for Food and
Development Policy
398 60th Street
Oakland, CA 94618
Tel: (510) 654-4400
Web site: <www.foodfirst.org>

Information and reader action guide for ending world hunger and poverty.

GENEWATCH
The Council for Responsible Genetics
5 Upland Road, Suite 3
Cambridge, MA 02140
Tel: (617) 868-0870
Web site: <www.gene-watch.org/

Publication which provides a forum for discussing, evaluating and distributing information and opinions about the social and environmental aspects of genetic engineering.

GLOBAL INFORMATION NETWORK
146 W. 29th Street, #7E
New York, NY 10001
Tel: (212) 244-3123
Web site: <www.globalinfo.org>

Global Information Network, a not-for-profit news and world media operation, is the largest distributor of developing world news services, including the award-winning Inter Press Service, in the U.S.

THE HIGHTOWER LOWDOWN
P.O. Box 20596
New York, NY 10011
Tel: (212) 741-2365
Web site: <www.Jimhightower.com>

A twice-monthly populist newsletter featuring Jim Hightower.

HUMAN RIGHTS TRIBUNE
Human Rights Internet
8 York Street, Suite 302
Ottawa, ON K1N 5S6
Canada
Tel: (613) 789-7407
Web site: <www.hri.ca>

Quarterly publication. Web site also has links to human rights Web sites worldwide; job postings from human rights organizations; databases.

IN THESE TIMES
2040 N. Milwaukee Avenue
2nd Floor
Chicago, IL 60647-4002
Tel: (773) 772-0100
Web site: <www.inthesetimes.com>

Provides independent news and views
you won't find anywhere else.

INDIAN COUNTRY TODAY
(LAKOTA TIMES)
P.O. Box 4250
Rapid City, SD 57709
Tel: (605) 341-0011
Web site: <www.indiancountry.com>

With subscriptions and store sales in
all 50 states and 15 foreign countries,
this weekly is reportedly the most
influential and widely read Native
American newspaper in the United
States. (It also has a regional section
covering the Pine Ridge Reservation.)

INDUSTRIAL WORKER
Industrial Workers of the World
P.O. Box 13476
Philadelphia, PA 19101-3476
Tel: (313) 483-3548
Web site: <www.iww.org>

The Industrial Worker is the monthly
newspaper of the industrial workers of
the world, or Wobblies. Every issue
contains news of the world labor strug-
gles, and analysis of the labor movement and economy from a Wobbly
perspective.

THE INSURGENT
Erb Memorial Union, Suite 1
Eugene, OR 97403-1228
Tel: (541) 346-3716
Web site: <www.theinsurgent.org>

A newspaper that seeks to provide a
forum for those working towards a
society free from oppression.

INTELLIGENCE REPORT
Journal of the Southern Poverty
Law Center
400 Washington Avenue
Montgomery, AL 36104
Tel: (334) 264-0286
Web site: <www.splcenter.org>

A quarterly journal that offers in-
depth analysis of political extremism
and bias crimes in the United States.
The Intelligence Report profiles far-
right leaders, monitors domestic terrorism, and reports on the activities of
extremist groups.

THE IRE JOURNAL
Investigative Reporters and Editors,
Inc. (IRE)
Missouri School of Journalism
138 Neff Annex
Columbia, MO 65211
Tel: (573) 882-2042
Web site: <www.ire.org>

The IRE Journal is published six
times a year and contains journalist
profiles, how-to stories, reviews,
investigative ideas, and background-
ing tips. The Journal also provides
members with the latest news on
upcoming events, training, and
employment opportunities in the field
of journalism.

LABOR NOTES
7435 Michigan Avenue
Detroit, MI 48210
Tel: (313) 842-6262
Web site: <www.labornotes.org/>

News and information for workplace activists. Aimed at rebuilding the labor movement through democracy and member activity.

LEFT BUSINESS OBSERVER
38 Greene Street, 4th Floor
New York, NY 10013-2505
Tel: (212) 219-0010
Web site: <www.panix.com/
~dhenwood/LBO_home.html>

A monthly newsletter on economics and politics in the U.S. and the world at large.

MONTHLY REVIEW
122 W. 27th Street
New York, NY 10001
Tel: (212) 691-2555
Web site:

An independent socialist magazine. A unique blend of scholarship and activism, critical understanding, and accessibility.

MOTHER JONES
731 Market Street, 6th Floor
San Francisco, CA 94103
Tel: (415) 665-6637
or (800) 438-6656
Fax: (415) 665-6696
Web site: <www.motherjones.com>

The magazine of investigative journalism; now with the online sister "mojowire."

MULTINATIONAL MONITOR
P.O. Box 19405
Washington, DC 20036
Tel: (202) 387-8030
Web site: <www.essential.org>

Tracks corporate activity, especially in the Third World.

NEW INTERNATIONALIST
P.O. Box 1143
Lewiston, NY 14092
Tel: (906) 946-0407
Web site: <www.oneworld.net>

An international journal that exists to report on the issues of inequality and world poverty; to focus attention on the unjust relationship between the powerful and the powerless in both rich and poor countries; and to debate the campaign for the radical changes necessary.

NEW UNIONIST
1821 University Avenue, S116
St. Paul, MN 55104
Tel: (651) 646-5546
Web site: <www1.minn.net/~nup>

A monthly paper dedicated to building a rank-and-file working-class movement for fundamental social change and to replacing the present competitive, class-divided system of capitalism with the cooperative industrial community we call economic democracy.

NEWSLETTER ON INTELLECTUAL FREEDOM
The American Library Association (ALA)
50 E. Huron Street
Chicago, IL 60611
Tel: (800) 545-2433
Web site:
<www.ala.org/alaorg/oif/nif_inf.html>

Newsletter of the ALA's Office of Intellectual Freedom.

NORTH BAY PROGRESSIVE
P.O. Box 14384
Santa Rosa, CA 95402
Tel: (707) 5251422
Web site:
<www.northbayprogressive.org>

National, international, and local news
for the San Francisco North Bay
region.

OUR TIMES
Canada's Independent
Labour Magazine
219-192 Spandina Avenue
Toronto, ON M6K 1G2
Canada
Tel: (800) 648-6131
Web site: <www.ourtimes.web.net>

Focuses on social change through
unionism and democratic socialism.

PEOPLE'S WEEKLY WORLD
3940 High Street, Suite B
Oakland, CA 94691
Tel: (510) 336-0617
Web site: <www.pww.org>

Reports on and analyzes the pressing
issues of the day: peace, social and
economic justice, workers' rights, civil
liberties, reproductive rights, protection of the environment, and more.

POOR MAGAZINE
Poor News Network
255 9th Street
San Francisco, CA 94103
Tel: (415) 541-5629
Web site: <www.poormagazine.org>

Poor is the publication of a literary,
visual arts–based community
organization that provides vocational

training, creative arts, and literacy
education to very low-income and
no-income adults and children in the
San Francisco Bay Area, with the goal
of deconstructing the margins of class
and race oppression.

PR WATCH
Center for Media and Democracy
520 University Avenue, Suite 310
Madison, WI 53703
Tel: (608)260-9713
Web site: <www.prwatch.org>

Investigates corporate and government
propaganda. The editors also wrote
Toxic Sludge is Good For You: Lies,
Damn Lies and the Public Relations
Industry.

PREVAILING WINDS MAGAZINE
The Center for the Preservation
of Modern History
P.O. Box 23511
Santa Barbara, CA 93121
Tel: (805) 899-3433
Web site: <www.prevailingwinds.org>

Devoted to exposing assassination,
political scandals, medical fraud,
crime, media manipulation,
corruption, mind control, and
high strangeness.

PRISON LEGAL NEWS (PLN)
2400 NW 80th Street, PMB 148
Seattle, WA 98117
Tel: (206) 789-1022
Web site: <www.prisonlegalnews.org>

PLN reports court rulings involving
prisoner rights as well as providing
news and commentary on criminal justice issues.

PUBLIC CITIZEN
1600 20th Street, NW
Washington, DC 20009
Tel: (202) 588-1000
Web site: <www.citizen.org>

Consumer rights, safety issues, corporate and business accountability, environmental issues, and citizen empowerment.

RACHEL'S ENVIRONMENTAL & HEALTH WEEKLY
The Environmental
Research Foundation
P.O. Box 5036
Annapolis, MD 21403-7063
Tel: (410)263-1584
Web site: <www.rachel.org>

Rachel's provides timely information on toxic substances and other environmental hazards.

REVOLUTIONARY WORKER
Box 3486, Merchandise Mart
Chicago, IL 60654
Tel: (773) 227-4066
Web site: <www.rwor.org>

The weekly newspaper of the Revolutionary Communist Party, USA.

SIERRA MAGAZINE
The Sierra Club
P.O. Box 52968
Boulder, CO 80321-2968
Tel: (415) 977-5500
Web site: <www.sierraclub.org>

The Sierra Club's grassroots advocacy has made it America's most influential environmental organization. Founded in 1892, we are now more than 700,000 members strong.

SOUTHERN EXPOSURE
P.O. Box 531
Durham, NC 27702-0531
Tel: (919) 419-8311, ext. 26
Web site: <www.southernstudies.org/>

Award-winning magazine focused on fighting for a better South. Heavily deals with the work force in the South and corporations.

THE NATION
33 Irving Place, 8th Floor
New York, NY 10003
Tel: (212) 209-5400
Web site: <www.thenation.com>

Investigative journalism; a leading forum for leftist debate; home of Radio Nation and the Nation Institute.

THE PROGRESSIVE
409 E. Main Street
Madison, WI 53703
Tel: (608) 257-4626
Web site: <www.progressive.org>

The Progressive discusses peace, politics, social justice, and environmental concerns from a liberal point of view.

THE PROGRESSIVE POPULIST
P.O. Box 487
Storm Lake, IA 78715-0517
Tel: (512) 447-0455
Web site: <www.populist.com>

The Progressive Populist provides monthly reports from the heartland on issues of interest to workers, farmers, and small business. It promotes the idea that people are more important than corporations.

THE TEXAS OBSERVER
307 W. 7th Street
Austin, TX 78701
Tel: (800) 939-6620
Web site: <TexasObserver.org/>

The Texas Observer writes about
issues ignored or underreported in the
mainstream press. Our goal is to cover
stories crucial to the public interest
and to provoke dialogue that promotes
democratic participation and open
government.

THIRD WORLD RESURGENCE
Journal of the Third World Network
228 Macalister Road
Penang 10400
Malaysia
Tel: (604) 226-6728 or 6159
Web site: <www.twnside.org.sg>

An international network of groups
and individuals involved in efforts to
bring about a greater articulation of
the needs and rights of people in the
Third World; a fair distribution of
world resources; and forms of development that are ecologically sustainable
and fulfill human needs.

THIS MAGAZINE
401 Richmond Street W., Suite #396
Toronto, ON M5V 3A8
Canada
Tel: (416) 979-9426
Web site: <www.thismag.org>

Thirty-five years and still going
strong, This Magazine is one of
Canada's longest-publishing
alternative journals. This focuses
on Canadian politics, literature,
and culture, but in keeping with its
radical roots, never pulls punches.

Subversive, edgy, and smart, *Th*is is
the real alternative to that.

TOWARD FREEDOM (TF)
The Independent Media
Convergence Project
Box 468
Burlington, VT 05402-0468
Tel: (802) 654-8024
Web site: <www.towardfreedom.com>

A progressive international news,
analysis, and advocacy journal that
helps strengthen and extend human
justice and liberties, TF opposes
all forms of domination that repress
human potential to reason, work
creatively, and dream.

UPPNET NEWS
Labor Education Services
437 Management &
Economics Building
University of Minnesota
271 19th Avenue South
Minneapolis, MN 55455
Tel: (612) 624-4326
Web site:
<www.mtn.org/jsee/uppnet.html>

Official publication of the Union
Producers and Programmers Network,
promoting production and use of TV
and radio shows pertinent to the cause
of organized labor and working
people.

URGENT ACTION NEWSLETTER
P.O. Box 1270
Nederland, CO 80466-1270
Tel: (303) 258-1170 or (303) 258-
7886
Web site:
<www.amnestyusa.org/urgent/>

The newsletter for Amnesty International out of the Urgent Action Program Office.

UTNE MAGAZINE
1624 Harmon Place, Suite 330
Minneapolis, MN 55403
Tel: (612) 338-5040
Web site: <www.utne.com>

A digest of alternative ideas and material reprinted from alternative and independent media sources.

WAR AND PEACE DIGEST
Journal of the War and Peace Foundation
United Nations Bureau
777 UN Plaza
New York, NY 10017
Tel: (212) 557-2501
Web site: <www.warpeace.org>

An antinuclear publication promoting peace, social justice, and media reform.

WAR TIMES
EBC/War Times
1230 Market Street
San Francisco, CA 94102
(510) 869-5156
Web site: <www.war-times.org/>

The terrorist attacks of September 11 marked the beginning of a new and frightening period in our history. But the response of "permanent war against terrorism at home and abroad" has further endangered the lives and liberties of millions of people everywhere. *War Times* is a free, mass produced, biweekly, and nationally distributed tabloid-sized newspaper. It will be a valuable outreach and education tool for organizers on the ground and an entryway for new people into the peace and justice movement.

WASHINGTON REPORT ON MIDDLE EAST AFFAIRS
P.O. Box 53062
Washington, DC 20009
Tel: (202) 939-6050
Web site: <www.wrmea.com>

The Washington Report on Middle East Affairs is a 140-page magazine published 10 times per year in Washington, DC, that focuses on news and analysis from and about the Middle East and U.S. policy in that region.

WILD MATTERS
Food & Water, Inc.
P.O. Box 543
Montpelier, VT 05601
Tel: (802) 229-6222
or (800) 328-7233
Web site: <www.wildmatters.org>

Formerly *Food & Water Journal*, *Wild Matters* is now published 10 times a year. A magazine that advocates for safe food and water, and a clean environment by educating the public on the health and environmental dangers of food irradiation, genetic engineering, and toxic pesticides.

Z MAGAZINE
18 Millfield Street
Woods Hole, MA 02543
Tel: (508) 457-0626
Web site: <www.zmag.org>

An independent political magazine of critical thinking on political, cultural, social, and economic life in the United States.

APPENDIX C

Censored 2004 Resource Guide
MEDIA ACTIVIST ORGANIZATIONS

ACME: ACTION COALITION
FOR MEDIA EDUCATION
6400 Wyoming Boulevard NE
Albuquerque, NM 87109
Tel: (505) 828-3377
Web site:

A national coalition for media
education.

ALL AFRICA GLOBAL MEDIA
920 M Street, SE
Washington, DC 27702
Tel: (202) 546-0777
Web site:

Disseminates stories from African
news organizations.

AMERICAN LIBRARY
ASSOCIATION OFFICE FOR
INTELLECTUAL FREEDOM
50 E. Huron Street
Chicago, IL 60611
Tel: (312) 280-4223
or (800) 545-2433
Web site: <www.ala.org/oif.html>

Organized to educate librarians and
the general public about the nature
and importance of intellectual freedom
in libraries.

ASIAN AMERICAN JOURNALISTS
ASSOCIATION (AAJA)
1182 Market Street, Suite 320
San Francisco, CA 94102
Tel: (415) 346-2051
Web site: <www.aaja.org>

Committed to ensuring diversity in
American journalism and expressing
the Asian-American perspective.

ASSOCIATION OF
ALTERNATIVE
NEWSWEEKLIES
1020 16th Street, NW, 4th Floor
Washington, DC 20036-5702
Tel: (202) 822-1955
Web site: <www.aan.org>

A coordinating and administrative
organization for 113 alternative
newsweeklies in the U.S. and Canada.

CALIFORNIA FIRST AMENDMENT
COALITION
2701 Cottage Way, Suite 12
Sacramento, CA 95825-1226
Tel: (916) 974-8888
Web site: <www.cfac.org>

CAMPUS ALTERNATIVE
JOURNALISM PROJECT (CAJP)
Center for Campus Organizing
2729 Mission Street #201
San Francisco, CA 94110
Tel: (415) 643-4401
Web site: <www.indypress.org/
programs/cajp.html>

CAPJ supports the work of campus
progressive activists who make their
own printed media. We provide
resource guides, training, and
consultation, and organize a 100+
network of publications.

THE CENTER FOR DEMOCRATIC
COMMUNICATIONS OF THE
NATIONAL LAWYERS GUILD
240 Stockton Street, 3rd Floor
San Francisco, CA 94108
Tel: (415) 522-9814
Web site: <www.nlgcdc.org>

Focuses on the right of all peoples to
have access to a worldwide system of
media and communications with the
principle of cultural and informational
self-determination. This committee
is an important force in microradio
advocacy and activism.

CENTER FOR INVESTIGATIVE
REPORTING
500 Howard Street, Suite 206
San Francisco, CA 94105-3000
Tel: (415) 543-1200

Web site: <www.muckraker.org/
pubs/papertrails/index.html>

CENTER FOR WAR, PEACE
AND THE NEWS MEDIA
New York University
418 Lafayette Street, Suite 554
New York, NY 10003
Tel: (212) 998-7960
Web site: <www.nyu.edu/globalbeat>

CHICAGO MEDIA WATCH
P.O. Box 268737
Chicago, IL 60626
Tel: (773) 604-1910
Web site:
<www.mediawatch.org/~cmw>

COMMITTEE TO PROTECT
JOURNALISTS
330 7th Avenue, 12th Floor
New York, NY 10001
Tel: (212) 465-1004
Web site: <www.cpj.org>

The Committee to Protect Journalists
is dedicated to safeguarding journalists and freedom of expression worldwide. It is a non-profit, non-partisan
organization that monitors abuses of
the press and promotes press freedom
internationally.

COMMON CAUSE
1250 Connecticut Avenue, NW, #600
Washington, DC, MD 20036
Tel: (202) 833-1200
Web site: <www.commoncause.org>

Supports open, accountable government and the right of all American
citizens to be involved in helping to
shape the nation's public policies.
Common Cause presses for the enact-
ment of campaign finance reform.

COUNCIL ON INTERNATIONAL
AND PUBLIC AFFAIRS
(CIPA, OR POCLAD)
P.O. Box 246
South Yarmouth, MA 02664-0246
Tel: (508) 398-1145
Web site: <www.poclad.org>

Instigating democratic conversations
and actions that contest the authority
of corporations to govern. Publication:
Program on Corporations, Law &
Democracy.

CULTURAL ENVIRONMENT
MOVEMENT (CEM)
3508 Market Street, Suite 30-030
Philadelphia, PA 19104
Tel: (888) 445-4526
Web site: <www.cemnet.org>

A broad-based international coalition
of citizens, scholars, activists, and
media professionals who promote
democratic principles in the cultural
environment. Publishes The Cultural
Environment Monitor.

ELECTRONIC FRONTIER
FOUNDATION
454 Shotwell Street
San Francisco, CA 94110
Tel: (415) 436-9333
Web site: <www.eff.org>

A leading civil liberties organization
devoted to maintaining the Internet as
a global vehicle for free speech.

ENVIRONMENTAL NEWS
NETWORK INC. (ENN)
2020 Milvia, Suite 405
Berkeley, CA 94704
Tel: (415) 459-2248
Fax: (208) 475-7986

E-mail: <mgt@enn.com>
Web site: <www.enn.com>

ENN produces news seven days a
week with continuous updates
throughout each day; a multifaceted
Web site aimed at educating about
environmental issues.

FAIRNESS AND ACCURACY
IN REPORTING (FAIR)
112 W. 27th Street
New York, NY 10001
Tel: (212) 633-6700
Fax: (212) 727-7668
E-mail: <Fair@fair.org>
Web site: <www.fair.org>

A national media watchdog group
that focuses public awareness on
"the narrow corporate ownership
of the press . . . ," FAIR seeks to
invigorate the First Amendment by
advocating for greater media pluralism
and the inclusion of public interest
voices in national debate.

FREEDOM FORUM
WORLD CENTER
1101 Wilson Boulevard
Arlington, VA 22209
Tel: (703) 528-0800
Web site: <www.freedomforum.org>

A non-partisan, international foundation dedicated to free press, free
speech, and free spirit for all people.

FREEDOM OF INFORMATION
CLEARINGHOUSE
P.O. Box 558
Topeka, KS 66601
Tel: (785) 272-7348
Web site: <www.freedomclearing-
house.org/>

FRIENDS OF FREE SPEECH RADIO
905 Parker Street
Berkeley, CA 94710
Tel: (510) 548-0542
Web site: <www.savepacifica.net>

Founded in April 1999, working to preserve community radio stations owned by Pacifica and to institute democratic practice in their governance.

GLOBAL EXCHANGE
2017 Mission Street, Suite 303
San Francisco, CA 94110
Tel: (415) 255-7296
Web site: <www.globalexchange.org>

Global Exchange publishes books and pamphlets on various social and economic topics; promotes alternative trade for the benefit of low-income producers; helps build public awareness about human rights abuses; and sponsors Reality Tours to foreign lands, giving participants a feel for the people of a country. Global Exchange is an active participant in the "50 Years Is Enough" campaign.

GLOBALVISION
1600 Broadway, Suite 700
New York, NY 10019
Tel: (212) 246-0202
Web site: <www.igc.org/globalvision/>

An independent film and television production company. Specializing in an "inside-out" style of journalism, it has produced Rights & Wrongs: Human Rights Television and South Africa Now along with other highly acclaimed investigative documentaries.

THE GRASSROOTS MEDIA NETWORK
1602 Chatham
Austin, TX 78723
Tel: (512) 459-1619
Web site: <www.geocities.com/root-media/links.html> or <www.cross-winds.net/~rootmedia/>

Grassroots News Network, Queer News Network, Pueblos-Unidos. Grassroots film and essential to understanding the South with the grassroots organizing needed to change it.

GREENPEACE USA
702 H Street, NW
Washington, DC 20001
Tel: (800) 326-0959
Fax: (202) 462-4507
Web site: <www.greenpeaceusa.org>

Its purpose is to create a green and peaceful world. Greenpeace embraces the principle of nonviolence, rejecting attacks on people and property. It allies itself with no political party and takes no political stance.

HISPANIC EDUCATION AND MEDIA GROUP, INC.
Laurn Ann Gee-Devitt
We Penguins
102 Crown Circle
South San Francisco, CA 94080
Tel: (415) 331-8560
Web site: <www.we-penguins.com/HEMG_page_1.htm>

Dedicated to improving the quality of life in the Latino community with main focus on high school drop-out prevention and health issues.

INDEPENDENT PRESS
ASSOCIATION (IPA)
2729 Mission Street, #201
San Francisco, CA 94110-3131
Tel: (415) 643-4401
Web site: <www.indypress.org>

A membership -based association
providing nuts-and-bolts technical
assistance, loans, and networking to
over 175 independent, progressive
magazines, and newspapers. Formed
during the first Media & Democracy
Congress in San Francisco (1996),
the IPA promotes a diversity of voices
of the newsstand.

INSTITUTE FOR
PUBLIC ACCURACY
65 9th Street, Suite 3
San Francisco, CA 94103
Tel: (415) 552-5378
Web site: <www.accuracy.org>

Serves as a nationwide consortium of
progressive policy researchers, scholars, and activists, providing the media
with timely information and perspectives on a wide range of issues.

INSTITUTE FOR ALTERNATIVE
JOURNALISM
77 Federal Street, 2nd Floor
San Francisco, CA 94107
Tel: (415) 284-1420
Web site:
<www.independentmedia.org/>

INSTITUTE OF GLOBAL COMMU-
NICATIONS
P.O. Box 29904
San Francisco, CA 94129
Tel: (202) 234-9382
Web site: <www.igc.org/igc/gateway
/index.html>

Formerly "Institute For Policy
Studies" (IPS). Since 1963, IPS has
been the nation's leading center of
progressive research link to activism.

INTERNATIONAL CONSORTIUM
OF INVESTIGATIVE JOURNALISTS
(ICIJ)
Center for Public Integrity
910 17th Street, NW, 7th Floor
Washington, DC 20006
Tel: (202) 466-1300
Web site: <www.icij.org>

ICIJ is a working consortium of leading investigative reporters from around
the world that sponsors investigations
into pressing issues that transcend
national borders.

INTERNATIONAL MEDIA
PROJECT
National Radio Project
1714 Franklin, #311
Oakland, CA 94612
Tel: (510) 251-1332
Web site: <www.radioproject.org>

Produces a half-hour, weekly, public
affairs radio program called Making
Contact, which is heard on 150 stations nationally, in Canada, and South
Africa. Shows also heard on the Internet as Radio for Peace International.
Their mission is to air the voices of
those not often heard in mass media.

INVESTIGATIVE REPORTERS
AND EDITORS, INC. (IRE)
Missouri School of Journalism
138 Neff Annex
Columbia, MO 65211
Tel: (573) 882-2042
Web site: <www.ire.org>

Investigative Reporters and Editors, Inc. is a grassroots non-profit organization dedicated to improving the quality of investigative reporting within the field of journalism.

MEDIA ALLIANCE
814 Mission Street, Suite 205
San Francisco, CA 94103
Tel: (415) 546-6334
Web site: <www.media-alliance.org>

Review and analysis of San Francisco Bay Area media issues. Publisher of MediaFile.

MEDIA COALITION/ AMERICANS FOR CONSTITUTIONAL FREEDOM
139 Fulton Street, Suite 302
New York, NY 10038
Tel: (212) 587-4025
Web site: <www.mediacoalition.org>

An organization that defends the American public's First Amendment right to have access to the broadest possible range of opinion and enter-tainment.

MEDIAVISION
P.O. Box 1045
Boston, MA 02130
Tel: (617) 522-2923
Web site: <mediavi@aol.com>

Working for wider exposure of progressive views through mass media, MediaVision provides strategic media consulting, training, and other services for organizations and individuals.

NATIONAL ASIAN AMERICAN TELECOMMUNICATIONS ASSOCIATION
346 9th Street, 2nd Floor
San Francisco, CA 94103
Tel: (415) 863-0814
Web site: <www.naatanet.org>

An organization seeking to increase Asian and Pacific Islanders' participation in the media and the promotion of fair and accurate coverage of these communities.

NATIONAL ASSOCIATION OF BLACK JOURNALISTS (NABJ)
University of Maryland
8701A Adelphi Road
Adelphi, MD 20783-1716
Tel: (301) 445-7100
Web site: <www.nabj.org>

Its mission is to strengthen ties among African-American journalists, promote diversity in newsrooms, and expand job opportunities and recruiting activ-ities for established African-American journalists and students.

NATIONAL ASSOCIATION OF HISPANIC JOURNALISTS (NAHJ)
1000 National Press Building
Washington, DC 20045-2001
Tel: (888) 346-NAHJ
or (202) 662-7145
Web site: <www.nahj.org>

NAHJ is dedicated to the recognition and professional advancement of His-panics in the news industry.

NATIONAL COALITION AGAINST CENSORSHIP (NCAC)
275 7th Avenue
New York, NY 10001

Web site: <www.ncac.org>

Founded in 1974, NCAC is an alliance of over 50 national non-profit organizations. It works to educate members and the public at large about the dangers of censorship and how to oppose it.

THE NATIONAL LESBIAN AND GAY JOURNALISTS ASSOCIATION (NLGJA)
1420 K Street, NW, Suite 910
Washington, DC 20005
Tel: (202) 588-9888
Web site: <www.nlgja.org>

NLGJA works from within the news industry to foster fair and accurate coverage of lesbian and gay issues and opposes newsroom bias against lesbians, gay men, and all other minorities.

NATIONAL WRITERS UNION (NWU) (EAST)
National Office East
113 University Place, 6th Floor
New York, NY 10003
Tel: (212) 254-0279
Web site: <www.nwu.org>

American Writer is NWU's national quarterly.

NATIONAL WRITERS UNION (NWU) (WEST)
337 17th Street, #101
Oakland, CA 94612
Tel: (510) 839-0110
Web site: <www.unionwriters.org>

American Writer is NWU's national quarterly.

NEW MEXICO MEDIA LITERACY PROJECT
6400 Wyoming Boulevard, NE
Albuquerque, NM 87109
Tel: (505) 828-3129
Web site: <www.nmmlp.org>

An organization whose goal is to be the most successful and the most dedicated media education organization in the U.S.

NEWSWATCH CANADA
School of Communication,
Simon Fraser University
8888 University Drive
Burnaby, BC V5A 1S6
Canada
Tel: (604) 291-4905
Web site: <newswatch.cprost.sfu.ca/>

Canadian media watch organization and freedom of information advocacy group.

PAPER TIGER TELEVISION
339 Lafayette Street
New York, NY 10012
Tel: (212) 420-9045
Web site: <www.papertiger.org>

A non-profit volunteer collective that has been pioneering media criticism through video since 1981, conducting workshops, creating installations, and producing videotapes. Its programs address issues of democratic communication, media representation, and the economics of the information industry. Smashes the myths of the information industry.

PROGRESSIVE MEDIA PROJECT
409 E. Main Street
Madison, WI 53703
Tel: (608) 257-4626
Web site: <www.progressive.org>

It provides opinion pieces from a progressive perspective to daily and weekly newspapers all over the country.

PROJECT CENSORED
Sociology Department,
Sonoma State University
1801 E. Cotati Avenue
Rohnert Park, CA 94928-3609
Tel: (707) 664-2500
Web site: <www.projectcensored.org>

A faculty/student media research project dedicated to building free democratic news systems. It produces an annual yearbook that discusses the year's top 25 best underreported news stories.

SOCIETY OF ENVIRONMENTAL JOURNALISTS
P.O. Box 2492
Jenkintown, PA 19046
Tel: (215) 884-8174
Web site: <www.sej.org>

Dedicated to supporting environmental journalists and furthering environmental journalism. Publisher of *SEJournal*.

SOCIETY OF PROFESSIONAL JOURNALISTS (SPJ)
Improving & Protecting Journalism
3909 N. Meridian Street
Indianapolis, IN 46208
Tel: (317) 927-8000
Web site: <www.spj.org>

SPJ is the nation's largest and most broad-based journalism organization. It is a not-for-profit organization made up of 13,500 members dedicated to encouraging the free practice of journalism, stimulating high standards of ethical behavior, and perpetuating a free press.

THE TELEVISION PROJECT
2311 Kimball Place
Silver Springs, MD 20910
Tel: (301) 588-4001
Web site: <www.tvp.org>

An organization to help parents understand how television affects their families and community, and to propose alternatives that foster positive emotional, cognitive, and spiritual development within families and communities.

WE INTERRUPT THIS MESSAGE
160 14th Street
San Francisco, CA 94103
Tel: (415) 621-3302
Web site:
<www.interrupt.org/witm.html>

Builds capacity in public interest groups to do traditional media and publicity work as well as to reframe public debate and interrupt media stereotypes.

WHISPERED MEDIA
P.O. Box 40130
San Francisco, CA 94140
Tel: (415) 789-8484
Web site: <www.videoactivism.org>

Provides video witnessing, video post-production and media resources for grassroots activist groups. Facilitates

Bay Area Video Activist Network (VAN). Specializes in direct action campaigns.

YOUTH MEDIA COUNCIL
1611 Telegraph Avenue, Suite 510
Oakland, CA 94612
Tel: (510) 444-0640
Web site:
<www.youthmediacouncil.org>

Eight youth organizations in the San Francisco Bay Area have partnered with We Interrupt This Message and the Movement Strategy Center to launch an organizing, youth development, media strategy and media watchdog project.

Our Favorite Web Site E-Zines

ALTERNET
Institute for Alternative Journalism (IAJ)
77 Federal Street
San Francisco, CA 94107
Tel: (415) 284-1420
Fax: (415) 284-1414
E-mail: <info@alternet.org>
Web site:

A news service for the alternative press, IAJ supports independent and alternative journalism and is best known for sponsoring the Media & Democracy Congress.

BLACKPRESSUSA.COM
2711 E. 75th Place
Chicago, IL 60649
Tel: (312) 375-8200
Fax: (312) 375-8262
E-mail: info@blackpressusa.com>
Web site: <www.blackpressusa.com/aboutus/aboutus.asp>

<BlackPressUSA.com> is your independent source of news for the African-American community. It is the joint Web presence of America's Black community newspapers and the NNPA News Service—the last national Black Press news wire. It is a project of the Black Press Institute, a partnership between the National Newspaper Publishers Association Foundation and Howard University.

BLUE EAR
Web site: <www.blueear.com>

Blue Ear is an editorial partnership publishing international journalism and writing in a variety of digital formats.

CENTRE FOR RESEARCH ON GLOBALIZATION (CRG)
Web site: <www.globalresearch.ca>

An independent research and media group committed to curbing the tide of "globalization" and "disarming" the New World Order. Based in Montreal, CRG publishes news articles, commentary, background research, and analysis on a broad range of issues, focusing on the interrelationship between social, economic, strategic, geopolitical, and environmental processes.

COMMON DREAMS
P.O. Box 443
Portland, ME 04112-0443
Tel: (207) 799-2185
Fax: (619) 798-6341
E-mail: <editor@commondreams.org>
Web site: <www.commondreams.org>

A national non-profit, grassroots organization whose mission is to organize an
open, honest, and nonpartisan national
discussion of current events. The Web
site is one of the best-organized on
national and international topics.

CORPWATCH
P.O. Box 29344
San Francisco, CA 94129
Tel: (415) 561-6568
Fax: (415) 561-6493
E-mail: <corpwatch@corpwatch.org>
Web site: <www.corpwatch.org>

CorpWatch counters corporate-led
globalization through education and
activism. They work to foster democratic control over corporations by building grassroots globalization—a diverse
movement for human rights, labor
rights, and environmental justice.

DEMOCRACY NOW!
WBAI
120 Wall Street, 10th Floor
New York, NY 10005
Tel: (212) 397-0886
E-mail: <mail@democracynow.org>
Web site: <www.webactive.com/
pacifica/demnow.html>

Launched by Pacifica Radio in 1996
to open the airwaves on a daily basis
to alternative voices traditionally
excluded from the political process.

Programs with Amy Goodman are now
available online.

ENVIROLINK NETWORK
5801 Beacon Street, Suite 2
Pittsburgh, PA 15217
E-mail: <support@envirolink.org>
Web site:

One of the world's largest environmental
information clearinghouses. In addition
to being an information resource,
EnviroLink provides environmental and
animal rights non-profit organizations
with free Internet services.

ENVIRONMENTAL MEDIA
SERVICES (EMS)
1320 18th Street, NW, 2nd Floor
Washington, DC 20036
Tel: (202) 463-6670
Fax: (202) 463-6671
Web site: <www.ems.org>

EMS is a non-profit communications
clearinghouse dedicated to expanding
media coverage of critical environmental and public health issues.

ENVIRONMENTAL NEWS SERVICE
E-mail: <news@ens-news.com>
Web Site:< ens.lycos.com/>
Newswire for environmental issues.

EYE MAGAZINE
P.O. Box 9145
Greensboro, NC 27429-0145
Tel: (910) 370-1702
Fax: (910) 370-1603
E-mail: <info@eyemag.com>
Web site: <www.eyemag.com>

A forum for underreported news and
a watchdog publication for coverups
and scandals in corporate America.

FREE SPEECH TV (FSTV)
P.O. Box 6060
Boulder, CO 80306
Tel: (303) 442-8445
Fax: (303) 442-6472
E-mail: <Programming@sftv.org>
Web site: <www.freespeech.org>

Progressive voice in the media revolution bringing activist and alternative media into 7 million homes each week.

GLOBAL ISSUES
E-mail: <comments@globalissues.org>
Web site: <www.globalissues.org>

This Web site looks into global issues that affect everyone and aims to show how most issues are interrelated. Over 3,000 links to external articles, Web sites reports, and analysis.

GLOBALSPIN
News & Views from Abroad
E-mail: <goto@globalspin.org>
Web site: <www.globalspin.org/>

GlobalSpin is dedicated to bringing more of those voices to you. It is a door to the thoughts and opinions of vast segments of the world outside the American media empire.

INDEPENDENT MEDIA CENTER
E-mail: <general@indymedia.org>
Web site: <www.indymedia.org>

The Independent Media Center is a network of collectively run media outlets for the creation of radical, accurate, and passionate tellings of the truth. We work out of a love and inspiration for people who continue to work for a better world, despite corporate media's distortions and unwillingness to cover the efforts to free humanity.

INTERNATIONAL
ACTION CENTER
Tel: (212) 633-6646
Fax: (212) 633-2889
E-mail: <iacenter@action-mail.org>
Web site: <www.iacenter.org>

Social Activism organization founded by Ramsey Clark former U.S. Attorney General.

INTER PRESS SERVICE (IPS)
E-mail: <online@ips.org>
Web site: <www.ips.org>

Inter Press Service, the world's leading provider of information on global issues, is backed by a network of journalists in more than 100 countries, with satellite communication links to 1,200 outlets. IPS focuses its news coverage on the events and global processes affecting the economic, social, and political development of peoples and nations.

LABOR BEAT
37 S. Ashland Boulevard, #W
Chicago, IL 60607
Tel: (312) 226-3330
Fax: (773) 561-0908
E-mail: <laborbeat@fs.freespeech.org>
Web site: <myweb.wwa.com/
~bgfolder/lb/>

An independent rank-and-file labor forum. Producers of labor television and radio. Advocates for labor media. Labor issues in today's news.

MEDIACHANNEL
1600 Broadway, #700
New York, NY 10019
E-mail: <editor@mediachannel.org>
Web site: <www.mediachannel.org>

Web site produced by Globalvision New Media. An online global media supersite.

MOTHERJONES.COM/ MOJO WIRE
Web site: <www.motherjones.com/about_us>

MotherJones.com's guide to undercovered news, commentary and resources.

PACIFIC NEWS SERVICE
660 Market Street
San Francisco, CA 94104
Tel: (415) 438-4755
Web site: <www.pacificnews.org>

TAO COMMUNICATIONS
P.O. Box 108, Station P
Toronto, ON M5S 2S8
Canada
Tel: (416) 812-6765
E-mail: <ao-www@tao.ca>
Web site: <www.tao.ca>

A Canada-based federation comprised of local autonomous collectives and individuals, Tao organizes networks in order to defend and expand public space and the right to self-determination. Host to an array of online movement networks and Web sites.

TOMPAINE.COMMONSENSE
Web site: <www.tompaine.com>

TomPaine.com seeks to enrich the national debate on controversial public issues by featuring the ideas, opinions, and analyses too often overlooked by the mainstream media. We promote these in our weekly advertisement on the op-ed page of *The New York Times*.

TRUTHOUT.COM
767 S. San Perdo Street
Los Angeles, CA 90014
E-mail: <comments@truthout.com>
Web site: <www.truthout.com>

An independent forum for investigative articles and editorials concerning issues important to the people of this society.

WIRED
P.O. Box 37705
Boone, IA 50037-4705
Web site: <www.wired.com/wired>

WORLD SOCIALIST WEB SITE
E-mail: <Editor@wsws.org>
Web site: <www.wsws.org>

The World Socialist Web Site is the Internet center of the International Committee of the Fourth International (ICFI). It provides analysis of major world events, comments on political, cultural, historical and philosophical issues, and valuable documents and studies from the heritage of the socialist movement.

ZENZIBAR NEWS SERVICE
E-mail: <dreamers@zenzibar.com>
Web site:
<zenzibar.com/news/newsarchive.asp>

Zenzibar Alternative Culture is an alternative portal and directory of alternatives to Western mainstream culture.

ZNet
Web site: <www.lbbs.org>
Z Magazine's news and links.

Index

1996 Telecommunications Act, 27, 87, 129, 210
48 Hours, 179, 229
50 Cent, 192
60 Minutes II, 285
60 Minutes, 179, 238, 249, 252
9/11. *See* September 11
ABC (American Broadcasting Company), 25-26, 166, 178, 190, 196, 220, 222, 226, 248, 287-290
  ABC News, 190, 289
  ABC World News Tonight, 248
  ABCNews.com, 45
ABM. *See* Anti-Ballistic Missile Treaty
abortion, 152-154, 211
Abrams, Elliot, 147, 149
ACLU. *See* American Civil Liberties Union
ACME. *See* American Coalition for Media Education
Adbusters, 327
Adelstein, Jonathan S., 26, 210
advertisers, advertising, 27-28, 87, 92, 167, 169, 175, 177, 179, 186-187, 192, 198-200, 207, 236, 245, 283-286, 289, 327
AEI. *See* American Enterprise Institute
Afghanistan, 7, 33, 35, 60-63, 68, 70, 99, 119, 136-138, 148, 155, 202, 221-223, 236, 256, 260, 275, 297-298, 300
AFL-CIO, 46, 52, 86, 160-161
AFP. *See* Agence France-Presse
Africa, 33, 35, 57, 64-67, 95, 111, 114, 127, 157-159, 194, 236, 241, 306, 339, 342-343
African Americans, 213-214
Against the Current, 327
Agence France-Presse (AFP), 307
Agent Orange, 59
AGR. *See* Asheville Global Report
Agribusiness, 122
AIDS, 189, 236, 324
air pollution, 82
air quality, 127
airlines, 46, 49
airports, 47, 84
airwaves, 26, 128-129, 164-165, 168, 182, 350
Al Jazeera, 201-202, 225, 234, 305
Al Qaeda, 138, 154-155, 168, 212, 223, 232-233, 238-239, 263, 294

ALA. *See* American Library Association
Albion Monitor, 327
Albright, Madeleine, 249, 252
alcohol, 165
Algeria, 300
All Africa Global Media, 339
Alternative Press Review, 327
AlterNet, 82, 219, 221, 226-227, 230, 349
AMA. *See* American Medical Association
American Broadcasting Company. *See* ABC
American Civil Liberties Union (ACLU), 39, 280-281, 329
American Coalition for Media Education (ACME), 181, 207-211, 309
American Enterprise Institute (AEI), 260-262, 264
American Idol, 164, 166
American Library Association (ALA), 19, 280-281, 333, 339
American Medical Association (AMA), 164
American Mineral Fields, 157
American Prospect, The, 37, 46, 91, 103, 237, 239, 319, 328
American Recreation Coalition (ARC), 92-93, 155
Amnesty International, 69, 156, 307-308, 337
Andersen, Arthur, 290
Andersen, Robin, 9, 11, 16, 18, 34, 219
Anderson, Pamela, 163
anhydrous ammonia, 27, 88
Animal People, 328
animal protection, 328
anthrax, 43, 138, 242
anti-abortion law, 153
Anti-Ballistic Missile (ABM) Treaty, 53-54
antitrust activities, 114
antiwar protests, 81
AOL Time Warner, 50, 172-173, 287-288, 291, 344
AP. *See* Associated Press
apartheid, 112, 204-205
Arabs, 205
Arafat, Yassir, 205
ARC. *See* American Recreation Coalition
Argentina, 8, 33, 86, 102, 107-110, 115
Armenia, 300
Arms Sales Monitor, 328
Arnett, Peter, 12, 224

art, 127, 163
artists, 25, 89, 187-188, 190-193, 196
ArtVoice, 42-43, 150
Asano, Kenichi, 9, 11, 16, 309, 315, 317
Ashcroft, John, 39, 266, 280, 298
Asheville Global Report (AGR), 52, 56-57, 68, 83, 113, 118, 133, 150-151, 319, 328
Asia Times, 45
Asia, 9, 45, 63, 95-97, 114, 118, 127, 174, 179, 304, 309, 316
Asian American Journalists Association, 339
Associated Press (AP), 136, 138, 170, 240, 307-308
Association of Alternative Newsweeklies, 340
Association of American Publishers, 273
asthma, 126-127
AT&T Broadband, 50-51
Atta, Mohammed, 238
Australia, 4, 16, 78-79, 174-175, 179
Azerbaijan, 297
Bachelor, The, 173, 288
Baghdad, 37, 82, 99, 150, 201, 224-225, 227-229, 237, 240, 248-250, 253-255, 257-258
ballistic missiles, 53
Baltimore Sun, 38, 254
Bangladesh, 300
banks, 101-102, 107-109, 123
Baraka, Ras, 188
Barnet, Richard, 18
Bates, Jerry, 259
BBC, 37, 66, 125-127, 134, 137, 154, 166, 224, 227, 250, 253, 255, 303, 307-308
Beastie Boys, 193
Bechtel, 43, 114, 157-158, 242, 261-263
Belarus, 297, 300
Berlin Wall, 228
Bernstein, Dennis, 195, 256
BET, 179, 182, 191, 193
Between the Lines, 39, 202, 204-205
bilingual education, 103, 143
Bill of Rights, 211, 281
bin Laden, Osama, 136, 168, 233, 239, 279, 291
biological agents, 118
biological weapons, 53, 55, 118, 200, 252
Biological Weapons Convention (BWC), 53, 55, 118
birth defects, 58, 60, 79, 248, 252
Black Hawk Down, 227
Black Panthers, 187
BlackPressUSA.com, 349

Blair, Tony, 234, 239
Bolivia, 86, 114
Bolton, John, 259
bombs, 99, 118, 140-142, 200, 248-249, 251, 259
booksellers, 267, 272-274, 277, 279
Booz Allen Hamilton, 263
Borgman, Marcus, 9, 16, 247, 257
Bosnia, 60, 99, 263-264, 301
Boston Globe, 121, 138, 166, 228, 294
botulism, 43
Brazil, 84, 86, 115-116, 149, 176, 185, 236, 301
Briarpatch, 64, 319, 328, 365
Britain, 16, 42, 78, 247, 311. *See also* U.K.
British Aerospace, 262
British House of Commons, 169
Brokaw, Tom, 220, 222, 224, 292
Brown, James, 187
Bruckheimer, Jerry, 222, 227
Bulletin of the Atomic Scientists, 141, 319, 328
Burma, 301
Bush, George H.W., 35, 42-43, 58, 71, 98, 147, 159, 242, 259-261
Bush, George W., 36, 45-46, 48-49, 54, 56, 59, 73, 81, 93, 106, 114, 135-136, 141, 143, 147-148, 154, 220, 231, 237, 242, 250-251, 260, 262-264, 277, 300
    Administration, 8, 33, 36-37, 39-40, 42-43, 47, 52-55, 57, 70-71, 80, 86-87, 92-94, 96, 99, 103, 105, 113, 118, 136-137, 142-147, 149, 154, 231-239, 241-245, 262, 264-266, 268, 276, 283, 292
BWC. *See* Biological Weapons Convention
cable television, 31, 51, 195
Caldicott, Helen, 58-59
Cameroon, 301
campus organizing, 340
Canada, 4, 16, 19, 37, 56, 84, 86, 117, 160, 178-179, 319, 321, 327-328, 331, 334, 336, 340, 343, 345, 352
cancer, 19, 58, 60, 79, 126, 153, 248-249, 252, 254
capitalism, 108, 333
CAQ. *See CovertAction Quarterly*
Carmona, Pedro, 71-72, 149
Caribbean, the, 84, 86, 111, 149, 236, 323
Carter, Jimmy, 35, 110
    Doctrine, 35
Caspian Sea, 260
Castro, Fidel 21, 45, 68
Catholic Conference of Bishops, 52
CBC-TV (Canada), 37

CBS, 25-26, 174, 179, 225-226, 229, 248-249, 285, 288
CBS Evening News, 248
CBS News, 179
censorship, 7, 9, 11, 17-18, 29, 31, 43, 51, 72, 82, 221, 296-300, 314, 344-345, 365
self-censorship, 43, 314
Center for Constitutional Rights, 221, 281
Center for Democracy and Technology, 275, 280
Center for Digital Democracy, 52
Center for Investigative Reporting, 340
Center for Law and Social Policy (CLASP), 105-106
Center for Public Integrity (CPI), 38, 88, 130, 278, 320, 343
Center for War, Peace and the News Media, 340
Central America, 73, 83-86
Central Asia, 95, 118
Central Intelligence Agency (CIA), 39, 66, 71-72, 118, 121, 137-138, 147, 154-155, 195, 237-241, 259, 262-263, 271
PSYOPs, 72
Chalabi, Ahmed, 237, 260-261
Challenge, 202, 205, 328
Chamber of Commerce, 48, 293
Charlie Rose, 285
Charter Forest Proposal, 8, 33, 91-93
Chavez, Hugo, 71-73, 297
Chechnya, 305
chemical weapons, 43, 53, 205, 242, 252
Cheney, Dick, 34-36, 39, 57, 95, 98-99, 238-239, 260-261, 263-264
Cheney, Lynne, 260
Chevron, 194, 260-261
Chicago Media Watch, 19, 340
Chicago Tribune, 229, 293
child care, 104-106, 130-131
Children of War, 57, 61, 320
Chile, 73
China, 37, 42, 57, 84, 118-119, 173, 301, 308, 310-311, 313
Chomsky, Noam, 315, 317
Christian Coalition, 244
Christian fundamentalism, 113
Christian Science Monitor, 60, 82, 104, 254, 256
Christianity, 206, 244-245
Chuck D, 182, 189-191
CIA. *See* Central Intelligence Agency
Citigroup, Citibank, 123, 157
civil disobedience, 192, 278
civil liberties, 31, 39, 197-198, 211, 268-269, 275, 277-281, 323, 329, 334, 341

Civil Liberties, 329
civil rights, 13, 39-40, 186-187, 214-215, 244, 323, 334
Clamor, 116, 329
Clark, William, 94-95, 242
CLASP. *See* Center for Law and Social Policy
Clear Channel, 8, 27, 33, 87-90, 129, 190-192, 216
Clinton, Bill, 36, 54, 92, 103-104, 114, 149, 262
Administration, 110, 114, 118
Clorfene-Casten, Liane, 19
cluster bombs, 248-249, 259
CTBT. *See* Comprehensive Test Ban Treaty
CNBC, 37, 220, 223, 290
CNN, 12, 26, 51, 156, 173, 190, 219, 221, 224-226, 249, 290, 303
coal, 117
Coast Guard, 38
cobalt, 157
Coca-Cola, 83, 285
cocaine, 73
Cockburn, Alexander, 120, 132-133
Coen, Rachel, 9, 11, 16, 83, 283, 296
COINTELPRO, 39, 187, 265
Cold War, 36, 55, 64, 150
Colombia, 42, 57, 71, 73, 86, 99, 120, 132-136, 301
colonialism, 7, 33, 64, 312
coltan, 157-158
Columbia Journalism Review, 284, 289, 295
Comcast, 51, 173
Committee on International Relations, 137
Committee to Protect Journalists, 307-308, 340
Common Cause, 52
Common Dreams, 74, 350, 365
Communist Party, 301, 335
Comprehensive Test Ban Treaty (CTBT), 53
Congo. *See* Democratic Republic of Congo
Congo War, 66
Congress, 28, 39, 45, 47, 50-51, 58, 78, 80, 87, 104-106, 117, 132, 137, 142, 145, 147-150, 189, 234, 236-237, 241, 250, 260, 265-266, 269, 276, 278-280, 289, 301, 324, 343, 349
Connections, 52, 184, 197, 220, 242, 261, 324, 366
Constitution, the, 40, 71, 74, 250, 275, 314
Consumer Broadband Deregulation Act, 51

consumer protection laws, 76
Consumer Reports, 19
consumer rights, 335
Consumer's Union, 2, 209
Contras, 45, 73, 147-148
Conyers, John, 268
copper, 157, 159
Copps, Michael J., 26, 130, 210
corporate media, 11-13, 26, 28-29, 34, 38, 44, 62, 74, 87, 90-91, 93, 129-130, 137, 139-140, 146, 150, 181, 189-190, 197-198, 202-203, 206-207, 212, 252, 292, 351
corporations, 25-26, 33, 42, 51, 74-77, 83-86, 92, 113, 115, 128, 130-132, 142, 157, 169, 200, 207-208, 215, 237, 265, 286, 320, 329, 335, 341, 350
  corporate personhood, 33, 74-76
CorpWatch, 83, 85, 98-100, 113, 116, 320, 350
Costa Rica, 43, 87, 149
Council on International and Public Affairs, 341
CounterPunch, 44-45, 49, 133, 259, 320, 329, 365
CovertAction Quarterly (CAQ), 66-67, 100, 110, 158, 320, 329
CPI. *See* Center for Public Integrity
crime, 90, 102, 107, 140, 159, 271, 273, 304, 334
Cruise, Tom, 163
C-Span, 37
CTBT. *See* Comprehensive Test Ban Treaty
Cuba, 44, 79, 86, 99, 155, 233
Cultural Environment Movement, 19, 341
Cultural Survival Quarterly, 329
Cyprus, 301
Czech Republic, 57, 300
Daily Mirror, 45
Dark Night Field Notes, 329
DARPA. *See* Defense Advanced Research Projects Agency
Daschle, Tom, 267-268
Dateline, 166
DaveyD, 9, 11, 16, 181, 184-186, 188, 190, 193
day care, 108
DEA. *See* Drug Enforcement Agency
dead prez, 191-193
Def, Mos, 188
Defense Advanced Research Projects Agency (DARPA), 147, 281
Defense Department, 38-40, 43-44, 80-81, 98, 116, 140, 261, 278, 281, 294
Defense Intelligence Agency (DIA), 139, 238

Defense Monitor, 329
deforestation, 120
Democracy Now!, 16, 25-26, 28, 42-43, 111, 181, 194-195, 197, 221, 223, 228, 350, 365
Democratic Left, 330
Democratic Media Legal Project (DMLP), 128
Democratic Republic of Congo (DRC), 66-67, 157-159
Democrats, 27, 35, 141, 210, 267
dengue fever, 43
Department of Agriculture, 43
Department of Defense (DOD). *See* Defense Department
Department of Energy (DOE), 43, 117, 141
Department of Homeland Security (DHS), 38-40, 47, 149
Department of Housing and Urban Development (HUD), 145-146
Department of Justice (DOJ), 38-39, 51, 80, 115, 138, 259, 265-268, 270-271, 274, 276-278, 280-281
Department of War, 38
depleted uranium (DU), 33, 57-61, 82, 248-249, 252, 254-255, 257, 259, 320
Desert Storm, 222, 239-241, 243
DHS. *See* Department of Homeland Security
DIA. *See* Defense Intelligence Agency
diamonds, 67, 157
Disney Corporation, 26, 51, 92, 178, 289
  Disneyland, 178
Dissent, 330
Dixie Chicks, 89
DMLP. *See* Democratic Media Legal Project
DOD. *See* Defense Department
Dodd, Christopher, 148
DOE. *See* Department of Energy
DOJ. *See* Department of Justice
Dollars and Sense, 50, 79, 82, 103, 158, 320, 330
Domestic Security Enhancement Act of 2003, 39, 278, 281. *See also* Patriot Act II; USA Patriot Act
Dominican Republic, 115
Dow Chemical, 83
Dow Jones, 143-144, 290
DRC. *See* Democratic Republic of Congo
Drug Enforcement Agency (DEA), 118
drugs, 90, 132-133, 136, 257, 305
  dealers, 301
  laws, 192
  trade, 133

trafficking, 149, 301
war on, 133
DU. *See* depleted uranium
DuPont, 43
DynCorp, 98-99, 120, 262-263, 301
E Magazine, 330
Early Show, 179, 288
Earth First!, 91, 93, 119, 321, 330
Earth Island Journal, 330
Earth Justice Organization, 133
Earthjustice, 135-136
East Timor, 119, 147, 151-152
Eastern Europe, 173
Eastman Kodak, 43
EC. *See* European Commission
ecological biodiversity, 83, 114
Ecologist, The, 45, 131, 330
ecology, 20
Economic Justice News, 331
economics, 21, 320, 330, 333, 336, 345
Ecuador, 86, 99, 149, 263
Edison schools, 143-144
education, 17, 19-23, 32, 65, 81, 103-104,
    112, 119, 131-132, 142-144, 159, 175-
    176, 181, 189, 196, 207-210, 278, 295,
    307, 319-320, 325, 328, 334, 336-337,
    339, 342, 345, 350
    privatized, 142, 144
    public, 81, 142-144
    teachers, 143, 208, 210, 298
Educational Management Organizations
    (EMOs), 142-144
Egypt, 154, 302
Eisenhower, Dwight, 98
El Salvador, 87
electricity, 117, 140
Electronic Frontier Foundation, 341
Elementary and Secondary Education Act
    (ESEA), 144
EMOs. *See* Educational Management
    Organizations
Enron, 113-116, 165, 290
environmental groups, 93
environmental issues, 330, 335, 341, 350
Environmental Protection Agency (EPA),
    81, 114-115, 293
Eritrea, 302
Ethiopia, 65, 302
EU. *See* European Union
euro, the, 8, 33, 94-97
Europe, 42, 69, 97, 99, 114, 117, 156,
    173-174, 176, 178-179, 202, 205-206,
    233, 235-237, 254, 308
European Commission (EC), 321
European Parliament, 69
European Union (EU), 57, 63, 96-97, 302

Extra!, 42, 83, 121, 147, 166, 173, 286,
    289, 296, 306, 321, 331
Exxon, 83
Fairness and Accuracy in Reporting
    (FAIR), 9, 11, 25-26, 28, 86, 161, 247-
    248, 259, 283, 292, 295-296, 321, 331,
    336, 341, 344-345
famine, 65
FARC. *See* Revolutionary Armed Forces of
    Colombia
farmers, 65, 86, 101, 111, 120, 122, 206,
    299, 335
fascism, 31
Feasta, 94, 321
Federal Bureau of Investigation (FBI), 39,
    136-138, 155, 187-188, 195, 265, 272-
    277, 280, 307
Federal Communications Commission
    (FCC), 19, 26-27, 50-51, 88-89, 128-
    130, 189, 191, 198, 209-210
Federal Emergency Management Agency
    (FEMA), 39
Federal Housing Administration, 145
Federation of American Scientists, 121,
    141, 328
Feingold, Russ, 267
Feith, Douglas, 260, 264
Fiji, 175, 297
Financial Times, 97, 142
First Amendment, 16, 30, 75-76, 265,
    273, 275, 278, 340-341, 344
FISA. *See* Foreign Intelligence Surveil-
    lance Act
Flashpoints, 181, 194-196
Fleischer, Ari, 148, 156
Fluor Corp., 263
Foerstel, Herbert, 11, 16, 265, 275
Foerstel, Lenore, 19, 34
FOIA. *See* Freedom of Information Act
food
    distribution, 108
    shortages, 65
Food First News, 331
Ford, Gerald, 35, 151
Foreign Intelligence Surveillance Act
    (FISA), 265, 267, 270, 272-273
Forest Service, 92-93, 286
forests, 91-92, 94, 119, 127, 286
Fortune, 27, 74, 98, 135-136, 172, 306
fossil fuel plants, 117
Fourteenth Amendment, 74-75, 279
Fourth Amendment, 278
Fox (TV), 12, 129, 166, 174-175, 178,
    182, 196, 226, 228, 249-250
    Fox News, 174, 182, 228, 249-250
Fox, Vicente, 83-85

France, 37, 42, 150, 173, 176-179, 229, 233, 235, 247, 302, 310
free press, 52, 79-80, 179, 209, 325, 341, 346
Free Speech TV (FSTV), 28, 181, 194, 196-198, 351
free speech, 13, 28, 74-76, 181, 194, 196-198, 276, 279, 297-298, 307, 329, 341-342, 351
Free Trade Area of the Americas (FTAA), 33, 83-84, 86-87
free trade, 83, 86-87, 101
Freedom Forum, 307-308, 341
Freedom of Information Act (FOIA), 47, 80-81, 115, 277, 280, 298, 306
Freedom of Information Clearinghouse, 341
Freedom to Read Committee, 273
Freedom to Read Foundation, 19
Friends of Free Speech, 342
FSTV. *See* Free Speech TV
FTAA. *See* Free Trade Area of the Americas
fumigation, 133-134, 136
fundamentalists, 238, 244
G8, 64-66, 96
gang activity, 183
gangrene bacteria, 43
gangsta rap, 182, 193
Gannett, 87, 140
GAO. *See* General Accounting Office
GATS. *See* General Agreement on Trade in Services
GATT. *See* General Agreement on Tariffs and Trade
gay men, 345
Gaza, 110-111, 201
gender, 23, 256
General Accounting Office (GAO), 80, 160
General Agreement on Tariffs and Trade (GATT), 130
General Agreement on Trade in Services (GATS), 130-132
General Electric (GE), 26, 114-115, 290
General Motors (GM), 122
Geneva Convention, 139-140
GeneWatch, 118, 122, 331
genocide, 53, 140, 158-159
Georgia, 5, 99
Gerbner, George, 19, 25
Germany, 173, 176, 189, 233, 235, 247, 302, 310
Global Exchange, 342
Global Information Network, 331
Global Outlook, 38, 52, 70, 118, 254, 321
global warming, 53, 232

globalization, 83, 85-86, 100, 102, 126, 320, 349-350
Globalvision, 342, 352
GM. *See* General Motors
gold, 43, 94, 144, 159, 175
Goldman Sachs, 261
Gonzalez, Juan, 26, 194, 197
Good Morning America, 287-288
Goodman, Amy, 16, 25, 28, 42-43, 89, 111, 194, 197, 350
Google, 301
Gore, Al, 27
Graham, Bob, 239
Grassroots Media Network, The, 342
Great Britain, 16, 78, 247. *See also* U.K.
Greece, 78
Green Party, 196
Greenpeace, 142, 342
Guardian, The, 66, 68-70, 129, 137, 147-148, 150, 155-156, 308, 321
Guatemala, 73, 84, 87
Giuliani, Rudolph, 291, 293
Gulf War, 36, 57-60, 139, 219-222, 240, 243, 247-248, 252-254, 260-261, 263
Gulf War I, 60, 253-254, 261, 263
Gulf War II, 57-58, 247, 252-253
veterans of, 58-59
Hackett, Robert, 19
Haiti, 84, 259
Halliburton, 98-99, 159, 260, 263-264
Halliday, Denis, 252
Harkin, 83
Harper's, 34, 100, 322
Hart, Peter, 9, 11, 16, 283, 296
Hartford Courant, 277, 280
Hatch, Orrin, 266
Head Start, 106
health care, 48, 100, 108, 119, 130-131, 145, 154, 283
Helms, Jesse, 148
Hewlett-Packard, 43
Hightower, Jim, 74, 76, 199, 219-220, 230, 322, 331, 365
Hightower Lowdown, The, 74, 76, 322, 331
Hill & Knowlton, 220, 241
hip-hop, 11, 89-90, 181-193
Hispanic Education and Media Group, Inc., 342
Hispanics, 344
historians, 186, 230, 311, 316
Hitchens, Christopher, 151-152
Hitler, Adolf, 291, 310
HIV, 236. *See also* AIDS
Houellebecq, Michel, 302

Homeland Security Department.
See Department of Homeland Security
homeless, 78, 89, 102, 106, 145, 160, 200
Honduras, 87, 147, 149
Honeywell, 43
Hong Kong, 130
Hoover, J. Edgar, 187
Hotmail, 184
House of Representatives, 47, 54, 105,
142, 268-269, 280-281
housing, 106, 145-146, 278
low-income, 145-146
Houston Chronicle, 142, 252, 256
HUD. *See* Department of Housing and
Urban Development
human rights, 32, 48, 56-57, 62-63, 66,
68-69, 72, 76, 79, 83-84, 99, 111, 132-
136, 147, 149-150, 154-156, 182, 238,
241-242, 253, 263, 302, 304, 307-308,
310, 320, 327, 331, 342, 350
abuses, 133, 147, 149, 342*Human Rights
Tribune*, 331
Human Rights Watch (HRW), 48, 63, 66,
79, 132, 134, 136, 308
Humanist, The, 42-43, 150
Hussein, Saddam, 34, 37, 42-43, 71, 140,
169-170, 212, 227-228, 233, 235, 237,
239-243, 248, 252, 260, 262-263, 303
Hustler, 57-58
IAO. *See* Information Awareness Office
ICC. *See* International Criminal Court
illegal aliens, 77
IMC. *See* Independent Media Center
IMF. *See* International Monetary Fund
immigrants,immigration, 26, 47, 78-79,
276
immigrant workers, 46-47
Immigration and Naturalization Service
(INS), 47
imperialism, 96, 310
In These Times, 19, 68, 77, 103, 105, 143,
145, 147, 322, 332
INC. *See* Iraqi National Congress
Independent Media Center (IMC), 203,
351
independent media, 88-89, 91, 181, 195,
201-203, 207-211, 307, 325, 336-337,
351, 365
journalists, 32, 224, 299-300
newspapers, 175, 302
press, 31, 306, 343
Independent Press Association, 343
Independent, The, 31, 89, 253, 304, 308,
336, 351
India, 16, 114-115, 126, 137, 173-174,
297, 302, 308

Indian Country Today (Lakota Times), 332
indigenous people, 329
rights, 197
Indonesia, 97, 151, 236, 303, 310, 315
Industrial Worker, 161, 332
infanticide, 120
Information Awareness Office (IAO), 147,
149, 281
information technology, 7, 13, 33, 50, 175
inner-city schools, 143-144
INS. *See* Immigration and Naturalization
Service
insider trading, 164-165
Institute for Public Accuracy, 20, 251,
343
Institute of Global Communications, 343
Insurgent, The, 332
Intelligence Report, 332
Inter Press Service, 56-57, 116, 135, 331,
351
International Atomic Energy Agency, 42,
55, 241
International Consortium of Investigative
Journalists, 343
International Criminal Court (ICC), 52-54,
56-57, 147
International Labor Rights, 120
international law, 53-54, 69, 77, 140, 156,
231, 251
International Media Project, 343
International Monetary Fund (IMF), 65,
67, 94, 100-102, 107-108, 115, 119-
120
International Paper, 83
International Resources Group, 264
International Security Assistance Force
(ISAF), 62-63
Internet Service Providers, 50
intifada, 201-205
investigative journalism, 169, 195, 316,
320, 322-323, 329, 333, 335
investigative reporters, 332, 343-344
Iran, 35, 43, 55, 73, 95, 97, 232, 241-243,
262, 299, 303
Iran-Contra, 45, 147-148, 150
Iraq, 7-9, 11-12, 20, 25, 32-37, 42-43, 49,
54, 56, 58-63, 71, 73, 78, 81-82, 94-99,
116, 121, 139-140, 148-150, 159, 168-
170, 189, 192-193, 202-203, 211-216,
219-226, 228, 230-235, 237-243, 247-
249, 251-252, 254-257, 259-264, 294,
303, 305, 320
Iraqi National Congress (INC), 76, 144,
160-161, 172-174, 177, 179, 237, 259,
260, 262, 291, 320, 325, 329-330, 332,
337, 341-344

IRE Journal, The, 332
irradiated foods, 200
ISAF. See International Security Assistance Force
Islam, 202, 204, 244, 275, 298, 304
  Islamic fundamentalism, 205
Israel, 33, 35, 110-113, 202-206, 211, 259, 303, 328
Italy, 78, 176, 178-179, 299, 303
Jackson, Janine, 9, 11, 16, 283, 296
Jagger, Mick, 187
Jamaica, 297
Japan, 9, 11, 118, 173-174, 178, 285, 309-317
Jayasekera, Rohan, 9, 11, 16, 297
Jay-Z, 192
Jefferson, Thomas, 31
Jennings, Peter, 220
Jensen, Carl, 15, 17, 19, 34
Jewish Institute for National Security Affairs (JINSA), 259-262
Jews; Judaism, 205-206, 233, 244-245
Jhally, Sut, 19
jihad, 233, 238
Jimmy's Internet Shack, 50
JINSA. See Jewish Institute for National Security Affairs
Joe Millionaire, 164, 167
Johnson & Johnson, 290
Johnson, Nicholas, 19
Jordan, 99, 259-260, 297, 305
Jordan, June, 192
JP Morgan Chase, 260, 262
junk food news, 163-170
Justice Department. See Department of Justice
Karpatkin, Rhoda, 19
Kazakhstan, 303
Kellogg, Brown & Root, 98, 260, 263
Kennedy, John, 44
Kenya, 175, 177, 303
Khalilzad, Zalmay, 260
Kharzai, Hamid, 70, 99, 263, 298
Kidman, Nicole, 163
kidney disease, 79
King, Martin Luther, 186, 330
Kissinger, Henry, 151-152
Klotzer, Charles L., 19
Knight Ridder, 238
Korea, 55, 232, 312-313, 316
Kosovo, 230, 264
KPFA, 5, 25, 181, 191, 194-196, 198
Kranich, Nancy, 9, 11, 16, 19, 265, 275, 280
Kristol, William, 35
Krug, Judith, 19

Kurds, 43, 241-243, 307
Kuwait, 36, 42, 99, 220-221, 240, 242, 258
Labor Beat, 49, 351
Labor Department, 47
Labor Notes, 49, 83, 322, 332
Labor Ready, 160-161
labor, 21, 33, 46-49, 75, 83, 86, 100-101, 113, 120, 160-161, 199, 206, 264, 319-320, 322, 325, 328, 332-333, 336, 350-351
  laws, 48, 113
  rights, 120, 320, 350
  unions, 46, 199
land mines, 232
Latin America, 86, 111, 115, 127, 134-135, 147-149, 159, 176, 178, 323
Latinos, 26, 213
  communities, 183
  youth, 183
Lay, Kenneth, 165
Le Pen, Jean, 310
Leahy, Patrick, 266, 273
Lebanon, 206
Lee, Spike, 185
Left Business Observer, 333
Left Turn, 61, 64, 110, 113, 322
Lennon, John, 89
lesbians, 345
leukemia, 60, 249, 254
Levy, Chandra, 207
Libby, Lewis, 261-262, 264
Liberia, 304
libraries, 130-132, 179, 267, 270, 272-277, 279-280, 307, 339
Libya, 233, 303
Livermore, 53, 55
Lockheed Martin, 260, 264
logging, 93
Lopez, Jennifer, 165
Los Alamos, 43, 55, 140-141
Los Angeles Times, 44-45, 74, 137, 149-150, 152, 253
Lough, Tom, 9, 16, 22, 34, 42, 94, 98, 247, 259
low birth weight, 79
Lucent, 264
Lugar, Richard, 148
lung disease, 126
Lutz, William, 19
Lynch, Jessica, 226, 230
magazines, 172, 175, 181, 201, 204-205, 249, 296, 312, 316, 323, 327, 343
mainstream media, 25, 28, 32, 34, 38, 45, 47, 49, 56, 58-60, 63, 75-76, 78, 82, 102, 112, 116, 121, 125, 127, 138, 145,

151, 153, 164-167, 169-170, 184, 191,
196, 201, 203-205, 293, 319, 324, 328,
336, 352
malnutrition, 62, 140, 159
Malveaux, Julianne, 20
manganese, 157, 159
Marable, Manning, 188
Marcos, Ferdinand, 315
marijuana, 164
Mauritania, 304
Mayfield, Curtis, 187
McChesney, Robert W., 20, 52
McConnell, Mitch, 264
MCI, 116
McKinney, Cynthia, 187
Media Alliance, 90, 195, 322, 344
Media Coalition, 344
MediaChannel, 351
MediaFile, 87, 129, 322, 344
Medicaid, 106
Meese, Ed, 242
Mexico, 55, 83-86, 123, 152, 236, 277,
297, 304, 345
microradio, 340
Miller, Mark Crispin, 8, 11, 16, 20, 171, 173
minerals, 83, 157-158
minimum wage, 46
mining, 67, 93, 120, 132, 159
miscarriage, 79
Mobil, 83
Mojo Wire, 352
Monsanto, 83, 122, 134
Montesquieu, 31
Monthly Review, 333
Moore, Michael, 199
Morocco, 304
mosques, 274
Mother Jones, 19, 34, 37, 61, 77, 103,
113, 115, 129, 153, 322, 333
Moussaoui, Zacarias, 138
Moyers, Bill, 87-88, 223
MSN, 50
MSNBC, 12, 37, 249, 290
MTV, 179, 182, 191, 193
muckraking, 320, 329
Mugabe, Robert, 299
multinational corporations, 83-85, 115,
157
Multinational Monitor, 123, 143, 333
murder, 45, 132, 134, 152, 158, 170, 177,
244, 279, 299, 304-305
Muslims, 192, 204, 242-245, 302
NAB. *See* National Association of Broad-
casters
NABJ. *See* National Association of Black
Journalists

NACLA Report on the Americas, 71, 323
NAFTA. *See* North American Free Trade
Agreement
NAHJ. *See* National Association of His-
panic Journalists
Nanjing Massacre, 310-311, 313, 316
Nas, 193
NASA, 158
NASDAQ, 143
Nation, The, 18-19, 52, 61-62, 94, 138,
147, 156-157, 179, 323, 335
National Academy of Sciences, 159
National Asian American Telecommunica-
tions Association, 344
National Association of Black Journalists
(NABJ), 344
National Association of Broadcasters
(NAB), 28, 209
National Association of Hispanic Journal-
ists (NAHJ), 26, 344
National Association of Television and
Radio Announcers, 186
National Coalition Against Censorship
(NCAC), 344-345
national forests, 92, 94
National Lawyers Guild, 340
National Lesbian and Gay Journalists
Association (NLGJA), 345
National Organization for Women (NOW),
42
national parks, 92
National Public Radio (NPR), 26, 28, 37,
220, 249-251, 268
National Rifle Association (NRA), 27, 52
National Security Archive, 241-242
National Security Council (NSC), 45, 147,
149
National Security Strategy (NSS), 36, 55,
57
National Writers Union (NWU), 345
Native American, 22, 332
NATO, 56-57, 66
Natsios, Andrew, 261
Nazi Germany, 310
Nazis, 244
NBC Nightly News, 248, 288
NBC, 25-26, 87, 129, 166, 220, 222, 224,
226, 248, 288, 290, 292-293
NCAC. *See* National Coalition Against
Censorship
Nelson, Jack L., 20
NEPAD. *See* New Partnership for Africa's
Development
Netherlands, the, 52, 54, 179
New Internationalist, 64, 323, 333
New Mexico Media Literacy Project, 345

New Partnership for Africa's Development (NEPAD), 64-65, 67
New Republic, The, 236
New Unionist, 333
New York Post, 175, 289, 291
New York Times, The, 18, 36, 39, 74, 76, 87, 112, 121, 138, 221, 224-225, 249, 256, 284-288, 291, 293, 312, 352
New Zealand, 134, 136
News Abuse, 163, 167-170
News Corporation, 174
Newsday, 138, 151-152
NewsHour with Jim Lehrer, 26
Newsletter on Intellectual Freedom, 19, 333
NewsWatch Canada, 19, 345
NGOs, 80, 132
Nicaragua, 87
Niger, 194, 241, 304
    Niger Delta, 194
Nigeria, 115, 194, 304
Nike, 75-76
niobium, 157
Nixon, Richard, 45, 94, 262
NLGJA. *See* National Lesbian and Gay Journalists Association
No Child Left Behind, 143-144
Nobel Peace Prize, 58, 152, 301
non-governmental organizations. *See* NGOs
nonviolence, 342
NORAD, 56
North American Free Trade Agreement (NAFTA), 79, 83-84, 86-87, 123
North Coast Xpress, 143
North Korea, 55, 232, 312-313
Northcom, 39
Northern Alliance, 68-69, 293
Northern Command, 40
Northwest Airlines, 46
NOW. *See* National Organization for Women
NOW with Bill Moyers, 87-88
NPR. *See* National Public Radio
NPT. *See* Treaty on the Non-Proliferation of Nuclear Weapons
NRA. *See* National Rifle Association
NSC. *See* National Security Council
NSS. *See* National Security Strategy
nuclear energy, 55-56, 117, 214
Nuclear Posture Review, 53, 55
nuclear weapons, 43, 53, 55, 59, 111, 137, 140-142, 232, 240, 313
    "mini-nukes," 141-142
Nuremberg, 54, 251
NWU. *See* National Writers Union
Occupational Safety and Health Administration (OSHA), 114-115

Office of Intellectual Freedom, 19, 333
Office of Management and Budget (OMB), 114
Office of National Drug Control Policy (ONDCP), 164-165
Office of Strategic Influence (OSI), 121-122
oil, 35-37, 64-65, 70-73, 83, 94-97, 101, 113, 117, 127, 132, 136-137, 150, 194, 242, 250, 260-263, 295
Olympics, 288
OMB Watch, 114
ombudsman, 30, 136, 288
ONDCP. *See* Office of National Drug Control Policy
O'Neill, John, 136-138
Operation Garden Plot, 38, 40
opium, 70, 133-134
Orange County Weekly, The, 285
O'Reilly, Bill, 182
Organization of Petroleum Exporting Countries (OPEC), 71, 95
Osbourne, Ozzy, 236
    Osbournes, The, 164-165
OSHA. *See* Occupational Safety and Health Administration
OSI. *See* Office of Strategic Influence
Our Times, 11, 334
overpopulation, 78
P. Diddy, 165
P2OG. *See* Proactive Preemptive Operations Group
Pacific News Service, 352
Pacifica, 20, 25-26, 28, 181, 194-196, 198, 342, 350
Pakistan, 57, 119, 137, 297, 304
Palestine, Palestinians, 33, 110-113, 159, 197, 203-204, 206, 211, 216, 303, 305
Panama, 83-84
Paper Tiger Television, 345
paramilitary groups, 132-133, 135, 147
Parenti, Michael, 11, 16, 20, 34, 100, 125, 128
Parents Advocating School Accountability, 144
Parsons Corp., 264
Pataki, George, 192
Patriot Act, 9, 11, 38-40, 211-212, 214-215, 265, 267-269, 272-278, 280-281, 298, 307. *See also* USA Patriot Act
    Patriot Act I, 268. *See also* USA Patriot Act
    Patriot Act II, 38-40, 281. *See also* USA Patriot Act
patriotism, 223, 227
PBS, 26, 285

Peace Watch, 194

Peacework, 64, 119, 323

Pearl, Daniel, 304

Pentagon, 8, 12, 33, 35-36, 38, 40-41, 44-45, 58-60, 69, 80-82, 98, 118, 121-122, 136, 139, 142, 148, 150, 169, 220-221, 225, 227, 236-239, 248-250, 253, 260-264, 294, 298

People's Weekly World, 70, 149-150, 323, 334

Pepsi, 236

Perkins, Dan, 20

Perle, Richard, 35, 238, 260-263

Perot, Ross, 27

Persian Gulf, 19, 35-37, 59, 95, 195

Peru, 297

pesticides, 58, 120, 325, 337

Peterson, Laci, 168, 170

petroleum, 159. *See also* oil

Philippines, the, 57, 236, 315

Pilger, John, 34, 45, 323

Plan Puebla-Panama (PPP), 33, 83-85

Planned Parenthood, 153

plastic surgery, 164, 166, 258

plutonium, 55, 141

PNAC. *See* Project for the New American Century

Poindexter, John, 147-150

Poland, 305

polling, 211, 214-215, 231, 236, 247, 310

pollution, 79, 82, 115, 117, 127, 305, 327

Poor Magazine; Poor News Network, 214, 334

porn, 51, 58

Posse Comitatus Act of 1878, 40

postal services, 130-131

poverty, 33, 61-62, 65, 67, 78, 83-85, 101, 103-107, 116, 119, 160, 323, 331-333

Powell, Colin, 25, 36, 128, 148, 209

Powell, Michael K., 88, 128, 209

POWs, 225

PPP. *See* Plan Puebla-Panama

PR Watch, 9, 11, 231, 237, 334

PR. *See* public relations

Press, Eyal, 156-157

Prevailing Winds Magazine, 334

print media, 45, 165, 184

Prison Legal News, 334

prisons, 68-69, 78, 99, 135, 155-156, 189, 192, 215, 301, 304, 306, 308, 334

privatization, 25, 37, 47, 67, 86, 91-94, 98-101, 107, 128, 130-131, 142-143, 207

    education, 142, 144

Proactive Preemptive Operations Group (P2OG), 44-45

product placement, 284, 288

Progress and Freedom Foundation, 128

Progressive Media Project, 346

Progressive Populist, The, 143, 160, 335

Progressive, The, 18-19, 46, 48, 139, 182, 189, 191, 199-200, 222, 324

Project Censored, 13-21, 28-30, 32-34, 43, 125, 163, 165, 167, 181-182, 184, 189, 194-196, 198, 200, 208, 251, 280, 346-347, 365-366

    how to Support, 366

    mission statement, 30

    national judges, 18-20

    to nominate a *Censored* story, 366

Project for the New American Century (PNAC), 35-36, 259-262

pro-life campaigners, 153

public access stations, 194

Public Citizen, 83, 86-87, 115-116, 324, 335

Public Enemy, 182, 189, 193

public lands, 8, 33, 91-93

public relations (PR), 12, 17, 23, 76, 90, 182, 220, 231, 233-234, 236-237, 241-242, 248, 289, 292, 295, 334

publishing, 15-16, 133, 144, 172, 175-179, 201, 205, 214, 272-275, 286, 289, 303, 306, 311, 322, 349

Puerto Rico, 82, 177, 179

    Isla de Vieques, 82

Qatar, 131, 202, 221, 305

Qualcomm, 264

Qur'an, the, 244

race, 83-84, 86, 214, 269, 288, 334

Rachel's Environment & Health Weekly, 133, 335

racism, 306

radiation, 252, 254-255

Radio Free Europe, 254, 308

radio, 12, 20, 25, 27-28, 30, 37, 43, 45, 51, 61, 82, 87-90, 127-129, 169-170, 175, 178-179, 181, 183-187, 190-191, 193-195, 198, 207-208, 211, 242, 249, 251, 254, 261, 268, 290, 295-296, 301, 303, 305, 307-308, 323, 335-336, 342-343, 350-351, 365

    low-power FM, 28

    short-wave, 28, 194

radioactive dust, 248, 255

Rampton, Sheldon, 11, 16, 231

Rand Corporation, 260-261

RAND Report, 133

rap, 182, 186. *See also* hip-hop

rape, 99, 158, 299, 316

Rather, Dan, 220, 225, 229

Raytheon, 264

Reagan, Ronald, 35, 42-43, 45, 110, 147-149, 242, 259, 262-263
    Administration, 147, 242
Recreation Fee Demonstration Program, 92
Red Cross, 155, 253, 258
Rehnquist, William, 75
Reich, Otto, 72-73, 147-149
Reid, Richard, 154
Reilly, Robert, 260-261
Republican Party, 35, 105, 214, 262-264, 269
Retro Poll, 181, 211-213, 215
Reuters, 56, 97, 130
Revolutionary Armed Forces of Colombia (FARC), 134
Revolutionary War, 259
Revolutionary Worker, 335
Rice, Condoleezza, 141, 261
Ridge, Tom, 47, 170
Rite-Aid, 165
Robertson, Pat, 244
Rockefeller Drug Laws, 192
Rockwell, 43
Roe v. Wade, 153-154
Rokke, Doug, 58, 60
Rose, Charlie, 285
Rumsfeld, Donald, 35-36, 43-45, 80, 121, 142, 233, 237-238, 241-242, 260, 262-263
Russia, 37, 42, 236, 247, 297, 305
Rwanda, 66, 157-159
Safire, William, 39
San Francisco Bay Guardian, 99, 256
San Francisco Chronicle, 214, 252, 256
San Francisco Examiner, 286
Sanders, Bernie, 279
Saudi Arabia, 35, 65, 73, 136, 222, 305
Sawyer, Diane, 165
School of the Americas (SOA), 132
Schorr, Daniel, 250
Scud missiles, 240
Seaman, Barbara, 20
Seattle Times, The, 140
Secret Service, 38, 270
Senate (U.S.), 48, 72, 88, 105-106, 141, 147-148, 150, 239, 252, 266-268, 277, 281
Sensenbrenner, James, 268, 273, 280
September 11 (9/11), 32, 38-40, 46-47, 77-78, 98, 101, 128, 136-138, 140, 145, 151-155, 168, 190, 192-193, 197-198, 204, 212, 231-233, 238, 265-266, 274-277, 279, 281, 292, 297-298, 325, 337
Shah of Iran, 35

Shakur, Afeni, 188
Sharon, Ariel, 112, 303
Sharpton, Al, 191
Shell Oil, 113
Shultz, George, 242, 260, 262-263
Sierra Club, 86, 335
Sierra Leone, 159, 306
Sierra Magazine, 335
Sierra Times, The, 94, 324
Simmons, Russell, 188, 192
Simpson, O.J., 211
single parents, 105-106
Sixth Amendment, 279
slavery, 159, 185, 306
Smith, Erna, 20
smoking, 127, 285
Snoop Dogg, 192-193
Society of Professional Journalists, 346
solar energy, 117, 127
Solomon, Norman, 11, 16, 20, 121, 199, 247, 251
soup kitchens, 108-109
South Africa, 342-343
South Korea, 312-313, 316
Southern Christian Leadership Coalition, 186
Southern Exposure, 255-256, 335
Soviet Union, 36-37, 95, 99, 297
Spain, 78, 176, 179, 247, 306
Spears, Britney, 236
Sperry, 43
Sri Lanka, 297, 306
St. Louis Dispatch, 153
St. Petersburg Times, 146
Stahl, Lesley, 249
standardized testing, 142-143
Star Tribune (Minneapolis), 146
Star Wars, 53
Starbucks, 284-285
starvation, 64, 67
State Department, 35, 65, 73, 99, 115, 133, 148, 150, 169, 234, 237, 241, 244, 259, 263, 293, 307
State of the Union, 232, 241
Stauber, John, 11, 16, 231
Steelabor, 133
Steve Doring Services of America, 264
Stewart, Martha, 164-165
Stewart, Rod, 187
Stone, Sly, 187
strikes, 47, 95, 294
    strikebreakers, 160
Sudan, 306, 308
surveillance, 149, 259, 265-267, 270, 272-281, 305
Survivor, 68, 179, 288

SUVs, 164
Taft-Hartley Act, 46, 49
Taiwan, 118-119, 174, 297, 310
Tajikistan, 306
Taliban, 8, 33, 62, 68-70, 136-138, 223, 260, 275, 293, 298
Talk of the Nation, 365
Targeted Regulation of Abortion Providers (TRAP) laws, 152-153
tear gas, 109
Telecommunications Act of 1996, 87, 128-129
television (TV), 12, 15, 17, 19, 28, 30-31, 37, 51-52, 59, 70, 72, 87-88, 90, 128-130, 149, 163-164, 166-167, 169-170, 172-179, 181-182, 185-186, 190, 192, 194-197, 207-211, 219-220, 222-229, 234, 261, 284, 288, 291, 294-296, 299, 301, 303, 305, 307, 312, 314-315, 320, 342, 345-346, 351, 365
children's television, 28
Television Project, The, 346
temp workers, 160
temples, 274
terrorism, 12, 33, 37-39, 40-41, 44-45, 77-78, 101, 128, 135-138, 140, 147, 153-158, 168, 170, 188, 192-193, 211-215, 231-233, 238, 240, 243-244, 265-269, 271-273, 275-276, 298, 306-307, 325, 332, 337
Texas Observer, The, 100, 324, 336
Thailand, 236, 297, 310, 315
Third World, 33, 100-101, 119, 125, 127, 157, 333, 336
Third World Resurgence, 336
This Magazine, 336
Thoreau, Henry David, 93
timber, 83, 159
Time, 172-173, 227-228, 250, 287-288, 291
Times of India, 137, 308
Times, The (London), 226, 308
tin, 159
tobacco, 127
Togo, 306
Tomorrow, Tom, 16, 20
"Top Gun" president, 11, 219-220, 224, 230
torture, 69, 120, 154-158, 215
Toward Freedom, 336
transportation, 47, 84, 108, 130-131, 142, 164, 258, 278
Transportation Security Authority (TSA), 47
TRAP laws. *See* Targeted Regulation of Abortion Providers laws
Treaty on the Non-Proliferation of Nuclear Weapons (NPT), 53, 55, 111

Tunisia, 229, 306
Turkey, 57, 99, 115, 243, 247, 306-307
TV Guide, 174-175, 288
Tyco, 165
Tylenol, 290
Uganda, 66, 157-158
U.K., 37, 45, 70, 140, 172, 174, 176-177, 179, 302, 321. *See also* Britain
Ukraine, 297, 307
U.N. *See* United Nations
underage drinking, 165
unemployment, 102-103, 106-107, 111
Union Carbide, 83
Union Pacific-Southern, 83
Union Producers and Programmers Network (UPPNET), 336
union, 2, 19, 36-37, 46-49, 56-57, 63, 83, 89, 95, 97, 99, 134, 160, 199, 209, 232, 241, 297, 302, 305, 329, 332, 336, 345
unions, 7, 33, 46-49, 89-90, 102, 199, 314
United Airlines, 46, 49
United Kingdom. *See* U.K.
United Nations (U.N.), 25, 32, 42, 53, 56, 58, 67, 69-70, 81, 99, 121, 139-140, 147, 149-150, 216, 241, 249, 251-252, 254-255, 257, 301, 337
UNICEF, 62, 252, 254
United Nations Security Council (UNSC), 56-57
UNSCOM inspectors, 121
United States. *See* U.S.
uranium, 33, 57-60, 82, 157, 159, 241, 248-249, 252, 254-255, 257, 259
Urgent Action Newsletter, 336
Uribe, Alvaro, 134-135
U.S., 12-13, 15-17, 20, 26, 29-30, 32-33, 35-45, 47-49, 52-60, 62-73, 75-88, 92, 94-101, 103, 108, 110-121, 123, 125, 129, 132-141, 145-161, 173-174, 179, 193-194, 196, 200, 202-203, 206, 211-213, 215-216, 219, 222-228, 231-245, 247-262, 265, 270-271, 273, 275-276, 278, 280-281, 290, 292-294, 298, 301-302, 304-305, 307, 312-316, 323, 328, 331-333, 337, 339-340, 345, 351, 366
Air Force, 38, 79-80, 316
Army, 38, 40-41, 58, 80, 98, 136, 158, 224, 229, 248, 256, 260, 263
Border Patrol, 38
Coast Guard, 38
Marines, 37-38, 226, 228, 250
Navy, 38, 80-82
war on terror, 41, 77, 97, 136-137, 156, 168, 170, 192-193, 211-215, 233, 268, 292, 298, 293
U.S. News and World Report, 223

USA Patriot Act, 11, 39, 211-212, 214, 265, 267, 269, 274-278, 280-281, 298, 307
USA Today, 74, 121, 228, 290
USAID, 259, 261, 264
USDA. *See* Department of Agriculture
USSR. *See* Soviet Union
Utne Reader, 82, 107, 117
vaccines, 58
Venezuela, 8, 33, 70-74, 149-150, 236
veterans, 58-60
Viacom, 26, 28, 129, 174, 176, 179, 191
Vidal, Gore, 138
Vietnam War, 219
Vietnam, 59, 133, 219-221
Village Voice, 112, 289
violence, 26, 90, 131, 134, 155, 189, 191, 224, 244-245, 255-256, 311, 313
Vivendi, 176-177
Voice of America, 261, 293, 303
Walker Lindh, John, 298
Wall Street Journal, 87, 90, 285, 304
Wall Street, 87, 90, 285, 289, 304, 350
Wal-Mart, 291
war, 11-13, 19, 25-26, 32-33, 35-38, 40-41, 43-46, 49, 53-55, 57-62, 64, 66-67, 69, 73, 77-79, 81-82, 94-99, 112, 132-133, 135-140, 147, 149-150, 152-153, 156-159, 164, 168-170, 189, 192-193, 197, 202-203, 211-216, 219-233, 237-244, 247-257, 259-263, 266, 268, 283, 292-294, 298-299, 302-303, 305, 310-311, 313-314, 320, 325, 337, 340
war crimes, 43, 53-54, 69, 112, 140, 215, 303*War and Peace Digest*, 337
war on drugs, 133
War Times, 46, 325, 337
Washington Free Press, 79-80, 325
Washington Monthly, 153, 236
Washington Post, 48, 91, 121, 133, 136-138, 152, 154-155, 157, 221, 227-229, 242, 249, 280, 285-288, 293-294, 308
Washington Report on Middle East Affairs, The, 337
water, 43, 68, 79, 83, 89, 101, 111-112, 130-131, 133, 139-140, 159, 177, 200, 230, 254, 325, 337
purification, 139-140
Watergate, 148, 265
WBAI, 5, 194, 350

We Interrupt This Message, 346-347
weapons of mass destruction, 37, 42, 58, 141, 239, 251-252, 263
Weekend Australian, 154
Weekend Edition, 250
Weekly Standard, The, 35
Weidenfeld, Sheila Rabb, 20
Weinberger, Caspar, 262
welfare, 8, 33, 103-106, 108, 130, 139, 142, 145
West Bank, 110-111, 201, 205, 303
West Nile fever virus, 43
Whispered Media, 346
White House, 35, 57, 98, 103-104, 155, 159, 202, 221, 235, 241-242, 250, 265-266, 292-294
white supremacy, 113
Whitman, Christine, 293
Wild Matters, 74, 79, 325, 337
Will, George, 137-138
Williams, Robin, 285
wind power, 117
Wired, 308, 352
wiretaps, 39, 276, 278
Witness for Peace, 136
Wolfowitz, Paul, 35-36, 80, 238, 260-262
women's health, 20, 152-153
women's rights, 7, 33, 61-62, 89
Woolsey, James, 261-263
World Bank, 65, 67, 100-102, 115, 119, 331
World Socialist Web site, 352
World Trade Center, 137-138, 265, 293
World Trade Organization (WTO), 123, 130-132
World War I, 230, 238
World War II, 25, 54, 66, 229-230, 251, 310, 313-314
World Wildlife Fund, 114
WorldCom, 113-114, 116, 165
WTO. *See* World Trade Organization
Wu-Tang Clan, 190
Yahoo, 97, 184
Yes!, 89, 107, 126, 165, 325
Youth Media Council, 90, 347
Z Magazine, 46, 67, 337, 352, 365
Zimbabwe, 299, 307
Zionism, 113, 205
ZNet, 49, 63, 110, 138, 352

About the Editor

Peter Phillips is a professor/department chair of sociology at Sonoma State University and director of Project Censored. He teaches classes in media censorship, power, political sociology, and sociology of media. He has published seven editions of *Censored: Media Democracy in Action* from Seven Stories Press. Also from Seven Stories Press is the Project Censored *Guide to Independent Media and Activism 2003*.

Phillips writes op-ed pieces for independent media nationwide, having published in dozens of publications newspapers and Web sites including *Z Magazine*, *CounterPunch*, *Common Dreams*, *Social Policy*, and *Briarpatch*. He frequently speaks on media censorship and various sociopolitical issues on radio and TV talks shows including *Talk of the Nation*, *Public Interest*, *Talk America*, *World Radio Network*, *Democracy Now!*, and the *Jim Hightower Show*.

Phillips is the national and international news editor of the *North Bay Progressive* newspaper in Santa Rosa, California. The *North Bay Progressive* is a monthly regional publication serving a five-county area north of San Francisco.

Phillips earned a B.A. degree in social science in 1970 from Santa Clara University and an M.A. degree in social science from California State University at Sacramento in 1974. He earned a second M.A. in sociology in 1991 and a Ph.D. in sociology in 1994. His doctoral dissertation was entitled *A Relative Advantage: Sociology of the San Francisco Bohemian Club*, <libweb.sonoma.edu/regional/faculty/Phillips/bohemianindex.htm>.

Phillips is a fifth-generation Californian, who grew up on a family-owned farm west of the Central Valley town of Lodi. Phillips lives today in rural Sonoma County with his wife Mary Lia-Phillips.

How to Support Project Censored

NOMINATE A STORY

To nominate a *Censored* story send us a copy of the article and include the name of the source publication, the date that the article appeared, and page number. For Internet published news stories of which we should be aware, please forward the URL to <Censored@sonoma.edu>. The final deadline period for nominating a most *Censored* Story of the year is March of each year.

CRITERIA FOR PROJECT CENSORED NEWS STORIES NOMINATIONS

1. A censored news story is one which contains information that the general United States population has a right and need to know, but to which it has had limited access.
2. The news story is timely, ongoing, and has implications for a significant number of residents in the United States.
3. The story has clearly defined concepts and is backed up with solid, verifiable documentation.
4. The news story has been publicly published, either electronically or in print, in a circulated newspaper, journal, magazine, newsletter, or similar publication from either a foreign or domestic source.
5. The news story has direct connections to and implications for people in the United States, which can include activities that U.S. citizens are engaged in abroad.

SUPPORT PROJECT CENSORED BY MAKING A FINANCIAL GIFT

Project Censored is a self-supported 501-c-3 non-profit organization. We depend on tax-deductible donations and foundation grants to continue our work. To support our efforts for freedom of information, send checks to the address below or call (707) 664-2500. Visa and Mastercard accepted. Review our Web site at <www.projectcensored.org>.

Project Censored
Sonoma State University
1801 East Cotati Avenue
Rohnert Park, CA 94928
E-mail: <censored@sonoma.edu>

0304